The Mediation Process

The Mediation Process

Practical Strategies for Resolving Conflict

Christopher W. Moore

Third Edition Revised

JOSSEY-BASS
A Wiley Imprint
www.josseybass.com

Published by Jossey-Bass
A Wiley Imprint
989 Market Street, San Francisco, CA 94103-1741   www.josseybass.com

Jossey-Bass books and products are available through most bookstores. To contact Jossey-Bass directly call our Customer Care Department within the U.S. at 800-956-7739, outside the U.S. at 317-572-3986, or fax 317-572-4002.

Jossey-Bass also publishes its books in a variety of electronic formats. Some content that appears in print may not be available in electronic books.

Library of Congress Cataloging-in-Publication Data

Moore, Christopher W., date.
    The mediation process: practical strategies for resolving conflict/
Christopher Moore.—3rd ed.
        p. cm.
Includes bibliographical references and index.
    ISBN 0-7879-6446-8 (alk. paper)
    1. Mediation.   2. Conflict management.   I. Title.
    HM136.M684 2003
    303.6'9—dc21

                                                        2003001775

Printed in the United States of America
THIRD EDITION
PB Printing   10 9 8 7 6 5 4

Contents

Preface

All societies, communities, organizations, and interpersonal relationships experience conflict at one time or another in the process of day-to-day interactions. Conflict is not necessarily bad, abnormal, or dysfunctional; it is a fact of life. Conflict and disputes exist when people or groups are engaged in competition to meet goals that they perceive to be, or actually are, incompatible. However, conflict may go beyond competitive behavior and acquire the additional purpose of inflicting physical or psychological damage on an opponent, even to the point of their annihilation. It is then that the negative and harmful dynamics of conflict exact their full costs.

But disputes are not inherently destined to follow a negative course; conflict can lead to growth and be productive for those who are involved. Whether this happens often depends on the participants' ability to devise efficient procedures for cooperative problem solving, on their capacity to lay aside distrust and animosity while they work together on resolving their conflict, and on the availability of solutions that will at least partially satisfy all of the parties' interests. Unfortunately, many people in conflict are unable to develop effective procedures, deal with the psychological barriers to settlement, or create integrative solutions on their own. They often need help to do so.

Mediation, one form of third-party assistance in the voluntary resolution of differences, has a long history. However, until relatively recently, there have been few works that detailed what mediators actually do to aid people in conflict.

For the past thirty years, I have been actively involved as a mediator of international, public policy, environmental, ethnic, organizational, personnel, community, and family disputes. I have practiced in the United States and worked as an intermediary, conflict manager, consultant, and trainer in more than twenty-five countries in

Africa, Asia, Latin America, Eastern and Western Europe, and the South Pacific. This broad experience has led me to believe that there are some common mediation principles and procedures that can be applied effectively to a wide range of conflicts. My belief has been confirmed by the expanding experience and literature in the field of mediation. There is a continuing need for an integrative "how-to" manual on the various ways that mediation is and can be practiced in a variety of settings and to address a range of problems and conflicts.

The Mediation Process: Practical Strategies for Resolving Conflict integrates my personal experience and research and that of others and details what is known about the mediation process as it has been applied in a variety of areas, types of disputes, and cultures. The contents have been greatly expanded since the first and second editions, to encompass some of the exciting new developments and applications of mediation in the commercial, interpersonal, and public disputes arenas and to incorporate some of what I have learned about the practice of mediation in different cultures. The book outlines how mediation fits into the larger field of dispute resolution and negotiation and then presents a comprehensive, stage-by-stage sequence of activities that can be used by mediators to assist disputants in reaching agreement.

AUDIENCE

I have written this book for several groups. First are the practicing mediators who work in a wide variety of arenas and who have repeatedly expressed their need for a comprehensive description of mediation process and theory. The book should be helpful to practitioners in international, public policy, environmental, organizational, community, family, and interpersonal mediation, as well as in many other areas of practice.

Second are professionals—lawyers, managers, therapists, social workers, planners, and teachers—who handle conflicts on a daily basis. Although those professionals may choose to become full-time mediators, they are more likely to use mediation principles and procedures as additional tools to help them within their chosen fields of work. The material presented here will aid any professional who wishes to promote cooperative problem solving between his or her clients.

Third are people who have to negotiate solutions to complex problems. Because mediation is an extension of the negotiation process and, in fact, a collection of techniques to promote more efficient negotiations, an understanding of the mediation process can be tremendously helpful to people directly involved in bargaining. Mediation can teach negotiators how to be cooperative rather than competitive problem solvers and how to achieve win-win rather than win-lose outcomes. An understanding of mediation can also aid negotiators in deciding when to call in a third party and what an intervenor can do for them.

Fourth are trainees and students in both mediation training programs and academic courses on dispute resolution. This book is suitable for use in law, business, social work, counseling, management, education, sociology, and psychology seminars. Undergraduates as well as graduates will find it useful in learning mediation concepts and skills.

OVERVIEW OF THE CONTENTS

Part One provides an overview of the entire process of mediation and dispute resolution. Chapter One describes the broad field of dispute resolution and details how mediation fits in as an important means of handling conflicts. In this chapter, I present a spectrum of conflict management approaches, identify when mediation is appropriate and when it has a high probability of success, and describe the history and range of mediation practice in a number of cultures around the world. Chapter Two examines the mediation process in more depth. I explore variations of mediator roles and procedures describe a number of types of mediators, introduce the twelve stages of the mediation process, and survey several variables that determine how directive the mediator should be in his or her interventions.

Part Two discusses mediator activities that occur *prior* to joint negotiations between the disputing parties. Chapter Three covers procedures for mediator entry and explores both how an intervenor becomes involved in a dispute and what impact being invited by a sole party, all parties, or an uninvolved secondary party has on the dispute resolution procedure. Chapter Four describes the process of searching for a dispute resolution approach and arena with the parties. Procedures that can assist disputants in evaluating the various methods of resolving their conflicts are covered, along with the means of deciding which approach to use. Chapter Five presents data collection techniques that mediators can use to gather information about the parties' preferred negotiation procedures and the substantive issues in dispute. Special emphasis is placed on identifying issues, interests, and potential options that may address the causes of the conflict. Chapter Six explores procedures for designing a conceptual mediation plan. The identification of participants, the physical setup of the session, and strategies for the first session are detailed. Chapter Seven examines procedures for conciliation, the process of emotionally preparing the parties for negotiation over substantive issues. Techniques for responding to strong emotions, perceptual problems, and communication difficulties are discussed.

Part Three explores mediation procedures in joint session with all disputants present. Chapter Eight focuses on beginning a joint session with the disputing parties. Strategies and opening statements for both the intervenor and the parties are described and analyzed. Chapters Nine and Ten examine the steps by which the issues in dispute can be identified; an agenda can be developed; and the substantive, procedural, and psychological interests of the parties can be explored. The useful technique of reframing, or defining, issues and interests is presented. Chapter Eleven examines procedures and strategies for generating settlement options. The technique of proposal-counterproposal is described, as well as more effective cooperative problem-solving methods.

Part Four covers the conclusion of mediation and the various steps involved in reaching a settlement. Chapters Twelve and Thirteen present procedures for assessing settlement options and reaching final agreements. In these chapters, I explore acceptable bargaining ranges, incremental convergence, leaps to agreement, procedures for building bargaining formulas, and the usefulness of deadlines. Chapter Fourteen discusses how agreements can be finalized. Procedures for drafting settlements, increasing compliance, and monitoring are examined. Chapters Fifteen and Sixteen address specific problems that are encountered in some but not all disputes and present techniques for dealing with them. Both the caucus and mediator power are examined, as are procedures for handling value differences, resolving disputes that involve multiple parties, and funding mediation. Chapter Seventeen explores some of the developments in the field that have promoted excellent practice. Some of these are the development of professional associations, the drafting of codes of ethics and model standards, the development of comprehensive training programs, and the identification of qualifications for specific areas of practice. A brief conclusion rounds out the text.

The resources in the appendix contain a code of professional conduct; a sample agreement; and a list of associations, organizations, and publications of relevance to practitioners.

ACKNOWLEDGMENTS

All knowledge is socially produced. Although I bear responsibility for the identification, elaboration, and development of the ideas presented in this book, I have clearly drawn on the experiences and advice of others engaged in the practice of mediation.

The first group of people to whom I am indebted is my fellow mediators. Since 1973, when I first became involved in mediating an intense interracial community dispute, I have worked with four active groups of mediators and conflict resolvers. Each group has contributed significant insights and pushed me to develop my thinking.

First and foremost are my partners at CDR Associates in Boulder, Colorado—Susan Wildau, Mary Margaret Golten, Bernard Mayer, Louise Smart, Judy Mares-Dixon, and Peter Woodrow—and our other program staff. They have been my colleagues in developing and practicing many of the ideas contained in this book. Susan Carpenter and W.J.D. Kennedy of ACCORD Associates also provided insights and support in researching and refining mediation theory and practice while I worked as a mediator and director of training for that organization. The members of the Training Action Affinity Group of the Movement for a New Society—Suzanne Terry, Stephen Parker, Peter Woodrow, and Berit Lakey—and my coauthors on the *Resource Manual for a Living Revolution*—Virginia Coover, Charles Esser, and Ellen Deacon—worked with me to develop intervention skills for multiparty disputes and effective training techniques in conflict resolution. Bill Lincoln provided my first excellent exposure to mediation training. Work with academic colleagues was also important. Norman Wilson, Paul Wehr, and Martin Oppenheimer encouraged and supported my research.

The individuals I have mentioned so far are the theoretical and experiential contributors. Just as important are the people who prepare the drafts and edit them. My sincere thanks to Nancy Wigington and to Benjamin and Bess Moore, who helped assemble the final draft.

A final word of thanks to Susan Wildau and Stephanie Judson for their faith in me as a scholar and reflective practitioner, and for emotional support during graduate school.

February 2003   CHRISTOPHER W. MOORE
Boulder, Colorado

The Mediation Process

Part One

Understanding Dispute Resolution and Mediation

Chapter One

Approaches to Managing and Resolving Conflict

Conflict or disputes seem to be present in all human relationships and in all societies. From the beginning of recorded history, we have evidence of disputes between spouses, children, parents and children, neighbors, ethnic and racial groups, fellow workers, superiors and subordinates, organizations, communities, citizens and their governments, and nations. Because of the pervasive presence of conflict and because of the physical, emotional, and resource costs that often result from disputes, people have always sought ways of peacefully resolving their differences. In seeking to manage and resolve conflicts, they have tried to develop procedures that are efficient; that satisfy their interests; that build or maintain relationships, where appropriate; that minimize suffering; and that control unnecessary expenditures of resources.

In most conflicts, the parties involved have a variety of means at their disposal to respond to or resolve their differences. The procedures available to them vary considerably in the *way* the conflict is addressed and settled and often result in different outcomes, both tangible and intangible.

This chapter begins with an analysis of a specific interpersonal and organizational conflict and explores some of the procedural options available to the parties involved for managing and resolving it. Mediation, one of those options, is examined in depth, and a detailed description is given of its historical and present-day applications and variations.

THE SINGSON-WHITTAMORE DISPUTE

Singson and Whittamore are in conflict. It all started three years ago when Dr. Richard Singson, director of the Fairview Medical Clinic, one of the few medical service providers in a small rural town, was seeking two physicians to fill open positions on his staff. After several months of extensive and difficult recruiting, he hired two doctors, Andrew and Janelle Whittamore, to fill the positions of pediatrician and gynecologist, respectively. The fact that the doctors were married did not seem to be a problem at the time they were hired.

Fairview liked to keep its doctors and generally paid them well for their work with patients. The clinic was also concerned about maintaining its patient load and income and required every doctor who joined the practice to sign a five-year contract detailing what he or she was to be paid and what conditions would apply should the contract be broken by either party. One of these conditions was a covenant not to compete, or a no-competition clause, stating that should a doctor choose to leave the clinic prior to the expiration of the agreement, he or she would not be allowed to practice medicine in that town or county during the time remaining on the contract; violation of this clause carried an undefined financial penalty. The clause was designed to prevent a staff doctor from building up a practice at the clinic and then leaving with his or her patients to start a private competitive practice in the community before the term of the contract had expired.

When Janelle and Andrew joined the Fairview staff, they each signed a contract and initialed all the clauses. Both doctors performed well in their jobs and were respected by their colleagues and patients. Unfortunately, their personal life did not fare so well. The Whittamores' marriage went into a steady decline almost as soon as they began working at Fairview. Their arguments increased, and the tension between them mounted to the point where they decided to get a divorce. Because they both wanted to be near their two young children, they agreed to continue living in the same town.

Every physician at the clinic had a specialty, and all relied on consultations with colleagues, so some interaction between the estranged couple was inevitable. Over time, their mutual hostility grew to such an extent that they decided one of them should leave the clinic—for their own good and that of other clinic staff. Because they believed that Andrew, as a pediatrician, would have an easier time finding patients outside the clinic, they agreed that he was the one who should go.

Andrew explained his situation to Singson and noted that because he would be leaving for the benefit of the clinic, he expected that no penalty would be assessed for breaking the contract two years early and that the no-competition clause would not be invoked.

Singson was surprised and upset that his finely tuned staff was going to lose one of its most respected members. Furthermore, he was shocked by Whittamore's announcement that he planned to stay in town and open a medical practice. Singson visualized the long-range impact of Whittamore's decision: the pediatrician would leave and set up a competing practice, taking many of his patients with him. The clinic would lose revenues from the doctor's fees, incur the cost of recruiting a new doctor, and (if the no-competition clause was not enforced) establish a bad precedent for managing its doctors. Singson responded that the no-competition clause would be enforced if Whittamore wanted to practice within the county, and that the clinic would impose a penalty for breaching the contract. He estimated that the penalty could be as much as 100 percent of the revenues that Whittamore might earn in the two years remaining on his contract.

Whittamore was irate at Singson's response, considering it unreasonable and irresponsible. If that was the way the game was to be played, he threatened, he would leave and set up a practice, and Singson could take him to court to try to get his money. Singson responded that he would get an injunction against the practice if necessary and would demand the full amount if pushed into a corner. Whittamore stormed out of Singson's office mumbling that he was going to "get that son of a gun."

This conflict has multiple components: the Whittamores' relationship with each other, their relationship to other staff members at the clinic, the potential conflict between Andrew Whittamore's patients and the clinic, and the relationship between Andrew Whittamore and Richard Singson. For ease of analysis, we will examine only one of these components: the conflict between Richard Singson and Andrew Whittamore and the various means of resolution available to them.

CONFLICT MANAGEMENT AND
RESOLUTION APPROACHES

People in conflict have a number of procedural options to choose from to resolve their differences. Figure 1.1 illustrates some of these possibilities, which vary in terms of the formality of the process, the privacy of the approach, the people involved, the authority of the third party (if there is one), the type of decision that will result, and the amount of coercion that is exercised by or on the disputing parties.

At the left end of the continuum in the figure are informal, private procedures that involve only the disputants or a process assistant (a mediator). At the other end, one party relies on coercion and often on public action to force the opposing party into submission. In between are a variety of approaches that we will examine in more detail.

Disagreements and problems can arise in almost any relationship. The majority of disagreements are usually handled informally. Initially, people may *avoid* each other because they dislike the discomfort that accompanies conflict, they do not consider the issue to be that important, they lack the power to force a change, they do not believe the situation can be improved, or they are not yet ready to negotiate.

When avoidance is no longer possible or tensions become so strong that the parties cannot let the disagreement continue, they usually resort to *informal problem-solving discussions* to resolve their differences. This is probably where the majority of disagreements end in daily life. Either they are resolved, more or less to the satisfaction of the people involved, or the issues are dropped for lack of interest or inability to push through to a conclusion.

In the Singson-Whittamore case, the Whittamores avoided dealing with their potential conflict with the medical clinic until it was clear that Andrew was going to leave. At that point, Andrew initiated informal discussions, but they failed to reach an acceptable conclusion. Clearly, their problem had escalated into a dispute. Gulliver (1979, p. 75) notes that a disagreement becomes a dispute "only when the two parties are unable and/or unwilling to resolve their disagreement; that is, when one or both are not prepared to accept the status quo (should that any longer be a possibility) or to

Figure 1.1. Continuum of Conflict Management and Resolution Approaches.

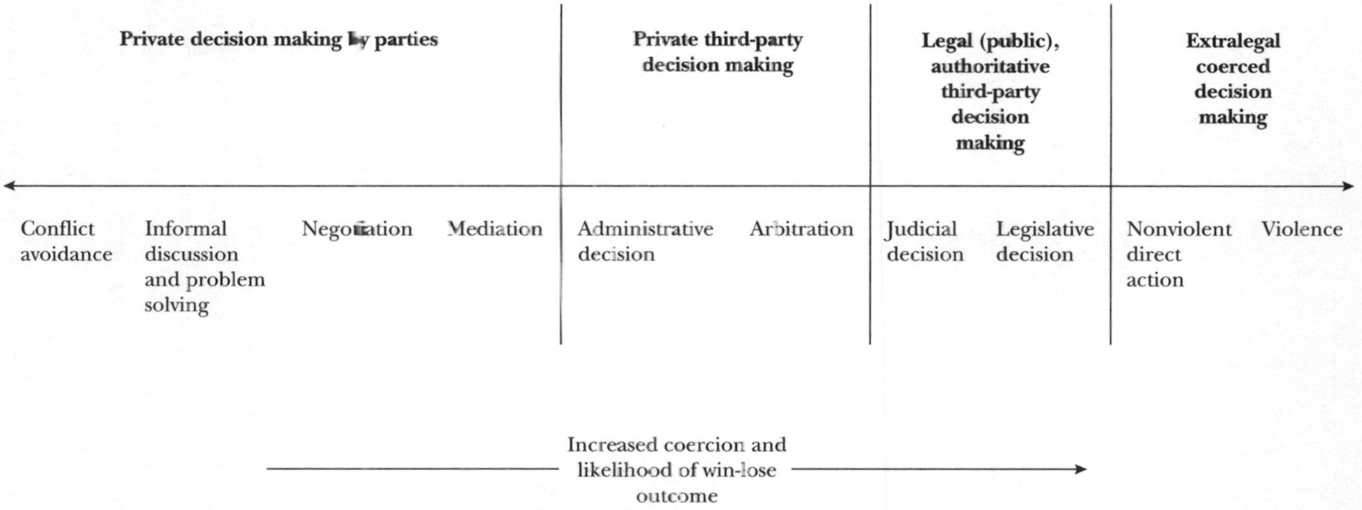

Private decision making by parties			Private third-party decision making		Legal (public), authoritative third-party decision making		Extralegal coerced decision making	
Conflict avoidance	Informal discussion and problem solving	Negotiation	Mediation	Administrative decision	Arbitration	Judicial decision	Legislative decision	Nonviolent direct action	Violence

Increased coercion and
——————————— likelihood of win-lose ———————————
outcome

accede to the demand or denial of demand by the other. A dispute is precipitated by a crisis in the relationship." People involved in a conflict that has reached this level have a variety of ways to resolve their differences. They can pursue more formal and structured means of voluntarily reaching an agreement, resort to third-party decision makers, or try to leverage or coerce each other to reach a settlement.

Other than informal conversations, the most common way to reach a mutually acceptable agreement is through *negotiation* (Fisher and Ury, 1981; Shell, 1999; Thompson, 2001). Negotiation is a bargaining relationship between parties who have a perceived or actual conflict of interest. The participants voluntarily join in a temporary relationship designed to educate each other about their needs and interests, to exchange specific resources, or to resolve less tangible issues such as the form their relationship will take in the future or the procedure by which problems are to be solved. Negotiation is clearly an option for Whittamore and Singson, although the degree of emotional and substantive polarization will make the process difficult.

If negotiations are hard to initiate or have started and reached an impasse, the parties may need some assistance from a party who is outside of the dispute. *Mediation* is an extension or elaboration of the negotiation process that involves the intervention of an acceptable third party who has limited (or no) authoritative decision-making power. This person assists the principal parties to voluntarily reach a mutually acceptable settlement of the issues in dispute. As with negotiation, mediation leaves the decision-making power primarily in the hands of the people in conflict. Mediation is a voluntary process in that the participants must be willing to accept the assistance of the intervenor if he or she is to help them manage or resolve their differences. Mediation is usually initiated when parties can no longer handle the conflict on their own and when the only means of resolution appears to involve impartial third-party assistance.

Whittamore and Singson might consider mediation if they cannot negotiate a settlement on their own. We will return to this process later on, once their other procedural options have been evaluated.

Beyond negotiation and mediation, there are a number of approaches that decrease the personal control the people involved have over the dispute outcome, increase the involvement of external decision makers, and rely increasingly on win-lose and either-or decision-making techniques. These approaches can be divided into public and private, and legal and extralegal.

If the dispute is within an organization or, occasionally, between an organization and members of the public, there is often an *administrative* or *executive dispute resolution approach*. In this process, a third party who has some distance from the dispute but is not necessarily impartial may make a decision for the parties in dispute. The process can be private, if the context within which the dispute occurs is a private company, division, or work team; or public, if the difference is a public dispute and is conducted by a governmental agency, a mayor, a county commissioner, a planner, or another administrator. An administrative dispute resolution process generally attempts to balance the needs of the entire system and the interests of individuals or concerned groups.

In the Singson-Whittamore dispute, both parties might choose to appeal to the board of directors of the Fairview Medical Clinic for a third-party decision. If both parties trust the integrity and judgment of these decision makers, the dispute might end there. However, Whittamore is not sure that he would get a fair hearing from this board.

Arbitration is a generic term for a voluntary process in which people in conflict request the assistance of an impartial and neutral third party to make a decision for them regarding contested issues. The outcome of the decision may be either advisory or binding. One person or a panel of third parties may conduct arbitration. The critical factor is that they are outside of the conflict relationship.

Arbitration is a private process in that the proceedings, and often the outcome, are not open to public scrutiny. People often select arbitration because of its private nature, and also because it is more informal, less expensive, and faster than a judicial proceeding. In arbitration, the parties frequently are able to select their own arbiter or panel, which gives them more control over the decision than if the third party were appointed by an outside authority or agency.

Whittamore and Singson have both heard of arbitration but are reluctant to turn their problem over to a third party before they are sure that they cannot resolve it themselves. Neither wants to risk an unfavorable decision. In addition, Singson fears an external decision that might erode the clinic's prerogative to control the contract process.

A *judicial approach* involves the intervention of an institutionalized and socially recognized authority in a dispute. This approach shifts the resolution process from the private domain to the public. In the judicial approach, the disputants usually hire lawyers to act as their advocates and the case is argued before an impartial and neutral third party—a judge, and perhaps a jury as well. These decision makers take into consideration not only the disputants' concerns, interests, and arguments but also the broader society's standards and values. The judge or jury is usually required to make a decision based on and in conformity with case law and legal statutes. The outcome is usually win-lose and is premised on a decision regarding who is right and who is wrong. Because the third party is socially sanctioned to make a decision, the results of the process are binding and enforceable. The disputants lose control of the outcome but may gain from forceful advocacy of their point of view and by a decision that reflects socially sanctioned laws or norms that are in their favor.

Whittamore and Singson have both considered using a judicial approach to resolve their dispute. Singson is willing, if necessary, to seek a court injunction that would enforce the no-competition clause in the contract by prohibiting Whittamore from establishing a private practice. Whittamore is willing to go to court to test the constitutionality of the clause. But both see a risk in this procedure, as the outcome may be highly detrimental to their underlying interests.

The *legislative approach* to dispute resolution is another public means of solving a conflict by recourse to law. It is usually employed for larger disputes affecting broad populations, but it may have significant utility for individuals. In this approach, the decision regarding the outcome is made by another win-lose process: voting. The individual has only as much influence on the final outcome as he or she, and those who share his or her beliefs, can bring to bear on legislators. Furthermore, the win-lose aspect of the outcome is only partly softened by the compromises that go into a bill.

Whittamore has considered using this approach to resolve his dispute. He believes there should be a law against no-competition clauses, and some of his patients agree with him. One patient has even suggested a campaign to pass a bill prohibiting this type of contract. But Whittamore also realizes that a legislative approach to this problem might take a long time—time he does not have at his disposal. Also a change in the law might not cover contracts entered into before the new law was passed.

Finally, there is the *extralegal approach*. The approaches examined so far are either private procedures the parties use alone or with the assistance of a third party to negotiate a settlement, or third-party decision making that is either privately or publicly sanctioned. The last category is extralegal in that it does not rely on socially mandated—or on occasion, socially acceptable—processes and generally uses stronger means of coercion to persuade or force an opponent into compliance or submission. There are two types of extralegal approaches: nonviolent action and violence.

Nonviolent action involves a person or group committing acts or abstaining from acts so that an opponent is forced to behave in a desired manner (Sharp, 1973). These acts, however, do not involve physical coercion or violence and are often designed to minimize psychological harm as well. Nonviolent action works best when the parties must rely on each other for their well-being. When this is the case, one of the parties may force the other to make concessions by refusing to cooperate or by committing undesirable acts.

Nonviolent action often involves civil disobedience—violation of widely accepted social norms or laws—to raise an opponent's consciousness or bring into public view practices that the nonviolent activist considers unjust or unfair. Nonviolent action can be conducted by an individual or by a group and may be either public or private.

Whittamore has contemplated nonviolent action on both the personal and group levels to resolve his dispute. On the individual level, he has considered fasting or occupying Singson's office until the director agrees to bargain in good faith and give him a fair settlement. He has also considered opening a private practice, challenging the terms of the contract, and forcing the clinic to either take him to court or drop the case. If he goes to court, he could exploit the publicity and place the clinic in a dilemma: dismiss a widely esteemed doctor and earn the wrath of the community and bad publicity, or reach a negotiated settlement favorable to Whittamore and avoid the bad press.

One of his patients has suggested organizing a picket or vigil outside the clinic to embarrass Singson and the clinic into a settlement. If that is unsuccessful, the patient has suggested a group sit-in. Whittamore is unsure of the likely effects of these approaches, as well as of the costs.

The last approach to dispute resolution is *violence* or *physical coercion*. This approach assumes that if the costs to the person or property of an opponent and the costs of maintaining his position are high enough, the adversary will be forced to make concessions. For physical coercion to work, the initiating party must possess enough power to actually damage the other party, must be able to convince the other side that it has the power, and must be willing to use it.

Although Whittamore and Singson are very angry with each other, they have not come to blows. Both are physically fit and could conceivably harm each other, but neither feels he could force the issue with a private fight. Whittamore, in the heat of anger, mumbled that he ought to sabotage some of the clinic's valuable equipment, but such an action would go against some of his deeply held values and would also hurt patients. Singson, in a moment of rage and fantasy, also considered violence and wondered what Whittamore's reaction would be if he were to be assaulted by agents Singson could hire for that purpose. He, too, has decided against physical violence as too risky, costly, unpredictable, and unreasonable.

The question remains: Which of the approaches represented in Figure 1.1 will Whittamore and Singson choose to resolve their dispute?

Whittamore wants to stay in town so that he can be near his children. He also wants to practice medicine. Establishing a new practice will be expensive, so he wants to minimize his dispute resolution costs. He hopes for a quick decision so that he may leave the clinic soon to avoid more adverse contact with Janelle and to minimize any harm to his personal relationships with other staff members. A positive ongoing relationship with the clinic and its staff is important because the clinic has the only laboratory and high-tech medical equipment in the town. Whittamore also needs to establish a private practice quickly so that he can generate income. Physical violence was a fleeting fantasy. Nonviolent action is still a possibility if the clinic does not yield. Judicial and legislative approaches seem unreasonable at this point because of the cost and the length of time they will take to effect a change.

Singson is also trying to decide what action he will take. He wants to keep management control over the contract process; seeks to solve the problem himself and not rely on outside agents; and wants to minimize such costs as legal fees, patient attrition, and bad publicity. He wants to find an amicable solution but feels that his interactions with Whittamore have reached an impasse.

Whittamore and Singson's conflict is ripe for negotiation. The two parties are:

- Interdependent and must rely on the cooperation of one another in order to meet their goals or satisfy their interests
- Able to influence one another and to undertake or prevent actions that can either harm or reward
- Pressured by deadlines and time constraints and share a motivation for early settlement
- Aware that alternatives to a negotiated settlement do not appear as viable or desirable as a bargain that they might reach themselves
- Able to identify the critical primary parties and involve them in the problem-solving process
- Able to identify and agree on the issues in dispute
- In a situation in which their interests are not entirely incompatible
- Influenced by external constraints—such as the unpredictability of a judicial decision, potentially angry patients or staff, costs of establishing a new practice, and expenses of recruiting a new physician—that encourage them to reach a negotiated settlement

These conditions are critical to successful negotiation. However, Singson and Whittamore's relationship also contains elements that will make unassisted negotiations extremely difficult. To overcome these problems, they will need third-party help, and in this case, mediation seems to be the most appropriate dispute resolution procedure to pursue. A mediator may be called into negotiations when:

- The emotions of the parties are intense and are preventing a settlement
- Communication between the parties is poor in either quantity or quality and they cannot change the situation on their own
- Misperceptions or stereotypes are hindering productive exchanges
- Repetitive negative behaviors are creating barriers
- There are serious disagreements over data—what information is important, how it is collected, and how it will be evaluated
- There are multiple issues in dispute, and the parties disagree about the order and combination in which they should be addressed
- There are perceived or actual incompatible interests that the parties are having difficulty reconciling
- Perceived or actual value differences divide the parties
- The parties do not have a negotiating procedure, are using the wrong procedure, or are not using a procedure to its best advantage
- There is not an acceptable structure or forum for negotiations
- The parties are having difficulties starting negotiations or have reached an impasse in their bargaining

Because Whittamore and Singson's relationship has some of the characteristics listed here, they will decide to use mediated negotiations as a means of resolving their differences. For the moment, let us leave this case and take a look at the process that they have selected to resolve their conflict. We will return to the Singson-Whittamore dispute in Chapter Two when we explore how the mediation process works.

THE MEDIATION PROCESS

Although mediation is practiced around the world in the resolution of interpersonal, organizational, commercial, legal, community, public, ethnic, and international disputes; and although techniques have been documented in particular applications and case studies, there has been until recently little systematic study or description of specific strategies and tactics used by mediators. The analysis that *has* been done has often been presented on the most general level or is so specific as to limit its broad application.

This book addresses the need for a systematic and practical general approach to mediation. It has three major goals: (1) to illustrate the effects and dynamics of mediation on the practice of negotiation; (2) to develop a theoretical explanation for the current practice of mediation as it has been applied in a variety of issues, arenas, and cultures; (3) to provide practitioners concrete and effective strategies and techniques to assist parties in dispute resolution. Let us first attempt to define mediation.

A DEFINITION OF MEDIATION

Consider these scenarios: a mediator from the United Nations enters an international conflict; a labor mediator engages in negotiations prior to a threatened strike; a commercial mediator settles a business dispute; a lawyer acting as a mediator settles a contentious legal suit; a family mediator assists a couple in reaching a divorce settlement. Who are these individuals, and what relationship do they have with the respective parties? What activities are they performing? What are their goals and objectives and those of the mediation process?

As stated earlier, *mediation* is generally defined as the intervention in a negotiation or a conflict of an acceptable third party who has limited or no authoritative decision-making power, who assists the involved parties to voluntarily reach a mutually acceptable settlement of the issues in dispute. In addition to addressing substantive issues, mediation may also establish or strengthen relationships of trust and respect between the parties or terminate relationships in a manner that minimizes emotional costs and psychological harm.

A mediator is a third party, generally a person who is not directly involved in the dispute or the substantive issues in question. This is a critical factor in conflict management and resolution, for it is the participation of an outsider that frequently provides parties with new perspectives on the issues dividing them and more effective processes to build problem-solving relationships. More will be said about the variety of possible relationships between the parties and "outsiders" in the next section.

The next aspect of the definition is *acceptability:* the disputants must be willing to allow a third party to enter the dispute and assist them in reaching a resolution. Acceptability does not necessarily mean that disputants eagerly welcome the involvement of the mediator and are willing to do exactly as he or she says. It does mean that the parties approve of the mediator's presence and are willing to listen to and seriously consider his or her suggestions on how to manage and resolve their differences.

Intervention means "to enter into an ongoing system of relationships, to come between or among persons, groups, or objects for the purpose of helping them. There is an important implicit assumption in the definition that should be made explicit: the system exists independently of the intervenor" (Argyris, 1970, p. 15). The assumption behind an outsider's intervention is that a third party will be able to alter the power and social dynamics of an existing conflict relationship by influencing the beliefs or behaviors of individual parties, by providing knowledge or information, or by introducing a more effective negotiation process and thereby helping the participants to settle contested issues. Rubin and Brown (1975) have argued that the mere presence of a party who is independent of the disputants may be a highly significant factor in the resolution of a dispute.

For mediation to occur, the parties must begin talking or negotiating. Labor and management must be willing to hold a bargaining session, business associates must agree to conduct discussions, governments and public interest groups must create forums for dialogue, and families must be willing to come together to talk. *Mediation is essentially dialogue or negotiation with the involvement of a third party.* Mediation is an extension of the negotiation process in that it involves extending the bargaining into a new format and using a mediator who contributes new variables and dynamics to the interaction of the disputants. Without negotiation, there can be no mediation.

Conflicts involve struggles between two or more people over values, or competition for status, power, or scarce resources (Coser, 1967). Mediators enter conflicts that have reached various levels of development and intensity—(latent, emerging, or manifest). These levels differ according to their degree of organization, the activities of the parties, and the intensity of expression of concerns and emotions. *Latent conflicts* are characterized by underlying tensions that have not fully developed and have not escalated into a highly polarized conflict. Often, one or more parties, usually the stronger one, may not even be aware that a conflict or the potential for one exists (Curle, 1971). Examples of latent conflicts are changes in personal relationships in which one party is not aware of the seriousness of the breach that has occurred; projected but unannounced staff cutbacks within an organization; developed but unimplemented plans for the siting of a predictably controversial facility such as a mine or waste disposal site; or potentially unpopular changes in public policy.

Mediators (or facilitators, another type of third party) working on latent disputes help participants identify the people who will be affected by a change or who may be concerned about a problem arising in the future. They assist in developing a mutual education process around the issues and interests involved, and they work with participants on designing, and sometimes implementing, a problem-solving process.

Emerging conflicts are disputes in which the parties are identified, the dispute is acknowledged, and many issues are clear. However, a workable cooperative negotiation or problem-solving process has not developed. Emerging conflicts have a potential for escalation if a resolution procedure is not implemented. Many disputes between coworkers, businesses, and governments illustrate this type of conflict. Both parties recognize that there is a dispute, and there may have been a harsh verbal exchange, but neither knows how to handle the problem. In this case, the mediator helps establish the negotiation process and assists the parties begin to communicate and bargain.

Manifest conflicts are those in which parties are engaged in an active and ongoing dispute. They may have participated in violent or nonviolent activities or may have started to negotiate and have reached an impasse. Mediator involvement in manifest conflicts often involves changing the conflict resolution or negotiation procedures or intervening to break a specific deadlock. International mediators intervene in wars. Labor mediators who intervene in negotiations before a strike deadline are working to resolve manifest conflicts, as are commercial mediators who handle a specific insurance claim over a personal injury. Child custody and divorce mediators also usually intervene in fully manifest disputes—a couple's initiation of separation proceedings.

A mediator generally has limited or no authoritative decision-making power; he or she cannot unilaterally mandate or force parties to resolve their differences and enforce the decision. This characteristic distinguishes the mediator from the judge or arbitrator, who is generally empowered to make a decision for the parties on the basis of a prior agreement by the disputants or societal norms, rules, regulations, laws, or contracts. The goal of a judicial or quasi-judicial process is not reconciliation or agreement between the parties, but a unilateral decision by the third party concerning which of the parties is right.

The judge examines the past and evaluates "agreements that the parties have entered into, violations which one has inflicted on the other," and "the norms concerning acquisition of rights, responsibilities, etc. which are connected with these events. When he has taken his standpoint on this basis, his task is finished" (Eckhoff, 1966–67, p. 161).

The mediator, on the other hand, works to reconcile the competing interests of the two parties. The mediator's tasks are to assist the parties in examining their interests and needs, to help them negotiate an exchange of promises, and to redefine their relationship in a way that will be mutually satisfactory and will meet their standards of fairness.

The mediator does not have decision-making authority, and this fact makes mediation attractive to many parties in dispute because they can retain the ultimate control of the outcome. However, mediators are not without influence. The mediator's authority, such as it is, resides in his or her personal credibility and trustworthiness, expertise in enhancing the negotiation process, experience in handling similar issues, ability to bring the parties together on the basis of their own interests, past performance or reputation as a resource person, and (in some cultures) his or her relationship with the parties. Authority, or recognition of the right to influence the outcome of a dispute, is granted by the parties themselves rather than by an external law, contract, or agency.

So far, we have examined some of the characteristics of a mediator. We will now explore some of the functions a mediator performs. Our definition states that a mediator *assists* disputing parties.

Assistance can refer to very general or to highly specific activities. We will examine here some of the more general roles and functions of the mediator; we will discuss specifics later, when analyzing intervention activities during particular phases of negotiation.

The mediator may assume a variety of roles to assist parties in resolving disputes (American Arbitration Association, n.d.):

- The *opener of communication channels,* who initiates communication or facilitates better communication if the parties are already talking
- The *legitimizer,* who helps all parties recognize the right of others to be involved in negotiations
- The *process facilitator,* who provides a procedure and often formally chairs the negotiation session
- The *trainer,* who educates novice, unskilled, or unprepared negotiators in the bargaining process
- The *resource expander,* who offers procedural assistance to the parties and links them to outside experts and resources (for example, lawyers, technical experts, decision makers, or additional goods for exchange) that may enable them to enlarge acceptable settlement options
- The *problem explorer,* who enables people in dispute to examine a problem from a variety of viewpoints, assists in defining basic issues and interests, and looks for mutually satisfactory options
- The *agent of reality,* who helps build a reasonable and implementable settlement and questions and challenges parties who have extreme and unrealistic goals
- The *scapegoat,* who may take some of the responsibility or blame for an unpopular decision that the parties are nevertheless willing to accept. This enables them to maintain their integrity and, when appropriate, gain the support of their constituents
- The *leader,* who takes the initiative to move the negotiations forward by procedural—or on occasion, substantive— suggestions

The last component of the definition describes mediation as a voluntary process to reach a mutually acceptable settlement of issues in dispute. *Voluntary* generally refers to both freely chosen participation and freely made agreements. Parties are not forced to mediate and settle by either an internal or external party to a dispute. Stulberg (1981b, pp. 88–89) notes that "there is no legal liability to any party refusing to participate in a mediation process. Since a mediator has no authority unilaterally to impose a decision on the parties, he cannot threaten the recalcitrant party with a judgement."

Voluntary participation does not, however, mean that there may not be pressure to try mediation. Other disputants or external figures, such as friends, colleagues at work, constituents, authoritative leaders, or judges, may put significant pressure on a party to make an attempt at negotiation with the assistance of a mediator. Some courts in family and civil cases in the United States have even gone so far as to rule that parties must make a good faith effort at mediation before the court will be willing to hear the case. Attempting mediation does not, however, mean that the participants are forced to reach agreements.

THE HISTORICAL PRACTICE OF MEDIATION

Mediation has a long and varied history in almost all cultures of the world. Jewish, Christian, Islamic, Hindu, Buddhist, Confucian, and many indigenous cultures all have extensive and effective traditions of mediation practice. Here are a number of examples indicating the extensiveness and development of mediation as a means of dispute resolution.

Jewish communities in biblical times used mediation—which was practiced by both religious and political leaders—to resolve civil and religious differences. Later, in Spain, North Africa, Italy, Central and Eastern Europe, the Turkish Empire, and the Middle East, rabbis and rabbinical courts played vital roles in mediating or adjudicating disputes between members of their faith. These courts were often crucial to the protection of cultural identity and ensured that Jews had a formalized means of dispute resolution. In many locales, Jews were barred by exclusionary laws of larger societies from other means of dispute settlement.

Jewish traditions of dispute resolution were ultimately carried over to emerging Christian communities, who saw Christ as the supreme mediator. The Bible refers to Jesus as a mediator between God and man: "For there is one God, and one mediator between God and man, the man Christ Jesus; who gave himself as ransom for all, to be testified in due time" (I Timothy 2:5–6). This concept of the intermediary was eventually adopted to define the role of clergy as mediators between the congregation and God and between believers. Until the Renaissance, the Catholic Church in Western Europe and the Orthodox Church in the Eastern Mediterranean world were probably the central mediation and conflict management organizations in Western society. Clergy mediated family disputes, criminal cases, and diplomatic disputes among the nobility. Bianchi (1978), in describing one mediated case in the Middle Ages, details how the church and the clergy made available the sanctuary where the offender stayed during dispute resolution and how they served as intermediaries between two families in a case involving rape. In the resulting settlement, the family of the rapist agreed to provide monetary restitution to the woman's family and promised to help her find a husband.

Islamic cultures also have long traditions of mediation. In many traditional pastoral societies in the Middle East, problems were often resolved through a community meeting of elders in which participants discussed, debated, deliberated, and mediated to resolve critical or conflictual tribal or intertribal issues. In urban areas, local custom (*'urf*) became codified into *shari'a* law, which was interpreted and applied by a specialized intermediary, or *quadi*. These officials performed not only judicial but also mediating functions. Hourani (1991, p. 114) notes that a *quadi* "might interpret his role as that of a conciliator, attempting to preserve social harmony by reaching an agreed upon solution to a dispute, rather than applying the strict letter of the law."

In Indonesia, one of the largest geographic areas influenced by Islam and Arab culture, traditional means of decision making and dispute resolution were blended with Islamic practices. The result was the *musyawarah* process, a consensually based conflict management procedure (Moore and Santosa, 1995). Variations of this process were used, and are still practiced today, throughout the island archipelago to make decisions and resolve disputes on both local and national issues (Von Benda-Beckmann, 1984; Slatts and Porter, 1992; Schwarz, 1994).

Hinduism and Buddhism, and the regions that they influenced, have a long history of mediation. The Hindu villages of India have traditionally employed the *panchayat* justice system, in which a panel of five members both mediates and arbitrates disputes; the panel also exercises administrative functions in addressing welfare issues and grievances within the community.

Mediation has been widely practiced in China, Japan, and a number of other Asian societies, where religion and philosophy place a strong emphasis on social consensus, moral persuasion, and seeking balance and harmony in human relations (Brown, 1982). Buddhist sacred texts describe at least three cases in which the Buddha acted as a mediator (*Dhammapada Commentary,* cited in McConnell, 1995; *Kosambi Jataka,* n.d.), and the sangha, or religious community of priests and nuns, has long played a mediation role in Buddhist communities and societies, first in India and China and later in Sri Lanka, Thailand, Nepal, Tibet, and Japan (McConnell, 1995).

With the rise of secular society in the West, mediation and the range of people acting as mediators expanded. In the business world, guilds and their members practiced mediation, as did burghers in disputes arising in the emerging cities. Though the clergy continued to play a role as intermediaries in local, intercommunal, and interstate relations, the rise of the rule of law and nation-states led to the growth of secular intermediaries. Secular judges both mediated and issued judicial rulings. Ambassadors and envoys acted to "raise and clarify social issues and problems, to modify conflicting interests, and to transmit information of mutual concern to parties" (Werner, 1974, p. 95).

Mediation also grew in the American and other colonies, and ultimately in the United States and Canada, where religious sects such as the Puritans and Quakers, and Chinese and Jewish ethnic groups, developed alternative procedures for dispute resolution that were of an informal and voluntary nature (Auerbach, 1983). These procedures functioned in parallel with preexisting dispute resolution mechanisms of Native Americans and First Nations peoples, who often used consensus-based council meetings, led by an elder or elders, to resolve disputes (LeResche, 1993).

THE CONTEMPORARY PRACTICE OF MEDIATION

For the most part, mediators in other ages and cultures learned their craft informally and fulfilled their role as intermediaries in the context of other functions or duties. Only since the turn of the

twentieth century has mediation become formally institutionalized and developed into a recognized profession. The modern
practice of mediation has expanded exponentially worldwide, especially in the last twenty-five years. This growth is due in part to a
wider acknowledgment of individual human rights and dignity,
the expansion of aspirations for democratic participation at all social and political levels, the belief that an individual has a right to
participate in and take control of decisions affecting his or her
life, an ethic supporting private ordering, and trends in some locales for broader tolerance of diversity in all its aspects. Change
has also been motivated by growing dissatisfaction with authoritative, top-down decision makers and decision-making procedures;
imposed settlements that do not adequately address parties'
strongly felt or genuine interests; and the increasing costs—in
money, time, human resources, and damage to interpersonal and
community solidarity—of more adversarial, win-lose procedures
of dispute resolution.

The use of mediation has grown significantly in many countries
and cultures, but it has perhaps grown most rapidly in the United
States and Canada. The first arena in which mediation was formally
institutionalized in the United States was that of labor-management
relations (Simkin, 1971). In 1913, the U.S. Department of Labor
was established, and a panel, the "commissioners of conciliation,"
was appointed to handle conflicts between labor and management.
This panel subsequently became the U.S. Conciliation Service,
which in 1947 was reconstituted as the Federal Mediation and Conciliation Service. The rationale for initiating mediation procedures
in the industrial sector was to promote a "sound and stable industrial peace" and "the settlement of issues between employer and
employees through collective bargaining" (Labor-Management Relations Act, 1947). It was expected that mediated settlements would
prevent costly strikes and lockouts and that the safety, welfare, and
wealth of Americans would be improved. Federal use of mediation
in labor disputes has been a model for many states. Numerous
states have passed laws, developed regulations, and trained a cadre
of mediators to handle intrastate labor conflicts.

The private sector has also initiated labor-management and
commercial relations mediation. The American Arbitration Association was founded in 1926 to encourage the use of arbitration
and other techniques of voluntary dispute settlement.

Mediation sponsored by government agencies has not been confined to labor-management issues. The federal Civil Rights Act of 1964 created the Community Relations Service (CRS) of the U.S. Department of Justice. This agency was mandated to help "communities and persons therein in resolving disputes, disagreements, or difficulties relating to discriminatory practices based on race, color, or national origin" (Civil Rights Act, 1964). The agency assists people in resolving disputes through negotiation and mediation rather than through recourse to street justice or the judicial system (Klugman, 1992). CRS works throughout the country on such issues as school desegregation and public-accommodation cases. There has also been a burgeoning of diverse state agencies, local civil rights commissions, and private agencies that use mediation to handle charges of race and ethnic discrimination in areas of employment, housing, accommodations, and consumer affairs (International City Managers' Association, 1966). In Canada, the Ontario Race Relations Directorate and other similar agencies in that province have provided dispute resolution services to manage differences between ethnic communities.

There have also been a number of specialized initiatives to utilize mediation to resolve disputes with ethnic or religious elements within and between various groups. The Navajo peacemakers (Bluehouse and Zion, 1993), Pacific Coast Salish tribes conciliators (Mansfield, 1993), Alaskan tribes intermediaries (Connors, 1993), the Mohawks' Akwesasne Peacemaking Program, and a variety of other tribal groups have developed traditional or modified means of resolving internal tribal differences. On the Hawaiian islands, traditional dispute resolution procedures, the Ho'Oponopono, are being revived to manage differences between a number of ethnic groups (Shook and Kwan, 1988; Barnes, 1994). Programs and projects have been developed in Los Angeles and Chicago to address disputes between Korean and African American communities, especially those related to conflicts between business owners and customers. In New York, initiatives have been taken to manage African American and Hasidic Jewish conflicts, and in a number of cities programs have been developed to respond to tensions among the dominant culture, traditional minority cultures, and newer Southeast Asian immigrants.

Since the mid-1960s, mediation has grown significantly as a formal and widely practiced approach to community dispute resolution (Bradley and Smith, 2000). In the early years of the field's growth, the federal government funded Neighborhood Justice Centers (NJCs) to provide free or low-cost mediation services to the public so that disputes could be resolved efficiently, inexpensively, and informally. In the early 1980s, many of these NJCs were institutionalized and became part of city-, court-, or district attorney–based alternative dispute resolution services. Some community programs also became independent nonprofit organizations and offered grassroots dispute resolution services in which community members served as solo mediators, co-mediators, or members of mediation or conciliation panels (Lemmon, 1984; Shonholtz, 1984). By 1997, there were over 550 NJCs across the United States (Ray, 1997).

In many U.S. and Canadian communities, mediation is being applied in landlord-tenant conflicts (Cook, Rochl, and Shepard, 1980); issues related to homelessness (Nelson and Sharp, 1995); police work with disputants (Folberg and Taylor, 1984); victim-offender issues (Umbreit, 1985, 1994, 2000); conflicts between citizens and police (Mayor's Office, City of Portland, Oregon, 1994); disputes among elderly residents, nursing home owners, and adult children of aging parents (Schmitz, 1998; Gentry, 2001); and consumer disputes (Ray and Smolover, 1983).

Canadians and Americans have developed community-based programs in a number of provinces. Of special note is the program of the Saskatchewan Mediation Service, based in Regina, which has focused on providing services to farm families. Centers such as this one mediate debtor-creditor and loan restructuring disputes and interpersonal and operations conflicts on family farms (Van Hook, 1990).

In addition to local mediation programs, there are statewide programs in many American states (Susskind, 1986; Drake, 1989). Initially spurred by the advocacy and funding by the National Institute for Dispute Resolution, the number of state-based programs jumped from four in 1984 to twenty in 1995, with some states having more than one program (Khor, 1995). Services provided by state programs include design and implementation of dispute resolution systems; training of state employees in alternative dispute resolution procedures; and mediation of interpersonal, group, and public disputes that involve state governments.

Mediation and other approaches to conflict resolution are also being introduced in primary and secondary schools and institutions of higher education (Araki, 1990; Sandy, 2001; Volpe and Chandler, 2001). Some of the initiatives have been teaching conflict management skills and integrating them into the general curriculum, while others involve developing direct peer mediation services (Compton, 2002; Ford, 2002; Batton, 2002). In this setting, disputes are mediated between students (Volpe and Witherspoon, 1992; Smith and Sidwell, 1990; Burrell and Vogl, 1990; Lindsay, 1998; Levy, 1989; Doelker, 1989), gangs (Wahrhaftig, 1995), between students and faculty, between faculty members, and between faculty and administration (McCarthy, 1980; McCarthy and others, 1984; Crohn, 1985). In the 1980s, the National Association of Mediation in Education (NAME) was founded, to link mediation practitioners and programs in the educational arena. In 2000, this organization merged with the Society of Professionals in Dispute Resolution (SPIDR) and the Academy of Family Mediators to become the Association for Conflict Resolution (ACR).

Another interesting effort in the area of education is the use of mediation and other collaborative problem-solving skills to handle problems related to decentralized decision making and school-based management (CDR Associates, 1993a). In this application, consensus-based decision making assisted by a facilitator/mediator is used as a strategy for anticipating, preventing, and managing conflict, as well as a process for fostering collaborative day-to-day decisions.

The criminal justice systems in the United States and Canada have used mediation to resolve criminal complaints (Felsteiner and Williams, 1978) and disputes in correctional facilities (Reynolds and Tonry, 1981). Mediation in the latter arena takes the form of both crisis intervention in prison riots or hostage negotiations and institutionalized grievance procedures. An interesting growth area in the criminal justice system has been victim-offender mediation programs in which intermediaries help concerned parties develop restitution plans or reestablish conflicted interpersonal relationships (Umbreit, 1985, 1994; Coates and Gehm, 1989; Umbreit and Greenwood, 1999).

One of the fastest-growing arenas in North America in which mediation is being practiced is family disputes (Fisher, 1991). Court systems and private practitioners provide mediation to families in child custody and divorce proceedings (Coogler, 1978;

McIsaac, 1983; Folberg and Taylor, 1984; Folberg and Milne, 1988; Haynes, 1981, 1994; Irving, 1980; Lemmon, 1985; Saposnek, 1983, 1998; Moore, 1988; McKnight and Erikson, 1998, 2002; Taylor, 2002), disputes between parents and children (Shaw, 1982; Wixted, 1982; Vorenberg, 1982), child protection cases (Mayer, 1985; Golten and Mayer, 1987), conflicts involving adoption and termination of parental rights (Mayer, 1985), spousal disputes in which there is domestic violence (Orenstein, 1982; Wildau, 1984; Ellis and Stuckless, 1992; Barsky, 1995; Corcoran and Melamed, 1990; Girdner, 1990; Erickson and McKnight, 1990), and as an alternative separation process for gay and lesbian couples (McIntyre, 1994; Gunning, 1995; Campbell, 1996). In family disputes, mediated and consensual settlements are often more appropriate and satisfying than litigated or imposed outcomes. Models of practice in this area include mandatory court-connected programs in which disputants must try mediation before a judge will hear the case; voluntary court programs; and forms of private practice such as the sole practitioner, the partnership, and the private nonprofit agency.

Mediation is also extensively used within public and private organizations to handle interpersonal and institutional disputes. The scope of mediation application ranges from one-on-one personnel disputes to problems between partners (for example, in law or medical practices), interdepartmental conflicts, altercations between companies, and other commercial disputes (Biddle and others, 1982; Bazerman and Lewicki, 1983; Blake and Mouton, 1984; Brett and Goldberg, 1983; Brown, 1983). In the late 1980s and early 1990s, there was a significant growth of mediation services and programs in the public and private sectors to mediate charges related to racial, ethnic, gender, and sexual-orientation discrimination in the workplace; sexual harassment (Rowe, 1994; Cloke and Goldsmith, 2000, 2001); and accommodation of people with disabilities (Roberts and Lundy, 1995), as well as to process complaints or grievances in nonunion and unionized settings (Skratek, 1990; Feuille, 1992; Goldberg, 1989; Valtin, 1993; Feuille and Kolb, 1994). Programs have been developed in a number of federal and state agencies, such as the U.S. Bureau of Reclamation and the Army Corps of Engineers ("Corps of Engineers Early Resolution Program," 1993), state governments (deLeon, 1994), and private sector firms (Westin and Feliu, 1988; Rowe, 1995; Mares-Dixon,

1999). The federal government, through the Administrative Dispute Resolution Act, presidential memorandums, and regulations for rule making, has actively promoted use of alternative dispute resolution and mediation (Susskind, Babbit, and Segal, 1993).

Closely related to the use of mediation within or by organizations is the growth of a wider practice of conflict management, institutional decision making, and dispute systems design:

> Decision making and dispute systems design is a systematic process for enabling people and developing mechanisms to make decisions and handle serious chronic disputes. The process involves (1) identification of types and causes of reoccurring issues and conflicts; (2) development and institutionalization of a range of decision-making, conflict management, and dispute resolution procedures that will assist parties to make decisions, lower the number of incidents of destructive conflict, and assist them to resolve their differences; (3) matching of issues and disputes with the appropriate decision making, conflict management or resolution procedure; (4) implementation of efficient operations and administrative procedures (of the system); (5) design of effective information programs to educate potential parties about how the range of decision making and dispute resolution processes can assist them to reach settlements and resolve conflicts; and (6) training cadres of people to work in the new system and provide needed services [Wildau and Mayer, 1992].

Many dispute resolution systems, whether newly developed or the result of expanding a previously existing system, have involved implementation of a mediation component. Settings in which systems have been developed include corporations; unionized mines; hospitals; social service agencies; natural resource management agencies; human resource departments; and federal, state, and local governments (Ury, Brett, and Goldberg, 1988; Ziegenfuss, 1988; Slaiku, 1989; Constantino and Merchant, 1995; Moore and Woodrow, 1999; Phillips, 2001).

Mediation has grown very rapidly since the mid-1980s in the corporate and commercial arenas, where in some types of disputes it has surpassed arbitration as the method of choice. Common types of disputes that have been mediated in this arena include contract disputes, failure to perform, product liability, patent infringement, trademark violations, intellectual property disputes, and a variety of insurance claim issues ("AAA Designs ADR Insurance Procedures," 1984). Leaders in promoting the use of alternative dispute resolution procedures, including mediation, to resolve corporate and commercial disputes have been the CPR Institute for Dispute Resolution, the American Arbitration Association, Jams/Endispute, and a number of other national and local private dispute resolution providers, as well as governmental agencies such as the U.S. Army Corps of Engineers. The CPR Institute for Dispute Resolution is a nonprofit coalition of general counsels of Fortune 500 companies and partners in leading law firms who are seeking alternatives to the increasingly high cost of litigation. Through publications, educational forums, and the Corporate Policy Statement (a pledge signed by corporations to explore and use alternative dispute resolution mechanisms as a first resort for settling commercial disputes), they have made a significant contribution to educating North American corporations about the utility of nonadversarial procedures (Henry and Lieberman, 1985).

Court-based mediation programs have been established in a number of jurisdictions in the United States to handle a variety of issues. Starting in the area of family disputes, these programs have expanded to address a range of civil cases. In some jurisdictions, courts have prescribed lower limits for financial claims, below which disputants must try mediation before the court will hear the case. Mediators working in these programs are generally either officials of the court or private mediators on contract. Another court-based mediation initiative that has gained popularity in a number of jurisdictions in the United States and abroad is "Settlement Week" (Dewdney, Sordo, and Chinkin, 1994). In this program, the court docket is set aside for a week, and cases are sent to voluntary mediation as an informal and expedited means of settlement. Mediations are conducted by trained professional mediators, lawyers, and judges. The record of success has led to the adoption of this mediation model by a number of jurisdictions across the United States and in other countries.

Mediation is also used extensively to resolve a variety of large public disputes over environmental and social policy issues (Susskind and Cruikshank, 1987; Laue, 1988; Bingham, 1984; Stamato and Jaffe, 1991; Grey, 1989; Moore, 1991; Susskind, 1994;

Dukes, 2000). In the environmental arena, mediation has been used to address site-specific conflicts such as those over water project construction, conservation, and operations (Carpenter and Kennedy, 1977; Meeks, 1988; Moore, 1989; Moore 1997; Viessman and Smerdon, 1989); facility siting and locational disputes (O'Hare, Bacow, and Sanderson, 1983; Lake, 1987; Tomain, 1989) and development issues (Sullivan, 1984); wildlife and fisheries management and habitat protection issues (CDR Associates, 1993b, 1995; Mayer, Moore, and Todd, forthcoming); waste management; highway, railroad, and airport siting; hazardous waste cleanup; land management and wetlands protection; and a variety of other local disputes (Bacow and Wheeler, 1984; Talbot, 1983; Cormick, 1976; Lake, 1980; and Mernitz, 1980).

Mediation is also being used extensively by a number of federal and state agencies to develop new regulations through a process of regulatory negotiations, or "reg-negs" (Bingham, 1981; Harter, 1984; Millhauser and Pou, 1987; Haygood, 1988). In this process, key stakeholders concerned about proposed regulations are convened, and negotiations are conducted by mediators or facilitators to develop consensus recommendations that can be submitted to the sponsoring agency or government entity. The federal agency that has sponsored the largest number of regulatory negotiations has been the U.S. Environmental Protection Agency (EPA), although a number of other agencies, such as the Department of Education, the Department of the Interior, the Federal Aviation Administration, the Occupational Safety and Health Administration, the Nuclear Regulatory Commission, and the Department of Agriculture, as well as a significant number of state governments, have implemented similar procedures.

Some of the topics for reg-negs have included aggregate resource mining regulations; standard setting for volatile organic compound emissions from finishes used in wood furniture manufacturing; use of disinfectants in drinking water; standards for the disposal of nonhazardous construction debris; rules for fossil collection on federal lands; accessibility of airplanes to people with disabilities; and air emissions standards from small engines.

Closely related to the development of regulations is the mediation of permitting and enforcement actions. Mediation helps concerned parties negotiate acceptable agreements over the conditions for future activity—for example, waste treatment and discharge plans for a new factory or mitigating or cleaning up past environmental problems. Allocating responsibility among potentially responsible parties at U.S. Superfund hazardous waste sites is a case in point; mediators have assisted concerned parties in apportioning financial responsibilities for cleanup and in negotiating remediation plans.

In the area of making public policy, mediation has been used to facilitate policy dialogues (Ehrman and Lesnick, 1988). Like regulatory negotiations, this process involves convening key stakeholder groups and negotiating consensus recommendations that can then be incorporated into policies or legislation. Some examples of policy dialogues are negotiations to develop growth management plans in California and New Jersey, policies and testing procedures for lowering volatile organic compounds in carpets and carpet-related activities, policies for the protection of oyster beds in the Chesapeake Bay, model national energy policies, and control of storm drainage systems.

In nonenvironmental areas, mediation has been used in site-specific cases; reg-negs; and policy dialogues to enable local, state, and federal agencies to coordinate their decisions on such matters as

- Block grants for program funding (Shanahan and others, 1982)
- Development of educational policies
- Closure or conversion of military bases or weapons production plants
- Policies on the release of drugs to the public
- Promotion of biodiversity and sustainability issues
- Historic preservation of valuable urban properties
- Municipal social service priorities
- Funding allocation priorities for the treatment of AIDS (Hughes, 1999)
- Resolutions of farmer-creditor disputes

One of the newest areas of growth in mediation is the health care industry (Reeves, 1994; Leone, 1994; Marcus and others, 1995; Currie, 1998). In the United States and Canada over the last decade, this industry has seen a growing number of disputes. Medical malpractice claims cost the industry roughly $15 billion annually in preventive insurance (Quayle, 1991). These suits are damaging to physicians and a threat to family financial security. Studies on the motivations of malpractice plaintiffs have shown that 40 percent felt humiliated by their experiences with the physician, more than 50 percent felt betrayed by their doctor, more than 80 percent felt embittered by the doctor's response to their complaints or questions, and more than 90 percent were "very angry" at their physician. In addition, 24 percent felt the physician was dishonest or misled them regarding the case or incident, 20 percent felt "court was the only way to find out what happened," and 19 percent felt the need to punish the doctor. When asked what could have been done to prevent litigation, 35 percent of plaintiff-patients responded "apologize or offer further explanations," and 25 percent responded "correct the error"; by contrast, only 16 percent responded "pay me compensation" (Dauer, 1994). Because malpractice disputes are often amenable to negotiation to resolve both emotional and financial issues, a number of insurers (Aetna, Allstate, Chubb, Cigna, Federated, Fireman's Fund, Hartford, Maryland Casualty, Nationwide, Royal, St. Paul Fire and Marine, State Farm, Wausau, and others) have begun to offer mediation as an alternative means of dispute settlement (Slaiku, 1989). To date, the process has been highly successful. In Austin, Texas, where a majority of malpractice claims are now mediated, there is an 80 percent settlement rate (Joseph, 1994).

In addition to malpractice cases, there are a number of other health care disputes in which mediation is being applied or explored. They include conflicts among doctors, administrators, and hospitals; HMO, group practice, and partnership difficulties; disputes between doctors and nurses; insurer denial of coverage; insurer denial of payment; bioethical disputes; credentialing conflicts; and labor-management relations (Joseph, 1994).

An emerging area of mediation practice is electronic or online dispute resolution (ODR). This form of mediation uses a "fourth party," the Internet or other electronic communications systems, to foster discussion, deliberation, and decision making by disputing parties (Rifkin, 2001; Katsh and Rifkin, 2001; Rule, 2002). The technological tools by which electronic dispute resolution is accomplished are highly diverse. Both synchronous and real-time interactions such as can be achieved through the use of chatrooms, decision rooms with multiple linked terminals, electronic mechanisms to collect input and identify areas of consensus, electronic voting (straw or weighted), and face-to-face videoconferencing and asynchronous communications such as e-mail or Web-based messaging may be used.

In online mediation, the role and function of the intermediary also varies, from being primarily a technical manager for information exchange to being highly influential in managing the negotiation process. Because of the limits on communications imposed by the use of electronic technology or the Internet, and the lack of face-to-face interactions, mediators have had to develop innovative approaches for working with disputing parties, including new ways of building trust and developing rapport, facilitating exchanges of emotions, dealing with the lack of verbal and nonverbal cues, coordinating the timing of message exchange, overcoming the tendency for parties to put forth extreme views or engage in "flaming" when communicating through the written word, and responding to the higher likelihood of deadlocks that occur more frequently in nonface-to-face interactions (Landry, 2000; Nadler, 2001; Rifkin, 2001).

Electronic and online dispute resolution have developed to address a variety of disputes, including intraorganizational differences (Landry, 2000) and e-commerce over the Internet (Nadler, 2001). Currently a number of companies have formed, among them Squaretrade (partnered with e-Bay), World Intellectual Property Organization Mediation and Arbitration (international disputes between commercial parties, including domain name disputes), ClickNSettle.com (insurance claims), Cybersettle.com (insurance claims), On-line Resolution (general), Mediate-net (family law), and Internet Neutral (commercial contracts)" (Nadler, 2001).

MEDIATION AROUND THE WORLD

The modern practice of mediation is not confined to Western societies, and in fact mediation procedures may be more widely practiced in non-Western countries than in the West (Augsburger, 1992). In general, the world can be divided into direct-dealing and nondirect-dealing cultures. Members of the former value face-to-face interactions, accept conflict as a given, are generally not uncomfortable with directly confronting those with whom they disagree; they are at ease with direct dialogue, debate, and negotiations. Members of the latter societies generally try to avoid overt conflict, strive to preserve face for themselves and others, and extensively use both informal and formal intermediaries. Many non-Western cultures, especially in Asia, Africa, and Latin America, have highly developed informal and formal mediation processes for resolving conflicts that are integrated into routine day-to-day interactions.

Asia

The Asia-Pacific region has been a particularly fertile area for mediation practice. The People's Republic of China has long practiced mediation to resolve interpersonal, community, and civil disputes through People's Conciliation Committees and court conciliation (Ginsberg, 1978; V. Li, 1978, M. Q. Li, 1988). The People's Conciliation Committees are institutionalized service providers established by the government; they offer mediation services primarily at the neighborhood, village, town, district, and county levels. The mediators are often retired village leaders with high prestige. The court conciliation occurs in the process of settling judicial cases and is often mediated by the hearing judge. More recently, mediation has been introduced to manage environmental and interjurisdictional disputes between governmental entities, which have been given increasing degrees of autonomy from the central government. Hong Kong and Singapore, too, have made significant strides in introducing and institutionalizing mediation in the commercial and family areas through the Hong Kong International Arbitration Centre; the Alternative Dispute Resolution Division of the Ministry of Law and Community Mediation Centers (CMC) in Singapore; and a number of social service agencies, religious and secular, in both locales (Ngoh-Tiong, 2002). In Singapore especially, there has been some effort to build upon the multicultural dispute resolution traditions of its Chinese, Malay, and Indian population. By incorporating Western models of mediation and traditional indigenous philosophies and procedures that engender a "*kampong* spirit" (a sense of community and being together), informal use of intermediaries (the *hong chin* among Chinese, *kampong kuta* or *penghulu* among the Malays), village meetings such as the *panchayat* (Indian), gift giving, and tea, Singapore has attempted to build a blended mediation approach.

Japan has a long history of using mediation at the informal level, with elaborate systems of go-betweens carrying communications between disputing parties. Mediation is embedded in the business culture, where intermediaries are used as introducers (*shokai-sha*) and as mediators (*chukai-sha*) to smooth business relationships (Graham and Sano, 1984). Japan also has an elaborate system of court-based mediation for both civil and family cases, which is extensively used to address a range of issues (Krapp, 1992). Family mediation is mandatory for most divorce proceedings and many parent-child issues. Generally, there is a mediation panel chaired by a judge and two other respected professional mediators, the latter handling most of the sessions.

Korea has developed mediation to address family and civil disputes through both independent and court-based mediation programs (Yang, 1988). In recent years, the ruling political party has established the People's Predicament Committee, which performs both ombudsman and mediating functions. The national environmental agency has also developed a mediating committee to address environmental issues.

Thailand, Malaysia, and Indonesia have developed a number of arenas where mediation is used (Muntarbhorn, 1988; Moore and Santosa, 1995; Ihromi, 1988). Thailand has experience in mediation primarily at the village level. Malaysia has developed a formal "conciliation" process, centered on government appointed mediators, for resolving industrial relations and trade conflicts (Aminuddin, 1990). Independent mediators are also used, though on rare occasions.

Indonesia, which has had a more restrictive government since the imposition of the New Order in 1965, still has maintained the *musyawarah* process for consensus decision making and dispute resolution in many villages and institutions. In addition, labor mediation is offered through a governmental body, the Committee for Labor Conflicts Settlements, which is part of the Ministry for Labor Affairs (Ihromi, 1988). The newest initiative in the area of *musyawarah* and mediation is in environmental dispute resolution. The Ministry for the Environment, the Bureau of Environmental Impact Management, and several nongovernmental public interest groups (Wahana Lingkungan Hidup Indonesia and the Indonesian Center for Environmental Law, among others) have supported and participated in a number of mediations over water pollution issues. The governor of the province of Kalimantan on Borneo has supported the design and institutionalization of a mediation system for resolving environmental disputes. The latter project is conducted in cooperation with the Deutsche Gesellschaft für Technische Zusammenarbeit (GTZ), a German technical assistance agency; and U.S. conflict management practitioners (Moore and Santosa, 1995).

The Philippines and Sri Lanka have developed highly elaborate community-based mediation programs for resolving civil and some minor criminal disputes. The Barangay Justice System in the Philippines, which was established by President Ferdinand Marcos in 1978, set up a nationwide system of mediation and arbitration panels in neighborhoods and districts to hear community disputes (Pe and Tadiar, 1988). The mediation panels handle cases in a multistep resolution process that includes efforts by the panel chair to settle the case, a mediation hearing, and (if these are not effective) the option of a decision by an arbitration panel. The system now has more than forty thousand boards throughout the country.

Sri Lanka's Mediation Boards Commission was authorized by law in 1988. This founding act set up an independent Mediation Boards Commission under the Ministry of Justice and promoted the establishment of mediation panels of respected citizens in districts throughout the island. With the assistance of U.S. experts in dispute systems design and in mediation, the boards have trained more than six thousand mediators and established more than 240 panels. Thousands of civil cases are processed each year (Herat, 1993).

On the Indian subcontinent today, the *panchayat* tradition described earlier is carried on in India, Nepal, Pakistan, and Bangladesh. In India, mediation is provided by legal aid programs in a number of states, and in Gujarat and Uttar Pradesh states by the *Lok Adalats,* or People's Courts, which offer mediation and conciliation services for matrimonial and civil disputes (Shourie, 1988).

In India, many of these systems have been strongly influenced by Gandhian principles of decentralized governance. Nepal, Pakistan, and Bangladesh have also taken steps to enhance, develop, and institutionalize mediation services, primarily at the local level (Afzal, 1988; Aryal, 1988; Islam, 1988). The Nepalese have developed mediation procedures to handle forest management disputes (Shrestha, 1995), marital conflicts, and financial transactions. Pakistan and Bangladesh have concentrated on mediating family and civil disputes.

Australia, New Zealand, Melanesia

Australia and New Zealand have followed a development path in mediation that in many ways has paralleled that of North America. Initially, mediation in several arenas in Australia was financially supported by government agencies. Community mediation centers have been established in most states and in large urban areas. These centers provide either solo mediation or co-mediation and have primarily addressed smaller civil and neighborhood disputes.

Mediation in Australia has also been developed in the courts— in the family arena (Faulkes, 1988; Renouf, 1991); as a component of a settlement week program; and as part of a Supreme Court pilot project on resolving personal injury, mortgaged property, and simple contractual disputes (Dewdney, Sordo, and Chinkin, 1994). Australia also has a very active community mediation sector, with programs in most states (Faulkes, 1990; Stevenson, 1990). Race complaints are also being mediated (Mulcahy, 1992). In addition, mediation is being used to resolve industrial disputes (Interim Rules, 1992) and conflicts between the majority culture and Australia's aboriginal peoples over social service and natural resource issues (Ross, 1995).

New Zealand has developed mediation services to handle a range of commercial, civil, small claims, criminal, family, labor, housing, land, and environmental disputes (Macduff, 1988). In the area of housing, the Housing Corporation of New Zealand has developed extensive services, provided by in-house and external mediators, for resolution of differences between tenants in public housing and between the authority and tenants. The Maori, the indigenous population of New Zealand, have their own traditional means of resolving disputes—*taha Maori*, or the Maori way—which until recently they used only within the clan or kinship group. This process involves a ritualized greeting invoking spirits, ancestors, and common bonds; creation of an atmosphere for dialogue; a fairly unlimited and open discussion; and recognition of agreement and reconciliation. More recently, some of these procedures have been used to address Maori altercations with non-Maori Pakiha (Macduff, 1988, 1995) and Maori land claims disputes (Wilson, 1992; Barnes, 2002).

In Melanesia, the Tolai villages in New Britain each have a counselor and committee that meet regularly to hear disputes (Epstein, 1971). The role of the counselor and committee is to "maintain conditions for orderly debate and freedom of argument by the disputants and anyone else who wishes to express opinion" (Gulliver, 1979, p. 27). The process is both a "mode of adjudication" and a "settlement by consensus" of the parties (Epstein, 1971, p. 168).

Latin America

Latin American indigenous and Hispanic cultures have used mediation historically, and they currently use it to address a range of disputes. Nader (1969) reports on the dispute resolution process in the Mexican village of Ralu'a, where a judge assists the parties in making consensual decisions. Lederach (1984, 1995) describes other mediation models from Hispanic culture that have been transposed to Latin America, such as the *Tribunal de las Aguas* (water court) in Spain. He also details informal mediations to resolve interpersonal disputes in Central America (Lederach, 1988). Riley and Sebenius (1995) and McCreary (1995) describe negotiation, fact-finding, and intermediary assistance in natural resource disputes in Ecuador, Honduras, and Cost Rica. Argentina is in the process of developing family, labor-management, and commercial mediation, and Brazil has a thriving mediation movement.

Africa and the Middle East

Mediation is used in both traditional and modern African societies, with practices varying from tribe to tribe and region to region (All Africa Conference on African Principles of Conflict Resolution and

Reconciliation, 1999; Ayendo et al., 2001). For example, the *moot court* is often a common means for neighbors to resolve disputes (Gulliver, 1971). The Tswana in Southern Africa use headmen and councils, and some tribes in Nigeria use chiefs, to accomplish negotiated resolutions (Comaroff and Roberts, 1981).

In Kenya and Somalia, mediation work has been undertaken by the Mennonite Central Committee and local secular and religious groups to address ethnic and clan disputes (Lederach, 1993). In these interventions, the emphasis has been to build on indigenous processes and develop culturally appropriate mediation mechanisms to address local disputes.

South Africa has experienced the most extensive development and use of formal mediation processes on the continent. In 1968, the Centre for Intergroup Studies (now the Centre for Conflict Resolution) was founded to create constructive, creative, and cooperative approaches to resolving conflict and reducing violence. In the mid-1980s, Independent Mediation Services of South Africa (IMSSA) was established to handle an increasing number of labor conflicts in various industries. Its success in that area has led to an expansion into the spheres of racial and political conflict.

In the 1980s and early 1990s, a host of highly effective groups and organizations emerged that were active in community and political conflict resolution. Most notable were the African Centre for the Constructive Resolution of Disputes (ACCORD), Vuleka Trust, Wilgespruit Fellowship, the Negotiation Skills Project (Funda Centre), the Institute for a Democratic Alternative in South Africa (IDASA), and a number of dispute resolution programs at the University of Port Elizabeth and the University of Witwatersrand.

In 1991, the major parties to the conflict in South Africa—the government, the African National Congress, and the Inkata Freedom Party—negotiated the National Peace Accord, a nationwide effort to address the growing violence in the country that was threatening progress toward democracy. This highly innovative accord established both regional and local peace committees that were to address actual and potential conflicts on the ground through a variety of conflict management approaches, one of which was mediation. Although it encountered enormous structural, political, resource, and logistical obstacles, this national system of dispute resolution made a significant effort in the peaceful transition of South Africa to democracy (Nathan, 1993; Moore, 1993). The boards, staff, and members of the peace committees successfully mediated numerous violent or potentially violent disputes and contributed significantly to the development of positive norms and procedures for peaceful conflict resolution in the country. Since the national elections in 1994, mediation has shifted from a focus on violence to an emphasis on development and reconciliation in South Africa and neighboring countries (Assefa, 1994).

Mediated settlements are also practiced in Arab societies (Salem, 1997). "A society in which conflicts are frequent must develop mechanisms for settling differences which, if allowed to get out of hand, can destroy the entire social fabric. In the Arab world, mediation on the tribal and village level has for centuries been the traditional method of settling disputes, and the same method has, in modern times, been adapted for settling political and military issues within and between Arab states" (Patai, 1983, p. 228).

Mediation is especially critical in Middle Eastern societies when honor is at stake and any concessions will appear to result in loss of self-respect or face. Face-to-face negotiations are often extremely difficult, and an intermediary is needed to separate the parties and work out an acceptable arrangement that preserves honor.

In many Middle Eastern and North African societies, intermediary services are performed by a mediator who is a person of respect. In Iraq and among tribal groups in Morocco and Algeria, he may even come from a special descent group with high status. Generally, mediators in the Arab world must be seen as neutral and impartial, and of high status so that neither of the parties can exert undue pressure on him (Patai, 1983).

Use of intermediaries in resolving business disputes is common across the Middle East. Villages in Jordan practice mediation using local community leaders as intermediaries (Antoun, 1972). Urban Cairo also has its own cultural approaches to dispute resolution (Murray, 1997). In Palestinian communities in the West Bank and Gaza, community and political leaders often mediate family, civil, and political disputes (Awad, 1994). These mediators are generally part of the disputants' social network, helping through the mediation process to assert community norms and reestablish social harmony. In Lebanon, especially during the time of the civil war, a number of political factions provided mediation as a means of

managing differences during the time the fighting either prevented access to the courts or inhibited them from functioning
(Hamzeh, 1994). Tunisia has an administrator or counselor, a
mouwafak el idri, who is attached to the office of the premier and
handles disputes that citizens have with government officials; and
market mediators, or *amine,* who resolve disputes between traders
and customers in the public markets.

Clearly, mediation has played a major role in Middle Eastern
societies in resolving serious diplomatic disputes and wars.
Whether in the Arab-Israeli peace process (Carter, 1982; Rubin,
1981), or in the ending of the American hostage crisis in Iran, intermediaries have played a valuable if not critical role.

In Israel, mediation has developed in its secular society to resolve commercial, community, and family disputes (Matz, 1991;
Sharon and Schwentzman, 1998). Several dispute resolution and
research centers have been started to study and apply intermediary processes to a range of disputes. Among religious Jews, spiri-
tual leaders often play intermediary roles in family, neighborhood,
and other community conflicts.

Europe

Western Europe, too, has begun to more widely adopt and develop
mediation processes and institutions. Business mediation has a firm
foothold in Great Britain, and family or community mediation services and centers have been developed in Great Britain, Ireland,
the Netherlands, Germany, France, and the Scandinavian countries (Acland, 1990). Norway has developed an elaborate system of
Boards of Conciliation, which mediate both civil and family cases
(Shaughnessey, 1992).

A number of programs and projects in Ireland have been initiated to address some of the sectarian tensions in the North (Morrow and Wilson, 1993). Germany is currently utilizing mediation
to address a variety of environmental, natural resource, and development issues (Weidner and Fietkau, 1995).

Since the end of communist rule in the early 1990s, Eastern
Europe and the Confederation of Independent States (CIS) have
begun to institutionalize mediation as a means of resolving a range
of disputes (Mayer and others, 1999). Dispute resolution centers,

which offer conflict resolution training and mediation services, have been established in Poland, the Czech Republic, Slovakia, Hungary, Bulgaria, Macedonia, the Ukraine, and Russia. Many of these centers have received significant assistance from U.S.-based practitioners who have traveled to the region to help in training and dispute systems design (Wildau, Moore, and Mayer, 1993; Votchal, 1993; Shonholtz, 1993). Specific areas of focus for practitioners and centers have been family disputes, conflicts in schools and universities, labor-management disputes, environmental conflict, and ethnic disputes. In this last area, a number of ethnic commissions have been established in Bulgaria and Slovakia, composed of majority and minority group members. These commissions advocate for fair treatment of minorities, conduct educational activities on multicultural relations, act as community problem-solving forums, and provide third-party mediation services (Mayer, Wildau, and Valchev, 1994).

Now that some of the history and applications of mediation in a variety of settings, situations, and cultures have been reviewed, we turn to an examination of the mediation process. In the next chapter, we will examine some of the variations in the roles of mediators, their orientations toward influence, the focus or goal of intervention, and the phases and tasks commonly used to achieve resolution of tangible issues and to address problematic relationships.

Chapter Two

How Mediation Works

This chapter examines the various roles of mediators and their relationships to parties. It also explores levels of directiveness of intermediaries and their choice of focus between problem solving and addressing relationship issues. An overview of general mediator approaches and activities is also presented.

VARIATIONS IN MEDIATOR ROLES AND PROCEDURES

The definition and description of mediation given in Chapter One generally outlines the role of mediators and the processes used to assist parties in reaching voluntary agreements. However, the fact that mediation is practiced in diverse situations, forums, conflicts, and cultures has led to variations in both roles and procedures.

In general, there are three broad types of mediators, defined by the relationship the mediator has with involved parties: (1) social network mediators, (2) authoritative mediators, and (3) independent mediators. Table 2.1 illustrates some of the characteristics of each type. To some extent, the type of relationship the intermediary has with disputants also influences the kind and degree of influence that is used to assist the parties. A variety of mediator types can be found in most cultures, although the development of mediation in a specific culture may emphasize or legitimize one form over another.

Social network mediators are individuals who are sought because they are connected to the disputants; they are generally part of a continuing and common social network. Such a mediator may be

Table 2.1. Types of Mediator.

Social Network Mediator	Authoritative Mediators		Vested Interest Mediator	Independent Mediator
	Benevolent Mediator	Administrative/ Managerial Mediator		
• Prior and expected future relationship to parties tied into their social network	• May or may not have a current or ongoing relationship with parties	• Generally has ongoing authoritative relationships with parties before and after dispute is terminated	• Has either a current or expected future relationship with a party or parties	• Neutral/impartial regarding relationships and specific outcomes
• Not necessarily impartial, but perceived by all to be fair	• Seeks best solution for all involved	• Seeks solution developed jointly with the parties, within mandated parameters	• Has a strong interest in the outcome of the dispute	• Serves at the pleasure of parties
• Very concerned with promoting stable long-term relationships between parties and their associates	• Generally impartial regarding the specific substantive outcome of the dispute	• Has authority to advise, suggest, or decide	• Seeks solution that meets mediator's interests and/or those of a favored party	• May be "professional" mediator
	• Has authority to advise, suggest, or decide		• May use strong leverage or coercion to achieve an agreement	• Seeks a jointly acceptable, voluntary, and non-coerced solution developed by the parties

- Frequently involved in implementation

- Generally has ongoing relationships with parties after dispute is terminated

- May use personal influence or peer/community pressure to promote adherence to agreement

- May have resources to help in monitoring and implementation of agreement

- May have resources to help in monitoring and implementation of agreement

- Has authority to enforce agreement

- May have resources to help in monitoring or implementation of agreement

- May use strong leverage or coercion to enforce agreement

- May or may not be involved in monitoring implementation

- Has no authority to enforce agreement

a personal friend, neighbor, associate, coworker, business colleague, or religious figure (priest, minister, rabbi, Moslem *'ulama,* shaman), or a respected community leader or elder who is known to all parties; the person is generally someone with whom those parties have an ongoing relationship. Lederach refers to network mediation using the Spanish term *confianza* mediation (1995): "Key to why people were chosen were the ideas of 'trustworthiness,' that 'we know them' and they can 'keep our confidences'" (p. 89). He continues: "*Confianza* points to relationship building over time, to a sense of 'sincerity' a person has and a feeling of 'security' the person 'inspires' in us that we will 'not be betrayed'" (p. 89).

The social network mediator often has a personal obligation to the parties to assist them as a friend—a desire to help them maintain smooth interpersonal relationships, both in the present and over the long run. He or she may also have a commitment to maintain harmony within the parties' broader social networks.

Social network mediator involvement with potential disputing parties often begins long before a specific conflict starts and may extend throughout the life of the resolution process, including the implementation of the agreement. The social network mediator's relationship with the parties is ongoing and enmeshed.

One example of a network mediator's activities comes from a dispute I observed in a Philippine community near Manila. A man and a woman had engaged in a heated public argument, the man claiming that money was due to him for his services as caretaker of the woman's garden and chauffeur of her children. He had come to her house twice to collect his pay; on the first occasion, she was out, and on the second, she told him she didn't have the money. When he came the third time and was denied payment, he created a noisy scene on the street in front of her home that roused her neighbors, and as he left he slammed her gate so forcefully that it came off its hinges. She in turn yelled at him and charged him with slandering her good name. They both ended this confrontation knowing that if the conflict was to be resolved, they would need some help.

The woman tried to think of a third person with whom they could talk, who could help them resolve their differences and restore the positive aspects of the relationship that they had maintained for several years. She decided on a respected community leader who was "related" to both of them: the woman was his *comadre* or godparent, and the man had grown up with him in the same village and had been his boyhood friend.

The woman approached the leader and obtained his agreement to mediate. He then approached the man and, after a long and informal chat, arranged for a joint meeting. This meeting involved discussion of the issues in dispute, the long-term relationship that the parties had with each other, the need to return harmony to the community, and the concern that each restore the good name of the other in the minds of their neighbors. After an extended discussion, the parties reached an agreement on all issues. Full payment was made for the gardener's services, apologies were exchanged, and each agreed to speak courteously and positively to the other in future conversations, as well as to use courteous language about each other when talking with neighbors about their past problem. (Some of the neighbors attended the open mediation session, saw the results, and were more than willing to spread the word that the relationship had been patched up by the respected leader.)

In this dispute, the authority of the mediator was embedded in the relationships he had with the parties, the trust and respect that the parties had for him as an individual, and his personal knowledge of their histories and the issues at hand. The relationship between the parties and the mediator was in fact the key to resolving the differences.

Although this dispute occurred in the context of Filipino culture, social network mediators are at work in almost all cultures. They are especially common in interpersonal disputes, whether in neighborhoods or organizations. However, they may also be found in larger public or political disputes; a respected communal or political leader is asked to intervene because of a past or ongoing personal relationship with the parties or because he or she occupies a particular position that engenders trust and respect on the part of the disputants.

The second broad category of mediator is a person who has an *authoritative* relationship to the parties in that he or she is in a superior or more powerful position and has potential or actual capacity to influence the outcome of a dispute. However, authoritative mediators, if they stay in a mediator role, do not make decisions for the parties. For any number of reasons—a procedural commitment to direct decision making by disputants, belief that a solution developed by the parties will result in greater satisfaction and commitment among their constituents, limits on the capacity or authority of the third party to unilaterally impose a decision—these intervenors usually try to influence the parties indirectly and attempt to persuade them to arrive at their own conclusions. This does not mean that they do not, on occasion, exercise significant leverage or pressure, perhaps with a view to limiting the settlement parameters. They may even raise the specter of a unilateral decision, as a backup to collaborative decision making if the parties cannot agree on their own.

The authoritative mediator's influence may have as its basis personal status or reputation, but it is also generally dependent on formal position in a community or organization, election or appointment by a legitimate authority, rule of law, or access to resources valued by the contending parties. Whether the authority, regardless of form, is actually exercised—and how it is exercised—depends very much on the situation and the intermediary's orientation toward influence.

In general, there are three types of authoritative mediators: benevolent, administrative/managerial (Kolb and Sheppard, 1985), and vested-interest (Rubin, 1981; Watkins and Winters, 1997). A *benevolent authoritative mediator* often has the ability to influence or possibly decide an issue in dispute but generally values agreement making by parties over his or her own role as a decision maker. A benevolent mediator wants a settlement that is mutually satisfactory; he or she is not particularly concerned with getting his or her own substantive needs or interests addressed in the resolution. (However, benevolent mediators may have procedural interests of fairness, efficiency, economy, and minimization of overt conflict; and psychological interests of maintaining a personal position, gaining respect from the parties and other observers of the dispute by effectively assisting the parties to resolve their differences, or being seen as a servant of wider community interests for peace and harmony.)

Examples of benevolent mediators are the interventions of highly respected religious or community leaders or elders into family or community disputes. The religious leaders or elders generally do not directly have the ability to decide the issue, but their status, knowledge, experience, reputation, and persona may highly influence the involved parties. A carefully measured statement by the respected benevolent mediator may significantly sway one or more of the disputants and move them toward agreement. It should be noted that benevolent mediators are very common, and in fact are more common in non-Western cultures than in the dominant cultures of Western societies.

A second type of authoritative intervenor is the *administrative-managerial mediator.* He or she has some influence and authority over the parties by virtue of occupying a superior position in a community or organization and having either organizational or legal authority to establish the bargaining parameters in which an acceptable decision can be determined (Kolb and Sheppard, 1985; Morril, 1995). This type of mediator differs from the benevolent type because he or she has a substantive interest in the outcome, albeit an interest that is institutionally or legally mandated.

Two brief examples of an administrative/managerial mediator, one within an organization and the other with concerned publics, illustrate this type of relationship with the parties. The first involved the services rendered by an executive who helped settle a workplace dispute. Two department heads were engaged in a hotly argued dispute over how a particular job, which required cooperation between the two departments, was to be handled and performed. They tried to talk directly about the issues but reached an impasse because of strong feelings about the problem and disagreements about how similar issues had been handled in the past. They both agreed to talk together with one of their colleagues, the chief executive officer of the company. Although the CEO could ultimately make a decision about the issue being brought before her, she did not at the time have a firm personal or "organizational" opinion about how the problem should be resolved. She was also not constrained by any organizational or legal requirements that would define the parameters of the solution. She did believe that it was better for the parties involved, for their subordinates, and for the organization as a whole if the two disputants reached their own decision on the question at hand. However, she was willing to provide procedural—and if necessary, substantive—advice. After a brief joint discussion with the CEO, who suggested some principles that might constitute a framework for an acceptable decision, the coworkers discussed the issues in more detail and developed a mutually acceptable solution to their differences.

A second example of managerial mediation comes from the Bureau of Environmental Impact Assessment, a government agency in Indonesia, though it could have occurred in any number of organizations or agencies around the world. The bureau was mandated to control and prevent water pollution from industrial plants and to protect environmental quality. A public interest law group brought a complaint to the agency that charged a particular company with polluting local waters and a claim that the releases were having an adverse impact on crops and the health of people downstream. The agency investigated and determined that the company was indeed releasing effluent that was above the legal limits. The company was notified that it had to control its releases, clean up past pollution, and possibly discuss past impact with the affected downstream parties.

Company representatives reluctantly agreed to meet with the agency and the affected parties. The meeting was chaired, and ultimately mediated, by one of the deputies in the agency. After being presented with the agency's test results, the company representatives agreed that they might be polluting and that measures needed to be taken to prevent these problems in the future. The government offered some technical assistance to the company and participated in the company's negotiations with the public interest group concerning the technology, procedures, and timing for installation of pollution control equipment. The company, however, was very reluctant to negotiate on compensation to the downstream interests. The agency could not mandate compensation but agreed with the public interest group that some action had to be taken to address past costs. It strongly suggested to the company that some form of acknowledgment needed to be made that the business had caused the local people serious problems.

Ultimately, in continuing negotiations with the public interest group, the company agreed to make a "contribution" to the community rather than paying "compensation." The company said it was not prepared to publicly admit fault or potentially adverse effects from its past pollution, but it would be willing, as a good neighbor, to aid the community in its time of need. The contribution that was ultimately agreed on was to haul fresh water into the community by truck, explore how the village could be hooked up to the water system of the adjacent municipality, and construct a new mosque and community center.

The third kind of authoritative mediator is a *vested-interest mediator*. This role is similar to that of the managerial mediator in that the intermediary has both procedural and substantive interests in the outcome of the dispute. What makes it different is the degree to which the intermediary's interests are advocated. Whereas the managerial mediator establishes the general parameters for a settlement that will meet organizational or legal norms and encourages and assists the parties to work within this framework, the vested-interest mediator often has specific interests and goals regarding all aspects of the dispute and pushes these objectives with enthusiasm and conviction (Smith, 1985). Some observers have noted that in this model the mediator is hardly an intermediary but merely another party who strongly advocates for his or her substantive interests.

The clearest examples of vested-interest mediators at work are probably found in the international arena. Henry Kissinger had strong vested interests when he acted as mediator for the Arab-Israeli disengagement negotiations in August 1975 (Rubin, 1981). So did President Carter in his role as intermediary in the Camp David Egyptian-Israeli peace talks (Carter, 1982; Princen, 1992), as did U.S. Ambassador Richard Holbrooke (Holbrooke, 1998) and the various UN mediators involved in the ethnonational conflicts of the former Yugoslavia. The United States has had longstanding political, economic, and strategic interests in the Middle East and assertively intervened as a broker in attempts to promote stability in the region. The United States has played the role of a mediator with muscle. Its representatives have at various times persuaded, cajoled, or aggressively pressured involved parties to seek a permanent peace; they have offered both arms and resources for development to help achieve these ends.

The U.S. and United Nations mediators in the former Yugoslavia, although representing national governments or an international organization, sought solutions that met the interests of key UN members as well as those of the parties on the ground. Much of their activity involved putting together proposals based on principles

established by either the United States or the UN and then trying
to persuade the combatants to accept these frameworks (Owen,
1995; Holbrooke, 1998).

Vested-interest mediation differs significantly from a number of
other forms of intervention that place a higher degree of emphasis on the parties' reaching their own decision. The latter view is
manifested particularly in the independent, impartial mediator,
who will be discussed next. Vested-interest mediation can be highly
effective in certain circumstances and is a common variety of mediation practice, but it might better be called "third-party advocacy."

The *independent mediator* is the final type to be discussed here.
The name derives both from the relationship that the intervenor
has to the parties—one of neutrality—and the stance that he or she
takes toward the problems in question—one of impartiality. The
independent intermediary is commonly found in cultures that
have developed traditions of independent and objective professional advice or assistance. Members of these cultures often prefer
the advice and help of independent "outsiders" (who are perceived
to have no personal vested interest in the intervention or its outcome) to assistance from "insiders" (with whom they may have
more complex and often conflicting relationships or obligations).
Members of cultures that favor independent mediators tend to
keep the various groups in their lives—family, close friends, neighbors, superiors and subordinates at work, business associates, recreational companions, civic associates, political affiliates, church
members—in separate compartments. They may rely on specialists
such as therapists, employee assistance counselors, financial advisors, legal counsel, golf pros, ward leaders, and clergy to help them
function well and handle potential or actual problems in each
area. An advisor or assistant in one arena may have little or no connection with another aspect of an individual's life, and members
of these cultures seem to like it that way.

Independent mediators are also most commonly found in cultures in which there is a tradition of an independent judiciary,
which is a model both for widely perceived fair procedures and impartial third parties as decision makers.

This type of intervention has in recent years been called the
North American model of mediation (Lederach, 1985). This label
is somewhat of a misnomer, as the roots of the process can be

found in Western Europe, and specifically Northern Europe, which during the Middle Ages and Renaissance produced Western models of compartmentalized relationships, professionalism, impartial advice, and independent procedural systems for resolving disputes. Although this type of mediation has been articulated, and perhaps most actively practiced, in North America, the model and its corresponding values are not culture-bound. They have spread around the globe and influenced the dispute resolution approaches of numerous cultures, which have either become acquainted with them as a result of colonial experience or selected them voluntarily because they have been seen to be efficient and fair.

Because impartiality and neutrality are often seen to be the critical defining characteristics of this type of mediation, it is important to explore these concepts in more detail (Young, 1972). *Impartiality* refers to the absence of bias or preference in favor of one or more negotiators, their interests, or the specific solutions that they are advocating. However, impartiality does not necessarily mean that the mediator is totally separate from the people or the conflict systems and issues in which they engage (Bowling and Hoffman, 2000). In many ways, a more accurate definition of impartial is "multipartial" or "omnipartial," in that mediators are involved with and concerned about how to help achieve satisfaction of all parties' issues and interests (Cloke, 1994). *Neutrality*, on the other hand, refers to the relationship or behavior between intervenor and disputants. Often, independent mediators have not had any previous relationship with disputing parties, or at least they have not had a relationship from which they could directly and significantly benefit. They are generally not tied into the parties' ongoing social networks. Neutrality also means that the mediator does not expect to obtain benefits or special payments from one of the parties as compensation for favors in conducting the mediation.

People seek an independent mediator's assistance because they want procedural help in negotiations. They do not want an intervenor who is biased or who will initiate actions that are potentially detrimental to their interests.

Impartiality and neutrality do not mean that a mediator may not have a personal opinion about a desirable outcome to a dispute or feel closer to one party than another or disconnected from people with home they work. No one can be entirely impartial.

What impartiality and neutrality do signify is that the mediator can separate his or her personal opinion about the outcome of the dispute or relationships that have developed during the mediation process from the performance of their duties and focus on ways to help the parties make their own decisions without unduly favoring one of them. The ultimate test of the impartiality and neutrality of the mediator lies in the judgment of the parties: they must perceive that the intervenor is not overtly partial or unneutral in order to accept his or her assistance.

Kraybill (1979) and Wheeler (1982) address the tensions between impartiality/neutrality and the personal biases of mediators by distinguishing between substantive and procedural interests. Wheeler argues that mediators generally distance themselves from commitments to specific substantive outcomes—the amount of money in a settlement, the exact time of performance, and so forth—but do have commitments to such procedural standards as open communication, equity and fair exchange, durability of a settlement over time, and enforceability. Mediators are advocates for a fair process and not for a particular settlement.

Let us take as an example an independent mediator in a personal injury claim case in North America. The parties, the insurance adjuster, and the plaintiff's lawyer corresponded and talked by telephone, reaching a decision to explore the use of mediation to resolve their differences. They agreed that the adjuster would seek the assistance of a mediation firm that had a reputation for impartiality and experience in resolving this kind of dispute. The firm gave them the résumés of three possible intervenors. After reviewing this information, the parties eliminated two of the candidates, one because she had previously acted as an arbiter in a case involving one of the parties and issued an unfavorable opinion, and the other because the number of years he had spent in the practice of mediation was considered inadequate. The mediator who was selected was not known personally to either party but had a significant reputation for being fair, impartial, efficient, experienced, and knowledgeable in handling this type of case.

A premediation interview was held with the chosen mediator, where the parties confirmed their decision to use his services and explained the background of the case. They then proceeded to a first joint session. During the subsequent half-day mediation session, the mediator asked both parties to explain their view of the case, helped them identify key issues and interests, assisted them in generating some possible settlement options in joint session, and then conducted a private meeting with each of them to explore which options were most viable and to break a deadlock on one particularly difficult issue. During both the joint sessions and the caucuses, the mediator asked the parties a number of questions, helped make their interests explicit, and assisted the parties in developing some fair and objective standards and criteria that offered a formula for settlement. He made few, if any, substantive recommendations on how they should settle and did not indicate his personal opinion or approval of the solution that they ultimately developed.

VARIATIONS IN MEDIATOR DIRECTIVENESS AND FOCUS

In addition to the diverse roles and relationships that mediators have with parties, intermediaries also differ with respect to the degree of directiveness or control that they exercise over the dispute resolution process and the relative emphasis they place on the substantive, procedural, and psychological or relationship interests of the parties.

In general, regardless of the type of mediator role being performed, intermediaries vary along a continuum from highly directive to highly nondirective with respect to substantive issues, the problem-solving process, and the management of relationships between the parties. Kolb (1983) described the ideal types at the ends of this spectrum: the "orchestrators" and the "dealmakers." In brief, orchestrators generally focus on empowering parties to make their own decisions; they offer mainly procedural assistance and occasionally help in establishing or building relationships. They are less directive than are deal makers and intervene primarily when it is clear that the parties are not capable of making progress toward a settlement on their own.

In contrast, deal makers are often highly directive in relation to both process and the substantive issues under discussion. Generally, they are very more prescriptive and directive with respect to problem-solving steps, questions of who talks and to whom, types of forum (joint sessions or private meetings), and the types of interventions made. Deal makers are also typically much more involved in substantive discussions and on occasion may give substantive information or advice, voice their opinion on issues under discussion, or actively work to put together a deal that will be mutually acceptable to the parties.

In addition to directiveness, intermediaries vary significantly in terms of the emphasis they place on the purpose or focus of the mediation. Here too, there is a continuum, with some mediators emphasizing problem solving and agreement making on tangible, substantive issues, and others (who sometimes call themselves "problem-solving facilitators") placing more stress on improving the parties' relationships. The latter generally work to establish or build cognitive empathy, trust, and respect. When necessary, they will seek to terminate a relationship with the least possible psychological harm (Bush and Folger, 1994; Rothman, 1992).

In recent years, some practitioners and academics writing about the field have locked themselves into rigid positions on the appropriate degree of intermediary directiveness or the optimal area of emphasis for mediators (problem-solving versus relationship orientation). This narrowness has not been productive. It ignores the range of successful models for practice, the variety of disputes, the specific capabilities of the parties, the expressed needs and goals of the disputants, and the diversity of cultural contexts in which interventions are practiced. A more productive approach would be to explore the specific situation and adapt the process to meet the needs of the parties. This would mean that in some disputes the intermediary might be highly directive, whereas in others he or she would merely orchestrate the process. Equally, in some conflicts the mediator would emphasize a more substantive problem-solving focus, whereas in others the emphasis would be placed on establishing or building relationships.

What is characteristic of good practice, and what is needed from effective mediators, is the ability to be a "reflective practitioner" (Schön, 1983). Such a person can match mediation theory and the learnings of others with his or her own past experience in resolving disputes, so that situation-specific approaches and interventions can be developed that assist parties in establishing and building respectful and trusting relationships and resolve the issues that divide them.

MEDIATION, CULTURE, AND GENDER

The earlier description of mediator roles and relationships to parties raised the issue of culture. Culture comprises a wide variety of wordviews, beliefs, assumptions, and behaviors that are characteristic of specific groups of people. Throughout this book, I will note a number of potential cultural mediation and negotiation patterns and practices that may be encountered with individuals and groups from specific cultures. It is important to note that members of any cultural group have both common and diverse ways of thinking and behaving. Therefore, clues or recommendations on possible mediation approaches or responses of either mediators or disputants from a cultural group are just that: clues. They are possible ways that people from a designated culture *may* think or behave in a conflict; but then again, they may not conform to common cultural norms. Clues should not be considered to be definitive or prescriptive about how any person or group mediates or will act as a disputant.

Closely related to culture is gender. In the mid-1970s, when Jeff Rubin and Bert Brown wrote *The Social Psychology of Bargaining and Negotiation* (1975), there were already a tremendous number of psychological studies that compared gender differences. Since that time, there has been a growing amount of research on this issue based on a variety of theoretical frameworks such as the direct study of difference in negotiation behavior or outcomes; the social factors that may contribute to gender differences in conflicts of efforts to resolve them; the deficit model that generally studies what men have and women don't; and studies that value difference and are more likely to present women's perspectives (Kolb and Coolidge, 1992; Kolb, 2000; Kolb and Williams, 2000).

Negotiation studies have been the focus of more gender-related research than mediation. To date, the final results are not conclusive regarding how much women and men differ in their negotiation approaches, styles, behaviors, or success rates (Menkel-Meadow, 2000). Some studies have found that "men negotiate significantly better outcomes than women (Stuhlmacher and Walters, 1999), while others have found that women are more cooperative than men (Walteres, Stuhlmacher, and Meyer, 1998). Still other studies find that "there are no statistically different differences in negotiation outcomes and performance between men and women" (Craver and Barnes, 1999).

On the topic of mediation, there are relatively few studies on gender differences in practice or outcome (Weingarten and Douvan, 1985; Maxwell and Maxwell, 1989; Stamato, 1992). A study by Maxwell (1992) of thirty-three male and twenty-seven female mediators who mediated the resolution of misdemeanors under the auspices of the Cleveland Prosecutor Mediation Program found that men and women were both effective in bring parties to a settlement, with women only slightly more so. Maxwell noted that the difference was not statistically significant. However, the research did find that women were more likely to reach conclusions that would ultimately be binding than were men, This was especially so in cases that involved actual or potential ongoing relationships between disputants and cases in which high emotions were present. As in the field of negotiations, research on gender difference in mediation, for either intermediaries or parties, is not conclusive. Nevertheless, it will be important as we examine various situations, power relationships, and ways that mediation is practiced that we be aware of when gender might or might not be salient in how mediators perform and in ways that disputants or different genders think and act.

THE APPROACH TO DESCRIBING THE MEDIATION PROCESS

As can be seen from the preceding descriptions, mediators can have many types of relationships with disputing parties, and the nature of the connection can significantly influence the process and the types of interventions that are initiated. Because this book is about general processes of mediation and describes a range of mediator intervention approaches that can be used in many situations, it will be helpful for me to describe my own orientation toward these processes and procedures.

Generally, my experience and orientation in mediation are those of the independent mediator who leans toward the orchestrator end of the directiveness spectrum (at least, by North American standards). However, I am familiar with and have worked extensively with intermediaries who have different orientations toward directiveness or the focus of the mediation process. I have also taught intervention approaches and skills to intermediaries who specialized in social network, authoritative, and vested-interest assistance. Because of this experience, I recognize the value, complexities, variations, and situational or contextual appropriateness of various orientations.

Writing a book that encompasses all types of mediators and mediation would be very difficult, if not impossible. Therefore, this text is primarily oriented toward describing the approach, strategies, and tactics of independent mediators who lean toward the orchestrator or moderately directive end of the procedural or substantive-directiveness spectrum, and with an emphasis on both problem solving as well as enhancing the parties' relationships. This emphasis should not be taken to imply that other types of mediators or their orientations are not valid or effective. However, for the sake of clarity and to facilitate a general understanding of how mediators work, I will describe a specific process that is widely practiced in a number of settings and cultures. In subsequent chapters, I will also describe some of the variations of practice that arise from differences among intervenors, kinds of disputes, and cultural contexts. It is my hope that this method of exploring the mediation process will present both a comprehensible and a cohesive approach to mediation for individuals who want to become effective practitioners.

MEDIATION ACTIVITIES: MOVES AND INTERVENTIONS

Negotiation is composed of a series of complex activities, or "moves," that people initiate to resolve their differences and bring the conflict to termination (Goffman, 1969, p. 90). Each move or action a negotiator performs involves rational decision making in which possible actions are assessed in relation to these factors:

- The moves of the other parties
- Their standards of behavior
- Their styles
- Their perceptiveness and skill
- Their needs and preferences
- Their determination
- The amount of information the negotiator has about the conflict
- The negotiator's personal attributes
- Available resources

Mediators, like negotiators, may initiate moves. A *move* for a mediator is a specific act of intervention or "influence technique" focused on the people in the dispute. It encourages selection of positive actions and inhibits selection of negative actions relative to the issues in conflict (Galtung, 1975). The mediator who is a specialized negotiator, generally does not directly effect changes in the disputants by initiating moves, as do the parties themselves; he or she is more of a catalyst. Changes are the combined result of the intervenor's moves and those of the negotiators (Bonner, 1959).

In negotiations, people in conflict are faced with a variety of procedural or psychological problems, or "critical situations," (Cohen and Smith, 1972) that they must address or overcome if they are to reach an agreement. The largest categories of critical situations and most frequent problems are hereafter referred to as *stages* or phases because they constitute major steps that parties must take to reach agreement. There are stages or phases for both negotiation and mediation, and for the most part they parallel each other.

Mediators make two types of interventions in response to critical situations: *general* or *noncontingent* moves or activities, and *contingent* moves or activities (Kochan and Jick, 1978).

Noncontingent moves are general interventions that a mediator initiates in virtually all disputes. These activities are responses to the broadest categories of critical situations and correspond to the stages of mediation. They are linked to the overall pattern of conflict development and resolution. Noncontingent moves enable the mediator to:

1. Gain entry to the dispute
2. Assist the parties in selecting the appropriate conflict resolution approach and arena
3. Collect data and analyze the conflict
4. Design a mediation plan
5. Initiate conciliation
6. Assist the parties in beginning productive negotiations
7. Identify important issues and build an agenda
8. Identify parties' underlying interests
9. Aid the parties in developing resolution options
10. Assist in assessing the options

11. Promote final bargaining, agreement making, and closure
12. Aid in developing an implementation and monitoring plan

I will examine these activities and stages in more detail later in this chapter.

Smaller, routine, noncontingent activities are also initiated by mediators within each stage. Examples of this level of intervention are activities to build credibility for the process, promote rapport between the parties and the mediator, and frame issues in a more manageable form, as well as develop procedures to conduct cost-benefit evaluations on settlement options.

Contingent moves are responses to special or idiosyncratic problems that occur in some negotiations. Interventions to manage intense anger, bluffing, bargaining in bad faith, mistrust, or miscommunication are all in this category of specific interventions. Though some contingent moves, such as the caucus—a private meeting between the parties and the mediator—are quite common, they are still in the contingent category because they do not happen in all negotiations.

HYPOTHESIS BUILDING AND MEDIATION INTERVENTIONS

For a mediator to be effective, he or she needs to be able to analyze and assess critical situations and design effective interventions to address the causes of the conflict. However, conflicts do not come in neat packages with their causes and component parts labeled so that the intervenor will know how to creatively respond to them. Causes are often obscured and clouded by the dynamics of the parties' interactions.

To work effectively on conflicts, the intervenor needs a conceptual road map, or "conflict map" (Wehr, 1979), that details why a conflict is occurring, identifies barriers to settlement, and indicates procedures to manage or resolve the dispute.

Most conflicts have multiple causes. The principal tasks of the mediator and the parties are to identify and take action to address them. The mediator and participants in a dispute accomplish this by trial-and-error experimentation in which they generate and test hypotheses about the sources of the conflict.

First, the mediator, in dialogue with the parties (either individually or together), observes and identifies elements of the parties' attitudes, perceptions, communication patterns, or ongoing interactions that are producing a negative relationship or hindering a positive one. The mediator tries to determine if lack of information, misinformation, the manner in which data are collected, or the criteria by which data are assessed are at the root of the conflict. He or she identifies both compatible and competing interests, while also exploring any structural causes of conflict, such as differences in authority or resources or the impact of time. Finally, the mediator ascertains similarities and differences in the values held by the parties. From all these observations, he or she tries to identify the central causes of the dispute. Often, a framework of explanatory causes and suggested interventions, such as that presented in Figure 2.1, will be used.

For example, in the Singson-Whittamore case presented in Chapter One, the mediator might determine that:

- There are relationship problems between the doctor and the clinic director that need to be addressed
- There is a significant amount of data missing on the cost of opening a new practice and on the potential adverse financial impacts on the clinic of losing a doctor
- Each of the parties has a variety of interests that need to be explored
- A major cause of the problem is structural proximity and day-to-day interaction between the Whittamores
- There might be common or dissonant values regarding parents' involvement with children that the clinic staff and Whittamore share

This information will help the mediator develop a strategy for approaching the problems faced by the disputants and a plan for sequencing his or her activities.

Once the mediator believes that one or more central causes have been identified, he or she builds a hypothesis: "This conflict is caused by *a and probably b,* and if either *a* or *b* is changed or addressed, the parties will be able to move toward agreement." The hypothesis must then be tested.

Testing hypotheses about conflicts involves designing preventions or interventions that challenge or modify the attitudes, behaviors, or structural relationship of the disputants. *Preventions* are activities that a mediator initiates *before* parties interact and that inhibit or prevent them from engaging in unproductive communication or problem solving. *Interventions* are activities undertaken by a mediator in response to unproductive communication or problem solving that arises in a joint session or private meeting after negotiations have begun. Preventions are proactive (and interventions reactive) initiatives by the intermediary.

Preventions and interventions are often grounded in a theory that identifies a particular cause of the conflict and suggests prescriptive actions. For example, one theory about the cause of conflict has communication as its base. Most communication theories propose that conflict is the result of poor communication, whether in quantity, quality, or form. The theory postulates that if the right *quantity* of communication can be attained, the *quality* of the information exchanged can be improved, and if this information is put into a mutually acceptable *form,* the causes of the dispute will be addressed and the participants will move toward resolution.

A mediator following the communication theory of conflict might observe disputants communicating very poorly: one barely begins to speak without the other interrupting, or they have difficulty focusing on present issues and constantly digress to arguments over past wrongs that tend to escalate the conflict, turning the dispute into a shouting match. The mediator hypothesizes that one cause of the dispute is the inability of the disputants to talk to each other in a constructive and restrained manner. He or she therefore proceeds to experiment with modifications of their communication patterns (quality, quantity, and form) to see if there is any resulting change in the conflict dynamics. The mediator may suggest preventions—that the parties discuss one topic at a time, may obtain permission to monitor the dialogue and prevent interruptions, or may establish ground rules about insults. The mediator may do an intervention, a caucus, to separate the disputants so that they can communicate only through the mediator.

Each intervention is a test of the hypothesis that part of the dispute is caused by communication problems and that if these difficulties can be lessened or eliminated the parties will have a better

Figure 2.1. Circle of Conflict: Causes and Interventions.

Possible Value-Related Interventions

Avoid defining problem in terms of value
Allow parties to agree and to disagree
Create spheres of influence in which
   one set of values dominates
Search for superordinate goal that all parties share

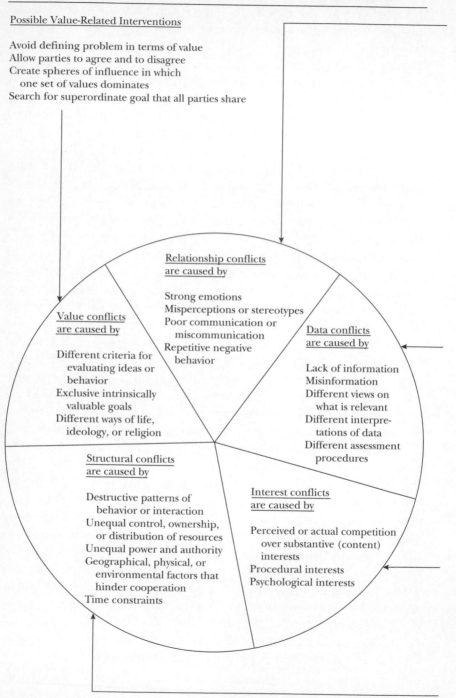

Relationship conflicts
are caused by

Strong emotions
Misperceptions or stereotypes
Poor communication or
   miscommunication
Repetitive negative
   behavior

Value conflicts
are caused by

Different criteria for
   evaluating ideas or
   behavior
Exclusive intrinsically
   valuable goals
Different ways of life,
   ideology, or religion

Data conflicts
are caused by

Lack of information
Misinformation
Different views on
   what is relevant
Different interpre-
   tations of data
Different assessment
   procedures

Structural conflicts
are caused by

Destructive patterns of
   behavior or interaction
Unequal control, ownership,
   or distribution of resources
Unequal power and authority
Geographical, physical, or
   environmental factors that
   hinder cooperation
Time constraints

Interest conflicts
are caused by

Perceived or actual competition
   over substantive (content)
   interests
Procedural interests
Psychological interests

Possible Relationship Interventions

Control expression of emotions through
   procedure, ground rules, caucuses, and so forth
Promote expression of emotions by legitimizing
   feelings and providing a process
Clarify perceptions and build positive perceptions
Improve quality and quantity of communication
Block negative repetitive behavior by changing structure
Encourage positive problem-solving attitudes

Possible Data Interventions

Reach agreement on what data are important
Agree on process to collect data
Develop common criteria to assess data
Use third-party experts to gain outside opinion
   or break deadlocks

Possible Interest-Based Interventions

Focus on interests, not positions
Look for objective standards and criteria to guide solution development
Develop integrative solutions that address needs of all parties
Search for ways to expand options or resources
Develop trade-offs to satisfy interests of different strengths

Possible Structural Interventions

Clearly define and change roles
Replace destructive behavior patterns
Reallocate ownership or control of resources
Establish a fair and mutually acceptable decision-making process
Change negotiation process from positional to interest-based bargaining
Modify means of influence used by parties (less coercion, more persuasion)
Change physical and environmental relationship of parties
   (closeness and distance)
Modify external pressures on parties
Change time constraints (more or less time)

chance of reaching an agreement. If the desired effect is not achieved, the intervenor may reject the specific approach as ineffective and try another. If several interventions based on one theory do not work, the intervenor may shift to another theory and begin trial-and-error testing again. The cycle of hypothesis building and testing is the basic process of intervention and conflict resolution (see Figure 2.2).

THE STAGES OF MEDIATION

Mediator hypothesis building occurs most intensively in the process of conceptualizing the stages or phases of mediation and designing appropriate preventions and interventions that are based on the causes of the conflict and the level of development that a particular dispute has reached.

Figure 2.2. Mediator Process of Building and Testing a Hypothesis.

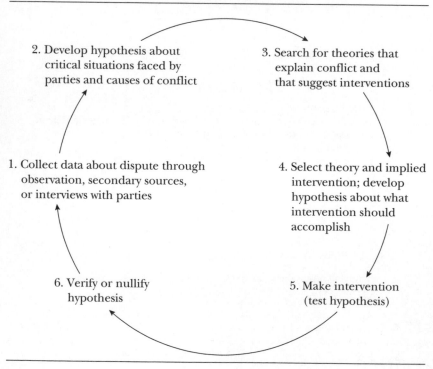

2. Develop hypothesis about critical situations faced by parties and causes of conflict

3. Search for theories that explain conflict and that suggest interventions

1. Collect data about dispute through observation, secondary sources, or interviews with parties

4. Select theory and implied intervention; develop hypothesis about what intervention should accomplish

6. Verify or nullify hypothesis

5. Make intervention (test hypothesis)

The stages of mediation are often difficult to identify; they frequently vary across cultures in sequence, emphasis, and approach. Mediator and negotiator activities seem to blend together into an undifferentiated continuum of interaction. Only through careful observation of negotiations and mediated interventions can distinct stages composed of common and predictable activities be identified. It then becomes possible to generate hypotheses about the critical situations and specific problems that a particular set of disputants may have to address in any given stage.

The stages of mediator interventions fall roughly into two broad categories: (1) activities performed by the mediator before formal problem-solving sessions begin; and (2) activities initiated once the mediator has entered into formal problem solving with the parties, either in joint session or by shuttling between them. Five stages occur in the prenegotiation work of the mediator, and seven stages occur after formal sessions have begun (see Figure 2.3).

In each of the twelve stages, the mediator designs hypotheses and appropriate strategies and executes specific activities. These initiatives are both sequential and developmental in nature and are designed to help disputing parties accomplish specific tasks and overcome barriers that commonly occur at particular points in the negotiation process. If a critical task appropriate at an earlier stage of negotiations has not been completed, either by the negotiators alone or with the assistance of a mediator, there are likely to be problems in moving on to the next stage of negotiation.

Regardless of when a mediator enters negotiations—at the beginning, middle, or end—he or she will usually perform most or all of the general activities characteristic of earlier stages, although if mediation begins late in negotiations the stages may be accomplished in abbreviated form. Naturally, the amount of time spent on the tasks of each stage will vary considerably, depending on factors that will be discussed in the remaining section of this chapter.

VARIABLES THAT INFLUENCE MEDIATION STRATEGIES AND ACTIVITIES

Although mediators make a variety of interventions to help parties move through the negotiation and mediation stages, their moves are not identical from case to case. Although there are general patterns

Figure 2.3. Twelve Stages of Mediator Moves.

Stage 1: Establishing Relationship with the Disputing Parties
- Make initial contacts with the parties
- Build credibility
- Promote rapport
- Educate the parties about the process
- Increase commitment to the procedure

Stage 2: Selecting a Strategy to Guide Mediation
- Assist the parties to assess various approaches
  to conflict management and resolution
- Assist the parties in selecting an approach
- Coordinate the approaches of the parties

Stage 3: Collecting and Analyzing Background Information
- Collect and analyze relevant data about the people,
  dynamics, and substance of a conflict
- Verify accuracy of data
- Minimize the impact of inaccurate or unavailable data

Stage 4: Designing a Detailed Plan for Mediation
- Identify strategies and consequent noncontingent moves that
  will enable the parties to move toward agreement
- Identify contingent moves to respond to situations peculiar
  to the specific conflict

Stage 5: Building Trust and Cooperation
- Prepare disputants psychologically to participate in
  negotiations on substantive issues
- Handle strong emotions
- Check perceptions and minimize effects of stereotypes
- Build recognition of the legitimacy of the parties and issues
- Build trust
- Clarify communications

Stage 6: Beginning the Mediation Session
- Open negotiation between the parties
- Establish an open and positive tone
- Establish ground rules and behavioral guidelines
- Assist the parties in venting emotions
- Delimit topic areas and issues for discussion
- Assist the parties in exploring commitments, salience,
  and influence

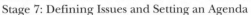

Stage 7: Defining Issues and Setting an Agenda
- Identify broad topic areas of concern to the parties
- Obtain agreement on the issues to be discussed
- Determine the sequence for handling the issues

Stage 8: Uncovering Hidden Interests of the Disputing Parties
- Identify the substantive, procedural, and psychological interests of the parties
- Educate the parties about each other's interests

Stage 9: Generating Options for Settlement
- Develop an awareness among the parties of the need for multiple options
- Lower commitment to positions or sole alternatives
- Generate options using either positional or interest-based bargaining

Stage 10: Assessing Options for Settlement
- Review the interests of the parties
- Assess how interests can be met by available options
- Assess the costs and benefits of selecting options

Stage 11: Final Bargaining
- Reach agreement through either incremental convergence of positions, final leaps to package settlements, development of a consensual formula, or establishment of procedural means to reach a substantive agreement

Stage 12: Achieving Formal Settlement
- Identify procedural steps to operationalize the agreement
- Establish an evaluation and monitoring procedure
- Formalize the settlement and create an enforcement and commitment mechanism

of moves, each mediator modifies his or her activities according to variables present in the case. These are the most critical variables that influence preventions and interventions:

- The level of conflict development and the timing of a mediator's entry
- The capability of negotiators to resolve their own dispute
- The power balance of the disputants and the mediator's role as an equalizer and agent of empowerment
- The negotiation procedures used by the parties
- The complexity of the issues negotiated
- The appropriate focus of the process of disputing and the substantive issues in question as jointly defined by the parties and the intervenor

I will examine each of these variables and how they affect the role of the mediator and his or her application of general and specific strategies.

Conflict Development and Timing of Entry

The level of conflict development, the stage reached in negotiations (or the resolution efforts previously made), and the degree of emotional intensity in the parties significantly influence the tasks that negotiators and mediators have to perform. If a mediator enters a dispute in its early stages, prior to extreme issue polarization or the development of intense emotions, he or she will use a different strategy and set of moves from those that would be used at a later stage, when the parties have been negotiating and have reached a substantive impasse or had a highly emotional interchange. If mediation is viewed as a total process, however, the difference in strategy and activities can be seen primarily as one of emphasis rather than substance; the types of initiatives are the same. For example, conciliation, preparing the parties psychologically to bargain effectively on substantive issues, generally occurs at the beginning of negotiations rather than later. If, however, a mediator enters in the later phases of a negotiation—after impasse—he or she will probably have to initiate some conciliatory activities to help overcome psychological barriers to settlement. The mediator will generally have to complete this phase prior to pursuing the substantive bargaining activities that belong to the stage the parties *believe* they have reached.

Capability of Disputants to Resolve Their Own Dispute

Whether the disputants are capable of resolving their own dispute also strongly affects the mediator's intervention strategies. Parties who are able to negotiate rationally, who are aware of problem-solving procedures, and who appear to be progressing toward a settlement will require less assistance from a mediator. In this situation, the mediator may lend support to the work of the parties merely by his or her presence or by minimal support of the principal negotiators (Perez, 1959; Kolb, 1983). On the other hand, if parties are in the grip of intense emotions, do not have skills or expertise in negotiations or problem-solving, or have reached an impasse on substantive issues, the mediator will probably be more active and more visible in the negotiations. He or she may assist the parties in productively expressing and/or handling strong emotions, framing the specific problems to be addressed, creating an agenda, educating each other about their interests, narrowing the bargaining range, generating and assessing options, and initiating a variety of other procedures or activities that assist the parties in reaching an agreement.

Power Balance Between Disputants

In order to derive mutually satisfactory and acceptable decisions from negotiations, all parties must have some means of influence, either positive or negative, on other disputants at the table. This is a prerequisite for a settlement that recognizes mutual needs (Lovell, 1952). Unless a weaker party has some power or influence, recognition of its needs and interests will occur only if the stronger party is altruistically oriented. If the power or influence potentials of the parties are well developed, fairly equal in strength, and recognized by all disputants, the mediator's job will be to assist the disputants in using their influence effectively to produce mutually satisfactory results. If, however, the influence of each side is not equal and one party has the ability to impose on the other an unsatisfactory solution, an agreement that will not hold over time, or a resolution that will result in renewed conflict later, the mediator will have to decide whether and how to assist the weaker party and moderate the influence of the stronger one.

To assist or empower the weaker party or to influence the activities of the stronger (contingent strategies that do not occur in all mediations) requires very specific interventions that shift the mediator's role and function dangerously close to advocacy. This problem has been debated among mediators (Bernard, Folger, Weingarten, and Zumeta, 1984). One argument states that a mediator has an obligation to create just settlements and must therefore help empower the underdog to reach equitable and fair agreements (Laue and Cormick, 1978; Susskind, 1981; Haynes, 1981). Another school argues that mediators should do little, if anything, to influence the power relations of disputing parties because it taints the intervenor's impartiality (Bellman, 1982; Stulberg, 1981b).

In examining this question and how it affects the mediator's choice of intervention activities, it is important to distinguish between the situation in which a mediator assists in recognizing, organizing, and marshaling the existing power of a disputant and that in which a mediator becomes an advocate and assists in generating new power and influence. The latter strategy clearly shifts the mediator out of his or her impartial position, whereas the former keeps the mediator within the power boundaries established by the parties. There is no easy answer to this strategic and ethical problem, but it does have an important impact on the types of moves a mediator initiates.

Negotiation Procedures

Negotiation is a form of joint problem solving. The topical problems that negotiators focus on are often called *issues*. An issue exists because the parties do not agree on a particular topic and because they have perceived or actual exclusive needs or interests.

In the Singson-Whittamore case described in Chapter One, these are some of the issues about which the two people will negotiate:

1. Can Whittamore continue to practice medicine in a town in which he wishes to live?
2. Will there be a penalty for breaking the contract?
3. If there is a penalty, how much will it be?
4. How will the penalty be calculated, and what factors should be considered?
5. Is there a way that Whittamore can stay at the clinic and still maintain some distance from his estranged wife (which is, after all, the crux of the problem)?

Note that the description of the issues is in neutral terms that favor neither party, and that the wording describes a problem to be solved rather than a particular solution to be forced by one bargainer on another.

Parties to a conflict select one of two major negotiation procedures to handle issues in dispute: *positional bargaining* or *interest-based bargaining* (Fisher and Ury, 1981). Positional bargaining usually occurs when a negotiator perceives that contested resources are limited and that a distributive solution, one that allocates shares of gains and losses to each party, is the only possible outcome (Walton and McKersie, 1965). Positional bargaining is generally a win-lose or compromise-oriented process. Interest-based bargaining, on the other hand, occurs when negotiators seek integrative solutions that meet as many of the needs of both parties as possible (Walton and McKersie, 1965). Generally, interest-based bargaining is pursued when parties do not see resources as limited, and when solutions can be found in which all parties can have at least some of their needs met.

Positional bargaining derives its name from the practice of selecting a series of positions—particular settlement options that meet the proposing party's interests—and presenting these to an opponent as *the* solution to the issue in question. A party's position may or may not be responsive to the needs or interests of other negotiators. Positions are generally ordered sequentially so that the first position is a large demand and represents a negotiator's maximum expectation of gain should his or her opponent acquiesce. Each subsequent position demands less of an opponent and results in fewer benefits for the initiating party. Characteristically, positional

bargaining commits parties early in negotiations to very specific solutions to issues in dispute and often reduces the flexibility to generate other equally acceptable options.

Positional bargainers generally reach agreement because they
have identified a solution that meets enough of an opponent's interests to induce settlement. However, positional bargainers often
fail to maximize the satisfaction of either party's interests because
the settlements are compromises or adoptions of one party's proposal, rather than the product of a joint effort to find mutually
beneficial solutions.

In the Singson-Whittamore case, one possible position for
Whittamore might be: "I refuse to pay any penalty for breaking the
contract because the no-competition clause is not constitutional."
Singson might respond with a counterposition: "Pay the penalty
fee immediately or move out of town," or "You must pay the penalty, but we can negotiate on the due date." If an agreement is
reached, the parties might settle at a point between these two extreme positions.

Disputants often adopt positional bargaining when:

• The stakes for winning are high
• The resources (time, money, psychological benefits, and so
  on) are perceived to be limited
• A win for one side appears to require a loss for another
• Interests of the parties are not or do not appear to be interdependent and are contradictory
• Future relationships have a lower priority than immediate substantive gains
• Parties assume that positional bargaining is *the* way to resolve
  problems or they are not familiar with other approaches to
  negotiation, or other approaches are deemed to be inappropriate or unacceptable (Moore, 1982b)

Interest-based bargaining differs from positional bargaining in its
assumptions about the issues to be negotiated, the contents of an
acceptable solution, and the process by which an agreement is to
be reached.

In interest-based bargaining, the negotiators do not necessarily assume that the substantive resource in question—money, other
resources, time, behavior, and so on—is limited. They do not as-

sume that the resource must be divided into shares in which one bargainer is a winner and the other a loser. The attitude of the interest-based bargainer is that of a problem solver. The goal of negotiation is to find a solution that is mutually satisfactory and results in a win-win outcome.

Interest-based bargainers believe that settlements in negotiations are reached because a party has succeeded in having his or her interests satisfied. *Interests* are specific conditions (or gains) that a party must obtain for an acceptable settlement to occur. They are of three broad types: substantive, procedural, and psychological.

Substantive interests refer to the needs that an individual has for particular goods such as money and time. Meeting substantive interests is often the central focus of negotiations.

Procedural interests refer to the preferences that a negotiator has for the way that the parties discuss their differences and the manner in which the bargaining outcome is implemented. Possible procedural interests might be that each person have the opportunity to speak his or her mind, that negotiations occur in an orderly and timely manner, that the parties avoid derogatory verbal attacks, that the process focus on meeting the mutual interests of all the parties rather than forcing a party to agree to a predetermined position advocated by another, that the plan for implementing the agreement be worked out in detail prior to final settlement, or that a written document or contract should result from bargaining.

Psychological interests refer to the emotional and relationship needs of negotiators both during and as a result of negotiations. Negotiators want to have high self-esteem, want to be treated with respect by their opponent, and do not want to be degraded in negotiations. If the relationship is to continue in the future, the negotiators may want to have ongoing positive regard from the other party for their openness to future communication.

In the Singson-Whittamore case, Whittamore's interests include:

- Remaining in town so that he can see and parent his children (substantive and psychological)
- Continuing to practice his profession (substantive and possibly psychological)
- Avoiding contact with his estranged wife (psychological and procedural)

- Maintaining amicable relations with the clinic and its staff (psychological)
- Minimizing the amount of initial penalty payments to the clinic so that he has enough money to start his own practice (procedural and substantive)

Some of Singson's interests are:

- Avoiding monetary loss and patient attrition when a doctor leaves the staff (substantive)
- Maintaining clinic management's prerogative to set the terms of an employment contract (procedural, substantive, and psychological)
- Avoiding a precedent in which a doctor leaves the clinic before the expiration of a contract and begins a practice in town (procedural)
- Avoiding a costly lawsuit (substantive and procedural)
- Maintaining, if at all possible, a positive working relationship with one or more of the Singsons (psychological)

Interest-based bargaining begins with joint education and development of mutual understanding of each of the interests of the parties, not statements of positions. Often, the parties identify their interests and those of other disputants in private and then participate in a joint meeting to share their results. Parties discuss and modify their interests on the basis of these early discussions. Once the interests have been described, explored, and accepted, at least in principle the parties can begin a mutual search for solutions that will meet their individual and joint needs. Reaching an agreement requires negotiators to develop settlement options that meet at least some of the substantive, procedural, and psychological needs of all parties.

Interest-based bargaining seeks to identify and address the particular interests of all parties rather than achieve a victory of one party at the expense of another, as is the case in positional bargaining. The procedure in interest-based bargaining is one of mutual problem solving, similar to what happens when two people work together on a puzzle. The parties sit side by side and attempt to develop a mutually acceptable picture or settlement.

Mediators can help parties conduct either positional or interest-based bargaining more efficiently and effectively. As the goal of mediation is to help parties reach a settlement that is acceptable to all, mediators generally have a bias toward interest-based and integrative procedures.

Parties often engage in a positional process that is destructive to their relationships, does not generate creative options, and does not result in wise decisions. One of the mediator's major contributions to the dispute resolution process is assisting the negotiators in making a transition from positional to interest-based bargaining. This process will be discussed in more detail in later chapters.

Complexity of the Issues

Disputes come in a variety of levels of complexity. The simple landlord-tenant case in which two parties argue over a simple issue, a security deposit, is very different from a child custody and divorce dispute that involves multiple issues and very complex psychodynamics between the disputants. The latter case may in turn be very uncomplicated in comparison with multiparty disputes, such as one involving the EPA, product manufacturers, and environmentalists over new federal air pollution regulations, or a complex commercial negotiation between major telecommunications companies over provision of services.

Mediators must design intervention strategies that respond to the complexity of the specific issues to be addressed. In one case, detailed data collection procedures involving multiple interviews over a period of months may be required to understand the causes and dynamics of the conflict, whereas in another a simple intake interview at the first joint session with the parties is sufficient. In some disputes, the mediator must break a particularly difficult impasse, and when successful he or she may withdraw and encourage the parties to continue and complete negotiations on their own. In others, the mediator may play an active role throughout negotiations and provide the major procedural framework. In exploring the stages of mediation in later chapters, it will be important to consider the complexity of the dispute to determine the amount of initiative and the level of intervention required from a mediator.

The Appropriate Focus: Process, Substantive Issues, or Relationships

Mediators vary significantly in the way they define their role and involvement in promoting successful negotiations. The differences are generally rooted in mediators' judgments about how much they should focus on process, substance, or relationships between the parties. More will be said about a relationship focus in later chapters.

Regarding substance, one school argues that mediators should focus primarily on the process of negotiations and leave substantive content as the exclusive domain of the parties (Stulberg, 1981b). Procedurally oriented mediators define their role this way for a variety of reasons. First, they believe that the parties are often better informed about the substantive issues in dispute than any third party could ever be. They maintain that the best decision is one arrived at by the parties. Second, they believe that what the parties need is procedural help, not substantive advice or a decision by an outsider. Third, they hold that the parties' commitment to implement and adhere to a settlement will be enhanced if those parties make the substantive decisions themselves, as opposed to having a deal forged by the intervenor. Finally, they believe that a focus on the process and an impartial stance toward substance build trust between the intervenor and the disputants, decrease the risk to the parties of involving another party (the mediator) in the substance of the dispute, and make the disputants more open to procedural assistance.

Many labor-management mediators (especially intervenors from the Federal Mediation and Conciliation Service) subscribe to this view (Kolb, 1983). They see themselves as orchestrators of a process that enables the parties to make their own substantive decisions.

Some environmental mediators also follow this procedurally oriented definition of the mediator's role. Bellman (1982), although raising concerns about a substantive agreement with which he disagrees, ultimately sees the terms of the settlement as the prerogative of the parties. He sees himself primarily as a process consultant.

The procedural orientation can be found among some family mediators, too. They argue that in a divorce, for example, the parents generally know what is best for both the children and the family system as a whole (conversation with W. P. Phear at a meeting of the Association of Family and Conciliation Courts, Ethics Working Group, Keystone, Colo., March 1984). The parents do not need a substantive expert to tell them what to do. What they need is procedural help to assist them in problem solving.

The alternative school of thought argues that although the mediator is impartial and neutral, this does not mean that he or she should not work with the parties on substantive matters to develop a fair and just decision (as fairness and justice are understood by the intervenor). Susskind (1981, pp. 46–47), an environmental mediator, argues that intervenors should be involved in substantive decisions when (1) "the impacts of negotiated agreement [will affect] under represented or unrepresented groups"; (2) there is "the possibility that joint net gains have not been maximized"; (3) the parties are not aware of the "long term spill-over effects of the settlements"; and (4) the precedents that they set "may be detrimental to the parties or the broader public." Susskind further notes that "although such intervention may make it difficult to retain the appearance of neutrality and the trust of the active parties, environmental mediators cannot fulfill their responsibilities to the community-at-large if they remain passive" (p. 47). Some labor-management mediators belong to this school. These deal makers intervene substantively when the parties are uninformed, ill-prepared to negotiate, or unaware of mutually acceptable substantive settlements (Kolb, 1983).

Child custody and divorce mediators also have representatives in the second school. Saposnek (1983) argues that the mediator should advocate the unrepresented interests of the children in negotiations between the parents and believes that the mediator should intervene and influence the substantive outcome if those interests are violated or not taken into consideration. Coogler (1978) advocates engagement in substantive negotiations and advocates that the mediator write a letter of nonconcurrence to the court if he or she seriously disagrees with the settlement.

There is a spectrum along which mediators place themselves in defining their degree of involvement in the procedure, substance, and relationships involved in negotiations. At one end are those who advocate mostly procedural interventions; at the other are advocates of substantive involvement by the mediator that may include actually forging the decision. Between them are mediators who pursue a role with mixed involvement in process and substance.

I lean toward the process end of the spectrum because I believe that the parties should have the primary responsibility for self-determination. On occasion, however, the mediator has an ethical responsibility to raise critical questions about substantive options under consideration by the parties. These occasions include cases where the agreement appears to be extremely inequitable to one or more of the parties, does not look as if it will hold over time, or seems likely to result in renewed conflict at a later date, or cases where the terms of settlement are so loose (or confining) that implementation is not feasible. I believe the mediator should also intervene in cases involving violence or potential violence to one or more parties, either primary or secondary.

Depending on the role that is assigned to the mediator (whether self-assigned or defined by agreement with the parties), he or she will have to determine which types of interventions to perform. In this process, the mediator must decide on (1) the level of intervention, (2) the individual or group to be targeted by the intervention, (3) the focus of intervention, and (4) the intensity of intervention.

The *level of intervention* refers to the degree to which the mediator concentrates on helping negotiators move through the general problem-solving stages, as opposed to a focus on particular idiosyncratic problems that are pushing the parties toward impasse. In some disputes, the parties may need assistance only to move through the broad stages, while in others, they may need help to break a particular deadlock. Sometimes parties need minimal help, and at other times they will need help throughout the bargaining process.

The *target of intervention* refers to the person or people to whom the mediator directs his or her moves. Should moves be directed to all parties, to a constellation within the group such as a subgroup or team, or to a particular person? In a postmarital dispute, for example, will it be best for the mediator to focus on changing the ex-wife's move, the ex-husband's, or both? Or should the focus be on the entire family system, including children, ex-spouses, stepparents, and grandparents? In a community dispute, should the mediator focus on the spokespersons, specific team members, the team as a whole, or the constituents of the parties?

The *focus of intervention* refers to the particular critical situations at which the mediator directs his or her moves. The mediator may focus his or her energies on changing the *psychological relationship* of parties to each other. This is often referred to as a conciliation. He or she may aim at creating the psychological conditions that are necessary for productive negotiations. Alternatively, the focus might be on changing the *negotiation process* or the procedure that is being used by one or more people to solve the dispute. Another option is to focus on the process for moving from one stage of negotiation to the next; for example, a mediator might help a party make a proposal that will be acceptable to the other side.

The focus could be on changing the *substance* or *content* of the dispute. The mediator may look for ways to explore data, to expand the number of acceptable options on the negotiation table, to narrow the choices when the parties are overwhelmed with possibilities, or to integrate proposals made by the disputants.

I will now turn to a detailed examination of the stages of mediation and the general moves mediators make in their efforts to promote agreement. Chapters Three through Seven describe activities that are often conducted prior to formal problem solving or a joint meeting of the parties. Some of these endeavors are generic conflict management initiatives that may be performed by the mediator and the parties as the means of deciding between a number of potential resolution processes; others, such as those in Chapters Six and Seven, are more mediation-specific. Chapters Eight through Eleven describe the mediation process in detail, from the first session to the final agreement.

Part Two

Laying the Groundwork for Effective Mediation

Chapter Three

Managing Initial Contacts with the Disputing Parties

Mediators enter disputes as a result of (1) direct invitation by one or more of the parties, (2) referrals by secondary parties, (3) direct initiation by the mediator, or (4) appointment by a recognized authority such as a government official or agency. Each of these means of entry poses specific strategic choices regarding mediator activities and may affect the quality, type, and probability of a settlement.

Direct invitation by a party or parties is probably the most common mechanism by which a mediator enters a dispute. The request for mediation may come from a single party, a subgroup or coalition of parties, or all the disputants. It may occur before or after the start of negotiations. The source of the request and the timing of the proposal for mediation may have a significant effect on the dynamics of negotiations. I will first explore requests for entry of a mediator made by single parties and subgroups of disputants and then examine requests made by all involved parties.

A request for mediation by a single party, whether an individual or a team, can have a variety of effects on the dynamics of negotiation and on subsequent strategies of the negotiators. One party commonly either proposes mediation to an opponent or takes unilateral action to obtain a mediator. For example, a husband may call a mediator and request help in negotiating custody arrangements with his estranged wife, or a government agency may request assistance in negotiating with a public interest group. If the parties have not started to negotiate, the request for mediation may mean that discussions are preferable to avoidance, stalemate, or alternative approaches to dispute resolution such as going to court. A request for mediation may also signal a desire to cooperate for mutual benefit, a willingness to make concessions, or a belief that total victory is not possible.

People in conflict are often reluctant to ask for a third party's assistance; they are afraid that their request for intervention may weaken their negotiating position and damage the possibility of a satisfactory outcome. Reluctance to call a mediator is especially strong once parties are in the midst of negotiations and have reached an impasse. Theodore Kheel, a labor mediator, describes the problem faced by a party who is initiating the entry of a mediator: "If you've reached an impasse, it can be assumed that both sides have put forth what they claim will be their final offers. In that situation a proposal by one side or the other to bring in a mediator is obviously a signal that side is willing to go still further"— and grant more concessions, for instance (Shapiro, 1970, pp. 41–42). Reluctance to appear weak or to make additional offers often discourages a request for a mediator. If such a request is made, the party from whom it comes has probably been following the traditional negotiator rule, "Always save something for the mediator" (Downing, 1960, p. 62).

Similar problems to those just described hold true for subgroups or coalitions of parties who request mediation. However, risks may be mitigated when more than one party makes such requests. The initiative can be framed in terms of the needs of all disputants rather than those of a single party, thus lowering the expectation of new concessions.

A proposal for mediation, especially in interpersonal or community disputes, also raises the possibility of procedural rejection by another party. Several studies have examined the rate of refusal to initiate mediation in community and interpersonal disputes. Cook, Rochl, and Shepard (1980) found that people refused mediation services in 1,898 of 3,911 cases—a refusal rate of 48 percent. Pearson (1982) found a rejection rate of 50 percent among divorcing couples in Denver, Colorado, who were offered free mediation services. Davis, Tichane, and Grayson (1980) found that in felony offenses among acquaintances, 32 percent of those referred to mediation failed to report, and 12 percent refused outright to participate in the process.

Researchers have attributed the rejection of mediation services to (1) unfamiliarity with the process, (2) rigid adherence to a win-lose approach to dispute resolution, (3) intense emotions that block communication, and (4) habitual attachment to judicial means of dispute settlement (Cook, Rochl, and Shepard, 1980). Single-party requests for mediation services generally seem to result in fewer instances of mediation.

Given such rejection rates, what should the mediator do if approached by only one party? After talking with the initiator, he or she must contact the other party or parties. In some situations, the mediator or agency will mail a letter to the responding party, explaining the process of mediation and its advantages, liabilities, and cost, and stating that the mediator will call within a short time to answer any questions and to discuss whether the party is interested in using the process. This letter serves to prepare the party for the mediator's call and creates an opportunity to consider the viability of mediation before any discussions with the mediator take place.

When calling the respondent, the mediator should not assume that there is a willingness to mediate. Most people are not familiar with the process, and the intervenor may therefore need to educate the respondent before a commitment to mediate can be elicited. Adequate time should be allowed for an explanation of the process and for questions. The approach should not be a hard sell; the party should be able to freely select or reject the process and should not feel pressured to use the mediator's services. This is important as the parties' personal commitment may ultimately be crucial for them to move toward settlement.

One mediator uses a paradoxical approach to demonstrate the merits of mediation. Instead of promoting the process himself, he asks the respondent to explain why he or she should use mediation. The respondent is thereby placed in the position of mediation advocate.

In some situations, especially those involving cultures in which writing or the telephone are not the preferred means of making an initial contact, the mediator may visit the disputants in person as a way of establishing a connection. This first visit may be facilitated by an introduction from a mutual friend or associate.

In cases in which both parties approach the mediator, a significant psychological step toward a cooperative resolution to the dispute has been made:

Implicit in such an invited third-party role are two assumptions: first, the disputants are sufficiently motivated to address their conflict and that one or both of them are willing to enlist the services of a third party; and second, the third party is regarded as sufficiently attractive by one or both disputants that this party is invited to intervene rather than some other individual. From the third party's vantage point, an invited role is desirable both because it suggests that the disputants are ready to work and because the third party is placed in a unique position to exercise influence [Rubin, 1981, p. 11].

To date, no data exist that correlate joint initiation of mediation with successful outcomes of interventions. However, mediators generally find that a cooperative initiation of mediation by all parties minimizes escalatory dynamics between the disputants at the beginning of the intervention and indicates willingness to solve the dispute to the satisfaction of all.

Referral by interested secondary parties is another way that mediation services are obtained. Secondary parties fall into two categories: first, persons or groups who have no direct stake in settling a dispute but are concerned about the general ramifications of continued conflict; and second, parties who, although they are not principal actors, do have tangible investment in settling a dispute.

Examples of the first type are close friends or neighbors who referred parties to a mediator—or vice versa—and a private foundation that was concerned about general community turmoil that could result from escalating conflict (Lansford, 1983). In each of these examples, the parties did not have a direct stake in the outcome but did want the dispute settled.

Secondary parties who have a more direct interest in the settlement also initiate activities that facilitate mediator entry. For example, in one particular workplace dispute two managers were in conflict over how a job was to be performed. A third manager—a peer—was uncomfortable with tension in the office. He talked to a fourth person in the office, a woman with no authority over the disputing managers, and asked her to intervene.

Lincoln (1976) described a school desegregation conflict in which a mediator was invited by the mayor and the school superintendent to mediate between two hostile groups of students—one black and the other white—that were threatening to vandalize school property and physically harm each other. Although the secondary parties were not directly involved in the negotiations, they clearly had high stakes in the outcome.

Occasionally, secondary parties have authority over the people in conflict and will intervene to encourage disputants to mediate. Mediation organizations often establish referral relationships with judges; lawyers; court clerks; police officers; and personnel in planning departments, social service agencies, and educational and public interest organizations to refer disputes to mediation.

Some secondary parties may not only refer cases to mediation but also influence the probability of settlement. Bench referrals by judges, prosecutors, public attorneys, and police officers generally have a higher rate of settlement than referrals by community social service agencies, legal aid organizations, or governmental agencies (Cook, Rochl, and Shepard, 1980). The prospect of a litigious alternative is undoubtedly a significant factor in the influence of certain referral sources on the probability of settlement. Parties know that if they do not reach an agreement in mediation, the case will probably go to court, an undesirable alternative in many instances.

Interventions initiated unilaterally by the mediator are not unusual in complex community disputes that are public in nature, involve multiple parties, and do not have a set of defined primary actors who can request mediation. In this form of entry, the mediator usually learns of the dispute from published written material or an interested secondary party. After careful examination of the dispute, the mediator takes the initiative to contact one or more disputants and offer his or her services. Entry of this type is complicated by the fact that the mediator may have difficulty building credibility with disputants, may lack their psychological commitment, may be subject to ethical issues related to the perception of "ambulance chasing," and will need to consider the possible effect of the intervention on the coalescence of power among the parties involved.

Gerald Cormick and Jane McCarthy, mediators of an environmental dispute concerning flood control and land use along the Snoqualmie River in Washington State, became involved in this way. They entered the conflict on their own initiative and assisted the primary parties in identifying and including additional disputants. "In determining whether mediation would be acceptable to the disputants, Cormick and McCarthy discovered who the key participants were by asking everyone involved: 'Can you name 10 or 12 persons who if they could agree on something, would have stature and influence enough so that you, who are in disagreement, could reasonably support them and any agreement they might reach?' Those named most often became part of the group that would meet with Cormick and McCarthy to work out a compromise" (Dembart and Kwartler, 1980, p. 47).

This uninvited form of entry is often the only one available to mediators who perceive that they may be helpful to disputants but also understand that the latter may not be aware of mediation as a means of dispute resolution.

Appointment is another means of entry. In institutionalized labor disputes, mediation is often legally required before the parties can proceed to other means of dispute resolution, and mediators are appointed by state or federal agencies. There are some interpersonal, community, civil, and court-related disputes in which government agencies may mandate the process, appoint mediators, or do both.

In the marital conciliation court system of California, for example, parties in child custody cases are required to try mediation before court action (Comeau, 1982). There are also numerous instances in which elected officials have appointed a mediator to respond to a community dispute (Dembart and Kwartler, 1980; Lansford, 1983; Clark-McGlennon Associates, 1982).

In the Singson-Whittamore case presented in Chapter One, both parties attempted unassisted negotiations and were not successful. Singson was familiar with mediation and had his lawyer ask a mediator to propose the process to Whittamore. The mediator sent Whittamore a letter of introduction, followed it up with a phone call, and then scheduled private meetings with both Whittamore and Singson to explore whether they wanted to use the process. When they indicated that they did, he instructed them to proceed with data collection on the case.

TASKS OF THE MEDIATOR IN THE ENTRY STAGE

Regardless of how a mediator enters a dispute, he or she must accomplish certain specific tasks in the first stage of the mediation process: (1) building personal, institutional, and procedural credibility; (2) establishing rapport with the disputants; (3) educating participants about the negotiation process, the role of the mediator, and the function of mediation; and (4) gaining a commitment to begin mediating.

Building Credibility

Mediators must build credibility with those in conflict by developing expectations that the mediator and the mediation process will help them successfully address the issues in dispute. In general, there are four types of credibility: personal, institutional, procedural, and substantive.

Personal credibility refers to the mediator's possession of certain personal characteristics that both mediators and disputants have long seen as crucial to the success of the intervention process (Davis and Gadlin, 1988). Landsberger (1956) found that disputing parties in labor negotiations, when asked to name desirable attributes of mediators, mentioned:

- Originality of ideas
- An appropriate sense of humor
- The ability to act unobtrusively in a conflict
- The ability to create the feeling of being "at one" with the disputants and concerned with their well-being
- A willingness to be a vigorous salesperson when necessary
- Control over his or her feelings
- Persistent and patient effort
- The ability to understand quickly the dynamics and complexities of a dispute
- Some specific knowledge of the field in which he or she is mediating

Activities by mediators that allow them to personally exhibit these qualities will generally reinforce beliefs held by disputing parties that the mediator has personal attributes that will assist them in resolving the dispute.

Institutional credibility refers to the reputation of the organization that employs the mediator. Such credibility is based on an organization's history of successful performance in the particular field of dispute resolution for which a mediator is needed, a history of unblemished impartiality among personnel, and often a background of neutral—or at least, not overtly biased—sources of funding. Institutional credibility may be a crucial factor in the acceptance or rejection of mediators or mediation organizations. Mediators wishing to build institutional credibility may:

• Produce brochures describing their organization's expertise and services
• Present a list of former clients to prospective users (subject, of course, to client approval and the limits of confidentiality)
• Offer examples and explanations of the types of disputes they have mediated
• Present credentials of membership in recognized dispute resolution associations
• Disclose organizational funding sources to demonstrate institutional impartiality

Two case examples illustrate the importance of building institutional credibility. A company executive considered using a mediation service to assist him in settling a community dispute to which he was a party. The mediation firm was asked to make a presentation about its services to some of the involved parties. During the meeting, the executive looked at the firm's brochure and began to put pluses and minuses next to the names of the firm's board members according to his perception of whether they would be positively or negatively disposed toward his interests in the dispute. When he counted the marks, he noticed that they came out even, and he accepted the firm's claim to impartiality.

In another case, an environmental group wanted the names and telephone numbers of other public interest groups that had used a mediation organization to settle conflicts over mining. The organization provided the data to build institutional credibility.

Procedural credibility refers to the belief of the disputants that the process the mediator has proposed has a strong likelihood of success. Some mediators are reluctant to describe the procedures by which they propose to resolve a dispute. By claiming that they respond differently to each conflict or by arguing that mediation is an art form rather than a series of scientific interventions, some mediators shroud their practice in secrecy and leave the disputants ignorant of the mediation process. Mediators following this approach argue that procedural credibility is enhanced by mystifying the process. However, this is not the majority view on the issue.

The practice of obscuring the mediation process has been sharply criticized by those who advocate a candid education of the parties about general mediation procedures that might be used in their dispute. Clear procedural descriptions enable the parties to make informed judgments about the viability of the process, and they demonstrate how the procedure might work in the particular case. In building procedural credibility, the mediator should stress that successful resolution rests primarily on the disputants themselves and that the best possible process will not guarantee that recalcitrant parties will come to terms.

An example of procedural credibility building occurred when mediators from my company, CDR Associates, were asked by the Public Utilities Commission of Colorado to intervene in a dispute over creating a new rule on telephone access charges. As the process of negotiated and mediated rule making had a very limited history in Colorado, and none of the major parties had ever engaged in such a process, the mediators conducted an educational session for the disputants in which case histories and procedures used for regulatory rule making in other settings were presented. Successful case studies built procedural credibility and enabled the parties to visualize how the process might work for them.

Substantive credibility refers to specific knowledge, expertise, or experience regarding the content of issues in dispute that the moderator can bring to assist the parties. For example, a background in handling personal injury cases may be helpful in aiding inexperienced parties to reach reasonable financial settlements. Similarly, knowledge and experience in resolving environmental cases over the protection of endangered species may be very beneficial to parties without such information.

Establishing Rapport with the Disputants

Personal, institutional, procedural, and substantive credibility is merely the starting point for a mediator's entry into a dispute. The greatest factor in the acceptability of an intervenor is probably the personal rapport he or she establishes with the disputants. *Rapport* refers to the degree of freedom experienced in communication, the level of comfort of the parties, the degree of precision in what is communicated, and the quality of human contact. Rapport is clearly influenced by the mediator's personal style; manner of speech, dress, and social background; common interests, friends, or associates; and the amount of communication between the mediator and the disputants. Mediators often talk about the need to develop some form of bond with the parties. This may be accomplished early in the mediation by identifying common personal experiences such as recreation, travel, children, and associates; by talking about common values; by genuinely affirming one or more of a disputant's attributes or activities; or by demonstrating one's sincerity through behavior.

In an intervention a few years ago, I was encountering significant difficulty in building rapport with a party over the telephone. He answered most questions, even open-ended ones, with yes-or-no answers or a grunt. Finally, he asked about the weather where I was in Colorado, and I knew that was the opening. On learning that it was snowing, he began to reminisce about time he had spent in the mountains. I followed up with a few open-ended questions about his experiences, and after a few minutes, we discovered that we had both done winter camping. The beginning of rapport had been established.

In another case, Kakwirakeron, a Mohawk leader in a dispute involving Native American land claims at Moss Lake in upstate New York, described the manner of Rowley, a mediator with the American Arbitration Association:

> When I first met Rowley I remember the white hair which he has, and the type of face he has is to me an honest face. And he always had the ready smile, which is a genuine smile, not just for the show of it. He had a manner, a very easy manner which is easy for us to identify. He really doesn't have a mask on. He is not trying to put on a show or an air of importance. He is just honest and straightforward and our first impression of him held up all the way through [Kwartler, 1980, pp. 15–16].

Educating Participants About the Mediation Process

To build initial procedural credibility, the mediator should explain enough about his or her role and the proposed mediation procedures to create a willingness on the part of disputants to try the process. In the later phases of a mediator's efforts to enter a dispute, he or she will spend additional time educating the parties about the particular negotiation and mediation process. This educational effort should be undertaken to (1) minimize surprises that might result from misunderstandings about the negotiation and mediation processes; (2) clarify the sequence of steps so that disputants know what to expect and know what roles they will be playing; and (3) gain both conscious and unconscious feedback from the participants, reflecting their feelings and reservations about the intervention procedure. Although the goal of mediation is not primarily an educational exercise, it is still a process designed to *teach* participants how to solve their problems. Disputants must thus have at least a minimal understanding of the process for the intervenor to be successful. Here are some of the matters that the parties should understand:

- The role of the mediator (neutrality and impartiality as appropriate for the particular type of mediator role being performed)
- The way information or data about the dispute will be collected
- The procedure that will be used to "work" on each issue
- The limits of confidentiality in the mediation process
- The potential use of joint sessions and of caucuses (private meetings)
- The possible forms that an agreement, if reached, might take

Before committing themselves to mediation, the parties should assess all the procedures available to them to resolve their dispute (Wade, 2001). Careful explanation and evaluation of the alternative approaches enhances the probability that mediation, if it is selected, will be successful.

Gaining a Commitment to Mediate

The mediator must believe that there is a common commitment by the parties both to the process of negotiation and mediation as a means of resolving their dispute and to the mediator as an assistant in this effort. The commitment to the process and to an intervenor has been referred to in organizational development literature as a "psychological contract" (Schein, 1969, pp. 81–88). A psychological contract is a tacit agreement between mediator and disputant that their relationship exists for the purpose of settling the dispute and that it will be based on certain core values, such as openness and honesty.

At this point, mediators usually have to make a strategic decision about how explicit or formal the commitment process should be and what form it should take. In some situations and cultures, oral agreements to participate may be all that will be necessary. In others, the contracting may be more formal.

Formal contracts often specify fees, expected time expenditure, and specific services to be or not to be performed. Mediators vary considerably in the degree of formality they introduce into mediation contracts. Some want an explicit signed statement that the parties are committed to achieving a jointly satisfactory solution with the mediator's assistance. Others rely exclusively on more informal documents.

In some disputes, an attempt to gain overt commitment to mediation, either oral or written, may lead to a failure to begin negotiations at all. Mediators occasionally delay asking the parties to formally commit to mediation until a series of successful procedural and substantive decisions have been made. In this approach to achieving commitment, mediators first seek agreement that they can talk with one or more parties alone or in informal joint meetings. In these conversations, the disputants may discover common interests that can be built on to develop rapport between the parties and later, perhaps, to form substantive agreements. Such common interests are used to initiate formal discussions.

Between the two extremes of explicit written commitment and informal oral commitment is a strategic third option. Through questioning of and discussion with the disputants, a mediator may discover specific conditions under which conflicting parties will be willing to negotiate. These might include understandings about how the parties will interact in negotiation, the timing and location of sessions, or specific symbolic gestures that are demanded before discussions can begin. The mediator may work with the parties to meet these behavioral preconditions for negotiation. By setting the stage and building a commitment contract, the mediator can encourage involvement without seeking a formal statement to that end. This approach has the advantage that parties do not have to overtly commit to the process to begin dialogue. However, it also has drawbacks: a precedent may be established that requires the mediator to constantly overcome limits or hurdles thrown up by participants who are not committed to the process; and the parties may balk at formalizing their commitment to any agreements.

In some large public disputes, the entry of an intermediary may initially be exclusively for data collection to conduct an analysis of a conflict and to gather information that can act as a catalyst for negotiation. A party's participation in data collection does not necessarily mean that a mediation will result or that the person or persons being interviews will necessarily be future participants in a dispute resolution initiative. This form of entry is often called "convening" and will be described in Chapter Five. In this scenario, the intermediary wants to collect data that will be used to determine if mediation is desirable and feasible; invitations to participate and the commitment process that has been described will occur later.

IMPLEMENTATION OF ENTRY

So far, I have explained the four general means of entry and the tasks to be accomplished by the mediator during this stage of intervention. I now turn to specific ways in which mediators initiate contact with disputants: letters, phone calls, personal visits, and third-party introductions. Depending on the mediator, institution, type of dispute, and characteristics of the disputants, various combinations may be effective. Some mediators and mediation organizations make first contact with clients by phone; others rely more heavily on personal interviews. Frequently, a combination of letter, brochure, and phone call is used to build credibility, describe the process, and gain commitment to mediate.

In complex disputes in which access to the main actors is tightly controlled or limited by some barrier such as race, channels of authority, or even physical inaccessibility (examples are volatile community conflicts and cases involving highly bureaucratic and hierarchical organizations), a secondary party may be used to introduce the mediator to one or more disputants. These introductions may be invaluable to the intervenor seeking entry into a closed dispute.

Two types of intervention activity should be considered when determining the timing of an intervention: data collection and problem-solving mediation activities. Although both types of intervention require entry by the mediator, their impacts on a dispute can be quite different.

Data Collection

Entry to gather preliminary data about a conflict can be initiated at almost any time in the development of a dispute, although it may be more difficult to collect information during certain phases of conflict development, such as the early escalation stage before the parties have decided to negotiate, or the stage in which negotiations have commenced but the parties do not believe a mediator is necessary.

The major strategic decisions about intervention for data collection focus primarily on whom to talk with, the sequence of interviews, the content of interviews, and the catalytic function that gathering and organizing information can play. More will be said about entry strategies and the function of data collection in Chapter Five.

Problem Solving

The timing of mediator intervention to solve problems, as opposed to collecting data, is one of the most intensely debated topics in the dispute resolution field (Simkin, 1971; Kerr, 1954; Carpenter and Kennedy, 1979; Pearson, 1984). Some mediators argue that early intervention limits hostility and emotional damage. It may also alleviate the tendency for parties to polarize on substantive issues. Early entry may enable the mediator to prevent the development of a hard-line commitment on one side to options that are unacceptable to the other.

Another argument for early intervention concerns procedural advantages. Polarization often results when disputants fail to understand productive means or procedures to resolve their controversy. Early intervention can discourage unproductive negotiation behavior, route the parties toward behavior or procedures that will result in settlement, and deter energy-draining responses that may escalate a dispute and create barriers to settlement through poor process rather than substantive differences.

Arguments for later mediator entry into a dispute center on parties' needs to mobilize their power, equalize the means they have to influence each other, and occasionally demonstrate their coercive power before negotiations. Later entry may also allow polarization to develop that often clarifies issues; give the parties time to vent emotions; and allow the parties themselves to request the assistance of an impartial mediator after they have exhausted their own procedural and substantive options.

Proponents of later intervention argue that parties need time to mobilize their forces and gather their means of influence in order to affect the other parties involved (Cormick, 1982; Crowfoot, 1980). They claim that early entry hinders this process; that the weaker party, who is not as well prepared for the conflict and therefore has less influence, may be overwhelmed; and that an unfair settlement may be either reached or imposed. Mobilization of resources might include visiting a lawyer and obtaining advice on the strength of a legal case, conducting research necessary for informed negotiations, mobilizing a community group to protest a particular policy, filing a case in court, or planning a strike.

Early-entry adherents generally do not disagree with those advocating late entry about the needs of parties to mobilize and, whenever possible, equalize power. Failure to gather the necessary data before negotiations is tantamount to playing a game of poker without looking at the cards. Failure to assess legal power or, when appropriate, extralegal action before negotiations can enable one party to take advantage of another.

Advocates of early entry diverge from their colleagues who advocate late entry on the question of demonstrating coercive power. They argue that mobilization and exercise of coercive options should be separated. Early-entry advocates point to experimental research (Rubin and Brown, 1975) demonstrating that the exercise of coercive power, although it may promote negotiations, does not necessarily promote cooperative behavior. This finding seems to be corroborated by research on outcomes of actual negotiations. Pearson (1984), for example, found that couples in divorce settlement mediation who had used coercive court mechanisms to obtain temporary orders had a lower rate of settlement than those who had not used legal coercion before settlement negotiations.

Late-entry advocates counter with valid case examples in which the exercise of force—by means of legal suits, strikes, or demonstrations—has been necessary to demonstrate a party's power and, in some cases, to force an opponent to negotiate. Last-minute pressure has clearly inclined parties toward agreement and has motivated them to request a mediator's assistance.

Mediators who look for easy answers regarding questions of power and timing of the impartial party's entry will probably find none. The best answer is that these factors depend on the case. If parties can mobilize information and resources so that they are informed and so that the other side knows that they are dealing with a prepared and powerful adversary, the power may never need to be exercised, and the mediator may be able to intervene before a crisis exacerbates relationship problems or inflicts costs that provoke escalation. Early entry in the case may prevent unnecessary damage to either of the disputing parties. On the other hand, if the parties have unequal power, need a confrontation to mobilize resources, or must test each other's strength before good-faith bargaining can begin, mediators are advised to delay entry.

The argument for a period to vent emotions is also not contested by early-entry proponents. They do, however, maintain that unstructured and prolonged venting, which may occur if the mediator delays entry, may result in hostile or unproductive behavior that causes unnecessary psychological barriers.

The final argument, which relates to the "ripeness" of a dispute for settlement, is an extremely important strategic issue that bears directly on the timing of intervention. Numerous mediators and negotiators have observed that disputes go through specific cycles, and that resolution of issues often cannot occur until disputants have performed ritual acts (Douglas, 1962). Mediator entry too early in a dispute, it is claimed, damages this developmental cycle.

Late-entry proponents argue that parties are not psychologically or strategically prepared to use an intervenor's services until they have reached an impasse and recognize that they cannot reach a settlement without third-party assistance:

> The safest rule for late entry proponents postulates that a mediator should not enter a negotiation until there is a bona fide deadlock. The reason is self-evident. A premature intervention by the media-

tor relieves the parties of the pressure under which they are working. The reciprocal pressure is the basic force that keeps the parties moving through proposals and counterproposals. Entering the situation before a genuine deadlock is reached creates an atmosphere of relaxation in the parties, and consequently, the mediator has no basic element to keep the parties moving. Requesting the services of a mediator before the bona fide deadlock is usually a trick used by one or both parties to extend the negotiations. An intervention at this time will discourage the parties from reaching an agreement. One or both parties will relax their efforts while the mediator gets his fingers burned [Perez, 1959, p. 717].

Proponents of early entry, on the other hand, argue that an efficient mediation process introduced early in a dispute can often accelerate the development of psychological readiness and motivation for settlement. Early introduction of mediation can decrease levels of frustration, diminish polarization, and promote positive results. Success, rather than mutual frustration, can then become the driving force in negotiations.

The timing of entry is clearly an important strategic decision for mediators. At the current stage of research, not enough is known to specify in an unqualified manner the conditions under which early entry is superior to later intervention. Mediators should assess whether early entry is likely to be more detrimental to the disputants than delay. If the answer is no, an early intervention is probably the safer route.

Chapter Four

Selecting a Strategy to Guide Mediation

In Chapter One, I presented several approaches to conflict management and resolution. They spanned a continuum, with conflict avoidance at one extreme and physical violence at the other. As one moves from left to right in the diagram (see Figure 1.1), the approaches become progressively more directive and coercive. My concern in this chapter is with the processes people in conflict use to select a particular approach or combination of approaches along this continuum. Key questions are how and under what circumstances people select mediated negotiation as the principal way to manage or resolve conflict.

Related to selecting the approach is the choice of arena. Arenas are locales for conflict management and resolution that vary on several dimensions: publicness and privacy, informality and formality, institutionalization and noninstitutionalization, and voluntariness and coercion. Any given approach can be acted out in a variety of arenas. For example, mediation can occur in a private setting that is informal, voluntary, and uninstitutionalized—as in child custody and divorce settlements conducted by a mediator in private practice. Alternatively, mediation can be conducted in a highly public setting with standardized behaviors and rituals, formal rules for participation, and an institutionalized structure. This is the type of arena used when the EPA and other concerned parties engage in a negotiated rule making (reg-neg) to formulate new, consensually based regulations.

Parties must select both the approach and the arena they think will best meet their needs and satisfy their interests. Approach and arena selection is a relational decision, in that it occurs as a result of interaction between the people in conflict. Parties may use the same approach and arena, or partially coordinate their approaches or arenas, or use entirely different approaches and arenas. For example, some disputants may use nonviolent direct action and others the courts. To achieve a termination of the conflict, the parties must usually coordinate at least some of their dispute resolution activities.

A mediator can assist parties in selecting and coordinating approaches and arenas. He or she is often more aware of approaches and arenas than are disputing parties and can therefore educate them about alternatives in the early stages of prenegotiation and assist them in selecting an appropriate means of conflict management and dispute resolution that will best meet their needs and capabilities.

THE MEDIATOR-DISPUTANT RELATIONSHIP AND DECISION MAKING

Mediator roles in helping disputants make decisions about conflict approaches and arenas are similar to those available to lawyers. Hamilton (1972, p. 41) outlines three philosophical stances that a lawyer may take in advising and counseling clients:

A. Collect the facts, explain how the law applies, analyze, recommend a best course, or courses, of action, and argue for its adoption.
B. Collect the facts, explain how the law applies, analyze, explain the course of action open to the client, and leave the decision entirely to him.
C. "B" above, except with discussion of the ramifications of the course of action and the situation until the client is able to make his decision.

Mediators must choose among the same three stances, with the exception that they do not interpret the law.

The majority of process-oriented mediators probably see their role as defined by option C, in which the task is to assist disputants in making their own decision on the basis of information supplied by the mediator about the opportunities available through various approaches and arenas. Most mediators view their relationship with the disputant as collaborative; information is shared to develop the wisest and most considered decisions possible.

THE APPROACH AND ARENA DECISION

Mediators do not automatically assume at the beginning stage of intervention that mediated negotiation is the best approach for conflict management or resolution. It is only through a careful assessment process that the disputants and the mediator may jointly arrive at this conclusion (Wade, 2001).

There is no one decision-making procedure that is appropriate in all disputes for determining whether mediation is the best approach. Mediators can, however, assist disputants in accomplishing some of these tasks:

1. Identifying the interests or goals that must be satisfied in a potential settlement
2. Considering the range of possible and acceptable dispute outcomes
3. Identifying the conflict resolution approaches that may assist disputants in reaching individual, subgroup, or collective goals
4. Identifying and assessing criteria for selecting an approach
5. Selecting and making a commitment to an approach and arena
6. Coordinating, if necessary, the approaches used by the disputants

In the next sections, I will explain each point in more detail.

INTERESTS TO BE SATISFIED

At this point, the mediator often talks with the parties separately and will encourage them to carefully examine their own interests and those of other parties to arrive at answers to these questions:

• What interests (substantive, procedural, and psychological) must be met by a conflict management approach and resolution?

- What interests are mutually incompatible or overlap with the interests of other parties?
- What interest is there in an ongoing relationship?
- What forms of actual or potential power do the parties have that would allow them to impose their will on other disputants in order to achieve their interests?
- How important or salient are the various interests to each actor in the dispute?

Analyzing interests enables the parties and the mediator to determine whether any common interests exist and to assess the purity of the dispute (Kriesberg, 1973). *Purity* refers to the degree of exclusivity of interests. A pure conflict is one in which all interests are incompatible—for example, no settlement options are available that can satisfy one party's interests without sacrificing those of another. A mixed conflict allows for some satisfaction of all interests. If a conflict is pure, parties have little to negotiate. If it is mixed, negotiation and mediation are appropriate approaches to dispute resolution.

For example, if divorcing spouses both demand legal custody of their child and there are no provisions in their jurisdiction for joint custody, the conflict could be pure: neither party could win legal custody without the other losing. On the other hand, if both parents want to share their relationship with the child and are interested in allocating time equitably, the conflict is mixed and suitable for negotiation.

POSSIBLE DISPUTE OUTCOMES

After identifying the interests involved in the conflict, mediators usually work with each party separately to assess potential—and in some cases, probable—conflict outcomes. Thomas (1976) identifies five possible outcomes to any given issue in dispute; Clark and Cummings (1981) elaborate on Thomas's themes. Their combined results are represented in Figure 4.1. For the sake of clarity, this figure represents a dispute with only two sides and illustrates a conflict from the viewpoint of Party A.

Win-lose outcomes occur in the upper-left and lower-right corners of the chart. The difference is in which party wins. Win-lose outcomes are most common when:

Figure 4.1. Possible Outcomes of a Dispute as Viewed by Party A.

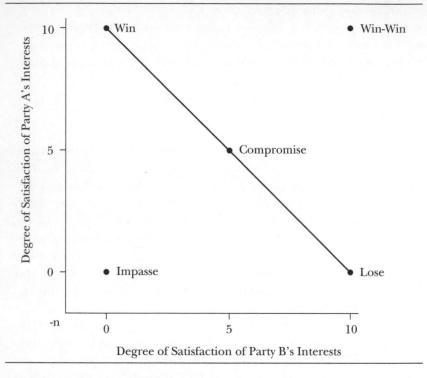

- One party has overwhelming power
- Future relationships are not of great concern
- The stakes for winning are high
- One party is extremely assertive and the other is passive or not as aggressive as the "winner"
- Satisfaction of the interests of the disputants is not dependent on their mutual cooperation
- One or more parties are uncooperative and are unwilling to engage in cooperative problem-solving negotiations in which interests can be mutually satisfied (Moore, 1982b)

Impasse outcomes are present in the lower-left corner. These outcomes result when parties are not able to come to an agreement. They occur when:

- Both parties choose to avoid the conflict for whatever reason
- Neither party has enough power to force the issue
- There is lack of trust, poor communication, expressive emotion, or an inadequate resolution process
- The stakes for winning are low, or neither party cares about the dispute
- The interests of the parties are not related
- One or more of the parties are uncooperative (Moore, 1982b)

Compromise outcomes are illustrated by the central portion of the diagonal line. Such outcomes occur when all parties give up some of their goals to obtain others. They are likely to happen when:

- Neither party has the power necessary to win totally
- The future positive relationship of the disputants is important, but they do not trust each other enough to work together for integrative solutions with mutual gain
- The stakes for winning are moderately high
- Both parties are assertive
- The interests of both parties are mutually interdependent
- The parties have some leeway for cooperation, bargaining, and trade-offs (Moore, 1982b)

Win-win outcomes occur when all parties feel that their interests have been satisfied. Conditions for win-win outcomes are present when:

- Both parties are not engaged in a power struggle
- A future positive relationship is important
- The stakes are high for producing a mutually satisfactory solution
- Both parties are assertive problem solvers
- The interests of all parties are mutually interdependent
- Parties are free to cooperate and to engage in joint problem solving (Moore, 1982b)

Mediators discuss with parties various possible outcomes and how they meet the interests of the disputants. Ideally, the outcomes and interests should match.

RANGE OF APPROACHES

Once a party has assessed its interests and those of other parties and reviewed potential dispute outcomes, it must select a particular approach to reach the desired end. Approaches are general procedures for resolving disputes; they include such options as unassisted negotiations, negotiations with the assistance of an advocate, conciliation to handle emotional or relationship barriers, facilitation, mediation, arbitration, and litigation.

Approach selection depends on a variety of criteria, including the outcome that is desired and the strategy that is to be used. Mediators review general strategy options open to the parties and how these strategies may be applied within the context of a given approach. The mediator usually conducts strategy assessment privately with each party.

There are five general strategy options: competition, avoidance, accommodation, negotiated compromise, and interest-based negotiation. Figure 4.2 describes strategy options as viewed by Party A.

Competition

In some situations, a party's interests are so narrow that they can be met by only a few solutions, none of which is acceptable to other parties. Such a party may choose a competitive approach and strive for a win-lose outcome, especially when it has more power than its opponent does. Competitive approaches include litigation, arbitration, and extralegal activities such as tactical nonviolent direct action and violence.

In deciding to use a competitive approach, a party should weigh the costs as well as the benefits of its conflict behavior:

- Will the party get what it wants over the long run as well as the short run?
- Will competitive behavior damage or destroy relationships that are important in the future?
- Does the party have adequate means of influence or power to guarantee a win? What happens if it loses?
- Will competition provoke competition in other areas?

Figure 4.2. Conflict Strategies as Viewed by Party A.

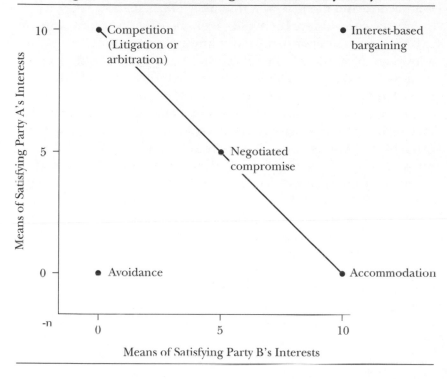

- Will a competitive strategy lead to the most desirable solution? (Moore, 1982b)

Avoidance or Stalemate

Conflict avoidance can be either productive or unproductive in satisfying interests. People avoid conflict for a variety of reasons: fear, lack of knowledge of dispute management processes, absence of interdependent interests, indifference to the issues in the dispute, absence of adequate influence or power over the outcome, belief that it is the wrong time for constructive engagement, or perception that agreement is not possible and overt conflict is not desirable.

Blake, Shepard, and Mouton (1964) noted that avoidance approaches have various levels. The first may be to claim a position of *neutrality.* Stating "We have no position on this issue at this time" is a way to avoid being drawn into a dispute.

At the second level of avoidance, *isolation,* disputants pursue their interests independently, with limited interaction. Groups are allowed to have their "spheres of interest" if they do not impinge on another's domain. This strategy is used frequently when a conflict of interest exists, but overt conflict is not desirable. For example, in organizational disputes, individual managers or departments may be assigned exclusive decision-making authority over specific matters. In divorce cases, some parents agree to spheres of interest regarding educational or religious upbringing for their children or different norms for the two homes; for example, at one parent's home the child is allowed to watch television three hours a day but at the other's the child may not watch at all. The parties agree to disagree on parenting styles, and they contract not to fight each other on the issue.

People or groups that have been repeatedly defeated frequently use *withdrawal* to ensure their continued existence and to avoid any conflict that might lead to another defeat. Withdrawal means total dissociation of disputants. This strategy does not encourage or promote mediated negotiations.

Accommodation

Accommodation occurs when one party agrees to meet the interests of another at the expense of its own needs. An accommodation strategy is pursued when:

- Sacrifice of some interests is required to maintain a positive relationship
- It is desirable to demonstrate or foster cooperation
- Interests are extremely interdependent (Moore, 1982b)

A positive accommodative approach may be pursued when there is hope that a more collaborative process or benefit trading may occur later on other issues. For example, when a developer voluntarily agrees to spend additional funds to add an amenity demanded by a dissatisfied homeowners' group, he is accommodating himself to their needs. He does not have to spend the money but decides that a positive ongoing relationship is worth the expenditure.

Accommodation may also be pursued for negative reasons:

- Parties lack the power necessary to pursue an alternative strategy.
- Parties are passive or unassertive.
- Parties have a lower investment in the outcome (Moore, 1982b).

Negotiated Compromise

Bargaining to reach a compromise is selected because:

- The parties do not perceive the possibility of a win-win situation that will meet their needs and have decided to divide and share what they see as a limited resource
- Interests are not seen as interdependent or compatible
- The parties do not trust each other enough to enter into joint problem solving for mutual gain
- Parties are sufficiently equal in power so that neither can force the issue in its favor (Moore, 1982b)

Many out-of-court settlements are negotiated compromises. A judicial decision is risky for both sides because it is not clear who will win. Parties and their advocates frequently split the difference to ensure that each gets some of what they want, and each party shares some of the loss.

Interest-Based Negotiation

In contrast to competition and compromise, in which the outcome is seen as division of fixed resources, interest-based procedures seek to enlarge the range of alternatives so that the needs of all parties are addressed and met to the greatest extent possible.

Interest-based procedures work best when:

- Parties have at least a minimal level of trust in each other
- Parties have some mutually interdependent interests
- Equal, but not necessarily similar, means of influence exist, or the party with the superior power is willing to curtail the exercise of power and work toward cooperative solutions

- Parties have a high investment in a mutually satisfactory outcome because of mutual fear of potential costs that might result from impasse
- Parties desire a positive future relationship (Moore, 1982b)

Each of the preceding strategies can be pursued in the context of several approaches and arenas.

Parties must match their strategy with their interests and link it with an approach that offers the best prospects of satisfying them. Mediators should help parties to decide if they want to compete, avoid, accommodate, compromise, or seek a cooperative settlement. Once the party has selected a general strategy, it chooses an approach that best implements the strategy. Of all the strategies described, compromise, accommodation, and interest-based negotiation are the most compatible with negotiation.

Selection of a general strategy to guide a negotiation approach does not mean that other strategies will not be used to respond to particular aspects of a dispute. For example, a party may choose to compete on a central or core issue but avoid or accommodate on others. Selection of a general strategy is merely a guide for subsequent negotiations. Strategy will often change once the parties have started discussions and become more informed about the issues, interests, and means of influence of other parties. Parties commonly select a competitive strategy, decide to negotiate, and then shift to a strategy of compromise or interest-based negotiations.

Mediators aid parties in matching interests, approaches, and strategies by helping them identify and assess an approach's potential for reaching a satisfactory outcome. Generally, a mediator should suggest, and help a party assess, more than one approach and strategy so that he or she does not seem to be advocating a particular method of resolution. The mediator may also discuss possible arenas that may be combined with an approach. For example, a party might have to initiate litigation as a means of forcing a party to negotiate. The mediator might explore with the party the use of the threat of potential costs of litigation to promote settlement negotiations.

CRITERIA FOR SELECTING AN APPROACH AND ARENA

After presenting possible approaches and arenas, the mediator can assist the parties in identifying relevant criteria that should be considered in making the selections. Criteria may be different for interpersonal, commercial, organizational, and public disputes. There are, however, many similarities. Some of the criteria or variables for selecting an approach or arena are cost, time, the relationship between the disputants, the internal dynamics of the dispute, and power.

The question to be asked with respect to *cost* is, What will be the costs (direct costs, salary costs, delay costs, lawyer fees, and so on) of pursuing each approach or arena?

As far as *time* is concerned, the questions include these:

- How long will it take to settle the dispute using each approach or arena?
- Is a rapid or a delayed settlement desirable?
- Are there any critical deadlines or time constraints to be considered? Does a deadline pose an opportunity or a crisis for one of the parties?
- What is the most advantageous time to settle?
- Do the parties need more time to mobilize resources or build credibility and commitment among a constituency for a particular course of action?

With respect to the *relationship between disputants,* the key questions are:

- Is the conflict a single-encounter dispute, or is it occurring in the context of an ongoing relationship?
- What type of relationship is desired at the end of the dispute?
- How will the use of various approaches and arenas affect the ongoing relationship?
- Do any of the proposed approaches and arenas seem unfair or in conflict with relationship or community norms?
- What effect will selection of an approach or arena have on the public image of the party or parties? Do the various options enhance or detract from public credibility?
- Will selection of a particular approach or arena affect future conflicts of this type?

The questions to be asked about *internal dynamics,* according to Crowfoot (1980), are:

- Is the individual or organization stable and effective enough to pursue various approaches?
- Will the approaches involve the membership of the organization? How, and at what costs or benefits?
- Will a particular approach or arena build or unify membership and the organization?
- Does a particular approach build self-acceptance, confirmation, essentiality, and a psychological feeling of success or failure (Argyris, 1970)?
- Do the individuals or organizations have the necessary leadership and skills to pursue a particular course of action?
- Do the individuals or organizations have the time, energy, and financial and emotional resources to pursue a particular course of action?

These are the relevant questions about *power,* as identified by Simokaitis (n.d.):

- What power or means of influence do disputants have to make the other side give them what they want?
- How powerful does the party believe the other side perceives it to be?
- What possible allies and other sources of power might the party be able to tap?
- What might happen to limit the party's power?
- What are the limits on the power of the other disputants?

Once relevant decision criteria or variables are identified, the mediator should assist a disputant in assessing how important each criterion is, and how it affects the selection of a particular approach and arena. Mediators may assist parties in making this assessment by providing a structure for a cost-benefit analysis (Moore, 1982b), by developing a decision tree (Behn and Vaupel, 1982) that identifies strategic choices and possible outcomes, or by helping participants assess probabilities of outcomes through an analysis of similar cases or trends (Bellows and Moulton, 1981).

An initial statement by parties that they want to mediate should not necessarily be taken at face value. A careful assessment of their interests and their criteria for selecting an approach and arena may reveal that they are not willing to make the substantive, procedural, or psychological offers that would be required for a negotiated settlement. In these situations, the mediator should advise the parties that other approaches to resolving the conflict may be more appropriate.

COMMITMENT TO APPROACH AND ARENA

Once all approaches and arenas have been compared according to the criteria, the mediator should assist the parties in making a final selection. Careful assessment of valid information about potential outcomes from each procedure usually helps people build internal commitment to a choice of action. "Internal commitment means the course of action or choice that has been internalized by each member so that he experiences a high degree of ownership and has a feeling of responsibility about the choice and its implications. Internal commitment means that the individual has reached a point where he is acting on the choice because it fulfills his own needs and sense of responsibility, as well as those of the system" (Argyris, 1970, p. 20).

Internal commitment to negotiation with the assistance of a mediator will help the parties in dispute struggle together to reach an agreement. If the mediator has done his or her job well, assisting the parties in selecting mediated negotiations will have moved them closer to a resolution.

COORDINATION OF APPROACHES AND ARENAS

Approach and arena selection by one disputant does not mean that other disputants will select the same approach or arena. The approach and arena assessment process must be conducted with all of the primary parties in a dispute.

Mediators may assist parties who are operating with different approaches or in different arenas in coordinating their conflict resolution efforts so that they can cooperatively reach a solution rather than spend unnecessary time, money, physical energy, or emotional effort on unproductive conflict activity. For example, Party A wants to negotiate a settlement on one issue, but not while litigation is being conducted on another. The mediator may help

Party B defer litigation until after the negotiable issues have been discussed.

In collective bargaining situations, where negotiation is the accepted and preferred means of settling conflicts, the parties are less likely to encounter the coordination problems that arise in interpersonal, organizational, or community disputes. In the latter types of conflicts, disputants often lack either a common approach or a common arena. They may in fact have no prior history of interaction and therefore no traditional or accepted way of resolving conflicts. In these types of disputes, the mediator can play a critical function in assisting the parties with coordinating their conflict resolution efforts.

There are, however, situations early in the negotiation process in which perfectly coordinated procedures are not attainable. These situations arise when parties:

- Are not psychologically prepared to commit themselves to a particular approach
- Are not dissatisfied with the approach currently being used
- Want to try noncoordinated activity, hoping for a win-lose outcome in their favor, before cooperating
- Feel that a coordinated approach offers them no advantage
- Feel that they do not have equal influence or power that could be effectively used if a coordinated conflict resolution approach were pursued
- Do not have the resources to engage in a coordinated effort

When faced with parties who are not prepared to coordinate their conflict resolution approaches, the mediator has several strategy options:

1. If coordination of efforts has no advantage for a disputant, the mediator can encourage the parties to pursue their chosen approaches and inform them that if it is advantageous to negotiate or mediate at a later time, the option remains open. In counseling the parties in this way, the mediator should refer to the various costs and benefits, identified by the disputant, of pursuing the uncoordinated course.

2. The mediator can negotiate a procedural approach to the dispute in which the parties agree to begin negotiations while retaining their right to pursue other approaches or arenas of dispute resolution, including continuation of hostilities.

3. The mediator may begin negotiations with fewer parties in the hope that others may be persuaded to join later or be impelled to join because of the fear that a settlement will be reached without them.

4. The mediator may obtain a tentative commitment to explore negotiation or mediation through a prenegotiation conference. This conference may have as its goal conciliation or negotiation of a mutual and cooperative conflict management procedure.

5. The mediator may continue with efforts to persuade the parties to begin negotiations.

6. The mediator may seek out additional parties who may be able to encourage the principal disputants to try negotiation.

Chapter Five

Collecting and Analyzing Background Information

Data collection and conflict analysis enable a mediator and disputants to identify the key parties in the conflict, determine the issues and interests that are important to them, and explore the relationships and dynamics—historical and current—that exist between them. The process of identifying the components and dynamics of a conflict is *data collection;* integrating and interpreting that information is *analysis.*

Through data collection and analysis, the mediator will:

- Develop a mediation plan or conflict strategy that meets the requirements of the specific situation and the needs of all parties
- Avoid entering a dispute with a conflict resolution or management procedure that is inappropriate for the stage of development or level of intensity that the dispute has reached
- Operate from an accurate information base that will prevent unnecessary conflicts due to miscommunication, misperception, or misleading data
- Clarify which issues and interests are most important to work on
- Identify the key people involved and the dynamics of their relationships

The first part of this chapter will examine methods of data collection. The second part will explore how information is integrated and analyzed. The chapter focuses primarily on data collection and analysis in disputes among more than two people or parties. However, the process is basically the same for conflicts between only two individuals.

The amount of time spent on data collection depends on the complexity of the dispute. An interpersonal conflict clearly requires less time to be expended in data collection—perhaps an hour or two with each party—than does a complex social policy dispute in which months may be needed to gather relevant information.

Data collection can be conducted before negotiation or once negotiation has begun. Because I prefer to perform preliminary data collection before joint sessions, I will assume in this chapter that the mediator is meeting with parties separately before starting formal mediation in joint sessions.

Useful and accurate data collection depends on six factors:

1. A framework for analysis and adequate background information
2. An appropriate method of data collection
3. An appropriate person to collect the data
4. A strategy for data collection and for building rapport and credibility with involved parties
5. Appropriate interviewing approaches that encourage valid responses
6. Appropriate questions and listening process during interviews

FRAMEWORK FOR ANALYSIS

All conflicts involve specific people, relatively predictable dynamics of development, competing interests, and tangible and intangible issues. These common components of disputes allow a general framework to be created that is useful in generating questions and explanatory hypotheses about a given dispute.

Mediators may use the categories in Figure 2.1 as a basic framework for analyzing a conflict. Relationship problems, data disagreements, competing interests, structural barriers, and value differences should be considered as potential causes of conflicts. In addition, factors that promote positive relationships, points of data on which the parties agree, compatible or nonexclusive interests, structural variables that enhance constructive interaction, and common or superordinate values should be identified as factors that may be encouraged or enhanced to promote agreement.

DATA COLLECTION METHODS

Mediators use several procedures to collect data: direct observation, review of secondary sources, and interviewing. These procedures are used either individually or in combination to produce more accurate or complete information about a given conflict.

DIRECT OBSERVATION AND SITE VISITS

A mediator may watch a couple fighting at the beginning of a mediation session, attend and observe a public meeting, visit a proposed development site, or attend a company briefing to gather firsthand information on how the parties react and interact in a conflict.

Observation goals vary from dispute to dispute. The focus can be on any of three levels: individual behavior, interaction within subgroups, and interaction between groups. From observation, the mediator can determine social class, status, power, and influence relationships; communication patterns; and group routines that will influence the conduct of a conflict.

Consultation of Secondary Sources

Secondary sources are materials that yield information about a dispute without direct observation or interviews. Helpful secondary sources could be financial records, minutes of meetings, maps, organizational or government reports, newspaper or magazine articles, tape-recorded or videotaped presentations, and research conducted on the issues or people involved in a dispute.

Interviewing

The most common way for many mediators to gain information is to interview involved parties. There are two broad types of interviews that may be used in mediation: data collection interviews and persuasive interviews (Stewart and Cash, 1974). The first type is used to collect relevant information, the second to persuade disputants that a particular procedure or outcome is desirable. The focus of this discussion will be on data collection interviews.

Such interviews may be conducted either before or during joint meetings. Some mediators prefer to hold a preliminary data collection interview with each individual or party before a joint meeting. This gives the interviewer information necessary to understand some of the people, issues, and dynamics of the conflict before interacting in a joint session. Preliminary interviews often provide the mediator with more information about the dispute than is known by any one party. This knowledge enables him or her to plan how the parties will educate each other about issues and interests in joint sessions; it also identifies information that needs to be exchanged to clarify misperceptions, fill in data gaps, and help the parties reach agreement.

Data collection interviews also serve to introduce the participants to the mediator. The personal and organizational rapport and credibility that are built during the interview strongly influence the amount and quality of information gathered and the receptivity of the disputant to the mediator's later interventions. Rapport is often more easily developed in one-on-one interviews than in joint sessions.

Finally, data collection interviews allow an exchange of information about the mediation process. A mediator can use the data collection interview to describe his or her proposed process in more detail and to solicit procedural or substantive suggestions from interviewees. A dialogue on processes for conflict management may be the first step toward an agreement on an approach for collaborative problem solving.

Data collection interviews may also be conducted at the start of joint meetings. Data collection is then performed in the presence of all involved parties. Such interviews allow the parties to educate each other; they create an opportunity for the mediator to watch how the disputants interact and enable the mediator to verify that information presented in the joint meeting is consistent with that from the earlier private interviews.

DATA COLLECTOR

Many mediators delegate the task of conducting the initial interview to an "intake" worker, whose findings form the basis of a case file. Although this arrangement may save time for mediators, it may also hinder the subsequent development of rapport and credibility between the mediator and the disputants. Usually, the mediator will have to follow up with his or her own brief data collection interview to build rapport with the parties.

In some conflicts, mediators or their agencies may prefer to collect data and mediate in teams. Male-female or lawyer-therapist teams are often used in child custody and divorce cases. In complex public policy or environmental disputes, interviewer-mediator teams may be involved. Co-mediators should take care in data collection to work together as much as possible, to frequently exchange any information that they obtain individually, and to minimize the possibility of working at cross purposes.

In some disputes, assignment of mediators to a particular type of conflict or interviewee may be an important move in securing fuller information from a respondent. Gender, age, race, social class, status, and previous relationship with the interviewer may affect the amount of information that can be obtained. For example, a woman disputant may feel more comfortable relating an incident of domestic violence if one of the mediators is a woman. In some interracial disputes, a minority mediator's presence has made a difference in the willingness of parties to be involved.

Usually, the more the respondent identifies with the interviewer or mediator, the better he or she will respond to the intermediary's influence. Mediators can often manage their own dress, speech, and manners, and use these attributes to enhance the possibility of interviewer-respondent identification.

DATA COLLECTION STRATEGY

A strategy is a conscious approach to addressing or solving a problem. In this context, the problem is how to get enough information about a dispute from the parties so that the intermediary can develop an intervention plan that will assist them. The information includes identification of key parties and a strategy for approaching them.

Identification of Parties

In many interpersonal and organizational disputes, parties are easy to identify, and the mediator can easily determine whom to interview. In divorce cases, for example, the husband and wife and perhaps the children will be targeted for interviews. The same is true in two-party commercial or insurance claim cases. But it is not always so in cross-cultural cases, where extended family members—parents, uncles and aunts of the disputants—and numerous other concerned parties may need to be involved in order to resolve a dispute.

In conflicts in which there are multiple disputants and the parties are not well organized or highly visible, the mediator may have to identify main actors before data collection can begin. In public disputes, mediators use procedures similar to those employed by researchers in community power-structure research (Aiken and Mott, 1970). The methods about to be described are used alone or in combination to assist mediators in identifying critical individuals, groups, and organizations that must be involved in a dispute resolution initiative.

The *positional approach* (Jennings, 1964; D'Antonio, Loomis, Form, and Erickson, 1961) identifies the main formal institutions or organizations involved and targets the people who fill their key positions. The chief executive officer of a company, members of a county commission, and the elected president of a public interest group all occupy positions of authority. The assumption of this approach is that those in key formal positions of authority in the institutions or organizations involved in a dispute are those who will make decisions about how the conflict is handled and resolved. In many cases, this may be true, although positional power holders may not have the authority to decide any given issue. Formal leaders of social, economic, and political institutions may not be as important as an individual without a formal position who can mobilize a group of supporters, make a technical decision, or initiate a lawsuit.

The assumption of the second identification method, the *reputational approach* (Walton, 1966; Hunter, 1953), is that people with a reputation for having power are indeed powerful. Mediators ask a group of reliable informants, "Who are the central people who should be interviewed about this conflict?" These informants are often knowledgeable observers of the dispute—but not active participants—or other primary parties. Names gathered in this process are cross-referenced, and the people who are most frequently mentioned are considered to be central to the dispute.

The weakness of this method, similar to that of the positional approach, is that perceived power does not necessarily mean actual power. Only through interviews can the two aspects of power be correlated.

The third identification method is the *decision-making approach* (Polsby, 1960; Dahl, 1961). In this method, the mediator seeks to ascertain who within an organization or group has been involved in previous decisions on issues similar to the one in question—and at what level they have been involved. The assumption is that certain people are likely to be repeatedly involved in the same type of issue. This method depends on the mediator's ability to review prior decisions and to identify the people who took part in them. It focuses on those participating in a conflict, the processes they have used in the past to influence decisions, and the development of conflict relationships over time.

All these approaches for identifying the key people in a conflict have merits and weaknesses, both in their theoretical assumptions and in their applications. Mediators will usually find that a combination of approaches produces the most reliable data from potential interviewees.

Sequencing of Interviews

After the interviewees have been targeted, mediators should consider the sequence of interviews. In interpersonal disputes and occasionally in other conflicts, the party that initiates mediation is interviewed first. These parties are often more amenable to sharing information than those who are responding to another's initiative.

Because the sources of data in conflict situations are individuals under actual or potential emotional stress, great care should be taken to determine a sequence of interviews that will not antagonize anyone.

In multiparty disputes, the mediator will have to develop a more detailed process for sequencing interviews. Often, he or she may have to contact secondary or less involved parties before talking to the principals. This helps to identify disputants, generate a more accurate picture of the conflict, practice questioning techniques, and obtain valuable information on the most suitable interviewing approach before talking with the main actors. Secondary parties are invaluable resources in disputes, because they often have a more objective view and may also be able to introduce the interviewer to other parties to the conflict. For example, in a university dispute, a department's secretary may be highly informative on the dynamics of faculty members and students and the critical interests and issues that concern them.

The mediator should frequently ask a secondary party, "Who is it important for me to talk with?" and "Who should be talked with first?" Inclusion of interviewees in interview sequencing decisions often gives the mediator valuable information about those most central to the dispute. In some instances, an interviewee may offer to call a friend and make an introduction.

Once secondary sources have provided sufficient data for the mediator, he or she should develop a strategy and a sequence for interviewing the central figures. These questions frequently guide the sequencing:

- Who are the most powerful or influential people in the dispute?
- Who will be offended if he or she is not interviewed, or is not interviewed first?
- Who should be interviewed earlier so that his or her cooperation can be used to induce others to participate in interviews?
- Who is the person most likely to talk about the problem?

Before interviewing the central individuals, the mediator may conduct research on what roles they play in the conflict, what positions they have held on similar issues, their likes and dislikes, and their personal traits. This information may expand the potential for data collection in the interview.

Timing of Data Collection Interviews

Data collection can be conducted before or at the time of joint sessions. Here are questions mediators can ask themselves to determine if a premediation data collection interview is necessary:

- Are the parties extremely hostile toward each other? Is there a potential for violence?
- Do the parties have widely divergent viewpoints on the issues in conflict?

- Do their styles of communication in joint session inhibit a clear exchange of views on the issues in dispute?
- Are multiple issues involved?
- Are issues extremely complex?
- Is there a likelihood that additional data or factual information may be needed before a joint session?
- Does one of the parties appear to be weaker than another?
- Does one party express fear of being dominated by another?
- Is one party unclear about the mediation process or the role of the mediator?

A yes to any of these questions indicates that a premediation interview for data collection may be appropriate.

If a mediator decides to use a premediation conference, he or she should carefully explain to all parties the purpose of the interview, its duration, the scope of issues to be covered, and limits of confidentiality of data revealed in the sessions. Most mediators hold to the standard that information exchanged in the premediation data collection meeting and in later separate caucuses is confidential and will only be revealed publicly or in joint session with the consent of the disputants. However, others make exceptions to this rule, most notably when criminal conduct, child abuse, or risk of physical harm is involved.

Some mediators opt to conduct all their initial interviews in joint session, with all disputants present. This choice may be based on strategy, convenience, time constraints, complexity, limits on confidentiality, or a desire to avoid suspicion on the part of the parties of partiality. The forum for data collection may also be constrained by the wishes of the disputants—one or more of whom may not wish to meet separately because of distrust of the mediator—or by political factors, such as rules on open meetings or sunshine laws. More will be said in Chapter Eight about conducting data collection interviews at the start of a joint session.

Development of Rapport and Credibility

The first five to ten minutes of any data collection interview may be the most critical to building rapport and establishing personal credibility. This has been called the "social" stage of the interview (Survey Research Center, 1969). (Clearly, the cultural context of the dispute and the relationship of the mediator to the party will greatly influence the length of time and the content of this activity.) In this brief period of informal conversation, the mediator should try to present himself or herself as an open, warm, intelligent, and interested person. A mediator should consider taking some time to have an informal conversation on noncontroversial topics of mutual interest as a means of building a positive relationship with a disputant. This conversation should not include subjects that might create distance or dissonance between the mediator and the party.

Once the initial phase of developing rapport has been completed, the mediator begins the process of credibility building referred to in Chapter Three. A mediator builds credibility from the moment he or she makes the first phone contact, but the face-to-face interview is an additional opportunity to do so. Mediators usually decide in advance how much to explain about themselves, the mediation organization, their relationship to the various parties, and the mediation process before going on to direct questioning. Disputants may need to know more about the process and the mediator with whom they will be working before they can enter into trusting communication.

The mediator must also motivate the participant to respond. This will be easy or difficult depending on the participant's disposition toward the issue in dispute, the procedure, and the mediator. Responsiveness is often facilitated by rapport building and by the discovery of commonalities between mediator and participant. For example, in collecting data for an environmental case on acid drainage from an old coal mine in rural Pennsylvania, I interviewed an elderly coal miner who sat as a member of a county water board. I asked him about his family's history in the area and then allowed lots of time for him to talk. I did this not only to learn more about the man and his background but also to give myself an opportunity to mention that my grandparents, too, had settled in the area; he could then feel that we had something in common.

These are some of the motivation strategies that mediators can use to elicit information:

- Explaining the importance and worth of the data to the mediation process so that the disputant feels that he or she can make a genuine contribution toward a positive change

- Stressing the need to hear all views, especially those of the interviewee
- Explaining the benefits of participation
- Answering questions that may decrease resistance to participation
- Demonstrating a positive personal interest in the disputant's concerns, problems, or viewpoints

Most mediators use a combination of these motivation strategies.

INTERVIEWING APPROACH

The interviewing approach often significantly affects the kind, form, and detail of the information that is collected. It also influences who is in control of the process and content of the data collection effort: the party being interviewed or the mediator.

Focused Versus Nonfocused Interviews

In some data collection interviews, the mediator determines specific areas about which he or she wants to obtain information through prior secondary source analysis. In other cases, mediators are more interested in conducting general exploratory interviews that may become more focused after the disputant has shared his or her perception of the conflict.

There are advantages to interviews with specific foci:

- The ability to focus on issues that are deemed relevant by the mediator
- The greater ease of filtering extraneous or irrelevant information
- The ability to gain the most helpful information in the shortest amount of time

The major drawbacks are that:

- The mediator may bias the information received by encouraging the disputant to give answers he or she thinks the interviewer wants

- The mediator may miss valuable information the participant would have revealed if the questioning were more comprehensive
- The mediator's conception of the conflict, rather than the participant's, may become the dominant framework for defining the dispute

A mediator should carefully decide what he or she needs to know and then design an interview format that will achieve those goals.

Structured Versus Nonstructured Interviews

Mediators usually use two types of interview formats to collect data from disputants or other parties with relevant information: structured and nonstructured.

Structured interviews are designed to collect the same or similar information from each of the disputants so that their answers are quantifiable and comparable. This requires a list of standardized questions or categories of information.

Nonstructured interviews are used for exploratory data collection if the same information is not required from each disputant, if there may be resistance to structure by the interviewee, or if the mediator has not accumulated enough information to narrow the focus to specific categories or questions. Nonstructured interviews resemble ordinary conversations except that they have more focus and less equal exchange. In this form of interview, both the mediator and the disputant have greater freedom to influence the direction of the information exchange.

In selecting the most appropriate form of interview, mediators consider which will produce the desired information, encourage the respondent to share knowledge, and create the rapport necessary for later information gathering or intervention.

The Interview Format

Mediators should plan a format for both individual and joint data collection interviews. Although formats may differ somewhat for these two interventions, many of the strategic questions are the same. These considerations should be addressed:

- In joint meetings, who should speak first, either to make an opening statement or to present his or her story?
- What information exchange format should be used?
- What time constraints should be placed on speakers?
- How will the mediator gain a procedural agreement on the data collection process?
- How acceptable is emotional expression?
- How will disagreements or discrepancies in data be managed?
- In joint sessions, how will the mediator prevent psychological burnout, or boredom in the party who is not speaking?
- How will interruptions be managed?

Although there is not enough space to answer all these questions, several of the most critical are addressed here.

Who speaks first? This question applies only to joint data collection meetings. Mediators use several criteria for determining who presents his or her view first:

- Who initiated the dispute or conflict?
- Who initiated the mediation?
- Who wishes to change the status quo?
- Who is not emotionally capable of waiting to explain his or her case?
- Who is the weaker party?

General practice allows the initiator or claimant to go first, as this party has brought the dispute to mediation (Stulberg, 1981a). Often, the first party to speak is the one who wishes to change the status quo. For example, in labor negotiations, the union generally goes first with proposals to change the current contract or initiate a new one. An exception to this practice may be made when one of the parties is so emotionally engaged in the conflict that he or she cannot wait for another party to present their viewpoint first, or when one party is weaker and may gain some internal psychological strength from going first, or by mutual agreement of the disputants.

What format should be used for information exchange and data collection? There does not seem to be one format that mediators use consistently. One common procedure is to allow each party a specific period of time in joint session to present its case to the mediator and the other party. The only interruptions allowed are requests from the mediator for clarification or more information. In joint meetings, other parties may often be allowed or encouraged to ask questions and obtain clarifications at the end of each interview.

Another procedure used in group disputes is for a disputant who has the trust of most parties to outline the dispute and its history, and for other parties to voice any disagreements with this account as it is proceeding. These points of disagreement may later become agenda items for discussion.

A third approach is to conduct a joint meeting with multiple parties or a team so that a group view of the problem may be obtained. Although group interviews are often a highly efficient way to get information from a number of people at one time, they can also result in the group view influencing or jaundicing the otherwise independent and diverse views of individuals. In group interviews, the accuracy of the views expressed should always be checked by giving participants the opportunity to contact the mediator privately to voice any privately held views. (I often give group participants my business card and encourage them to call me if they have any new thoughts on the subjects we have discussed.)

How are anger, interruptions, and disagreements over data to be managed in joint session? Because data collection usually occurs either before joint sessions, at the start of negotiations, or after the mediator has entered a dispute as the result of an impasse, the parties are usually experiencing significant feelings during the time allotted for information exchange. In individual interviews, mediators may accept emotional expression more than in joint sessions. More will be said about this in Chapter Seven.

INTERVIEW QUESTIONS AND THE LISTENING PROCESS

Effective interviews require both good questions and good listening on the part of the mediator. The balance between these communications skills, of course, depends on the purpose and structure of the interview. In both structured and nonstructured interviews, there is a great degree of variety in how questions are asked and the degree of mediator directiveness (see Table 5.1). Questions generally are of two types: closed and open-ended (Stewart and Cash, 1974).

Table 5.1. Question or Response Types.

Type of Response	Definition	Example
Elaboration Question	A request for more information related to something respondent has already said.	A. We are interested in co-parenting but don't know what it entails Q. Can you say more about what concerns you?
Active Listening	An exact statement or paraphrase of what the respondent has said. The restatement often focuses on the emotional content of a message and is more of a response than a question.	A. I'm very upset about the condition of the road and what they did to it. A. You are very angry that they damaged your property.
Direct Clarification Question	A direct request for information to clarify vague or ambiguous information.	A. We do not want multiple-family homes in our neighborhood. It spoils our single-family-home lifestyle. Q. Is it the idea of multiple-family homes that bothers you or the number of people or units in each one that is important?
Inferred Clarification Question	Clarification or information that was implicit in previous response.	A. The meeting was held over at the Federal Bulding. Q. At Frank Williams's office?
Summary Question	A question that summarizes previously stated information and requests that the respondent verify the data.	A. We purchased the property as a cooperative venture, wrote an agreement that required an equal input of money, and they subsequently violated it by not making agreed payments. Q. You purchased property, made a financing agreement, and then the partners failed to follow through?

Table 5.1. Question or Response Types, Cont'd.

Type of Response	Definition	Example
Confrontation	A question that points out a discrepancy in data presented by the respondent. (This should be used with care because it can create resistance from the interviewee.)	A. I want to have Smith pay for the cost of replacing my windshield and all the trouble he has caused me. That amounts to $250. Q. You say you want to have him pay $250 in damages, yet you stated earlier that your brother handled the installation and that the glass cost only $100. What exactly were your time and energy expenditures on this problem?
Repetition Question	An exact restatement of a previous question.	Q. How much will impact mitigation cost to restore the land to its previous state? A. Oh, I'm not sure with the price of water, seed... Q How much will impact mitigation cost to restore the land to its previous state?

Closed Questions

Closed questions, which call for a yes-or-no answer or a specific statement of fact, allow the mediator to narrow the focus so that he or she may obtain concrete information on a particular aspect of the dispute. The most closed format is a leading question, such as "Didn't you see the people move the truck onto the site the afternoon of August 27?" Mediators often avoid closed or leading questions early in interviews because they may create animosity toward the mediator on the part of the interviewee and therefore reduce the amount and quality of information that is offered (Richardson, Dohrenwend, and Klein, 1965).

Open-Ended Questions

A mediator wants to gather as much information about the conflict as possible and to identify the disputant's perceptions about
the problems to be addressed. That information is frequently difficult to obtain because of distrust or guardedness on the part of
those in conflict, or because the respondents have not defined the
situation in the same terms as the mediator. Mediators use open-
ended questions to help overcome these limitations. Such questions allow the interviewee to share as much information as he or
she wishes without feeling pressured. In addition, they enable the
interviewee to share his or her perception of reality without being
subjected to an alien framework of analysis; there are no probing
questions with an implied or prescribed answer.

In interviews based on open-ended questions, mediators
should not create a highly structured discussion. The goal is for
the interviewee to do most of the talking. After asking an open-
ended question, the mediator should simply listen. Active listening (see Table 5.1) with content or emotional feedback may also
be useful as a clarifying technique (Gordon, 1978).

Here are sample open-ended questions:

- What is the background to this situation? (*Situation* is preferable to *conflict* because of the negative connotation of the latter term.)
- What are the issues (or problems) that concern you?
- What kinds of decisions are to be made?
- Who (individuals, agencies, or groups) would have to be involved to reach a wise and implementable decision? What does
  each party think about the problem?
- What common interests and concerns do you and other people in this situation have?
- What do you think should be done to avoid or resolve this situation? Under what conditions would you be willing to work
  with the other people on this problem?

Note that many open-ended questions begin with *what* and *how*
rather than *why*. Asking "why" questions may make a person feel
that his or her beliefs have to be justified and may put him or her
on the defensive (Richardson and Margulis, 1984).

Failure to Answer Questions

Occasionally, an interviewee will fail to answer a mediator's question. The possible reasons are numerous:

- Failure to understand the question
- Overly complex wording of the question
- A multiplicity of questions in one sentence
- Excessive scope or complexity of the problem posed
- Reluctance to reveal private or privileged information
- Effects of intense emotion on thinking capacity
- Lack of trust between disputant and mediator

By carefully analyzing responses to previous questions that have been answered, observing nonverbal behavior, or asking more direct questions, the mediator should be able to determine why a respondent does not answer specific questions.

A mediator often receives more information in an interview than can possibly be remembered. To prevent losing important data, mediators usually decide before the session what data-recording methods they will use. The two primary recording techniques are written notes and sound or video recordings. Each method has its benefits and costs.

Written notes require rapid notation so that content and emotions can be easily retrieved during analysis. The writing method must be accurate enough that points of information are not lost but unobtrusive enough that the writing does not distract from the interview. Here are some guidelines for mediators relying on written recording:

- Ask the disputants for permission to take notes.
- Clarify with the disputants how notes will be used and whether they will be confidential or open to the public.
- If an interview has a planned sequence of informational categories, have a prelabeled page for each category.
- Take notes in an abbreviated or shorthand form.
- Maintain eye contact with the respondent as much as possible during the interview (if this is culturally appropriate), and do not concentrate on taking notes.

- Take notes consistently throughout the interview. Do not write in a noticeably different manner when an especially important or complex point is explained by the respondent. This prevents biasing the disputant by giving special attention to a particular area of questioning.
- Read the notes back to the interviewee, when appropriate, to verify accuracy.
- If appropriate, use a team consisting of one interviewer and one recorder. The roles can be reversed during the interview.

Sound or video recording of interviews is another way to obtain complete interview records. Tape recording is by far the most accurate data collection and storage system, but is often time-consuming to listen to and costly to transcribe, and it may inhibit interviewees.

   If sessions are to be tape-recorded, mediators should obtain permission from disputants, explaining how the tape will be used and who will have access to it. Mediators may gain greater cooperation by offering to turn off the recorder if a disputant is uncomfortable discussing a particular subject.

CONFLICT ANALYSIS

Conflict analysis is the synthesis and interpretation of data collected by the mediator from interviews, direct observation, or examination of secondary sources. The mediator's central task during this stage is to integrate and understand the elements of the dispute: people, dynamics, issues, and interests.

   Conflict analysis activities are often difficult to identify as a separate component of mediation because many mediators, working alone, do not perform any visible or external activities to indicate that they are analyzing a dispute. From all appearances, they often move from data collection to proposing an acceptable mediation procedure. However, when a group of mediators is working together on dispute analysis, their activities are more visible.

Data Reporting Between Co-Mediators

Data reporting refers to the exchange of interview information between interviewers or mediators if more than one person is collecting data. Several techniques are used to facilitate reporting.

The simplest is probably a periodic team meeting in which mediators make brief oral reports on people they have interviewed and information they have obtained. Time should be allowed for questions from other interviewers and for suggestions on improving the interview procedure and format. Such formal meetings, however, may take up too much time if there are many interviewers or interviews and the dispute demands rapid intervention.

Information may also be disseminated by circulation of written transcripts or recordings of interviews or reports of the interviewer's impressions. Mediators often find that writing down their reflections while traveling from an interview is an effective procedure for interpreting data and sharing them with others. This technique promotes synthesis and summarization of salient points, making the information more manageable.

Integration of Data

In complex disputes, interviews often generate a tremendous quantity of information. Structured recording and cross-referencing systems may have to be used. There are a variety of tools that mediators use to integrate their data.

Data About People

One way to organize data about the people in a dispute is to make a *participant list* showing names of potential and past interviewees and the organizations with which they are associated. Such a list helps mediators keep track of those who have been interviewed, when they were interviewed, and who remains to be questioned. It also allows mediators to determine when individuals representing a particular category of disputant—such as a family member, a company representative, a city council member, a lawyer, or a federal regulator—should be interviewed to balance views on an issue and to ensure that all viewpoints have been presented. Among the helpful elements that may be included in participant lists are the name of the interest group to which the person belongs and the degree to which he or she can influence the course or outcome of the dispute (Table 5.2).

Data About Relationships and Dynamics

The second category of information to be integrated is that concerning the relationships of the conflicting parties. In order to

Table 5.2. Interest Group of Individual Participant List.

	Industry Group		Government Group		Public Interest Group	
	Person	Interview Date	Person	Interview Date	Person	Interview Date
Main Groups or Individuals (High Influence)	1 _____	__/__/__	_____	__/__/__	_____	__/__/__
	2 _____	__/__/__	_____	__/__/__	_____	__/__/__
	3 _____	__/__/__	_____	__/__/__	_____	__/__/__
	4 _____	__/__/__	_____	__/__/__	_____	__/__/__
Secondary Groups or Individuals (Moderate Influence)	1 _____	__/__/__	_____	__/__/__	_____	__/__/__
	2 _____	__/__/__	_____	__/__/__	_____	__/__/__
	3 _____	__/__/__	_____	__/__/__	_____	__/__/__
	4 _____	__/__/__	_____	__/__/__	_____	__/__/__
Interested Parties with No or Low Influence	1 _____	__/__/__	_____	__/__/__	_____	__/__/__
	2 _____	__/__/__	_____	__/__/__	_____	__/__/__
	3 _____	__/__/__	_____	__/__/__	_____	__/__/__
	4 _____	__/__/__	_____	__/__/__	_____	__/__/__

understand a dispute, a mediator must have a grasp of historical events and trends that have led to the present conflict. Two tools are often used to describe the development of conflict relationships: time lines and case study scenarios (Coover, Deacon, Esser, and Moore, 1977).

The time line is a chart on which a mediator records significant events that have influenced a conflict's development (see Figure 5.1). Time line entries include specific communications, failures to communicate, interviews, press releases, public meetings, elections, direct actions, and initiation of litigation. In addition, they may include larger events, such as changes in public awareness on an issue, economic trends, a major government policy change, or international events that influence the dynamics of the dispute. Time lines may also project into the future and identify critical data or action that will affect the conflict dynamics.

Some mediators write brief dispute case histories to help them identify and order historical events. Later, these case studies or scenarios may be used to present to the parties a view of how the conflict developed, so that a common understanding of the background of the dispute can be cultivated.

Data About Substantive Issues

The final category of data that must be organized and integrated pertains to the substance of the dispute: issues, interests, positions, and potential settlement options.

One tool that mediators use to order and analyze conflicting interests is an issue, position, interest, and option chart. This chart is used to plot a disputant's stated issues and positions in an organized manner and then identify the underlying interests behind those positions. The chart also identifies potential settlement options. By identifying interests, the mediator can assist the parties in generating a range of solutions that may be mutually acceptable.

Verification of Data

Data collection, especially when conducted in separate meetings, may generate contradictory information. Data may have been incorrectly heard or recorded by the mediator, or the respondent may have intentionally or unintentionally given misinformation.

Figure 5.1. One-Month Time Line.

Parties	Time and Events			
	Week 1	Week 2	Week 3	Week 4
1. Company	Files plans with planning department	Visits affected homeowners		Attends public hearings
2. Planning Department	Receives plans			Holds public hearings
3. Public Interest Group	Meets to discuss company plans	Develops counter-position and press release	Meets with homeowners	Attends public hearings
4. County Commissioners		Notified by planning department of citizen opposition to project	Talk with citizens	
5. Local Landowners	Meet to discuss company plans	Meet with company	Meet with public interest group	Attend public hearings

Disputants also have different perceptions or definitions of the problem. The mediator must try to understand and correct information discrepancies if a successful intervention is to be launched.

The first step in investigating discrepant data is to determine if the incongruity is due to a problem in the questioning or recording process. This may entail reviewing original notes, cross-referencing interviewee responses, referring to secondary sources, or initiating follow-up interviews or questions.

Occasionally, mediators may recontact a disputant to clarify a point. This is usually done in a low-key manner, without placing judgment or blame on the disputant. For example, "I don't understand, there seem to be two explanations of this point. Can you clarify this for me?" would be appropriate to challenge a discrepancy in the information. The respondent always needs a way to maintain dignity in the process of clarifying conflicting data.

Interpretation of Data

So far, most of the conflict analysis procedures discussed have pertained to data organization. I will now discuss the most difficult aspect of conflict analysis: interpreting information. In order to proceed, the mediator must create a conceptual map of the conflict and develop a set of hypotheses such as those discussed in Chapter Two. There is no one procedure used by mediators to interpret information about a dispute. Listed below are several thought processes that may be useful, depending on the type of dispute. These procedures are linked to the categories presented in Figure 2.1.

Some mediators begin to dissect and analyze a conflict by dividing the unnecessary or unrealistic causes from those that are genuine or realistic (Coser, 1956). *Unrealistic causes of conflict* include:

- Strong emotions that are not based in objective reality
- Misperceptions about motivations of other parties
- Stereotypes
- Miscommunication
- Unproductive repetitive behavior that negatively affects another party

- Attempts to force an agreement on values when such concurrence is not required for settlement
- Confusion over data
- Competitive behavior induced by a misperception that interests are mutually exclusive

Genuine causes of conflict include:

- Real disagreements over what data are important or how they are collected or assessed
- Actual competing substantive, procedural, or psychological interests
- Structural constraints on the parties, such as competing roles or unequal power or authority
- Destructive behavior patterns caused by external forces such as environment or time constraints
- Different value systems that are difficult to reconcile but must be addressed to reach settlement

By dividing the causes of conflict into unnecessary and genuine categories, the mediator makes it possible to first address the problems that are tangential—the unrealistic ones, for instance—and then focus on the realistic causes of the dispute.

A second analysis process requires the mediator to carefully analyze the causation categories represented in Figure 2.1 and then target the cause that will be central to successful dispute resolution. For example, consider a case where poor communication and inadequate communication structures are a primary cause of the conflict. In a complex dispute involving closure of a local school because of declining enrollment, the only means by which parents can express their grievances is a hearing process before the school board. But public hearings frequently promote conflict because of their one-way communication structure and the tendency of participants to voice extreme positions. A new forum or structure is needed that will enable the community and education officials to effectively discuss the impact of the closure will have on the neighborhood and the system. Creation of a new structure may induce productive dispute resolution.

This same procedure can be used if a dispute over data is deemed to be the primary cause. For example, in a complex water dispute in Colorado, the parties disagreed over critical basic data: how much water was available, how much was needed, and where resources were located. Negotiations could not proceed until these issues were resolved. One party had much of the information in a computer model but would not disclose it because it was proprietary and would affect the party's economic capacity to obtain additional resources. The mediator worked with the parties to help develop a parallel computer model that would answer the necessary questions about water resources but would not require disclosure of privileged information. The two models were submitted for comparison to an independent and mutually acceptable water resource consulting firm. It verified that each model was based on valid premises and came up with similar conclusions regarding the amount of water available and the location of sources. The disputants were able to use assumptions developed through the computer modeling process to agree on basic data without violating proprietary constraints.

Conflict analysis is complex and will differ with the case. This step, however, is critical to designing an intervention plan.

PRESENTATION OF DATA AND ANALYSIS TO DISPUTING PARTIES

In most two-party mediations, the mediator will use the data collected in individual interviews and organized in his or her own mind to design a mediation strategy. Often, the information will never be directly shared with the parties.

However, in complex multiparty or public disputes, the mediator may want to organize the data into a "situation assessment" or "convening report" that is shared with the parties, to help:

- Organize their thinking
- Increase their understanding of the dispute
- Make them aware of each other's interests
- Describe the issues to be discussed
- Identify possible problem-solving processes for future joint sessions

- Build a commitment to begin exploring possible settlement options by mentioning options suggested by parties

Situation assessments or convening reports can be effectively used to identify both points of agreement and issues that need to be discussed.

Convening reports are often expected or required by public agencies that are considering initiating mediation as means to resolve public disputes. In fact, such agencies may divide the dispute resolution process, and contracts for intervention, into a convening portion and a mediation portion. They may also use the convening report to determine if adequate conditions have been met to proceed with formal mediation. For example, the U.S. Bureau of Reclamation and the Department of Interior used a convening report that analyzed the dynamics of a contentious water dispute over use of Klamath River Basin water for agriculture, by tribes, and to protect endangered species in Oregon and California, to decide whether and how the government should engage in negotiations to address long-term environmental sustainability and legal issues (Klamath Basin Issues, 2001).

The U.S. EPA has developed criteria that are used to evaluate information in a situation assessment and determine whether to proceed with a negotiation process. The EPA will generally proceed to mediation in reg-negs or policy dialogues only if (1) there are a limited and identifiable number of parties, (2) the issues are clear and definable, (3) there is a limited time period or deadline by which action must occur, and (4) there is some sort of political pressure that encourages parties to reach an agreement.

If the agency's criteria for proceeding are known by the mediator prior to preparing the convening report, the report's content can be structured to address the specific concerns and considerations that the agency will use in its decision making. If these criteria are not known, the mediator may suggest appropriate criteria and list the pros and cons of proceeding. Ultimately, of course, it is up to the parties to decide whether they will move forward to the next stage of the mediation process.

Chapter Six

Designing a Detailed Plan for Mediation

Once a mediator has collected and analyzed information and gained a commitment from the parties to mediate, the task that remains before any direct intervention to conduct problem solving is to design a mediation plan. A *mediation plan* is a projected sequence of procedural steps initiated by the intervenor that will assist negotiators in exploring and reaching an agreement. The plan's detail depends on the type and complexity of the conflict, the extent of the mediator's knowledge of the dispute, available planning time, and the amount of control over the negotiation process the disputants have delegated to the intervenor.

Mediation planning occurs throughout a dispute, but in the beginning of the intervention the mediator may be especially active. If the mediator has scheduled separate data collection interviews with disputants before joint negotiations begin, he or she may have time to reflect and develop a plan before the parties come together. If, however, the first data collection is performed with all the parties assembled, and if they expect progress in the same session, the mediation plan may have to be designed at the first meeting.

Many mediators prefer a more deliberative planning process that allows them time to consider all the options and formulate a comprehensive strategy. Others prefer to design the plan as the issues and dynamics unfold. Clearly, there is no one right way to design a mediation plan. Mediators must select the process with which they are most comfortable or that is best suited to the particular situation.

The mediator may develop a mediation plan either in cooperation with the disputants or, if one of two conditions is met, without consulting or involving the parties (Argyris, 1970). First, if the issue or problem under discussion is not very important and "does not involve the clients' feelings of self-acceptance and competence and where the problem is clearly out of range of competence of the clients" (p. 27), the mediator may decide to intervene unilaterally. Second, if the dispute is extremely intense and the disputants feel hopeless or paralyzed in their efforts to change their interactions, the mediator may take control of the process.

Whenever possible, the parties should be involved in designing the mediation plan, since this strengthens their commitment to the dispute resolution process. If the mediator alone designs the procedures, the parties may feel that it is external to them. An example of joint procedural planning by the mediator and the parties occurred during the negotiation of a growth management plan for the state of California. The mediators asked each party to designate a representative to sit on a small process design task group whose function was to design, with the mediator, the procedures for discussion of the issues in dispute. Once developed, procedural proposals were submitted to the group as a whole for approval and implementation. Involvement in designing the negotiation procedures and mediation plan increased the parties' ownership of, and commitment to, the process and created stronger advocates for the interventions that were suggested by the mediators.

In designing a mediation plan, mediators should consider certain critical questions:

1. Who should be involved in the mediation effort?
2. What is the best location for mediation?
3. What physical arrangements need to be made?
4. What procedures will be used?
5. What issues, interests, and settlement options are important to the parties?
6. What are the psychological conditions of the parties?
7. How will rules or behavioral guidelines be established?
8. What is the general plan for the first joint negotiations in the mediator's presence? How will specific agenda items be identified and ordered?

9. How will parties be educated about the process, and how will they arrive at agreement to proceed with negotiations?
10. What possible deadlocks could occur, and how will they be overcome?

This chapter will examine these questions and discuss planning activities assuming that they will be accomplished before the first joint session conducted in the mediator's presence. This approach will be an opportunity to examine the design of mediation plans in some detail. Later chapters will focus on implementing the activities designed during this stage.

PARTICIPANTS IN NEGOTIATIONS

In many disputes, the parties who should participate in negotiations are readily apparent. In divorces, husband and wife should be present; in labor-management disputes, union and management representatives should attend. In other disputes, however, the identities of the central parties are not as clear. For example, in a child custody case concerning revision of visitation rights, the second wife of the divorced husband may want to participate in negotiations. In commercial cases involving bankruptcy, multiple creditors may want to be involved. In large-scale community land use disputes, multiple parties may be interested in the issues and may want to participate.

Although the mediator usually should not decide who the disputants are or who will participate in negotiations, he or she may help the parties decide who should be present and when. Occasionally, a mediator may assist a party in selecting a spokesperson to represent a group, or in identifying a person who will be both effective in communicating a group's interests and acceptable to the other side. If a group or organization is disorganized, the mediator may also assist in designing an internal decision-making process to select a negotiating team or spokesperson.

A case in which a mediator played a role in helping a group determine who should be at the table to represent their interests was a federal regulatory negotiation. The formal leader of one of the parties, a coalition of groups, was perceived by other parties as being verbally abusive, unreasonable, and untrustworthy. They announced that if this person represented the coalition, they would refuse to participate. The mediator persuaded the coalition to increase the number of spokespersons it would send to the negotiations, as a means of broadening the "voices" at the table, providing wider credibility, and controlling the member perceived as difficult.

In general, participants in the negotiations should include those who:

- Have the power or authority to make a decision
- Have the capacity, if they are not involved, to reverse or damage a negotiated settlement
- Know and understand the issues in dispute
- Have negotiating skills
- Have control of their emotions
- Are acceptable to other parties
- Have demonstrated commitment or are willing to commit to bargaining in good faith and seeking mutually acceptable solutions
- Have the backing and support of their constituents

One mediator was asked by city officials to intervene in a dispute between a landlord and numerous tenants in a large apartment complex. She entered the apartment building's common room, where the residents had gathered, and found them vocal, angry, and prepared to harass the landlord. She asked them who their spokespersons were. They had not thought to select any. She then asked for a list of issues they wanted to discuss, and they shouted out a few items. She told the group that their meeting and show of force had demonstrated their seriousness to the landlord, but that they now had to organize themselves to be effective in negotiation. She suggested that they select four or five people who could speak for the group and would have authority to negotiate. She mentioned some of the criteria listed earlier in this chapter for selecting spokespersons, and after some resistance and milling around the tenants picked a team. Compromises had to be made on membership to ensure that all views were represented and that no one would work against the group's interests. Once the team was selected, the mediator asked the representatives to identify the issues deemed important and to prepare to negotiate on them.

As part of a bargaining strategy, one party occasionally may refuse to send a representative who has the authority to make a final decision. This action may be an attempt to insult the other party or to deny them recognition or legitimacy—a signal that one's own party does not consider the issue as important as the other party does, or a means of insulating a decision maker from the dynamics and direct pressure of negotiation (Schelling, 1960). Negotiation etiquette usually requires people of equal rank or status to be present. When faced by a discrepancy in decision-making authority between negotiators, mediators may (1) push for substitution of a decision maker with equal authority or (2) make explicit the differences in authority between two or more sides and develop an understanding of the decision-making and ratification structure to be used by the party without a decision maker present. To thus clarify the decision-making process before negotiations begin can minimize unnecessary conflicts and later claims of bargaining in bad faith.

Friends, Witnesses, Constituents, and Secondary Parties

Parties often want to have friends, witnesses, constituents, or secondary parties present at negotiations. (This is especially true in cultures that value collectivism and group decision making, in contrast to those that emphasize individualism and individual decision making.) There is no one rule or practice mediators follow to respond to such requests. Some mediators ask that friends, witnesses, and constituents remain outside negotiations unless they have a particular function or role to perform (Stulberg, 1981a). Others allow observers, who are then informed of the limits of their participation. This occurs commonly in cultures other than those dominant in North America and Western Europe; in such cultures, friends and observers are often used by the mediator and the parties as option generators, witnesses to ensure the fairness of the agreement, and ensurers of the implementation of or compliance to an agreement. Occasionally, the mediator will not have a preference or procedural rule regarding the presence of additional parties at negotiations and may leave the final decision to the disputants.

Lawyers, Therapists, and Other Resource Persons

Disputants often want resource persons with specialized skills present at negotiations. These secondary parties may assist the disputants in exchanging accurate information, extending emotional support, or participating as surrogate negotiators.

Lawyers are a special category of resource persons. They provide numerous types of services to disputants (Bronstein, 1982; Riskin, 1982). They may be legal advisers offering information about possible settlement ranges or judicial decisions should the dispute be brought to court; they may act as strategists, general advisers, or surrogate negotiators for disputants who are disinclined or unable to represent themselves.

Lawyers who advise or coach disputants may or may not be present at negotiation sessions. If they are not, and if the issues being negotiated involve legal questions, the mediator should encourage parties to consult with them before, during, and after negotiations so that there is a clear understanding of disputants' legal rights and of possible settlement parameters. The mediator may request that lawyers who are not directly negotiating on behalf of a client remain silent in joint session and confine their activities to consultations with their clients in caucuses or private meetings. Alternatively, lawyers may be allowed to participate fully as either co-negotiators or as direct advocates for parties, the latter retaining only final decision-making authority. The degree of lawyer involvement depends on the case, the will of the parties, and the mediator's style.

Lawyers who negotiate on their clients' behalf may create special problems for mediators. Although many lawyers have a cooperative style and are experienced in interest-based bargaining, others are familiar only with hard-line positional bargaining (Williams, 1983). Lawyers who have been trained to develop an argument that supports a singular outcome may couch settlement options in right-or-wrong, yes-or-no terms. Negotiation depends on cooperative and integrative decisions rather than either-or options for success. The differing demands of litigation and negotiation may on occasion make a lawyer a liability to the process of seeking a mutually acceptable resolution.

Mediators may sometimes decrease adversarial tendencies in mediation by encouraging parties to retain lawyers for legal advice but not for service as surrogate negotiators.

From time to time, disputants in North America request the presence of therapists in negotiations. This is not unusual in family or interpersonal disputes. Although mediation is not a therapeutic process, it may benefit from the presence of resource persons who can provide emotional support or psychodynamic insight. Mediators should be open to the involvement of therapists in negotiations if it is acceptable to all parties and if it can be demonstrated that the therapist can help disputants with emotional and psychological problems (Haynes, 1981). However, some restrictions on therapist participation may be appropriate.

Disputants may also request that accountants, engineers, financial planners, technical experts, or researchers be allowed to participate in negotiations. Such resource persons may give disputants a helpful professional perspective on issues (Fisher, 1978), with information that will prevent unnecessary conflict over inaccurate or conflicting data, or give them a way to mediate data disputes (Straus, 1979). Mediators often suggest that specialized resource persons (such as property assessors, accountants, and scientific experts) be introduced into mediation to present new information to disputants.

Media

Mediation in the United States is generally considered to be a private means of dispute resolution. In fact, research evidence indicates that negotiation is often effective because of the private nature of the controlled communication (Folberg and Taylor, 1984; Freedman, Haile, and Bookstaff, 1985). Private negotiations may allow greater candor and decrease the posturing so often found in public adversarial relationships.

However, before mediating a dispute of public interest, the mediator and the parties should decide if the meetings are to be open or closed, and how inquiries from the news media about media presence and provision of information will be handled. On occasion, the media have been excluded from negotiations because of potential negative effects they may have on the behavior of disputants or the public. The presence of reporters can on occasion encourage posturing for a constituency rather than serious negotiation. Premature or inaccurate revelation to the public of the substance of negotiations can also create conditions that make joint problem solving impossible.

In other public disputes, in which large interested and involved constituencies want to be present, it may be difficult or impossible to maintain privacy by means of closed meetings. Furthermore, public decision makers may be precluded from participating in closed negotiations by "sunshine laws" that require all discussions to be public. Although mediators and many negotiators assume that closed negotiations are crucial, a large number, and probably the majority, of public disputes have been successfully negotiated in the public view. There has also been significant experience with open negotiations on the interpersonal level. The Community Boards in California (Shonholtz, 1984) and several Canadian mediators (conversations with R. McWhinney and K. Metcalf at the annual meeting of the Association of Family and Conciliation Courts, Denver, May 1984) have conducted open mediation with significant success. Most interpersonal mediations conducted by the Mediation Boards in Sri Lanka and the Barangay Justice System in the Philippines are also conducted in open meetings. However, in North America such meetings for interpersonal disputes are the exception rather than the rule.

Mediators should assist the parties in determining whether negotiations are to be closed or open to the public and to design, when appropriate, methods of public education about the substance of a dispute and the procedure disputants are using to resolve their differences. If meetings are to be closed, the mediators may propose specific procedures to release information (Lansford, 1983). Parties often agree to a common press release that is issued on their behalf by the mediator. Other publicity about mediation progress may include periodic meetings with the press and public presentations by the parties outside the negotiation sessions.

LOCATION OF NEGOTIATIONS

The location chosen for negotiations may significantly affect the interaction of the negotiators. In considering where to meet, a mediator should select, or persuade the parties to select, a neutral location where neither party has strong emotional identification or physical control of the space. The benefits to the parties and the mediator of neutral locations are as follows:

- Interruptions can be controlled.
- Neither side can manipulate the use of space.
- Distance from the site of the conflict and from other distractions can be maintained.
- Distance from the usual environment may promote the psychological distance needed for an open-minded exploration of issues.
- Potential for bugging or eavesdropping is limited.
- All parties have the same psychological handicap of being in a new location.

The costs of a neutral location:

- Negotiators may be separated from necessary information.
- Parties are separated from their emotional support system.
- Parties may have to bear the cost of renting facilities.

Disputants occasionally refuse to negotiate at a neutral site and want to mediate in their own territory. Or they may want to continue negotiations at a site established before the mediator's entry. Mediators have two major strategic options when confronted with a demand by one party to negotiate in its territory. They can (1) discuss and make explicit the costs and benefits of such a decision, stressing the possible negative impacts on settlement; or (2) persuade other parties to accept the recalcitrant party's request while identifying costs or benefits to the parties who are not in their own territory.

There are benefits to a nonneutral territory:

- The guest party can demonstrate its good faith and willingness to be flexible.
- Asking the host party for information may be easier, and it may be more difficult for him or her to refuse.
- The guest party can more easily make demands on the host party's time and space if the host party does not cooperate.

There are, however, also costs:

- Unfamiliar surroundings may disorient the guest party.
- Lack of access to sources of information may weaken the guest party's case.

- The host party can be interrupted and called away at any time.
- The host party can receive strategic phone calls.

The mediator may also refuse to mediate the case, but this response is extremely rare.

PHYSICAL ARRANGEMENT OF THE SETTING

Physical arrangement of the negotiation setting may also affect the dynamics and outcome of negotiations. The disputes that erupted over seating arrangements and the shape of the table at the Vietnam peace negotiations held in Paris in the early 1970s indicate the impact that physical arrangement can have on negotiations.

Physical arrangement refers to seating patterns, the shape of the table, the amount of physical space allocated to and between disputants, physical objects that indicate authority or differences in power, and space for public or private interaction. Social science research presents important findings on seating arrangements and conflict behavior. Filley (1975) observes that adversaries tend to seat themselves opposite each other, and that this physical arrangement seems to produce more polarized and competitive behavior than side-by-side seating. Sommer (1965, 1969) postulates that undifferentiated seating locations for disputants, so that they neither are arranged opposite each other nor possess seats that indicate greater or lesser power, produce more evenly distributed leadership and less one-sided exercise of power.

Barriers such as tables between disputants are another variable. To illustrate how, consider that in U.S. culture tables are often equated with doing serious business. One mediator conducted several sessions in an informal setting without a table. Then, one day, mediation was scheduled in a conference room with a large wooden table. A disputant remarked, "Well, we now have a negotiating table. We can get down to business." They did—and settled that day.

The table's shape may be used to indicate the status of a party as a discrete entity with its own "side." Furthermore, a physical place at the table may grant recognition and legitimacy to a party and its views. Such was the case in the Vietnam peace talks held in Paris, where the independent role and status of the South Vietnam–based National Liberation Front, an ally of the North Vietnamese, was in question.

In volatile disputes, maintaining a safe distance and using a table as a physical barrier may be crucial in preventing dispute escalation and physical violence. Several years ago, the U.S. Air Force Academy negotiated with a union that provided services to the facility. The negotiations were protracted and became heated. Finally, one negotiator reached across the narrow negotiating table, seized the position paper of his opposite, and tore it into small pieces. The table prevented physical violence but was not large enough to prevent this negative interchange.

In addition, the shape of the table and seating arrangements may be used to blur differences between disputants. Mediators often use round tables because there is no physical indication of a boundary between representatives of the disputing parties.

In some disputes, mediators may eliminate tables or barriers between disputants to increase physical proximity or to promote informality (Stulberg, 1981a). In interpersonal disputes, a living-room setting without a table may be more appropriate than a formal conference room. One mediator reported that in a deadlocked interpersonal dispute that had been mediated in the intermediary's office at a table, a shift of venue to her living room, with sofas, a coffee table, and finger food during the discussions, changed the whole tone and dynamics of the session.

Additional important physical arrangements are waiting rooms and facilities for caucuses (Stulberg, 1981a). Mediators need waiting rooms so that they do not have to associate publicly with one of the parties before joint meetings; disputants may perceive such fraternization as partial behavior. In volatile situations, mediators may also use separate waiting rooms for antagonistic or hostile parties.

Caucus rooms are facilities where mediation participants can meet privately during negotiations. Caucus rooms should be near the site of joint negotiations but far enough removed so that they afford visual and auditory privacy.

It is important when working in separate caucus to ensure that the parties are really separated. In one of my earlier cases, I requested a caucus with the parties and asked one party to leave and wait in a conference room down the hall. He left, I closed the door and completed the private meeting with the other party. When I went to the door and opened it to bring the absent party back for his caucus, he fell into the room. He had not gone to the waiting room at all but had remained in the hall outside the mediation room, where he could listen. This underlined for me the importance of ensuring that the parties and the mediator really are in a private setting.

Caucus rooms are crucial in managing conflicts in which intense emotions are displayed or in which a potential for violence exists (Schreiber, 1971). Mediators often use entirely separate rooms for each party in disputes that involve actual or potential violence. The mediator can shuttle between parties, carry messages, and work out a settlement between disputants. If appropriate, the parties may be kept permanently apart throughout the mediation process.

Mediators should consider the type of dispute and the psychological and emotional condition of the disputants; they should select a physical arrangement that will be conducive to resolution. When negotiations have been held before the mediator's entry, the mediator may try to make minor modifications to the physical setting to induce psychological shifts in the disputants, or move them to an entirely new setting.

NEGOTIATION PROCEDURES

Before developing a mediation plan for joint negotiations, mediators should evaluate what the conflicting parties know about negotiation procedures and ascertain what approaches—positional or interest-based bargaining—have been used or are likely to be used. If the mediator conducts private meetings to collect data before the joint sessions, this information is usually easy to obtain. If it is not possible to gain information on the preferred negotiation procedure of the parties, the mediator should design a series of contingency plans that will enable him or her to respond to any combination of negotiation procedures.

There are four possible combinations in a two-party dispute:

1. Both parties use positional bargaining.
2. Both parties use interest-based bargaining.
3. One party uses predominantly positional bargaining and the other uses predominantly interest-based bargaining.
4. Both parties use a mixed procedure depending on the issue and their interests.

If the dispute involves more than two parties, the number of combinations and permutations increases.

If it is expected that one or more parties will use positional bargaining, and a mediator wants to help them transition to a focus on interests, there are a number of tactics that the intermediary can use:

- Ignore positions and keep on talking.
- Do not ask for specific solutions early in the negotiations.
- Do not allow or encourage "opposing parties" to respond to positions with counterpositions.
- Ask whether the problem has to be solved in a win-lose manner. State that you want to look for a solution that will be advantageous to all parties.
- Ask why a position is important to a party. Try to identify underlying issues.
- Conduct trial-and-error hypothesis testing to indirectly identify interests.
- Verbalize and make interests explicit.
- Separate substantive, procedural, and psychological interests contained in a stated position.
- Look for general principles behind positions, to which both parties can agree.
- Reframe the problem as a search for means to satisfy interests rather than a way to persuade the other party to agree to a position.
- Reframe the problem to emphasize commonality of interests or the possibility of joint gain.
- Separate the problem from the people involved.
- Ask for principles by which to evaluate positions offered.
- Respond with several suggestions or options, and suggest that they all merit further investigation to see how they meet the parties' interests.
- Don't be positional about the use of interest-based bargaining.

When mediators encounter parties who have previously engaged or are planning to engage in positional bargaining, they should, if possible, develop a mediation plan that will shift the parties toward interest-based bargaining as rapidly as possible. This may involve a briefing or discussion about the interest-based bargaining process or, in multiparty disputes, training sessions on how cooperative negotiations can be initiated. Mediators from CDR Associates and several other conflict management firms have conducted a number of successful joint training seminars in the industrial relations and public policy arenas that have presented interest-based bargaining procedures and skills to parties preparing for negotiations. Participants have reported that these workshops greatly assist them in making a more rapid transition from positional to interest-based bargaining.

ISSUES, INTERESTS, AND SETTLEMENT OPTIONS

Designing a mediation plan requires a mediator to identify issues and interests with which disputants are concerned, the salience or importance of these issues and interests, and potential settlement options. Anticipating these components of a dispute enables the mediator to design an effective procedural plan, but *not* a specific mediation settlement. Mediators differ greatly on how specifically they link the interests of the parties to the mediation plan. Some intervenors (deal makers) design a plan that will lead toward specific solutions addressing interests that they have identified and consider important to the parties. Other mediators (orchestrators) design a plan in which the parties identify their interests and develop their own outcomes (Kolb, 1983). I usually prefer the latter procedure.

PSYCHOLOGICAL CONDITIONS OF THE PARTIES

An assessment of the psychological readiness of the disputants to negotiate should accompany a mediator's consideration of the parties' substantive concerns and procedural preferences. The mediator should review some of the relationship variables—level of emotion, accuracy of perception, amount of miscommunication, and extent of repetitive negative behaviors—that have influenced or will influence the dynamics of the negotiations. He or she should then design appropriate procedures to reduce potential negative impacts and enhance positive ones. More will be said on these topics in Chapter Seven.

The mediation plan should include a tentative sequence of activities for the first joint negotiations, responsive to potential psychological or relationship issues. The sequence is tentative because it cannot be implemented before the parties accept the proposed activities. I will now describe a number of activities that can help a mediator set the tone, define an agenda, establish rules or behavioral guidelines, and obtain commitment to negotiate.

It is generally important to establish a positive and harmonious tone at the start of negotiations. Positive working relationships between the parties depend on their attitude toward themselves and each other. The presence of a neutral third party can often significantly assist in developing a positive, open, direct, and businesslike approach.

Tone setting usually begins with introductions. Setting the stage for the first joint session should include scheduling time for the mediator and the parties to introduce themselves to one another. In cases in which parties in dispute are groups or organizations, the mediator may also make time for descriptions of group affiliation and concerns.

After introductions, the mediator will usually schedule time for his or her opening statement—a description of what is to come. Stulberg (1981a, pp. 42–43) lists the advantages of conducting an effective opening statement:

A. It establishes the ground rules and your role in the hearing.
B. It establishes your control over the hearing.
C. It serves to put people at ease.
D. It conveys to the parties a sense that the mediator is confident and skilled, thereby inviting them to trust both the mediator and the process.
E. It serves to reconcile any conflicting expectations regarding what the party believes he could obtain through mediation and the reality of it.

Mediators often begin their opening remarks with a congratulatory statement that affirms the willingness of the disputants to negotiate and to try to cooperatively solve their problems. A reference to their interdependence is often mentioned at this time. Stulberg maintains that "the very first sentence or question in mediation needs to address what the individuals have in common or what they like and respect about each other. Emphasizing mutual dependence on one another heightens the need for overcoming the obstacles that brought them in. It also helps participants to look for the good in each other rather than letting their anger blind them. Conflict is much easier to handle if it rests on a positive foundation" (Stulberg, 1981a, p. 22).

After tone-setting activities, the mediator may allow time to review how he or she was asked to assist the parties in the dispute. If the mediator represents a mediation agency, he or she may explain the procedures and goals of the agency and the services it provides. The mediator may also describe his or her background and qualifications, but mediators usually try to convey their qualifications by their manner rather than reviewing their professional work, educational background, or affiliations.

At this time in intervention planning, mediators should demonstrate personal credibility, trust, and a businesslike manner by explaining, for instance, what mediation is and the mediator's role. The manner and process of explanation will convey the mediator's command of negotiation procedures.

Mediators commonly cover certain items in their description of mediation and the mediator's role (Moore, 1981):

- Mediation is a process whereby a third party helps people identify issues that they need to talk about, uncover needs that must be met by a settlement, generate possible solutions, and reach decisions.
- Mediation is voluntary. The people are there by choice, and the mediator has no power to force a decision on the parties involved.
- The people in the conflict will decide how the conflict is terminated.
- A mediator is impartial (this is optional, or even inappropriate in some situations or cultures). He or she has no investment in a particular substantive settlement. The mediator is a facilitator of the process, not a judge on the issues.
- A mediator is neutral in that he or she has no relationship with any of the parties that will bias his or her impartiality or commitment to all of them (this too is optional or inappropriate in some situations or cultures).

Mediators should also inform parties of their right to use legal procedures and seek legal advice (if appropriate). Offering this information should not, however, be construed as providing legal advice or practicing law. Disputants retain their right to terminate negotiations and pursue a legal route to redress their grievances until they sign an agreement that may become a legal contract. Participation in negotiation or mediation does not deny a party the right to consult legal counsel. Disputants can confer with a lawyer at any time, and many mediators request that all decisions be reviewed and perhaps be drafted by counsel before the parties sign the document (Folberg and Taylor, 1984).

In addition, mediators should explain the limits of confidentiality of the proceedings. Information exchanged between negotiators, or between the negotiators and the mediator in joint sessions or in caucuses, is usually confidential. On occasion, mediators have parties sign release forms in which the parties state that they will not subpoena a mediator or records of the negotiations for a later court case.

GROUND RULES AND BEHAVIORAL GUIDELINES

In some negotiations, a carefully designed procedure may be enough to incline disputants toward a productive resolution. In others, the negotiators may need to establish behavioral guidelines that detail how they will act toward each other and how the parties will handle particular problems that arise in the course of negotiations.

Certain behavioral guidelines should be considered by mediators and parties:

- Agreement on the speaking order of the disputants
- Rules on how disagreements over data will be managed
- Agreement on the time frame for the negotiation session or sessions
- Agreements on observers and witnesses
- Rules preventing attribution of motives or slanderous statements
- Rules regarding interruptions
- Procedures for breaks or intermissions
- Procedures for initiating caucuses or private meetings

Behavioral guidelines may be proposed either by the mediator or by disputants. If the mediator initiates them, the parties must agree to their implementation. The mediator should be careful not to create a dynamic in which he or she is the authority and the parties are obedient subjects. To work effectively, guidelines must be agreed on by consensus.

Behavioral guidelines may be made the subject of the first negotiations to occur in mediation. Parties may be willing, for a variety of reasons, to discuss behavioral guidelines and agenda formation procedures prior to discussing substantive issues. Doing so:

- Enables the parties to establish rules for interaction that will make them feel safer
- Allows parties to practice making agreements on issues that are not as substantively important or as emotionally charged as the issues in dispute
- Demonstrates that agreement is possible (Moore, 1982b)

I will explore the process of negotiating behavioral guidelines in more detail in Chapter Eight.

The amount and detail of guidelines vary tremendously among mediators. Coogler (1978), an early leader in divorce mediation, has turned explanation of procedures and guidelines into an elaborate component of the mediation process: disputants with whom he mediates must accept a list of sixty rules before negotiations can begin. Although Coogler occupies an extreme position, establishing behavioral guidelines is common practice, and most mediators may suggest a few to ensure safety and direction for the parties.

DEVELOPING A CONCEPTUAL AGENDA FOR FIRST JOINT NEGOTIATIONS

Once the mediator has planned the first joint session's general format, he or she should define the process for identifying specific agenda items. The mediator usually has enough information from data collection and conflict analysis to be able to formulate a proposed negotiating agenda.

In most cases, mediators should give the parties an opportunity to make their own opening statements—presentations at the start of negotiations in which the parties present the problem or conflict history, identify the needs they must have met for a satisfactory settlement, and (occasionally) express strong emotions. Opening statements may be the first opportunity for the mediator to watch the disputants interact face-to-face. Mediators learn much about disputants, issues, interests, positions, options, and conflict styles by observation at this stage. Foreknowledge of the issues and interests that parties will focus on in the opening statement assists the mediator in planning the order in which issues will be managed and what the subsequent problem-solving process will be for each item. Here is one agenda-planning procedure (adapted from Moore, 1982b, pp. VII–18–19) that many mediators use to develop a tentative mediation plan:

1. The mediator should gather all potential agenda items from disputants prior to the negotiation session. This may be done orally or in written form.

2. The mediator should clarify in his or her own mind the goals or outcomes desired by the parties for each item. He or she then should determine which items are information-sharing items, which are discussion items, and which are items that require a decision.

3. The mediator should make a tentative division into high-priority, medium-priority, and low-priority items, as well as those that can be held over for a later session. In defining priority, the mediator should take into consideration the time value of the item (does this decision have to be made tomorrow so that work can proceed next week?), the importance of the item (substantive importance and emotional importance), and the parties to whom it is important (all parties, a subgroup, an individual, or a superior). High-priority items should usually be scheduled for discussion, at least in principle, at the first session and should not be deferred.

4. The mediator should make an estimate of how long it will take to achieve the defined goal for each agenda item and establish possible time blocks for the topics.

5. Agenda items should be ranked according to the likely difficulty of achieving the defined goal: hard, medium, and easy.

6. The first item on the agenda should usually be one of high or medium priority—substantively, emotionally, or in terms of time

value—to most of the disputants and one the mediator expects will not require a long time to reach agreement on or to achieve the stated goal. This item should be easy for the parties to work on. The mediator should place the item with these qualities first because he or she wants the disputants to have a chance to achieve success in a short time early in negotiations. An early success will make the disputants feel more positive toward the process and toward their ability to work together, and it will indicate the possibility of future success in negotiations.

7. The second item often concerns a more difficult topic and may take longer to reach its goal. Successful completion of the first item will have prepared people for work on more complex issues.

8. Short and long items, and hard and easy ones, may be alternated so that the participants feel that the negotiations are progressing toward a productive end.

9. The agenda should allow some time for identification of issues to be addressed at a later session and for discussion of future logistics.

EDUCATION OF PARTIES

After completing a mediation plan, the mediator should decide how he or she will educate the parties about the process and gain their commitment to try it. If the mediator has worked with disputants on the design of the plan, gaining final approval is not a problem; but if disputants are not familiar with negotiation and mediation procedures or are too embroiled in the substantive issues in the dispute to focus on process, the mediator may have to educate the parties about the procedure he or she has designed.

Mediators occasionally take an active educational role before joint sessions to prepare disputants for what is likely to occur. The goal is to obtain the commitment of the parties to the procedure before the joint session. Other mediators make their procedural proposals or suggestions during the first session and assume that they will be accepted or that alternative procedures will be negotiated with disputants. The procedure for agreement on process usually depends on the particular parties involved, the issues in dispute, and the conflict dynamics of the case.

POSSIBLE DEADLOCKS

The final aspect of designing an intervention plan is the mediator's identification of potential problem areas that may cause an impasse. Fisher (1978) identifies several problem areas that often deadlock negotiations: (1) substantive problems, such as too few or too many favorable options; (2) procedural problems, such as an absence of process or the wrong process; and (3) problems with people, such as strong emotions, stereotypical labeling, or miscommunication. Early identification of potential problems and contingency plans to avoid or overcome them is central to mediation planning. Mediators can prepare themselves by imagining problems that might occur in the joint session and then developing several contingency plans for responding to each of them. I will discuss a variety of problems and the moves mediators use to handle them in later chapters.

Chapter Seven

Building Trust and Cooperation

Negotiation has long been recognized as a psychological process. As early as the mid-1970s, Rubin and Brown (1975) had identified more than five hundred studies on negotiation that examined individual psychological variables and group dynamics. In this chapter, I will discuss mediator activities that minimize unnecessary conflict and build a positive psychological relationship between disputing parties. This process is called conciliation.

"Conciliation is essentially an applied psychological tactic aimed at correcting perceptions, reducing unreasonable fears, and improving communication to an extent that permits reasonable discussion to take place and, in fact, makes rational bargaining possible" (Curle, 1971, p. 177). *Conciliation* is the psychological component of mediation, in which the third party attempts to create an atmosphere of trust and cooperation that promotes positive relationships and is conducive to productive negotiations.

Although I will discuss conciliation here as if it were a separate stage of negotiation and mediation, conciliation in practice is an ongoing process that occurs throughout negotiation and mediation. Five problems commonly create negative psychological dynamics in negotiations:

1. Strong emotions
2. Misperceptions or stereotypes held by one or more parties of each other or about issues in dispute
3. Legitimacy problems
4. Lack of trust
5. Poor communication

I will discuss each of these problems in turn and explore some common intervenor moves employed to respond to and change them.

STRONG EMOTIONS

There is no doubt that emotions play a central role in conflict and mediation. Jones (2001) argues that conflict is in many ways emotionally defined. She posits that disputes occur when people perceive incompatible goals when relating with each other, and that these trigger events cause conflict *and* elicit emotions. She also posits that expression of emotions is culturally linked in that culture defines what is emotionally important or relevant for the involved parties, establishes parameters for the strategic orientation of parties to conflict, circumscribes communication patterns, and defines appropriate and proper disputant behavior.

Strong negative feelings can drive parties apart and make agreement very difficult. Conversely, cultivating and enhancing positive emotions between parties can help them relate more positively toward each other and greatly facilitate arriving at mutually agreeable accords. Thus learning about the causes, development, dynamics, management, and regulation of emotions is often critical for effective mediation.

A number of researchers have noted the emotional stages that disputants move through in the process of conflict development, deescalation, and settlement (Douglas, 1962; Kessler, 1978; Ricci, 1980; Daily, 1991). Others have examined the sequences of escalatory behavior related to negative emotions in negotiations (Pruitt, Parker, and Mikolic, 1997) in divorce mediations (Donahue, 1991; Jones, 1985, 1988) and in crisis negotiations (Rogan, Donahue, and Lyles, 1990). At the start of negotiations, people often feel angry, hurt, frustrated, distrustful, alienated, hopeless, resentful, betrayed, fearful, or resigned to unsatisfactory conditions. As talks proceed, emotions may escalate and come to the fore, remain hidden or in the background, or ebb and flow as positive progress slows or is accelerated in processing feelings and issues or situations that have helped cause the conflict. Continued physiological experience of change in emotions, their behavioral expression, and ongoing disputant assessment of their relationship to the situation or issues in question is dependent on highly complex interactions between the individual or group involved, actions and behaviors of its counterpart, and the interventions of mediators. For feelings to be productively managed, processed, understood, and processed, and for rational discussions on substantive issues to occur, the impact of negative emotions must often be managed and minimized by either the disputants themselves or an intervenor. If not handled early in negotiations, negative feelings— whether openly manifested or felt and not spoken—may later block a substantive agreement or inhibit formation of more positive relationships. For mediators to assist parties in reaching acceptable solutions, they must work at least to minimize or neutralize the effects of negative emotions and, if possible, to create positive feelings between disputants.

Before examining conciliation approaches or specific ways to help parties handle and process their emotions, we need to examine the behavioral, physiological and cognitive components of emotions in disputes, and two sources of emotions, unrealistic and realistic sources of conflict.

COMPONENTS OF EMOTION

Researchers of emotions have identified three components of feeling: behavioral or expressive, psychological, and cognitive (Lazrus, 1994). The behavioral component refers to the expression of feelings, generally as part of communications with another party. The psychological component involves physical or biological changes in the body as a result of the party's "feeling" strong emotions. The cognitive component is an evaluation or appraisal process that occurs when people feel emotions such as shame or disgust.

The *behavioral component* of emotions can be expressed noverbally, verbally, or through actions. Facial expressions, body language, or specific behaviors are often the major indicators of a person's (or group's) emotional condition. Nonverbal expression of feelings may be either involuntary or strategically made to deliver a specific message. Verbal expression of emotions may also be involuntary and spontaneous, or finally calculated to make just the right impression or communicate a specific message.

In order to respond to the expression of emotions, parties and intermediaries need to be able to decode from the behavior the specific underlying emotion being communicated and respond appropriately to it. Since emotions are culturally defined, behaviors may mean and be interpreted differently by diverse cultural groups. For example, in some cultures, such as Japan, when people feel discomfort or disagreement, they laugh and smile, which may be interpreted by members of other cultures, such as the dominant U.S. culture, as agreement or enjoyment.

Accurate decoding of the meaning of emotional expression is not easy, and intermediaries need to use caution when interpreting nonverbal (or even verbal) cues. More accurate decoding can often be achieved by careful observation, asking multiple clarifying questions, or "active listening": stating perceived feelings and eliciting clarification or confirmation of accurate interpretation from emotionally expressive parties. More will be said about the latter technique later.

The *physiological component* of feelings refers to the "felt" experience within the body. Emotions are highly complex physiological and psychological responses to external stimuli. When a person feels emotions, the heart may race; hot or cold flashes may occur; vision may blur; perspiration often increases; hands involuntarily sweat or shake; and the body may be wracked by uncontrollable shaking, sobs, or rage. Emotion causes physiological changes in the body's chemistry, which prepare the person to either engage in the conflict and fight, or else to flee to safety (Adler, Rosen, and Silverstein, 1998).

When the body is physiologically overwhelmed by feelings, it is likely to exhibit emotional flooding or emotional contagion (Jones, 2001). Emotional flooding occurs when the physiological system is overloaded, as may commonly occur when a person or group feels "threatened . . . unfairly attacked, misunderstood, wronged, or righteously indignant" (p. 228). Flooding may also occur when a person dwells on repetitive negative thoughts, such as reliving a particularly distressing event, encounter, or feelings from the past. When emotional flooding happens, it inhibits the brain from accessing information from the neocortex, and it limits creative thinking, innovative responses, or problem solving. It may also take a significant amount of time for the body to return to equilibrium or homeostasis. Strategies for responding to emotional flooding will be presented later in this chapter.

Emotional contagion, another physiological response to emotions, occurs when a person or group takes on the feelings that are or have been felt or expressed by another party. When emotional contagion occurs, parties may begin to "mimic and synchronize facial expression, vocalizations, postures, and movements with those of another person and, consequently, to converge emotionally" (Hatfield, Cacciopo, and Rapson, 1992, pp. 153–154). Emotional contagion may indicate empathy or understanding of another's feelings, but more frequently it is a subconscious emotional response and connection to the other party. Emotional contagion in highly antagonistic disputes may result in escalatory mirroring of emotions and a spiral of conflict feelings and behaviors. In instances where parties feel depressed or hopeless, it can result in a downward spiral of dispair. Strategies for responding to this emotional dynamic will be discussed later in this chapter.

The *cognitive component* of emotions refers to the interconnection between feelings and logical-rational reappraisals of the interests, needs, issues, tensions, disagreements, problems, or conflicts that contributed to the rise to the emotions. The premise underlying a cognitive approach to feelings is that if people or parties can better understand their feelings and how they are linked to the substantive and procedural components of the dispute, they will be better able to manage or change their emotions and develop a course of action to modify their situation.

Responding to the cognitive component of emotions involves assessing the emotions and situation by asking and answering a series of questions that help determine whether the event that has caused the feelings is personally relevant, how it affects the achievement of goals, whether it blocks or facilitates goal achievement, and if and how it affects a party's identity (Lazrus, 1991). These primary appraisal questions are often followed by series of secondary appraisal questions. More will be said on cognitive approaches to responding to emotions later in this chapter, when I examine open-ended questioning.

UNREALISTIC AND REALISTIC CONFLICT AND EMOTIONS

Coser (1956) distinguishes between unrealistic and realistic conflict. Unrealistic conflict exists when parties act as if they are in dispute even though no objective conditions for a conflict exist. Realistic conflict is the result of genuine conflicts of interest. Coser's concepts of unrealistic and realistic conflict can also be applied to human emotions. Frequently, parties in conflict have unusually strong feelings that may not be merited by the actual situation. A conflict without a realistic base for negative emotions is in direct contrast to a dispute in which emotional responses are the realistic responses to the circumstances.

Many people have had the experience of meeting someone for the first time and immediately forming an intense dislike for that person. There is no previous relationship between the people, yet there is a strong negative reaction. This dynamic has been variously referred to as restimulation (Jackins, 1978) and negative transference (Freud, [1920] 1943).

Restimulation refers to the surfacing of feelings similar to those generated by a relationship or events in the past. Old feelings are triggered by a new encounter, which may or may not be similar to the earlier relationship or event. Although the new situation may not be an objective base for restimulated feelings, it is the mechanism that resurrects past emotions.

An example may illustrate restimulation more clearly. An environmental group had for several years struggled with a public utility over the terms and conditions for operating a hydropower dam. During the negotiations, personal relationships between the environmentalists and the company's spokespersons became tense and fairly hostile. Ultimately, the utility agreed to take some of the group's interests into consideration and reached a hard-fought negotiated agreement. A year later, a new public relations director at the utility—a man who was very open and committed to good company-community relations and public involvement in decision making—announced that the company planned to revise the operations of a second dam, which was unlike the first in both its construction and its situation. He also stated that the utility wanted to employ some of the operations procedures that had been hotly debated during the previous negotiations. The environmentalists, who launched a personal attack on the public relations director, met the announcement with outrage. Even though he had values and approaches to problem solving that were very different from those of his predecessor, he was treated just the same way. Old feelings had been restimulated by a situation that looked like the earlier one but was in fact dissimilar. The new situation may have merited a strong response from the environmentalists, but the intensity of their emotions was more than likely provoked by restimulated feelings related to past events.

Transference, and in particular *negative transference,* is the carryover or generalization of learned responses from one particular relationship to another. In the Freudian sense, transference occurs when the power dynamic of a previous relationship is transferred to a new one. The new relationship may or may not be similar to the earlier one. For example, in a couple's dispute, the wife may transfer emotions about a controlling father onto her husband even though the husband may be quite unlike the father in his personality and manner of relating.

Restimulation and transference may result in an escalation of feelings that may or may not be merited by the objective conditions of the disputants. Mediators need to know how to respond to these sources of strong emotions. More will be said on this point later in the chapter.

Realistic feelings, in contrast to restimulated feelings, are the direct result of clear and present conditions that could normally be expected to intensify emotions. For example, if two parties in negotiation begin to yell at each other and make derogatory remarks about each other's integrity, the direct insults will usually result in strong emotions. This is not restimulation but a direct response to the immediate circumstances. (Obviously, a person could also be restimulated if he or she has been directly insulted in the past, but the current events do merit the strong emotions that the disputant feels.)

Ideally, parties will manage both realistic and restimulated feelings. However, when people experience and express strong negative emotions, a third party may be needed to mitigate or manage their adverse impacts. Although the mediator is not a therapist, he or she must be familiar with psychological techniques to assist parties in managing their emotions.

RESPONSES TO NEGATIVE EMOTIONS

Mediators are often called upon to respond to the behavioral, physiological, and cognitive basis of emotions. Feelings cannot be "resolved," as is the case with substantive or procedural problems or issues, but they can be regulated, managed, understood, and worked through to the point that they do not totally control participants. They may also be neutralized or changed for the positive. There are four general strategies for responding to parties' negative emotions: (1) approaches that afford creative opportunities for parties to express their feelings; (2) strategies for reappraisal of emotions; (3) procedures for suppressing or controlling escalatory behavior or expression of emotions; and (4) strategies for removing the objective cause of the emotions by meeting substantive, procedural, or psychological needs or interests. I will discuss the first three strategies in this chapter. Strategies for removing the objective cause of emotions will be discussed in Chapters Nine through Fourteen as part of the problem-solving component of the mediation process.

There are a number of approaches for intermediaries and parties to creatively respond to strong emotions. Since for the most part conflicts involve at least initially negative feelings rather than positive ones, I will focus attention on mediator interventions that regulate or lower negative emotions. The management of negative feelings can often foster the emotional space for, or result in the emergence or development of, positive sentiments.

Mediator responses to emotions consist of three separate steps: recognizing that a party has a strong emotion, diagnosing the emotion, and selecting an appropriate intervention strategy to assist the party in handling and creatively responding to the behavioral, psychological, or cognitive components of the feelings. Responses to emotions generally fall into two categories: strategies for creative expression and understanding of feelings, and strategies for emotional suppression or control.

Strategies for Expressing and Gaining Greater Understanding of Emotions

Strategies for expressing or venting strong emotions are usually pursued because the mediator believes that (1) the party needs a physiological release for unexpressed feelings and will probably be unable to focus on substantive issues until this discharge of feelings has occurred (Jackins, 1978; Bach and Goldberg, 1974); or that (2) the party needs to express his or her emotions to another party to demonstrate how strongly he or she feels about an issue;

or that (3) expressing and exploring will result in greater insight into the relationship between feelings and contested issues; or that (4) direct expression of emotions is culturally expected and acceptable. If a mediator decides that parties need to vent emotions for any of these reasons, he or she has to decide when, where, and how a party's emotions might best be expressed.

Expressing strong negative emotions may threaten and be highly destructive to a delicate negotiation process. For this reason, strong emotions that are the result of restimulation, or manipulative emotional outbursts, are often best expressed in private meetings between a party and the mediator. Emotions may also be channeled into a caucus when a party has been the target of strong feelings of another disputant and is unable to effectively handle or creatively respond to them. In a caucus, emotions can be vented safely, beyond the presence of other parties; physiological release can be attained; an assessment can be made of what is genuine emotion and what are restimulated feelings; greater understanding can be achieved regarding the links between emotions and substantive issues; and expression of manipulative comments can be curbed without risking further damage to the parties' relationships. Mediators often initiate a caucus for venting emotions once parties have begun negative interactions in joint session. Mediators also initiate caucuses specifically for the purpose of provoking parties to release emotions.

It should be noted that strong expression of emotions in joint session may be a functional process and important for achieving productive negotiations. Douglas (1962) observed that ritualized venting in the early stages of labor-management disputes appeared to be almost a prerequisite for the parties to move toward negotiation of substantive issues. If the mediator decides to encourage the parties to express their emotions, or if venting occurs spontaneously in joint session, his or her central concerns should be how to prevent the expression of feelings from escalating the conflict and how to limit negative dynamics and negative damage to the relationship of the parties.

Mediators use several intervention strategies to respond to this problem. Mediators may encourage parties to establish ground rules regarding acceptable behavior. These rules may exclude such practices as character assassination, attribution, projections regarding motivations, and direct personal attacks. Mediators may also encourage parties to express their feelings about the *interests* in dispute and not about the *people* who advocate them (Fisher and Ury, 1981). A third approach is for the mediator to verbally identify and preempt unproductive venting, and to encourage or suggest ways in which disputants can express the same concerns in a less volatile manner. This strategy often means preparing a party in caucus for a verbal interchange in joint session. Humor is a fourth way that mediators can assist parties in venting and yet limit the negative effects of anger (Landsberger, 1956).

Expression of strong negative emotions in joint session has value only if it permits a productive physiological release for one or more parties without damaging the delicate relationship between disputants, or if it serves to educate a party about the source or intensity of emotion around a particular issue. When venting is conducted to punish another party, it will probably result in a deterioration of relationship. If this occurs, the mediator should encourage the parties to move to a caucus, both as a defensive measure and as a means of directing the destructive feelings into safe channels.

So far, we have discussed expression of emotions on the assumption that verbalizing or physically acting out feelings may lead to a positive physiological release, or greater insight for a party or parties about the links between emotions and contested issues. However, expression alone may not be enough to achieve this end. Mediators may need to further help parties by using more explicit procedures for responding to and processing emotions. Some of the procedures that need to be examined are active listening, open-ended questioning, and strategies to prevent and respond to emotional flooding and emotional contagion.

Active Listening

Mediators frequently have little difficulty recognizing that a party is experiencing an emotion, but neither they nor the party may be able to specifically define it, determine how intensely the disputant feels about the subject under discussion, or understand the link between the feeling(s) and the issues in question. Active listening often facilitates identification and diagnosis of emotions, by parties and by intermediaries. Rogers (1945) first identified this form of interaction as a means of conducting social research; Gordon (1978) and Creighton (1972) later elaborated on it as a method of responding to the emotions of people in conflict. Active listening is a communication technique in which a listener decodes a verbal message, identifies the emotion being expressed, selects a word or phrase with the same meaning and emotional intensity as that conveyed by the speaker, and restates the feeling content of the message to the sender for confirmation or clarification. For example, the mediator might respond, "You were really frustrated and hurt when the city did not respond rapidly to your permit request." The disputant then has an opportunity to verify the accuracy of the mediator's perceptions of his or her feelings: "Yes, I felt frustrated! I had complied with all the requirements, but they still wanted more data." It is important that the listener accept the speaker's emotions without necessarily agreeing with the speaker or holding the same beliefs about the issues in question.

Active listening performs several functions when responding to people's feelings:

- It assures the speaker that he or she has indeed been heard.
- It allows the speaker and listener to verify that the precise meaning of the message has been heard.
- It demonstrates the acceptability of expressing emotions.
- It allows the speaker to explore his or her emotions about a subject, and to clarify what he or she really feels and why.
- It can facilitate appraisal of the link between the emotion and the substantive or procedural content of the conflict.
- It may also perform the physiological function of encouraging release of tension through expressing emotion.

Mediators can use active listening in caucuses and joint sessions to assess if expression of emotions is a negotiation tactic to influence another party to make concessions, if it is posturing for other disputants or constituents, or if it is a genuine expression of feelings. The more the mediator and disputant interact, the more difficult it is for disputants to maintain insincere emotional postures.

It should be noted that active listening may be a culture-specific process in that it will not work or be appropriate with certain individuals or groups or within particular cultures. Members of cultures that prefer to avoid overt display or discussion of emotions in front of parties with whom they disagree will resist active listening and may feel that responding to its use will result in loss of face for themselves or their opponent. Mediators should take care when using active listening in an indirect-dealing culture or in one that is not comfortable with direct expression of emotions.

Once the mediator has accurately diagnosed the content and intensity of a disputant's emotions, he or she may decide how to assist the party in understanding and handling the feelings. Although conciliatory moves are close to the practice of therapy, the mediator is in fact not attempting to change or rehabilitate a disputant through a clinical or casework approach. The mediator merely assists parties in managing their emotions so that they can negotiate on the specific issues in dispute.

Open-Ended Questioning

The second technique for helping parties identify, cognitively understand, and work through feelings is open-ended questioning. This approach assists disputants to understand and appraise the emotional link between feelings and the issues or interests in conflict, and cognitively decide what to do about the dispute. Open-ended questioning by a mediator can help participants explore this link and determine an effective course of action.

Lazrus (1991) posits that there are two kinds of appraisals that can be made by parties in conflict: primary and secondary. Primary appraisals occur when an individual or group focuses on the question "Is the event or situation personally relevant?" To answer this question, three elements must be considered. First, an individual or group wants to assess how the situation affects his or her personal goals. Second, the individual or group needs to determine if the situation makes it harder to achieve desired goals. Finally, the involved party needs to evaluate if the situation is related to its identity, or in the case of an individual his or her ego. If the individual or group answers all of these questions in the affirmative, the situation is likely to elicit significant emotions and such behavior as "avoidance, hostile attribution, verbal and-or physical aggression, blaming, building coalitions, intransigence, etc." (Jones, 2001).

Secondary appraisals expand the analysis of the situation and assist in determining the specific feeling or bundle of feelings experienced by a disputant. To promote secondary appraisals, Lazrus (1991) identifies a number of additional questions:

- What or who is to blame for the event/situation? (judgements of accountability)
- How well can one solve the problem and manage one's feelings? (coping potential)
- How likely is it that things will get better or worse? (future expectancy)

The combined results of an individual's or group's answers to the two sets of appraisal questions help to determine the form of emotion— such as frustration, sadness, shame, anger, outrage, contempt, fear, and so on—and the intensity of the emotions that may be felt and expressed. It is important to note that the emotion may be more directly related to how an individual or group perceives a situation than to the event itself. This insight relates to the concepts of realistic and unrealistc conflicts and realistic and restimulated feelings, described earlier in this chapter.

If parties are to effectively reassess their situation and emotions, they require a safe place to do so, must be talking about the right questions, and need a process that helps promote accurate and affective assessment (Jones, 2001). Effective mediation helps parties involved in conflict and enmeshed in strong emotions by setting up a safe venue where people feel free to talk and analyze their situation and feelings; helping individuals talk about the right issues, either in caucus or with other parties; and aiding a process that promotes productive reappraisal of the conflict and feelings while at the same time preventing or inhibiting severe emotional flooding.

However, positive assessment or reassessment does not just occur because people are in a safe place, are talking about the right issues, and have a productive process. Mediators may need to help focus parties on their feelings, both those from the past and those that they are currently experiencing, and help the parties process them by using procedures such as active listening (which will be described later in this chapter) or guided questioning. Jones (2001) suggests a number of questions that may help parties work through and reevaluate their feelings and the situation they are experiencing:

- What are you feeling?
- Do you know why you are feeling this way?
- Did something specific happen to make you feel this way?
- How did that event help or hurt you?
- Do you think someone or something is to blame? (Jones, pp. 236–237)

By asking open-ended questions that are focused on feelings, intermediaries can help parties identify, name, and clarify feelings and how they are related to their situation. Once feelings are identified, the mediator will be in a better position to help a party work through them and possibly change the situation, or their appraisal of the situation that caused them.

This phase of the appraisal can be accomplished by asking further questions:

- This issue or situation and the related feelings seem to be very important to you; how important are they?
- Are they important now? Will they be important in the future?
- What might increase or decrease their importance?
- Do you want to continue to have these feelings toward the other person or party?
- What do these feelings do for you?
- Are there any costs or benefits to you of continuing to feel the way that you do?
- What would you have to do to change your feelings?
- What would you need from the other party to have a shift in your feelings?
- What have you tried to change the situation that has helped cause your feelings?
- Has this worked?
- What additional or new steps might you take to have a change in your emotions?
- Is a change in your feelings what you want, and is it in your interest for this to happen?

Preventing and Responding to Emotional Flooding

Prevention of emotional flooding on the part of disputants or intermediaries is not always easy. Some intermediaries have tried to identify a disputant's potential flooding patterns (Jones, 2001). By talking with a party before a joint session or in a caucus and asking him or her about what has triggered this response in the past—specific words, events, or situations—the intervenor and party may be able to identify what is likely to elicit a flooding event and prevent it from happening. Mediators can also coach parties on how to identify when flooding is beginning to occur, and to let the mediator know when it is happening. Possible responses may include taking a brief time-out or moment of quiet in session, or calling a caucus or longer break to prevent the escalation of emotional flooding. Additionally, mediators may coach other parties on how they can avoid messages or behaviors that trigger emotional flooding in another party.

Once emotional flooding has occurred, mediators may need to take more concerted action. It should be noted that brief breaks or short caucuses alone may not afford adequate time to physiologically or cognitively respond to severe emotional flooding. Gottman (1994) notes that it may take as much as twenty minutes for a person to become physiologically unflooded after a particularly significant emotional event. During this time, intermediaries may need to use active listening and open-ended questions to help parties process their strong feelings.

When emotional flooding is caused by the internal psychodynamics of a party, such as when a disputant is overcome by a negative script or a repeated playing back or dwelling on a negative experience or feeling, the mediatior may assist the party in revising the script (Jones, 2001). Intermediaries can ask a party to identify what role he or she has played in the development and continuation of the feeling, what alternative feelings would be desirable, and what the new script and consequent emotions or behaviors might look like. Jones (2001) suggests that this is a possible approach to help disputants move from an innocent-victim script and emotions to those of a person in control of his or her life.

Responding to Emotional Contagion

Mediators wishing to prevent or respond to emotional contagion on the part of parties—or mediators themselves—who may also be susceptible to this effect should closely observe when parties begin to mirror each other's emotional behavior and take measures to interrupt the pattern. This may include taking breaks, caucuses, or identifying and verbally articulating what seems to be occurring. Jones

(2001) suggests that in highly emotional disputes, co-mediators may be desirable so that both can monitor the changing emotions of the parties, help shift the disputants from an emphasis on negative emotions to positive ones, and prevent each other from getting hooked by the intense feelings of the parties.

Strategies for Suppressing Negative Emotions

So far, I have discussed mediator strategies that encourage emotional expression as a means of improving communications, promoting physiological discharge, increasing understanding of the emotions and the conflict, and possibly removing sources of unnecessary conflict. However, in some situations encouragement of expression of emotions, in joint session or in caucus, may be counterproductive and lead to unnecessary escalation (Berkowitz, 1973; Hokanson, 1970; Steinmetz and Straus, 1974). Straus (1977, p. 233) argues that "in general, aggression against another (either verbally or physically) tends to (a) produce counter aggression, (b) impedes getting to the real problem, and (c) if it does succeed in squelching the other person, reinforces the use of aggression as a mode of interaction." If there is a history of violence, if one or more parties have a low degree of impulse control, if the mediator does not believe that he or she can control an escalation of emotions, or if expression of strong emotions is culturally unacceptable, it may be preferable to structure negotiations so as to limit emotional expression. Structures that limit emotional exchange include explicit guidelines about how parties will communicate, rules that limit communication between disputants and encourage them to talk only to or through the mediator, and physical separation of the parties so that they have few face-to-face meetings or none. In this last instance, the mediator performs a type of shuttle diplomacy and conveys messages between the parties that further the resolution of substantive, procedural, and psychological or relationship issues.

Strategies for Identifying, Developing, and Enhancing Positive Emotions

Although a significant amount of a mediator's effort in a serious dispute may be focused on minimizing the impact of negative feelings, he or she should not forget the importance of helping parties recognize, cultivate, and expand their positive sentiments toward each other. When parties enter into disputes they are usually in one or more emotional states: they feel negatively toward each other, they feel neutral or numb, or they feel some mix of negative and positive emotions. The earlier sections in this chapter focused on how to help people handle negative feelings. We should now examine what can be done with neutral or mixed emotions.

When faced with parties with neutral or mixed sentiments about another party or the issues in question, the intermediary may want to help shift the parties toward more positive views. He or she can do this by several methods, which can be conducted either in joint session or in private meetings between the intermediary and a party.

Identify Positive Past Interactions and Feelings

The mediator can ask parties to identify and describe a time or times in the past when there were more positive feelings than negative ones toward the other disputant or the issues in question, and where they were able to interact and cooperate in a productive manner. An example of this technique is when a divorce mediator asks separating partners to describe why they originally married and what attracted them to each other. Remembering positive feelings from the past can counteract the totally negative emotions and perception of the dispute in the present.

Discuss How a Positive Past Was "Supposed to Be"

A mediator can ask parties to discuss how what happened in the past was "supposed to be" if the interaction, emotions, or outcomes that resulted from the situation or conflict were positive. By re-telling a negative story in the affirmative, a party may be able to get in touch with what the positive feelings might have been. They may also induce the other party to acknowledge that differences should have been handled in another way, express regret at the negative feelings that have resulted, or make other conciliatory gestures that enhance positive feelings between the disputants.

Identify Positive Events That Contradict Negative Feelings

Creating a contradiction between positive and negative feelings may make it more difficult for a party to cast his or her "opponent" in a totally negative light. A mediator can ask a party to identify positive occurrences as a catalyst toward a shift of views.

Envision a Positive Future

A mediator can ask one or more parties to identify and discuss positive visions for what the desirable future relationship and emotions between the parties might be. By identifying and making tangible a positive future, parties may be able to let go of negative, neutral, or mixed emotions and move toward the affirmative vision.

MISPERCEPTIONS AND STEREOTYPES

Conflicts are often escalated or deescalated on the basis of parties' perceptions of each other. The mediator's role in the conciliation phase is to decrease perceptual barriers to negotiation. This is usually accomplished in four stages:

1. Identifying perceptions held by a party
2. Assessing whether the perceptions appear to be accurate or inaccurate
3. Assessing whether the perceptions are hindering or furthering a productive procedural, substantive, or emotional settlement
4. Assisting parties in revising their perception of other disputants when they have characterized the disputants with stereotypes or other image distortions, and in minimizing the negative impacts of such misperceptions

THE MASK-MIRAGE ANALOGY

Curle (1971, p. 209) observes that "many of man's feelings about others derive from his feelings about himself. Since these feelings are often intricate, contradictory, and not fully grasped at the conscious level, his attitudes towards others are correspondingly obscure and irrational." Curle explains that individuals conceal from themselves and others true representations of themselves and, in place of them, present a mask that expresses how they would like to perceive themselves or how they would like to have others perceive them.

Curle argues that when a person uses a mask, the image he or she holds of other disputants is often that of another mask or mirage. A mirage is an image based on the psychic needs of the observer rather than on real or objective characteristics of the observed.

How does the mediator recognize this mask-mirage dynamic? First, through interaction with disputants, the mediator will often be able to penetrate the fronts the disputing parties present and to identify the discrepancies between who the disputants really are, how they want to be seen, and how other combatants perceive them. Because the mediator does not have an investment in a particular outcome and cannot dictate a settlement, disputants are often honest with him or her; they have little to lose in exposing their real selves to the mediator (Goffman, 1959). (This does not mean that parties always let down their masks for mediators—and when they do not, mediators may accept the false images being projected. Mediators should take great care not to be drawn into believing that the image is the real person.) Because mediators possess this access, they may have an unusual opportunity to view disputants speaking and acting sincerely. Such observation allows them to identify misperceptions between disputants and assess the accuracy of their views.

Several types of action are available to parties and mediators seeking to modify the way parties are perceived. The disputants or mediator can (1) demonstrate that parties share similar attitudes toward an object, event, idea, or third person; (2) encourage association between parties to create an opportunity to reveal undisclosed commonalities; and (3) encourage a party to associate with (or disassociate from) objects, ideas, or people that his or her opposite likes (or dislikes).

Demonstrating Similar Attitudes

"Similar attitudes toward an object (event, idea, third person) set up forces toward attraction between persons" (Walton and McKersie, 1965, p. 225). Similar attitudes can be cultivated by identifying personal points in common, encouraging use of similar language, defining a common problem, focusing on the benefits to both parties that will result from mutual success, emphasizing a common view of outsiders, and deemphasizing differences between the parties.

Personal points in common may include geographical or educational background, or intellectual, recreational, or religious concerns. For example, several disputants in an energy development project modified their perceptions of each other when they discovered that they had all been involved as participants in, or coaches of, high school wrestling teams! The common experience of an enjoyable sport blurred the adversarial relationship between them. Parties themselves can often identify personal points in common, but if they do not, the mediator may initiate moves that make the parties aware of their commonalities. Mediator moves may be either indirect (such as the casual mention of a common factor) or direct and structured. Some family mediators, for example, ask divorcing couples to describe how they first met and what they liked about each other, to create a sense of positive history for a currently negative relationship.

Parties often hold misperceptions of each other because they use different language. They may be using different words to convey the same meanings or may actually be speaking from an entirely different world view. Coordination of the language of the parties may also align their perceptions.

The mediator can encourage parties to use the same language or can translate the communications of the various parties to foster mutual understanding. The mediator may often assist a party in reframing or restating a message in another way to facilitate accurate communication and positive reception. This process will be explored in more detail in Chapter Nine.

Identifying a dispute as a common problem that can be resolved for any party only through mutual cooperation can also induce a positive attitudinal shift. For example, identifying common problems of landlords and tenants as issues of predictability and "stability of living situation and rent" may enable the parties to reach agreement on the terms of a lease. Mediators often must point out common problems to a party who is trapped in an adversarial mirage and sees little in common with an opponent.

Identifying mutual benefits of success is closely related to identifying common problems. Divorcing parents may modify their perception of each other if they believe that their children benefit from an amicable divorce rather than a hostile one. Disputing spouses may see happy and well-adjusted children as a mutual benefit. Mediators must often directly identify the mutual benefits to be gained by common action because the parties may not recognize them.

The way an event, idea, or third person is described can also promote either discord or attraction between parties. By deemphasizing differences, a party can minimize the amount of negative perception an opponent has of him or her. Mediators often perform the valuable function of minimizing differences by reframing the description or wordings of disagreements between parties.

Encouraging Common Association

Parties can be induced to change their perception of each other by developing common positive associations. Mediators should determine if parties have undisclosed commonalities that are likely to be revealed or enhanced by increasing their interaction. If this is the case, parties may be encouraged to work together. The opposite, however, may also be true. If the parties have few similarities, association may increase polarization. Mediators may separate and maintain the distance of parties who have little in common, or traits or beliefs that may escalate the conflict.

Encouraging Association/Disassociation with Objects, Ideas, or People

Parties can either associate themselves with, or disassociate themselves from, objects, ideas, or people that another disputant likes or dislikes. Mediators may encourage association or disassociation, depending on their assessment of various perceptions of the parties. In some instances, association may be more important and positive than disassociation, while in other disputes the opposite may be true.

REINFORCEMENT OF PERCEPTUAL CHANGE

Another approach to perceptual change focuses on rewarding or punishing a party's behavior to induce perceptual change. This approach has three central premises: (1) the more frequently one person's activity rewards the behavior of another, the more often the latter will demonstrate the behavior; (2) the more valuable the reward activity is to a person, the more often the person will demonstrate the rewarded behavior; and (3) if one person's activity punishes the behavior of another, the punished behavior will probably be suppressed (Walton and McKersie, 1965).

This approach assumes that by rewarding positive behavior and punishing negative behavior a person can influence the behavior, if not the perception, of another. Procedures for rewarding an opponent's behavior include extending compliments, expressing appreciation, returning favors, and increasing or stressing positive benefits (Walton and McKersie, 1965). Punishment behaviors include reminding an opponent of his or her role obligations, threatening the opponent's self-concept, and issuing direct threats and sanctions (Walton and McKersie, 1965).

Positive reinforcement or rewards are moves usually preferred by both mediators and negotiators because they do not trigger as many negative reactions (Stevens, 1963). In general, mediators should elicit and stress the benefits of reaching an agreement with the other party before detailing the costs of not doing so. Emphasis on the positive can incline parties toward agreement, whereas emphasis on the costs of not settling may set up resistance because of negative pressure or sanctions.

Occasionally, however, mediators must direct the attention of the parties to negative measures of reinforcement. The utility of a mediator's reference to a party's use of negative means of reinforcement or possible negative consequences of a continued behavior depends on several variables. Generally, the threat of punishment, or the risk of incurring costs for rejecting terms for agreement, will only under certain circumstances induce a party to change his or her mind.

Punishment or threat of punishment seems to work only in specific situations. If, for example, a party has anticipated the costs or punishment that he or she might receive as a result of a particular action, has factored them into the overall calculation of whether the action should be undertaken, and has found the punishment to be manageable, the threat is likely to have little effect.

Fisher (1964, p. 32) observes that "other considerations . . . suggest that inflicting pain on an adversary may be worse than useless. There is a common tendency to treat sunken costs as invested capital. The greater the costs we impose upon our adversary, the greater the amount they will regard themselves as having committed to this course of action." Parties therefore resist settlement because of the energy and resources they have invested in a conflict. Mediators may assist parties in rationalizing a change in resource expenditure so that settlement can be reached. Mediators should take great care when emphasizing the negative consequences of a failure to settle. Stressing the negative, even when one party has the capacity and will to carry out a coercive threat and the other is incapable of defending himself or herself, may create resistance on the part of the latter and escalate the dispute. Mediators often use soft negative reinforcement by implying, not directly stating, that another party may pose a threat. For example, the mediator might say, "I don't know whether he will go to court, but he could, and that might hurt you." This phrasing uses negative coercion, creates doubt, and pressures the party to reevaluate his or her view without directly threatening the party.

LEGITIMACY PROBLEMS

The most difficult perceptual problems, for both negotiators and mediators, are probably those that deal with legitimacy and trust. *Legitimacy* refers to a party's acceptance and recognition that an opponent, an opponent's issues or interests, and even an opponent's emotions are genuine, are reasonable, and conform to recognized principles or accepted rules or standards. Without a perception of legitimacy, negotiations may never begin.

A classic case in point is the perceptual change on the part of the government of Israel and the Palestine Liberation Organization (PLO) regarding each other's legitimacy. From the founding of the Israeli state in 1949, these parties repeatedly refused to recognize each other's legitimate right to exist and to have a state in the Middle East. This condition led to wars, terrorist bombings, assassinations, economic sanctions, forced removals, imprisonment, property destruction, and various nonviolent actions on the part of each party to convince the other to recognize its legitimate interests. In the early 1990s, a shift of perception, which had been developing over time, suddenly became more visible and explicit. How did this happen?

The changes appear to have resulted from (1) protracted interaction, both formal and informal, between the parties; (2) the stubbornness of each side in pressing for the recognition of its rights; (3) mobilization of power by each party (accompanied by increasing risks and costs) to force the other to recognize the legitimacy of its interests; and (4) recognition that a continuation of the status quo was unsatisfactory to all sides. This led to a breakthrough due to informal mediations in Oslo, Norway, and ultimately to the formalization of a phased peace accord process. Although at the date of this writing a final accord has not been totally formalized or implemented, the process does demonstrate how shifts in perception regarding legitimacy can change.

This chapter is most concerned with persuasive rather than coercive means of perceptual change and with encouraging parties to accept the legitimacy of the other party's issues, interests, and emotions. I will explore the use of coercion in Chapter Fifteen. Here I will explore each of the areas of legitimacy—party, issues, interests, and emotions—and the ways in which disputants shift perceptions by means of persuasion.

Legitimacy of Person or Party

A party recognizes another party as legitimate when the former is willing to talk with the latter. Negotiations often fail because one party does not perceive another as the legitimate spokesperson or bargaining agent for the opposing view. This can be the case in family disputes, union disputes, or international relations. The refusal of the United States and Israel to recognize the PLO as the legitimate bargaining agent for Palestinians and the corresponding refusal of the PLO to recognize Israel stood in the way of peace talks in the Middle East for years. The refusal of one birth parent to recognize the legitimacy of a stepparent's participation in negotiations may hinder or block postdivorce negotiations between birth parents.

Changing perceptions about the legitimacy of a person or party as a bargaining agent for one side of an issue can be accomplished in several ways. First, if the unacceptability of the negotiator is due to misperception, clarification of communication may remove the barrier.

Second, if the problem with legitimacy results from the procedure by which negotiators were selected to represent a conflict group, the procedure can be explained or the mediator can assist the parties in developing a procedure acceptable to all of them. Acceptable procedures ensuring that a negotiator genuinely represents and can ensure the commitment of a constituency often remove barriers to recognizing legitimacy. Mediators can and should assist the parties in improving procedures.

Third, perceptions about a particular negotiator can often be changed if parties organize direct unassisted discussion about images and perceptions. Blake, Mouton, and Sloma (1961) have succeeded with this approach in labor management disputes. Mediators can also assist parties in changing their personnel and thus changing an opponent's perceptions. Bush and Folger (1994) posit that legitimacy issues regarding the recognition of people, issues, and interests and emotions can be achieved through "perspective talking":

> Starting with parties opening narratives, mediators look for places that would allow each party to consider the other's point of view. . . . To aid perspective taking, mediators reinterpret, translate, and reframe parties' statements, not to shape issues or solutions but to make parties more intelligible to each other. They then ask parties to consider the significance of such reformulation, pointing out opportunities for recognition (of a party's capacity to consider another's situation, what they are experiencing, the reason why he or she acts the way he does, and possible merit in their view) without forcing them [Bush and Folger, 1994, p. 101].

Some parties may not be persuaded to change legitimacy perceptions, and coercion may be the only way to obtain recognition. When this perceptual deadlock occurs, mediators occasionally discuss with the party whose legitimacy is questioned what coercive means will be likely to be the most effective in persuading the other party to shift his or her views and to cause the least damage to their relationships.

Legitimacy of Issues and Interests

Legitimacy of issues and interests can be created in a variety of ways. Fisher (1964), drawing from his observations of international negotiations and mediation, suggests that a party can:

- Change the wording of the issue
- Redefine the issue in terms that are favorable or acceptable to the other party
- Ask that another person with authority recognize the legitimacy of an interest
- Have another person advocate an interest
- Ask for a focus on another issue that has a greater chance of being recognized as legitimate
- Be more specific
- Be more general

Mediators can assist parties in making all these moves by indirect or direct suggestions.

Legitimacy of Emotions

Legitimacy of emotions refers to the acceptance of a party's right to hold or possess specific feelings, not to whether another party agrees with them (Gordon, 1978). As long as a dispute persists about whether the substantive issues or behavior of an opponent objectively merits a particular emotion, the possibility of productive negotiations will remain low. The mediator should try to interpret the emotions to the other side and explain why they are appropriate or important to the person expressing them. He or she should also inform the party that is denying legitimacy that it is not necessary to agree with the emotions in order to proceed with negotiations. All that the party must do is accept that they exist and acknowledge that, for whatever reason, an opponent does feel a particular way. Acknowledgment may be all that the person having the feelings needs in order to proceed with a productive dialogue.

LACK OF TRUST

Conciliation involves not only minimizing the impact of negative emotions and perceptions but enhancing positive feelings and perceptions. Numerous researchers and practitioners have identified the importance of trust in conducting productive negotiations.

Trust usually refers to a person's capacity to depend on or place confidence in the truthfulness or accuracy of another's statements or behavior.

In negotiations, trust is very closely related to the mask-mirage images of disputants. "To believe everything the other person says is to place one's fate in his hands and to jeopardize full satisfaction of one's own interests. On the other hand, to believe nothing the other says is to eliminate the possibility of accepting any arrangement with him" (Kelly, 1966, p. 60). At the start of negotiations, when the mask-mirage dynamic is strongest, the parties and the mediator face the challenge of creating perceptions, if not actual behavior, that induce trust between disputants.

Base of Trust

Trust is based on the experiences of the negotiators with past negotiations, the similarity of current issues to those in past negotiations, past experience with a particular opponent, rumors about a current adversary's trustworthiness, and the opponent's current statements or actions. Mediators often must respond to all these variables in the process of building minimal trust between the parties.

The past experience of a negotiator, his or her personality, and his or her needs, beliefs, values, and predispositions toward other parties will strongly affect his or her ability and willingness to trust another party. Mediators usually do not make any efforts to change or modify a negotiator's psychological makeup on the basis of experience with previous and different negotiating opponents. However, the mediator may attempt through careful questioning to modify and clarify a negotiator's perceptions of the current negotiation, and another party may assist him or her in identifying similarities and differences between the present situation and the past. Because mediation is future-oriented, in that the goal is to establish a new relationship or define future terms of agreement, the mediator often pushes parties to defer judgment about a present situation or party and to limit the intrusion of past judgments or biases into the current case until they are proved to be valid.

A negotiator's past interaction with an opponent can constitute a base for either trust or distrust. Mediators negotiating with parties who have a history of negotiations between them may begin the trust-building process by asking questions that assess whether a positive or negative relationship has been built over time. If the parties have a positive trust relationship, and have been able to depend on the other party's veracity and count on the other party to follow through on agreed commitments, the mediator's task becomes simpler. In this case, the mediator may merely remind the parties of their positive and productive history or may ask them to recount transactions in which trust in each other has been rewarded.

The latter technique may often be used effectively even when little trust exists between the parties. For example, in difficult divorce mediation cases, mediators have asked spouses for specific instances when they were in conflict, trusted each other, and found the other spouse to be trustworthy. By this means, the disputants are reminded of occasions when the other has responded to cooperative gestures with reciprocation rather than exploitation.

Should the mediator discover that parties have a highly negative relationship and there are few instances where past trust has been reciprocated, he or she can assist the parties in determining if the breach of trust arose from a joint misinterpretation of the situation or an unintentional misunderstanding. If either of these is the cause, accurate communication may remove the perceptual barriers to a new trusting relationship. If, however, the trust of one party was misplaced and intentional exploitation rather than reciprocity resulted, the mediator must pursue another strategy and start from a point of no or little trust to build a positive relationship between the parties.

Mediator-Negotiator Moves to Build Trust

Trust in relationships is usually built incrementally over time. Through a succession of promises and congruent actions that reinforce the belief that commitments will be carried out, negotiators gradually build a relationship of trust. Mediators may assist negotiators in building a trusting relationship by encouraging them to make a variety of moves designed to increase credibility. Here are some moves that encourage negotiators to increase their trust in each other:

- Make consistently congruent statements that are clear and do not contradict previous statements (Creighton, 1972)
- Perform symbolic actions that demonstrate good faith in bargaining (Fisher, 1978)—for example, providing for an adversary's physical comfort, negotiating at a time or place that is convenient for another party, making a minor concession that indicates a willingness to negotiate
- Place themselves in a subservient position in relation to another party so that they incur a minor risk. This demonstrates trust because it places a party's well-being in the hands of an opponent (Pruitt, 1981)
- Ask for help, thus acknowledging the need for assistance from other participants (Fisher, 1978)
- Exhibit a genuine concern to help other participants reach their objectives while retaining the ability to reach their own (Zartman and Berman, 1982)
- Demonstrate that there will be an earlier return of benefits to the agreeing party than was previously expected (Zartman and Berman, 1982)
- Show that they are willing to undergo punishment or incur costs if they do not follow through on their promises (Zartman and Berman, 1982)
- Avoid making threats to an opponent or making promises that are unbelievable or unrealistic (Zartman and Berman, 1982)
- Make incremental agreements in which success can be measured along the way (Fisher, 1978; Zartman and Berman, 1982)
- Demonstrate an understanding of the other side's concerns, even if they do not agree with those concerns

All these moves should be carried out by the parties. The mediator, however, can be a catalyst for them.

Mediators can also make specific interventions that will build trust between parties and change their perceptions. Among these moves are creating situations in which the parties must perform a joint task, translating one party's perceptions to another, vocally identifying commonalities, verbally rewarding parties for cooperation and trust, and facilitating a discussion of their perceptions of each other (Fisher, 1978).

Structured Procedures to Address Issues of Trust and Respect

On occasion, intermediaries may want to introduce more elaborate and explicit procedures to address issues of trust, respect, and cognitive (as opposed to emotional) empathy. Although not historically common in problem-solving mediation, and although more akin to therapeutic or group dynamic interventions, these procedures can, when appropriate, be incorporated into a mediation process if it appears that attitudinal issues or extremely difficult historical relationships between parties are likely to block discussion or agreement making, thereby perpetuating the conflict.

In general, these approaches involve parties in explicit dialogue about their relationships and attitudes toward the issues in question and each other. Here are two common approaches:

1. Parties can be asked to develop a profile, in list form, of how they perceive *their* attitudes toward the other party and motivations in a situation, how they perceive the other party's attitudes and motivations, and how they think the other party perceives them. The results can then be shared in joint session and act as a catalyst for discussion about the bases of the perceptions, the past history that has given rise to them, and the actions necessary to change them and build more respectful and trusting relationships (Blake and Mouton, 1961).

2. Individuals in a two-party dispute or stakeholder groups in a multiparty conflict can be asked to privately develop a vision of an ideal working relationship between the parties, expressing this in terms of attitudes and behaviors. The parties are then asked to work in joint session, sharing their visions with each other and seeking a general consensus on the attitudes and behaviors they would like to see in their future relationship. The parties then separate and develop privately a list of attitudes and behaviors that have historically blocked, or are currently blocking, achievement of their joint vision. Once this task is completed, the parties come together again to share their ideas. They discuss the barriers, reach agreement on those they consider to be the most important, and then move to the third phase of the process: problem solving. The problem-solving phase has the parties identifying and agreeing on

concrete actions that they can take to improve their working relationship. The final phase of the process is working out ways to implement and monitor the jointly developed solutions and setting a time to reconvene, discuss progress being made, address any new problems that may have emerged, and if necessary fine-tune earlier agreements (Blake and Mouton, 1984).

Other procedures for dealing with attitudinal, respect, trust, and cognitive empathy problems have been developed by Burton (1969), Kelman (1991), Fisher and Brown (1988), and Rothman (1992, 1997) for use in large group disputes. The goal of the problem-solving workshops designed by these practitioners is to create a positive environment conducive to conflict resolution and to transformation of the relationship between the conflicting parties to one of understanding and cognitive empathy—both in the short run and the long run (Kelman, 1991). Other practitioners, including Bush and Folger (1994), describe transformative strategies for small-group and interpersonal disputes.

POOR COMMUNICATION

Communication is certainly a central component in negotiation. The amount, form, and quality of communication, as well as the identities and qualities of the communicators, are usually strong influences on the outcome of negotiations.

The common assumption that if parties are talking, they will work out their differences is not necessarily true. Deutsch (1969, p. 12) describes the communication of people in conflict: "Typically a competitive process tends to produce the following effects: communication between the conflicting parties is unreliable and impoverished. The available communication channels and opportunities are not utilized or they are used in an attempt to mislead or intimidate the other. Little confidence is placed in information that is obtained directly from the other; espionage and other circuitous means of obtaining information are relied upon. The poor communication enhances the possibility of error and misinformation of the sort which is likely to reinforce the pre-existing orientations and expectations toward the other."

Unproductive communication can lead to a breakdown of interaction between the parties or the inability to start negotiations at all. Mediators often structure communication or assist parties in doing so. Mediator moves to modify communication involve controlling or assisting the parties in determining:

- What is communicated
- How a message is communicated, in terms of both syntax and means of transmission
- By whom the message is communicated
- To whom the message is delivered
- When a message is delivered
- Where a message is delivered

I will examine each one of these points in detail.

What Is Said to Another Party

The content of a message that a speaker conveys to a listener can be substantive information, such as data regarding issues, interests, or positions; procedural information concerning the way a negotiator does or does not want an activity to be conducted; or information about the negotiator's emotional state.

Mediators manage what negotiators say in several ways. First, the mediator may meet with the party before joint sessions or during caucuses to assist him or her in determining what information should or should not be shared with other disputants. The mediator's knowledge of the likes and dislikes of other parties often assists him or her in making suggestions about the communications in joint meetings that will best meet the needs of all parties. The coaching role of the mediator is often important.

Second, the mediator can influence what a party says in joint session by translating it into language that is both understandable and acceptable to another party. This process, often called reframing, will be discussed in more detail in Chapter Nine. After a message is delivered, the mediator may make efforts at clarification to ensure that the listener fully understands its content and implications. I discussed active listening, one means of message clarification, earlier in this chapter, and I will discuss other clarification techniques in Chapter Nine. It is enough to say here that clarification usually includes restatement. If the message has been restated in one of a variety of forms, the speaker, whether negotiator or mediator, can determine if it has been accurately received. Restatement allows for corrections and modification by the speaker to ensure accurate communication. The mediator's role in clarification may extend to interpreting messages.

Third, the mediator can shift what is being said by structuring communication channels so that parties are allowed to make only limited and managed statements (Young, 1972). For example, the mediator may allow parties to talk only on particular subjects, may interrupt parties making statements that another party will not positively receive (for reasons either of substance or of emotional tone), or may even prevent direct communication by keeping the parties in a caucus. If a caucus is used, the mediator may filter information that flows between the parties, allowing through only content that builds toward agreement (Maggiolo, 1972). He or she may also suppress communication on issues that do not seem important to the parties, or that might antagonize them.

How Messages Are Communicated

Mediators may also help determine how a message is communicated. *How* refers not only to the medium—written, oral (in person or by phone), and so on (Cohen, 1980)—but also to the sender's syntax.

By managing how parties communicate, the mediator can vary both the substantive and the emotional content of a message. For example, written messages eliminate unproductive nonverbal communication and may be more explicit. They also take more time to prepare and respond to, thus allowing parties to deliberate longer on what they send and receive.

Direct oral communication between parties may be good for some negotiations and poor for others. In some cases, the mediator may want to deliver a message because the recipient is more likely to accept it from him or her than from the other party. In such cases, the mediator is also able to control and formulate what is to be communicated.

Who Communicates a Message

Mediators often take the initiative to manage who communicates in negotiations. In some disputes, a negotiator may deem a message more or less acceptable depending on who sends it. If, for example, a mediator discovers that one group is disconcerted by a leader of another group, he or she may advise the initiating group that their message will be better received if delivered by someone other than that person.

Who Receives a Message

Communication may be accepted or rejected, depending on whom it is directed to. Because the mediator is aware of the structure of negotiating teams or their constituents, he or she may be able to suggest to whom a communication should be addressed. Variables that mediators should consider are:

- Who has the power to decide?
- Who is psychologically ready to hear the message?
- Who are the moderates in the group?
- To whom in the bureaucratic hierarchy should the message be addressed?
- What is the protocol for delivering messages?

When a Message Is Delivered

Timing of communication is often important. *When* something is said is frequently more important than *what* is said. In one case, a manufacturer entered contract negotiations with his workforce. After careful analysis, he determined what wage increases the union wanted and decided to comply. In his opening offer, he proposed to meet the union's demands. The union rejected the offer, not because it did not meet their expectations but because it was offered too soon. The union had expected to fight for the increase. The offer's timing led to a strike that damaged both labor and management.

Mediators can often control communication timing by either encouraging or inhibiting discussion by one party until the other party or parties are most receptive. For example, one labor mediator kept parties apart in caucus and delayed joint meetings until their private discussions had progressed to the point that they would be able to agree in joint session (Shapiro, 1970).

Where a Message Is Delivered

Where a message is delivered may also be important. An extreme demand made in joint session when the opposing party's entire group is present may meet with a stronger objection than if the proposal is made in a private and more informal setting.

Similarly, a psychologically relaxing setting may enable a party to keep an open mind, whereas in others an uncomfortable setting may induce resolution. For example, mediators occasionally conduct all-night negotiating sessions in unfamiliar settings. Former Congressman Timothy Wirth used this strategy in his efforts to induce agreement between the Denver Water Board, the EPA, and environmental groups on the siting of the Foothills water treatment facility in Denver (Burgess, 1980). Time and setting can be used to influence recalcitrant negotiators. Mediators can often manage the negotiation and communication settings to enhance productivity.

NONVERBAL COMMUNICATION

Nonverbal communication—gestures, use of space, and manipulation of objects—may be intentional or unintentional, but it still conveys messages (Givin [website]; Hecht [website]; Massip [website]; Madonik, 2001; Remland, 2002). Henley (1977) argues that nonverbal communication may be the principal way that people communicate dominance, authority, and status. If a mediator is to assist parties in effective nonverbal communication, he or she must be aware of all its various forms and how it can be channeled to the benefit of all parties.

Gestures, Eye Contact, and Demeanor

Nonverbal gestures clearly can communicate a tremendous amount of information about a disputant's attitude and data about the power relationship between disputants. Hinde (1972) reported that people often communicate superior attitudes toward others with unsmiling or disdainful facial expressions, erect posture, and staring. People may communicate anxiety, on the other hand, by tense, rigid posture and hand wringing.

Gestures are often difficult for parties—and mediators—to control, being frequently initiated by the subconscious. Mediators may attempt to control nonverbal communication either directly or indirectly. Direct control may take the form of asking parties variously to (1) face or look at each other when they are speaking (if strategically or culturally appropriate); (2) look at and speak only to the mediator to avoid eye contact with an opponent; (3) stop tapping feet or fingers when they are frustrated; or (4) adjust their body positions so that they are sitting in a posture likely to induce cooperation rather than competition. Handshakes at the conclusion of negotiations are in some cultures one way to nonverbally affirm an agreement.

The use of caucuses is one way to eliminate the effects of gestures and other nonverbal signals. When negotiations are conducted through caucuses, the mediator transmits all messages.

Although controlling gestures and eye contact of disputants may be difficult, the mediator may engage in nonverbal communication that conveys particular messages to the parties. The mediator can use eye contact, handshakes, and body language to convey to disputants either engagement and approval or disengagement and disapproval.

In one case, a contractor and a homeowner were engaged in an intense conflict over compensation for a fault in house construction. They became verbally abusive and pointed and shook fingers at each other. The mediator stood up very slowly, took off his glasses, and began to slowly pace around the room. He suggested that the parties look at the issue another way. He stopped and pointed to a chart on the wall that listed information about the house in question. The mediator's movements and gestures, because they were more active and interesting than those of either of the disputants, attracted their attention, drawing their focus away from each other. The mediator's manner—calm, deliberate, rational, serious, and focused—also changed the emotional tone of the disputants and encouraged them to seek a more rational approach to their problem.

In conclusion, mediators can manage the gestures of disputants by direct requests or separation or by means of indirect signals transmitted by the mediator's own gestures or eye contact. There is a caveat, however. Nonverbal communication is often culturally or racially bound; signals take on meanings according to culture and race (Kochman, 1981; Van Zandt, 1970). Mediators should take great care to adhere to cultural norms when they attempt to modify their own gestures or eye contact, or those of disputants. A violation of such norms can lead to a deterioration or breakdown in communication between disputants, or between disputants and the mediator.

Use of Space

Mediators also initiate moves that control the environment in which parties negotiate. *Environment* refers to physical distance between the parties, or between the parties and the mediator, and also to the way individuals are physically positioned in relation to each other.

In a seminal work on nonverbal communication, Hall (1966) observed that Americans have norms regarding acceptable proximity between people for particular types of interactions. He identifies four general categories of relationships: intimate, personal, social, and public. The first three are relevant to negotiations. A distance of zero to six inches indicates extremely intimate interaction. It often includes body contact and may result in playful wrestling, affectionate touching, or gestures that comfort or protect. A distance of 1.5 to 2.5 feet is the acceptable proximity for people who have a close personal relationship, and is characteristic of parents and children or close friends. Henley (1977) notes that this is also the limit of physical domination. Social distance—four through seven feet—is the normal distance for working colleagues. It is a distance for more formal settings in which people do not engage in intimate or personal relationships.

Although these zones are culturally based, mediators must be familiar with them because they establish norms that, if violated, may trigger changes in the dynamics of disputes. Parties tend to become uncomfortable if acceptable distances are violated and will usually initiate behavior to reestablish a spatial norm; they may even become hostile.

A case illustrates the role of physical space and settlement. Two co-mediators were talking with a party in caucus. One of the mediators stressed the negative impact of not settling the case and crowded the physical space of the party by leaning toward him. There was no room for retreat, because the party was literally up against the wall. The party refused to change his negotiating demands. The other co-mediator suggested a break to allow time for consideration of the proposal. During the recess, this co-mediator suggested that the other mediator allow the party more physical space. The other mediator agreed, and when the caucus was resumed the party began to move around, leaned forward, and accepted the proposal.

Mediators often take the initiative to maintain spatial norms in order to prevent conflict escalation. They may allow parties enough room in the negotiating setting to avoid crowding; they may ensure that there is enough space between disputants so that they cannot harm each other; and they may even position themselves midway between the parties to impose a physical buffer and physically demonstrate the mediator's impartiality.

Occasionally, however, a mediator may violate spatial norms for negotiations in order to destabilize parties.

Certain aspects of spatial organization (such as seating arrangements, discussed earlier) and the location's degree of formality are both closely related to physical distance between negotiators or between negotiators and the mediator.

Some mediators manage the degree of formality to promote more cooperative negotiation or to emphasize the seriousness of the issues. Some court-related mediation programs may tend to reinforce a quasi-judicial perception of the mediation process by locating negotiations in a courtroom or judicial building, a lawyer's office, or a police station and maintaining a highly formal setting: sparse furnishings, few personal items, institutional furniture, and so on. Such an environment seems to reinforce formality, seriousness, and a businesslike approach to negotiation. It may subliminally suggest the gravity of the proceedings and may psychologically reinforce commitment to the agreement later.

Some mediators, however, prefer informal settings such as their personal offices, a neutral and uninvolved third-party's home, a restaurant, or a relaxing public setting such as a resort or retreat center. Mediators assume that informal settings will encourage parties to be more relaxed and comfortable, as the parties will not be forced to manage an alien environment as well as controversial issues.

Mediator moves to either increase or decrease the formality of the negotiating setting are, of course, contingent on the situation.

Use of Objects

Messages in negotiations are often conveyed by physical objects, such as clothing, sunglasses, handkerchiefs, documents or reports, briefcases, and even firearms. Mediators may attempt to enhance conciliation by either (1) promoting or inhibiting the use by negotiators of objects that may adversely influence settlement or (2) using objects themselves to influence disputants toward settlement.

The most important objects that negotiators use to influence other parties are their clothing. Clothing can produce either affinity or alienation between negotiators. Mediators may suggest to parties appropriate attire that may encourage another party to settle. In cross-cultural disputes, personal attire may often be a barrier to a party's acceptance of another's trustworthiness or seriousness.

Clothing can also influence the mediator's acceptability and credibility with a party. Several years ago, a group of professionals asked me to intervene in an interracial high school dispute. I wore jeans and a work shirt to the interview with conflicting students. My attire reduced the differences between myself and the students. The same attire, however, caused a controversy when I went to discuss the intervention with the professionals right after speaking to the students. They did not equate professional mediation services with informal attire.

Mediators also may request that the parties bring to sessions particular objects that may enhance psychological cooperation— financial records or contested objects (televisions, cars, clothing, and so on)—so that parties can refer directly to the objects. Mediators must also occasionally discourage the use of objects that have negative effects on negotiation. For example, certain negotiation projects require that all firearms be left at home or checked on arrival.

CULTURAL APPROACHES

A comprehensive description of cultural influences on emotions and ways they should be addressed, misperceptions and stereotypes, legitimacy problems, trust, and communications patterns is impossible in one book or chapter. However there are some points on a few of these factors that should be noted.

Emotions, as mentioned earlier, are culturally defined. Culture influences what is emotionally important or relevant for the involved parties, establishes parameters for the strategic orientation of parties to conflict, circumscribes communication patterns, and defines appropriate and proper disputant behavior. Several specific cultural variables are important to consider when mediating between or in cultures. First, is the culture of the disputants direct-dealing or indirect-dealing when it comes to conflict? Are members of the culture emotionally expressive or emotionally reserved? Are parties comfortable working through conflicts using unassisted or mediated face-to-face conversations with one another, or do they abhor direct talk or confrontation?

If the culture is direct-dealing and one that is emotionally expressive, especially when it comes to negative feelings, chances are good that many of the approaches and procedures described earlier for responding to feelings and emotions will be useful for both parties and intermediaries. But if the culture is generally indirect-dealing, and its members are uncomfortable with face-to-face expression of negative (or positive) emotions, or even talking about feelings, much more indirect procedures will have to be used. In some cases, active listening and asking open-ended assessment questions may be appropriate, especially in private meetings with individuals or in caucus. In other situations, the process for addressing emotions may need to be even more indirect, conversational, and nuanced, almost to the point of verbally ignoring emotions altogether. In this situation, periods of silence, breaks, or some physical activity may be needed to allow time for disputants to internally process feelings.

A second cultural factor when working with emotions has to do with which emotions are acceptable to have and express, and when. For example, in many cultures it is unacceptable for men to express fear or sadness. Conversely, women may be expected not to feel or express anger. Cultural definitions and parameters regarding acceptable feelings and their expression often force members of one culture to express a feeling one way, and members of others in yet another. For example, in some cultures it is OK for men to cry when they are hurt. In others, men may display anger when they are sad. Conversely, in cultures where women are not expected to have, much less express, negative or angry emotions, they may respond by crying when they are angry.

Closely related to the kind of emotion that is culturally accept-able to have and express is the level of intensity acceptable for dis-play. For example, a study of working-class African Americans and middle-class whites found that the former were much more com-fortable with (and in fact expected) emotional expression of strong feelings in conflict situations. The middle-class whites viewed the exhibition of strong feelings as an indication of being out of con-trol, a factor that could escalate dispute, and behavior that should be avoided (Kochman, 1981). When these two groups talked and tried to resolve their differences, the African Americans perceived the whites as being disengaged, and the whites saw the African Americans as being unnecessarily emotional and confrontational.

Mediators working interculturally need to become familiar with the expectations and patterns regarding emotions of the cultures they are working in so that they will better be able to identify, read, and accurately interpret what is being emotionally conveyed, and develop culturally appropriate intervention strategies.

Like emotions, the concept and operationalization of trust is culturally defined. In his classic study of the development of de-mocracy and collaborative commercial relationships, Putnam (1993) distinguished between the concepts, acceptability of, and actions that defined and established trust in various parts of Italy. Fukuyama (1995) distinguished and described the differences be-tween high-trust and low-trust societies. For some societies and cul-tures, verbal or written statements engender trust, while for others actions or performance of certain rituals may be expected. When working across cultures, mediators will need to either research or explore with parties what trust means, what it actually looks like in action, and how it can be developed in order to help disputants develop culturally relevant and appropriate trusting relationships.

Cultural patterns of communication are extremely diverse. Some of the most common variations and important considera-tions in the context of conflict and its resolution are (1) the par-ties' orientations and preferences regarding engaging in direct face-to-face discussions or negotiations, or working indirectly through intermediaries; (2) how high-context or low-context the cultures of the disputants are, which generally determines how many shared assumptions they have in common, and how explicit (low-context) discussions and agreements will have to be; (3) how willing disputants are to deal directly and explicitly with issues, as opposed to indirectly through circuitous and circumspect discussions; (4) whether parties are from a monochronic or turn-taking culture where one individual or group speaks at a time, or a polychronic one where multiple people speak at the same time and talk often overlaps; (5) the kinds of logic and sequences that conversation and problem solving takes, such as linear, linear with looping social diversions, circular, inductive, or deductive; and (6) different meanings of yes and no, maybe, and "very difficult to do." For example, in many indirect, high-context and inexplicit "dealing" Asian cultures, by saying "it would be very difficult" a party often means that the option is totally impossible.

When working interculturally, the major communication tasks of mediators are to make sure that they understand the communications patterns in play, how they can help parties understand differences in patterns and meanings of talk, and to provide communication coordination assistance. This may include activities such as using more caucuses with members of indirect-dealing cultures; helping members of more direct-dealing cultures be less confrontational, and members of indrect cultures to be more explicit; working with parties that are monochronic and polychronic to agree on procedures so that all can talk, feel respected, and not run over or bored; and clarifying what yes and no really mean.

Part Three

Conducting Productive Mediations

Chapter Eight

Beginning the Mediation Session

In this stage of intervention, the mediator assists the negotiators in beginning a productive exchange of information about issues in dispute and, when appropriate, feelings resulting from them. If the parties have been meeting before the mediator's entry, the intermediary may abbreviate some of the component moves of this stage. Nevertheless, most of these moves will appear near the start of the first joint meeting held in the mediator's presence. My discussion of the various moves and strategies mediators use in this stage will assume that the parties have not yet held a joint meeting.

The mediator's major tasks in this phase of intervention parallel those of the negotiators. The mediator wants to:

- Begin establishing a positive tone of trust and common concern
- Externally offer, or assist the parties in developing, a procedure that encourages emotional expression but prevents the destructive expression of emotions
- Externally provide, or assist the parties in developing, a structure for mutual education about their key interests and the issues they would like to discuss
- Develop a structure that enhances the possibility of accurate and productive communication

In Chapter Six, I discussed the general strategy or conceptual plan that mediators pursue when opening negotiations. I will now examine implementation of the plan in more detail.

OPENING STATEMENT BY MEDIATOR

Disputants usually enter negotiations in various states of emotional stress. Argyris (1970) notes that people are more likely to accept change—and negotiation means change—voluntarily if the negotiating climate enhances self-acceptance, a confirmation of personal worth, feelings of essentiality, and a psychological sense of success. Maslow (1968) points out that an individual's safety needs must be met before higher needs can be addressed.

The mediator's first activities in this phase of intervention should set a positive tone and meet the basic needs of the parties for comfort and safety. A mediator accomplishes this nonverbally through the physical arrangement of the parties in the room and verbally with his or her opening statement. The opening statement usually contains about eleven elements:

1. Introduction of the mediator and, if appropriate, the parties
2. Commendation of the willingness of the parties to cooperate and seek a solution to their problems and to address relationship issues
3. Definition of mediation and the mediator's role
4. Statement of impartiality and neutrality (when appropriate)
5. Description of the proposed mediation procedures
6. Explanation of the concept of the caucus (private meetings)
7. Definition of the parameters of confidentiality (when appropriate)
8. Description of logistics, scheduling, and length of meetings
9. Suggestions for behavioral guidelines or ground rules
10. Answers to questions posed by the parties
11. Securing a joint commitment to begin

In Chapter Six, I discussed the general content of the mediator's opening statement. I will now explain how it is presented in practice, using as an example the Singson-Whittamore case presented in Chapter One.

Mediator Introduction

First, the mediator introduces himself or herself and the parties (if applicable) and explains how he or she became the mediator in this negotiation:

Good morning, Dr. Whittamore and Dr. Singson. My name is Rita Montoya, and I have been asked to be your mediator and to assist you in discussing the issues that have brought you to mediation. I work as a mediator for CDR Associates and have a background in helping people work out their own solutions to situations they would like to change.

The mediator, by choosing to refer to herself with a social or professional title such as *Ms.* or *Dr.*, to give her full name, or to use only the first name, sets the tone for the degree of formality in the proceeding.

Affirmation of Willingness to Cooperate

Second, the mediator should commend the willingness of the parties to cooperate and to try mediation to settle their differences:

I would like to congratulate you both for coming here today and trying to reach your own agreement on some issues that may have been hard in the past to discuss. It is an affirmative indication on your part that you want to take responsibility for making your own decisions.

The mediator may want to ask people how they feel (if culturally appropriate), ascertain their emotions through their verbal or nonverbal messages, and acknowledge their emotional condition. The mediator may acknowledge or restate what she sees and hears to test perceptual accuracy and demonstrate that she understands the emotions of the disputants. The point of recognizing emotions here is not to make a therapeutic intervention but to release stress by talking about emotions. Early acknowledgment that disputants are uncomfortable often helps them dissipate tension so that they can relax and focus on the substance of negotiations.

Definition of Mediation and the Mediator's Role

Third, the mediator should define mediation and the mediator's role in dispute resolution. The mediator may have discussed this with each party in prenegotiation interviews, but it is psychologically important for all parties to hear the same information from the mediator in the presence of other disputants. This ensures that everyone has the same information and minimizes the risk of differing interpretations of what the mediator has previously said.

If the parties are extremely tense at the start of negotiations, they may not be able to hear or retain all the mediator's comments. Although this is a drawback to presenting the information at this time, the mediator should still explain to the parties why she is there and what she proposes to do. This can protect the mediator from later charges of having brought the parties together under false pretenses and outlines precisely what the parties can expect from the intervenor. An explanation of mediation and the mediator's role at this stage may also give the mediator leverage later in negotiations, when she can refer to the role definition or procedures presented at the start of the session.

Mediators in the community sector and in interpersonal disputes usually try to explain mediation and the mediator's role in the most informal language possible. Explanations vary considerably, but they usually cover (1) a brief description of what the parties will do during the current session; (2) what a mediator is; (3) what the mediator can do for the parties; and (4) the potential outcome of mediation. For example:

During the next meeting or two, you will be engaging in discussions and searching for a joint solution that will meet your needs and satisfy your interests. We will also be discussing how your mutual relationship, and your individual relationships with other clinic staff, can best be handled so that the current situation does not adversely affect other people, the functioning of the clinic, or the provision of quality services to patients, which both of you mentioned in premediation discussions as being important. My role as mediator will be to help you identify problems or issues that you want to talk about, help you clarify needs that must be met, assist you in developing a problem-solving process that will enable you to reach your goals, keep you focused and on the right track, and generally help you define a new relationship that each of you will find more comfortable and acceptable.

Next, the mediator should describe her authority relationship with the disputants:

As I mentioned to each of you previously, mediation is a voluntary process. You are here because you want to see if you can find solutions to issues that concern you and to discuss your future relationship. My role is to assist you in doing this. I do not have the authority, nor will I attempt, to make decisions for you. I will try to stay out of discussions of specific substance or content. My role is to advise you on procedure, and on how you might best talk about these issues. If you reach an agreement, we (or I) will write it down in the form of a memorandum of understanding. This agreement can become legally binding if it involves issues covered by law, or it may be left as an informal agreement. If you want to make your settlement legally binding, you may want to consult a lawyer at the end of mediation. He or she can draft the agreement and put it into the form of a contract. If you do not reach a settlement, you are free to pursue other means of dispute resolution that you feel are appropriate. You do not lose any rights to go to court if you use mediation and are unable to reach an agreement.

Statement of Impartiality and Neutrality

When acting as an independent mediator, the intermediary should explain that she is impartial in her views and neutral in her relationship to the parties:

> *Before proceeding, I would like to clarify both my position on the issues at hand and what my relationship has been with both of you. During this mediation, I will be impartial toward the substance of issues. I do not have any preconceived biases toward any one solution or toward one of you over the other. My relationship with each of you has consisted of [preconference meetings, business association, a previous advisory role, and so on]. I do not believe that this relationship will jeopardize my capacity to act as an impartial assistant to you in resolving this dispute. If at any time you feel that I am acting in a partial or one-sided manner, please bring this behavior to my attention, and I will try to change it. If at any time you feel that I am not able to remain impartial and am unable to assist you, you may cease negotiations, find another mediator, or pursue another means of settlement.*

In claiming impartiality toward issues and neutrality toward the parties, the mediator should disclose any relationship with one or more disputants that might bias her behavior or raise a question in the minds of the disputants as to whether the mediator can in fact remain impartial while assisting in discussions of the issues at hand. If disputants feel uncomfortable about the mediator's relationship with one or more parties, the mediator's past experience with similar issues, or a known aspect of the mediator's private life (political activity, professional or economic relations, or social affiliations that might jeopardize neutrality), they should have the opportunity to ask questions, obtain clear answers, and select a replacement mediator if necessary.

Disputants may not initially believe a claim of impartiality in a highly polarized conflict. There is a tendency to see the dispute in bipolar terms—"You are either for us or against us"—and anyone not taking a vocal position toward one side or another is suspect. Naturally, the parties will have to see impartial behavior before they believe that a mediator is unbiased in attitude. The goal of the mediator at this point is to gain nominal approval from the parties to proceed with negotiations.

Description of Mediation Procedures

Next, the mediator should describe the procedures to be followed. If she has worked these out with the disputants in the prenegotiation interviews, this description is no more than a reiteration of what has been previously agreed. However, if the mediator has taken the initiative to design negotiation and mediation procedures independently of the parties, she should present the proposal in a way that the parties are most likely to accept. The strategy, of course, must be adjusted to meet the idiosyncrasies of the particular parties. Here is a common description of negotiation procedures:

At this time, I would like to briefly describe the process that I propose you follow to begin the session. This proposal is based on your suggestions in our premeeting discussions. Both of you have a significant amount of information about the situation that you are responding to. Although I have briefly spoken with each of you about these matters, I do not have the detailed understanding that each of you does. I suggest that we begin the discussion today with a brief description from each of you about the situation and issues that brought you to mediation. This will educate all of us about the issues you want to discuss and the interests that are important to you and give us a common perception of the problem. Each of you will have a chance, roughly fifteen to twenty minutes [or other specified time], to present your view of the situation. I request that you not interrupt the other while he is explaining a viewpoint, and that you hold your questions until the end of the presentation. A pencil and a pad have been provided for each of you. I would suggest that you note observations or questions as they arise so that they do not get lost prior to the question-and-answer time.

During your presentations, I may ask some clarifying questions or probe your description so that I can gain a greater understanding of how you perceive the situation. My probing is not to put you on the spot but rather to broaden our mutual understanding of the problem. At the end of each of your presentations, there will be a time for the other person (or parties) to ask questions of clarification. This is not a time to debate the issues, but an opportunity to clarify issues and perceptions about the problem(s) at hand.

At the end of the presentation and questions, we will turn to the other [or next] person [or party] to repeat the process until a representative of each view has had an opportunity to speak. At that point, we will clearly identify both the issues that you would like to discuss in more depth and the interests that you would like to have satisfied. Once we are clear on the interests and have described our task in terms of meeting as many of your individual and joint interests as possible, we will develop some potential solutions and assess whether one or more of these options will meet your needs. Note that your goals will be to develop mutually acceptable options that will address the issues at hand and your current and future relationship. Mine will be to assist you with a process that will help you accomplish this end.

The mediator should clearly explain the stages of the problem-solving process and should take care not to present herself as an authority figure. It is the disputants' process, not the mediator's. The process description is a procedural suggestion, not an order.

Explanation of the Caucus or Private Meetings

Next, the mediator should explain the concept of the caucus with each party:

There may be a need, at some time in the course of our meetings, for each of you to take some time for yourself away from the joint meeting [and confer with other members of your group, if it is a group dispute] or to meet with me individually as a mediator. This type of break or meeting is not unusual. It allows you time to refocus and reflect on your short-term and long-term goals, handle strong emotions, explore options or proposals, gather your facts to develop new settlement options, or reach a consensus within your group [if applicable]. At times, I may call such a meeting, but you may initiate one also. If I call a separate meeting, it is not to make a deal but to explore issues that might be more comfortable for you to discuss in private. What is discussed in these separate meetings will be considered by me to be confidential. I will not reveal what we have talked about with the other party [or parties] unless you instruct me to do so.

Little more is said about caucuses at this time because in some situations the thought of private meetings may make one or more of the parties uncomfortable. Disputants often fear a clandestine deal or coalition between the other party and the mediator. I will explain the use of caucuses in more detail in Chapter Fifteen.

Definition of Confidentiality Parameters

At this point, the mediator should describe her understanding of the confidential nature of the negotiation session. Confidentiality, though often considered to be both an important aspect and indeed a functional necessity of mediation, is not universally guaranteed or necessary. Some states in the United States make legal guarantees of confidentiality between disputants and mediator (Freedman, Haile, and Bookstaff, 1985; Comeau, 1982; Folberg and Taylor, 1984). Other states do not provide for confidentiality and on occasion may request data or subpoena mediators to testify in postmediation court proceedings if the parties have failed to reach an agreement. Mediators should describe the limits of confidentiality as it is provided for in their state or agency so that disputants know the limits of their privacy. Here is an example of a statement concerning confidentiality:

These sessions will be considered by me to be confidential in that I will not discuss them publicly with any person not involved in this dispute. I will attempt to maintain this confidentiality to the best of my ability. On occasion, I may want to discuss this problem confidentially with a colleague so that I may gain greater insight into the conflict. I request that you grant me this privilege as it will enable me to better assist you in reaching an agreement. If I do so, I will not use either of your names in describing the situation.

At this point, some mediators ask parties to sign a confidentiality statement or a waiver and consent form (see Resource B) designed to protect the mediator from a future subpoena demanding either an appearance in court or the presentation of her notes as evidence in a lawsuit.

Description of Logistics

The mediator should now describe any relevant logistics: the time schedule for the entire process, the length of sessions, and note taking. The mediator often estimates how much time will be necessary to settle the dispute. Parties need to know this in order to assess the costs and benefits of mediated negotiations. An initial commitment should be gained from the parties for allotting a specific period of time to the first session. Later meeting dates and times can be established and defined as needed. Some mediators in complicated cases have obtained a time commitment for several sessions, as such cases require more time for data collection and for educating the parties about the issues in dispute. It may also take several sessions to achieve any substantive progress or to lower the psychological barriers to settlement.

The mediator should seek permission from the parties to take notes, explaining that the notes are for her own reference and that they will remain confidential. The notes are not an official transcript of the meeting but might at a later time be used to construct a written memorandum of understanding or a settlement document.

Suggestions for Behavioral Guidelines

At this time, the mediator should shift her focus to behavioral guidelines that will facilitate an orderly discussion. Guidelines that mediators may suggest include procedures to handle interruptions, agreements about the role of witnesses and relationships with the press, conditions for smoking, identification of those with whom disputants may discuss negotiations, delineation of what can or should be disclosed by the parties, and so on:

At this point, I would like to suggest several procedural guidelines that other negotiators have found helpful in their discussions. I would like to suggest that each of you have some uninterrupted time to talk. If one of you has a question about what is said, I request that you hold it until the question period. If you agree to this procedure, I request your permission to hold you to it. Is this acceptable? Do you have other guidelines that might help you discuss more productively?

Some mediators who wish to establish behavioral guidelines for negotiations list the rules under which they will work and are inflexible on changing them, whereas others ask the disputants to identify and generate their own guidelines to aid them in holding productive discussions. The latter strategy is a first step toward making mutual procedural decisions and developing habits of agreement.

There is clearly no one way to establish behavioral guidelines. In tense situations, disputants may need the mediator to be more directive, whereas in less polarized disputes, the parties themselves may be in total control. Mediators, in establishing guidelines, should be careful not to use authoritarian or command-ridden language. Terms such as *rules* or *terms for negotiation* or even *behavioral ground rules,* which imply regulations that are being forced on the group, should generally be avoided. Noncommanding terms such as *guidelines* or *suggestions for procedure* are often more acceptable to the parties and avoid putting the mediator in an authoritarian position. Once guidelines are established, the mediator should secure an agreement that she will be empowered to enforce the agreed terms or procedure.

Answers to Questions

The mediator is now nearing the end of her opening statement. At this point, she should answer any questions that the parties may have about the procedure to be followed. Questions should be answered to the satisfaction of the disputants before proceeding further. Lack of understanding by a disputant or dissatisfaction with a mediator's answer may lead to a decreased commitment to the process or later resistance.

Commitment to Begin Mediation

Gaining a commitment to begin is the mediator's last move before turning the session over to the parties. The mediator's concluding remarks should outline what has been discussed, set the information-sharing process in motion in a positive way, and motivate the parties to begin discussing their issues. Here is a sample statement concerning commitment and consent:

If there are no more questions about the process, I suggest that we are ready to move on to discuss the issues at hand. It is my understanding that you are both [or all] here voluntarily, and that you are committed to bargain in good faith, explore and develop settlement options that will be mutually acceptable, and to try to achieve a settlement. I also assume that your discussions will help redefine your relationships. We will explore ways that they can be improved if there are to be ongoing relationships, and if not how to end them with as much respect and comfort as possible. Are you ready to begin?

After gaining either verbal or nonverbal assent, the mediator should turn the session over to the disputants.

OPENING STATEMENTS BY PARTIES

Parties in dispute generally start with opening statements of their own. These statements are usually designed to outline their substantive interests, establish a bargaining procedure, and build rapport with the other side.

Disputants enter negotiations with a variety of levels of information about their own and other parties' issues and preferred solutions. In some disputes, issues and outcome possibilities may be very clear, and negotiators will have to spend little time exploring details of contested issues. In other conflicts, the parties may lack information on a number of dimensions.

Young (1972, p. 57) notes that at the beginning of negotiations, a negotiator may be unclear about:

- "The basic issue(s) at stake"
- The "range of alternative choices or strategies" available
- The solutions that will best meet his or her interests or needs
- The number and identity of people who should be involved in the negotiations (or whom they will affect)
- The way that other negotiators will make decisions

The degree of clarity at the start of negotiations varies greatly. At one end of the spectrum are disputant relationships that are very ill defined. At the other are situations in which strategies, issues, options, and potential outcomes are well known to all negotiators.

Parties use opening statements to present and test their views and assumptions at the onset of negotiations.

Mediators should be familiar with the variety of ways in which parties make opening statements so that they are ready to respond. Parties may open negotiations by focusing on substantive issues, negotiation procedures, or moves designed to improve the psychological conditions of disputants.

Openings Focused on Substance

The most common (but not necessarily the most effective) way to open negotiations is to focus immediately on the substantive issues of the dispute. In this approach, the negotiator usually selects several variables—the history of the problem, the reasons for seeking change, the issues, and possibly interests or positions—and orders them in a way that will have the maximum positive effect on the opposing party or parties. Moore (1982b) and Lincoln (1981) list possible combinations:

• *Focus on history, need, and position.* This combination is quite common in many situations and cultures. The negotiator reviews the background of the dispute, outlines how the status quo has caused damage, tells why change is needed, and then proceeds to detail an opening position that he or she feels would solve the problem. This type of opening frequently forces the parties into hard positional bargaining. Singson might use this approach for opening and detail the history of the Whittamores' coming to the clinic, the legal basis for their contract, and a statement that the contract should be enforced.

• *Focus on issues.* The negotiator may dispense with the history of the problem and proceed directly to a discussion of the issues. The issues may be presented in several ways:

• They may be left to each side to identify through a verbal presentation of the development of the dispute.
• They may be outlined by the negotiator in the form of a list that presents the most important issues first, indicating which items deserve the most attention.
• They may be outlined by the negotiator in an order that places simple and small issues first.

- They may be presented in random order so that the parties may later jointly organize them.
- They may be presented in an exhaustive manner that includes the stated or expected issues of the other side—an approach that demonstrates an interest in the opponent's viewpoint.

Whittamore might take the last approach to opening and list all of the issues that he wants to discuss, as he wants Singson to be aware of all the potential ramifications of the latter's actions.

- *Focus on merit.* In this approach, the negotiator tries to educate the other party about the need for change without disclosing or proposing a position. The major assumption behind this strategy is that if a party can make a convincing case that his or her situation is intolerable and that change is needed, it will be easier to reach an agreement later on a particular solution.

- *Focus on interests.* In this strategy, the negotiator discusses the interests or needs he or she seeks to have satisfied through negotiation. By focusing on interests instead of positions, the groundwork is prepared, but not guaranteed, for possible interest-based negotiations. This approach could be taken by either or both negotiators on their own initiative but might also be initiated by a suggestion from the mediator.

- *Focus on nonnegotiable position.* In cases in which parties are extremely polarized or feel that they have little room for bargaining, the negotiator may dispense with the history of a conflict and the issues involved and present an extreme position instead. This position may or may not be reasonable or negotiable. The tactic can often stalemate negotiations and may force parties to pursue other means of dispute resolution, such as litigation or direct action. If either of the parties in the Whittamore-Singson dispute took this approach, the mediator would probably have to caucus and help him back off of his initial position.

Openings Focused on Procedure

Another way of opening negotiations, which is not as common as substantive openings, is to focus on the negotiation procedure. With this strategy, the time in which the disputants focus on behavioral guidelines is expanded into an extended discussion of procedural steps that the parties will take to resolve their dispute. As discussed in Moore (1982b) and Lincoln (1981), advantages to opening negotiations in this way are that such a focus:

- Presents a jointly developed sequence for the negotiation to which all parties are committed
- Allows the parties to practice making decisions as a team
- Provides information about the behavior, attitudes, and trustworthiness of other parties
- Allows parties to practice making agreements on problems that are neither substantively important nor as emotionally charged as the issues in dispute
- Creates an opportunity to build "habits" of agreement
- Demonstrates that agreement is possible and that the situation is not hopeless

Central areas of procedure in which parties may make agreements include these (Moore, 1982b; Lincoln, 1981):

- How an agenda will be developed
- Negotiation procedures to be followed
- Time frame and schedule for sessions, including beginning and ending times
- How information will be shared among disputants
- Information sharing procedures with constituents or nonparticipating parties
- How legal rights and administrative mandates will be recognized and protected
- Parties' relationships with lawyers
- Parties' relationships with media
- Acceptable and unacceptable behavior (for example, respect for values, personal attacks, attribution of motivation, emotional displays, attitudes toward win-lose solutions)
- How commitment to the procedure and to potential agreements will be maintained
- Determination of participants
- Role of substitutes and observers
- Role of task forces or small work groups

- Size of negotiating teams
- Location of meeting sites
- Maintenance of meeting records
- How procedural and substantive agreements will be enforced

Mediators sometimes encourage negotiators, implicitly or explicitly, to focus on procedural agreements before delving into substance. This is done if the intervenor feels that parties need to build trust or experience in working with one another or would benefit from a more extensive set of procedural guidelines. Parties occasionally begin with this type of opening on their own.

Opening Focused on the Relationships of Disputants

In formal negotiations, the opening that is focused on the psychological conditions of disputants is not as common as substantive or procedural openings. It is more frequently observed in transformative mediation (Bush and Folger, 1994), a form of third-party consultation practiced by organization development specialists (Blake and Mouton, 1984) and by social scientists working in international peace making (Rothman, 1992; Kelman, 1991; Burton, 1969; Fisher, 1982; Walton, 1969).

This approach aims to improve the relationship of the disputants before, or as a major element in, discussions of substantive issues or procedure. In its most informal mode, some of the conciliation techniques mentioned in Chapter Seven may be initiated. If the process is conducted more formally, experiences may be planned in which disputants engage in unstructured social activities or take field trips that focus on the topic under discussion, thereby gaining an opportunity to establish and build personal connections. Other means of drawing disputants closer are general personal-sharing groups (Dubois and Mew, 1963), focused-topic discussion groups (Levinson, 1954; Levinson and Schermerhorn, 1951), intergroup training laboratories (Blake and Mouton, 1984), joint-skill training (Hunter and McKersie, 1992), discussions oriented toward mutual recognition and empowerment (Bush and Folger, 1994), and performance of common tasks unrelated to the issues in dispute (Fisher, 1978). For example, in one mediation of a public policy dispute, the mediators arranged for all parties to meet the night before the opening session for a casual dinner. The negotiators rode atop a double-decker bus to a Mexican restaurant, where they ate, drank, and came to know each other as individuals and not representatives of an interest group. In another dispute involving timber cutting on national forest land, the parties participated in a weekend retreat in which they hiked on land earmarked for a timber harvest. The hike built interpersonal relationships and raised awareness of the land involved in the dispute.

Mediators in marital disputes occasionally spend time before formal divorce negotiations discussing and processing courtship and the beginning, development, and decline of the marriage (Milne, 1981). It is argued that this procedure helps the couple adjust to the fact that they are divorcing.

In their attempts to build more flexible and open attitudes in disputants, mediators often initiate informal moves to promote conciliation. They might encourage active listening, affirmation of some quality of a party that is not related to the issues in conflict, a communication structure that promotes safety, or a deliberate focus on feelings.

Choice of Opening

The choice to focus on substance, process, or the psychological conditions of the disputants depends on:

- The type of dispute
- The abilities of the disputants to focus on substantive issues
- The level of emotional intensity of disputants
- The degree of authority the disputants have given to the mediator to design and regulate the process of the meeting and opening procedures or statements
- The internal and external pressures that are on the negotiators to settle promptly

The mediator should work with the parties to focus on an opening process that will be most successful for them. If the internal or external pressures to reach agreement are high or moderate and emotional tensions are high, the mediator will usually encourage procedural or psychological openings. Parties will often accept this emphasis if they can be convinced that such moves will later enhance the possibility of reaching a substantive settlement.

Transition to Parties' Opening Statements

The mediator now shifts from her opening statement to a focus on the disputants with a transition statement. Here is a sample transition statement from the Singson-Whittamore case in which the mediator proposes a focus on substance:

> *At this time, I propose that we move into a discussion of the situation that brought you to mediation.* [The mediator turns to the party that she has previously decided should begin presenting first.] *Dr. Whittamore, will you please begin by describing the situation as you see it? Please include some of the historical background of the problem, the issues that you would like to discuss, and the interests or needs you want to have satisfied. At this point, it will be helpful not to identify specific solutions but to merely focus on defining the problem.*

The mediator now turns the session over to the first party, who begins his opening statement.

FACILITATION OF COMMUNICATION AND INFORMATION EXCHANGE

The most critical task for disputants making opening statements is to maximize accurate information exchange. They may be hindered in doing so by a number of factors:

- Excessive posturing
- Extreme demands designed to signal how intensely the parties feel about the issues or how much they want the other party or party to move
- Jumbled or unstructured communication
- Inaccurate listening
- Intense emotional outbursts
- Total dysfunction of one or more parties

The mediator's main tasks, therefore, are to help the parties communicate about substantive issues in dispute and positive aspects of their relationship and minimize the psychological damage resulting from emotional exchanges. To facilitate this communication, mediators use a variety of communication techniques, some of which were described in Chapters Five and Seven. Additional communication techniques are:

Restatement. The mediator listens to what has been said and feeds back the content to the party in the party's own words.

Paraphrase. The mediator listens to what has been said and restates the content back to the party using different words that have the same meaning as the original statement. This is often called reframing.

Active listening. The mediator decodes a spoken message and then feeds back to the speaker the emotions of the message. This is commonly used in conciliation.

Summarization. The mediator condenses the message of a speaker.

Expansion. The mediator receives a message, feeds it back to the listener in an expanded and elaborated form, and then checks to verify accurate perception.

Ordering. The mediator helps a speaker order ideas into some form of sequence (historical, size, importance, amount, and so on).

Grouping. The mediator helps a speaker identify common ideas or issues and combine them into logical units.

Structuring. The mediator assists a speaker in organizing and arranging his or her thoughts and speech into a coherent message.

Separating or fractionating. The mediator divides an idea or an issue into smaller component parts.

Generalization. The mediator identifies general points or principles in a speaker's presentation.

Probing questions. The mediator asks either open-ended or focused questions to encourage a speaker to elaborate on an idea.

Questions of clarification. The mediator asks questions to obtain clarification of particular points.

Mediators use these communication tools to help parties communicate more accurately with each other. Ideally, the parties use them too. Mediators may encourage them to do so by explaining how the tools are used and by commending parties whenever they apply them.

CREATION OF A POSITIVE EMOTIONAL CLIMATE

In addition to facilitating communication, the mediator often must create an emotional climate conducive to clear communication and joint problem solving. Interventions related to promoting a positive emotional climate include:

- Preventing interruptions or verbal attacks
- Encouraging parties to focus on the problem and not on each other
- Translating value-laden or judgmental language of disputants into less emotionally charged language
- Affirming clear descriptions or statements, procedural suggestions, or gestures of good faith while not taking sides on substantive issues
- Accepting the expression of feelings and being empathic, though not taking sides
- Reminding parties about behavioral guidelines that they have established
- Defusing specific threats by restating them in terms of general pressure to change
- Intervening to prevent conflict escalation

CULTURAL VARIATIONS

The cultural context—professional, educational, ethnic, gender, and national—may significantly influence the process of beginning the mediation process. It is important for an intermediary to start the discussions in a manner that will be both culturally appropriate and acceptable to the parties. Although it is impossible to describe the range of procedures that are used in this stage, there are some approaches that appear quite frequently.

In situations and cultures in which social network mediators play a predominant role, more time may be allocated at the beginning of the mediation session for informal conversation, which is often focused on building connections between the mediator and the parties and between the parties themselves. This time helps to establish or reestablish the relationship between the parties and may also identify mutual bonds or obligations that will encourage settlement. In some cultures, such as many in Latin America and the Middle East, the opening of mediation or negotiations is also accompanied by the consumption of a beverage (and in other cultures, food), which may be provided by the mediator. For example, drinking tea is common in the Middle East, Iran, Pakistan, India, Sri Lanka, and in many societies in Africa (Senger, 2002). In a number of cultures, such as China, Japan, and Indonesia, this opening or social phase of the mediation may actually be separated in time and space from the later focus on substantive issue identification and problem solving (Graham and Sano, 1984).

In situations where the mediator is in a hierarchical relationship with the parties, or the parties are in a vertical relationship with each other, the opening statement and corresponding process may be more formal and emphasize the authority of the mediator, the superior-subordinate relationship of the parties to the intermediary, and the differences between the parties themselves. This formality may be seen as a means of leveraging the parties toward an agreement. In some cultures, such an approach may also be necessary to demonstrate respect for the positions of the parties. Although this may go against norms of more egalitarian societies, it is both acceptable and expected in more hierarchically organized cultures.

The level of detail in which the process and behavioral ground rules are spelled out also varies across cultures. In high-context and fairly homogeneous cultures, where members have many common and unspoken assumptions about how the negotiation process will be conducted, the degree of process explicitness will be less than in low-context cultures composed of members from diverse backgrounds, where parties expect and require detailed descriptions of procedures (Hall and Hall, 1987). For example, intermediaries in Japan, a high-context society, may be less procedurally explicit than U.S., Canadian, or Australian mediators, who often work in multicultural settings. In intercultural mediations, the mediator will have to decide how explicit he or she needs to be to adequately inform the parties about how they will proceed.

Patterns of communication may also differ across cultures. Some cultures, such as the majority culture of the United States, are monochronic (as described in Chapter Seven), in that events or activities within a human group occur one at time (Hall, 1983). One person talks and the other listens. A number of other cultures, such as many found around the Mediterranean, are polychronic, in that multiple activities and conversations may occur at once. These communication patterns can significantly affect the type of dialogue that occurs between the mediator and the parties during the opening statement, as well as the discussion or argumentation between the parties. What for one culture appears to be rudeness, interruption, and poor listening will be acceptable overlapping discussion in another. Mediators may need to adjust their communication patterns when working within or between monochronic and polychronic cultures by adopting or adapting to the culture of the parties, by openly discussing and reaching an agreement on communication norms that will be used in the session, or by switching cultures as different parties are related to.

TRANSITION TO THE NEXT STAGE

If the parties and the mediator have communicated successfully and built some positive feelings between them in this first stage of joint meetings, the groundwork for productive future dialogue has been established. This stage terminates as soon as the parties or the mediator focuses on building an agenda or on a particular issue or sphere of discussion and moves to explore it in depth. Shifts between stages of negotiations are often the most difficult for parties and mediators (Wildau, 1987). As we move to the next chapters, we will explore how mediators can help smooth these transitions and promote productive problem solving.

Chapter Nine

Defining Issues and Setting an Agenda

Negotiation and mediation are problem-solving processes, but they are also, at least potentially, opportunities for establishing, defining, building, or terminating relationships. Both the problem-solving and the relationship-defining aspects of mediation occur in the context of discussing issues and interests that may be substantive, procedural, or psychological in nature. It is generally helpful to both the parties and the mediator if, early in the negotiations, some if not all of the key issues or topics to be addressed are identified, so that the parties and the intermediary can develop an effective process for discussing them.

If parties are to move toward a settlement of their differences, they must shift procedurally from contention to cooperative interaction. Building a mutually acceptable agenda can help them achieve this goal. The three critical tasks negotiators and mediators must accomplish in this stage are to (1) identify broad topic areas of concern to the parties, (2) agree on the subtopics or issues that will be discussed, and (3) determine the sequence for discussion of the topics or issues. Coordinated activity by negotiators at this point in the process does not mean that they agree substantively. *Coordination* refers solely to an agreement on the procedure that will be used to handle a topic area or particular issues.

Several variables influence how rapidly and how easily this stage in negotiations can be dealt with:

• The number and complexity of issues involved

- The negotiators' understanding of the conflict's substantive matter
- The clarity of presentation by the parties of each topic or issue
- The capacity of the negotiators to recognize a distinct topic area or issue when it is presented
- The extent of parties' power to persuade other negotiators to accept a topic or issue for inclusion on the agenda
- The degree of psychological or other resistance to collaboration exhibited by one or more parties

Mediators who enter a dispute before topics and issues have been identified and the agenda has been drawn up can help the parties complete these tasks. At this stage, the mediator and the negotiators have similar procedural goals.

TOPIC AREAS AND ISSUES

The content of negotiation varies considerably in terms of the degree of specificity or conceptual definition of topics under discussion. For example, in a community dispute between a group of neighbors and a social service organization that plans to site a health clinic for low-income clients in the group's middle-class neighborhood, the parties may have some conceptual boundaries for the dispute. The neighbors, who oppose siting the clinic in the neighborhood, might define the boundaries of the discussion as being whether the facility should be sited there at all, what the process for decision making will be, and how their voices can be heard and respected by those in power who will ultimately decide the question. The clinic staff, on the other hand, are probably not concerned with discussing *whether* the facility should be sited in the neighborhood. They want to discuss *how* a building can be leased, how to lower the resistance they are encountering, how to begin to provide services to a clientele in need (and make other community members see this need), and how to establish a positive relationship with the neighbors of the clinic that will enable them to carry out their medical goals. If a representative of each group were asked to identify what the context and range of the negotiations should be, each would answer differently. The neighbors' spokesperson would cite a general topic area: *whether* the clinic should be built. The representative of the clinic staff, however, would focus the discussion on issues related to *how* the clinic could be located in the neighborhood, with community concerns and interests taken into consideration.

The degree of specificity of topic areas or issues that the parties want to discuss varies, of course, from dispute to dispute. Some conflicts begin with a disagreement over a particular point and then move from the specific issue to a more general level of contention, whereas others begin with very general topics of disagreement and gradually become more specific. More will be said about these two dynamics in Chapter Eleven, when we consider what problem-solving technique should be applied to handle a dispute.

Aside from the level of specificity of the dispute, a second kind of distinction can be made: issues can be classified as consensual (interest-based) and dissensual (value-based; Aubert, 1963).

Consensual or Interest-Based Conflict

Conflicts of interest usually exist in conditions of perceived or actual scarcity in which one or more parties believe that gains for one party may mean a loss for another. Conflicts of interest are often referred to as "competitive cooperation," in that the disputants are collaborating to compete for potentially the same set of benefits.

Because there are numerous types of interests that any given party may have in a dispute, there is often great latitude in trading satisfaction of one set of interests for another so that all parties can reach and accept a settlement.

Dissensual or Value-Based Conflict

In contrast to conflicts of interest in which a consensus exists between parties about competition for the desired end result, or in which enough differing interests exist to facilitate a trading process to minimize loss on all sides, dissensual conflicts are based on differences in values. Value disputes focus on such issues as guilt and innocence, what norms should prevail in a social relationship, what facts should be considered valid, what beliefs are correct, who merits what, and what principles should guide decision makers. Disputes over whether to build a shelter for the homeless in a middle-class neighborhood, whether to cut down an irreplaceable old growth forest, whether divorcing parents should invite new lovers over when the children live at home, or whether a party should be punished for committing a theft (as opposed to being compelled to make restitution) are generally disputes over values.

Values disputes are extremely difficult to resolve, and intermediaries are usually very careful when working with them to ensure that their actions do not increase the parties' intransigence and adherence to hard-line positions. More will be said about how to manage these difficult conflicts in Chapter Fifteen.

IDENTIFYING AND FRAMING ISSUES

In the process of defining the parameters of a dispute, the parties and the mediator engage in a preliminary definition of topic areas and issues that will be the focus of future negotiations. This process has been referred to variously as *framing* or *reframing* (Watzlawick, 1978; Mayer, 2000), *characterizing* (Stulberg, 1981a), *reconceptualizing*, or *redefining* (Boulding, 1962; Sawyer and Guetzkow, 1965) the issues in dispute. Before exploring the moves of framing or reframing a situation, I will briefly explain how parties arrive at their viewpoint of the conflict.

Each disputant comes to the conflict with his or her own individual and subjective picture of what issues are in dispute and what the basis of conflict is (Berger and Luckmann, 1967). Watzlawick (1978, p. 119) describes the individual's condition: "Let us remember: We never deal with reality *per se*, but rather with *images* of reality—that is, with interpretations. Although the number of potentially possible interpretations is very large, our world image usually permits us to see only one—and this *one* therefore appears to be the only possible, reasonable, permitted view. Furthermore, this one interpretation also suggests only one possible, reasonable, and permitted solution."

Framing is summed up in the familiar saying about the difference between an optimist and a pessimist: "The optimist says of a bottle that it is half full; the pessimist sees it as half empty. The same bottle and the same quantity of wine—in other words, the same first-order reality—but two very different world images, creating two very different (second-order) realities" (Watzlawick, 1978, p. 119).

More in line with our focus is the classic dispute in child custody over which parent will receive legal custody of a child. Both parents want to ensure that they will have a high level of involvement in their child's life. They, and in many cases the judicial system, often define the resolution procedure as a court decision determining who can legally possess the child. There are, however, alternative ways that these parent-parent and parent-child relationships can be framed. If, for example, the struggle over legal custody is defined in terms of maximizing the parent-child relationship, and the concept of legal custody or ownership of the child is reframed in terms of parental rights and responsibilities toward their offspring, the bipolar struggle with only a win-lose outcome is transformed into a more complex issue with multiple variables that may be traded off one against another (Haynes, 1981; Ricci, 1980). By reframing how a dispute is seen and defined by the parties, the parties and the mediator can open the door to more collaborative and mutually satisfactory solutions.

For example, in the Singson-Whittamore case, Singson may frame the problem as "how to enforce the terms of the contract and determine the amount of penalty Whittamore must pay for violating the terms of the agreement." Whittamore might frame the dispute thus: "What is the least amount of compensation I must pay to the clinic that will enable me to practice medicine in the town where my children live?" The mediator, after exploring the issues and interests with the parties, might assist them in reframing the problem in several ways: "How can the clinic and Dr. Whittamore have a mutually beneficial future relationship?" or "If compensation is to be paid so that Whittamore can stay in town, how might fair and objective standards be identified that could guide this calculation?" or "Are there ways that allow Whittamore to achieve the separation and distance he wants from his wife, yet still continue a working relationship with the clinic?"

VARIABLES IN FRAMING AND REFRAMING ISSUES

When negotiators frame issues in a way that will facilitate productive problem solving, the mediator may be merely an interested observer. However, some disputes become deadlocked because disputants have not discovered a mutually acceptable definition or framing of the issues that will allow them to cooperate. At this point, the mediator's intervention can be invaluable. The mediator may either frame the issues before the parties restrict themselves by a particular definition or may assist the parties in reframing their issues by moving them away from an unproductive definition toward one that will lead to successful problem solving. It should be noted that framing and reframing, by either the parties or the intermediary, may (and often does) happen throughout the negotiation process.

When taking the definition of issues put forth by one or more parties and reframing it in terms that are subjectively acceptable to all disputants, the mediator should consider (1) the meaning or essence of truth that is contained in the framing of a viewpoint, problem, or issue, which must be recognized and preserved in the reframing; (2) the level of reframing needed; (3) the potential need for reframing issues, positions, and interests: (4) techniques for reframing value-related issues; (5) the explicitness and timing of reframing; and (6) the appropriate language or syntax used in redefining the situation.

Reframing and Meaning

Every framing of a conflict situation, problem, issue, position, or interest has some kernel of the truth as the advocating party sees it. "Even in the most hostile, negative presentation of an issue, there is information about a person's concerns and attitudes that can be useful in moving the resolution process forward. Similarly, even in the most collaborative-sounding presentations, there are challenges to be faced in clarifying and addressing key concerns" (Mayer, 2000, p. 113). The essence of reframing, whether by a party or mediator, is to clarify and uncover the essence of the meaning, needs, interests, or concerns from an unproductive framing and present it in a new way so that it can be more easily addressed and handled by the parties.

Levels of Framing

Mayer (2000) notes that there are three levels of reframing: detoxification, definitional, and metaphorical reframing. Detoxification framing refers to changing the verbal presentation of a comment, idea, or proposal to remove toxic judgmental, derogatory, and negative attributions, negative emotions, or extreme positions. This often means changing wording or syntax. Reframing toxic language to make it more neutral while still maintaining the essence of feelings or underlying interests or needs can help both the presenter of the initial framing and its recipient get past the strong emotions or perceived negative language that may inhibit further discussions. Let's look at a reframe of toxic emotional language. The first party says of another, "You must be a moron to consider that kind of solution. It would have been acceptable twenty years ago, but times have changed. We have been damaged and ground down by your foolishness for years!" The reframe might be, "You would like to consider a wider range of solutions than the one that has been proposed because the circumstances that you are now facing are different than in the past, and the past impact on you may also need to be factored in."

Definitional reframing refers to changing the conceptualization of a conflict or situation to make it easier to conduct collaborative problem solving. This may involve defining the problem in a way that all parties can subscribe to. For example, in a debtor-creditor dispute a bank, represented by Ms. Ross, may define the problem as "getting paid back the full amount due now, or foreclosure will follow." A farmer, Mr. Brubaker, who owes the creditor, may define the problem as "how to get the creditor off my back, and keep on farming on the land that has been in my family for three generations." Neither of these frames will probably be acceptable to the other. The mediator, after carefully examining the underlying interests of the parties, might reframe the problem in this way: "What we are looking for is a way that the bank can be paid back the money it has loaned and not have to get into land ownership, which is not its primary business; and at the same time try to find ways to schedule the repayment of the loan in a way that repayment is possible, and make the farm a viable operation so that Mr. Brubaker can continue the family tradition and preserve his lifestyle." The reframe, which is also a joint problem-solving statement, redefines the problem that the parties are working on in a jointly acceptable way.

Metaphoric reframing "attempts to find a new or altered metaphor for describing the situation or concept, thus changing the way in which it is viewed. Sometimes this means finding a metaphor that all parties can use or translating one party's metaphor into a metaphor recognized by the other party" (Mayer, 2000, p. 136). For example, negotiation is described by one party as a competitive "game" in which participants are either a jerk or a sucker, and no negotiator wants to be "a sucker." The other party described negotiations as being dropped into an ocean without a life jacket, with the potential for going down and drowning. Looking at these two apparently contradictory metaphors, the mediator might reframe the problem in this way: "Survival is important to you both. Neither of you wants to be taken advantage of by the other and lose. Perhaps we need to imagine this situation as both of you being in a boat that is leaking. In order to survive, you will need both of your strengths to bail. This not an game or issue of who is a jerk or a sucker, but how you will both be survivors and come out of this conflict in the best shape possible." The reframing takes elements of both of the parties' metaphors and transforms them into a new joint definition of the problem.

Reframing Issues, Positions, and Interests

The act of reframing in itself raises some important questions regarding the mediator's neutrality. The general assumption of mediators when reframing an issue is that they are making such a move "based on some conception (implicit or explicit) of a more constructive or desirable relationship for the original players than the one that they see themselves engaging in at the outset of the interaction. And in this context, the terms 'constructive' and 'desirable' inevitably carry normative content. Be this as it may, mediators constantly redefine the context of disputes in ways that disputants find to be extremely helpful to avoid or overcome impasse" (Young, 1972, p. 59).

In general, reframing issues, positions, and interests is easier than reframing value conflicts over such issues as guilt, rights, or facts. In reframing issues, positions, and interests, mediators often use a technique that expands issues to leave the parties more room to bargain or trade. For example, in a labor-management dispute, the union and management are bargaining to a deadlock over a wage increase. The union negotiators must bring to their constituents some tangible benefits from the negotiations. They have selected salary increases as their goal. The mediator can assist the parties in reframing the issue from the problem of a wage increase to the problem of how the union can obtain multiple benefits that its constituents will see are the result of the negotiations. This reframing of the situation allows the negotiator to look for other means of meeting union needs than obtaining an increase in pay.

Reframing positions requires a careful analysis of position statements put forth by parties and the interests underlying and met by those positions. Sometimes this involves looking for either broad or narrow interests. Shifting from specific interests to more general ones may widen the number of settlement options available.

Occasionally, reframing issues and interests in narrower terms is also effective. For example, consider a case in which several people agreed to purchase together a piece of property that was to be used for cooperative housing. Several months after the purchase, the relationships among the owners deteriorated and one of the partners decided that he wanted his money back. However, this would be possible only by revising the financial contract all the owners had agreed on. The initial issue, stated in the form of a demand, was "I want my money back." The problem as the disputants described it was that one person wanted his money back and was withdrawing from the contract, but the others felt that they could not reimburse him without selling the property. Sale of the property was not acceptable to the other owners. From this either-or situation, the mediator and the parties mutually reframed the issue into smaller, more manageable subissues: How much money? When? In what form? With interest? And so on. The parties were then able to reach agreement on trade-offs for these subissues.

Reframing Value-Related Issues

The difficulty in reframing value conflicts arises from the fact that such issues have a strong tendency to become bipolar, with one side representing right and the other wrong. Disputants place great emphasis on normative judgments, which often make it difficult to compromise and trade, as can be done with interest-related issues. Even proposing such solutions may provoke escalation; People will claim that their "ideals are not for sale" or that one "can't bargain with the truth" (Aubert, 1963).

Mediators accomplish identification and framing of value-based issues in a number of ways: (1) translating value disputes into interest disputes, (2) identifying superordinate goals, or (3) avoidance. I will briefly discuss these approaches here and elaborate on a number of other approaches in Chapter Fifteen when examining strategies for specific kinds of problems.

Pure dissensus in conflicts over values and facts is relatively rare. Usually, value disputes are mixed disputes, in that participants also have some common interests. Mediators who work with value disputes often try to translate values into interests so that the parties have more tangible issues. For example, if a value dispute over who has power or authority can be translated into a conflict over the division of responsibilities, there are some possibilities for compromise based on a formula for a fair division. In a hypothetical case, two employees are rivals for promotion in their organization. There is only one position available at the next grade above their current rank. Both employees want the job and claim to be the better candidate. If it is in the company's interest to satisfy both employees, those responsible may explore how the tasks, authority, and status of the job could be divided between the two equally qualified employees. Thus struggle over who is better becomes moot as each employee is rewarded on the basis of interest.

In a real-life dispute, an association of single-family homeowners was confronting a planning department over construction of multifamily dwellings on the edge of their neighborhood. The single-family homeowners charged that the new construction would change the neighborhood's ambiance and that it would mean an entire shift in lifestyle. On careful examination, lifestyle values were translated into interests: limited noise, no abrupt transitions from single-family to multifamily homes, minimizing the height of new construction to preserve views, and maintaining privacy by avoiding building complexes that overlook the backyards of single-family homes. Given the interests of all parties, a mutually satisfactory development plan was negotiated that met most of the needs described.

A second approach to reframing value disputes is to identify larger superordinate goals with which all parties can identify (Sherif and others, 1961). For example, in a dispute over locating a dam, one party may argue that the proposed construction site damages a pristine wilderness area, whereas the other party argues that it has a mandate to provide water to a nearby city and that the dam allows the party to fulfill contractual obligations. The mediator looks for a superordinate goal to join the parties in a cooperative effort. A consensus might be obtained on two points: the city needs a certain amount of water, and the wilderness is to be protected. The parties can then participate in a joint search for potential sources of water.

The third strategy for managing value-based issues is to avoid identifying or responding to them directly, or to reframe the situation so that parties agree to disagree. Because it is difficult to mediate guilt or innocence, right or wrong, respect or lack of respect, and so on, the mediator may want to avoid these questions entirely and focus only on the components that can be turned toward interest-based bargaining. If enough issues can be solved with interest-based bargaining, the importance of value differences may fade and be dropped from a list of demands or topics for discussion.

Explicit-Implicit Reframing and Timing

To resolve disputes over interests or values, parties must often be explicit about the topic areas that divide them. The degree of explicitness, however, may vary over time because of the dynamics of the negotiation process itself or the conscious strategies of the negotiators or the mediator. The mediator should manage the timing of issue identification so that the parties will be most receptive to the way an issue is framed. Parties are often vague at the start of negotiations about the specifics of issues in dispute. Only through a process of discussion and mutual education can the parties jointly define and make explicit the concrete issues that must be resolved.

One party will often precisely name an issue, only to have another party repeatedly reject it. After several rounds of proposal rejection and exploration, the parties may finally be able to agree to discuss the issue. The final framing of the issues by the parties, or reframing by the mediator, may be identical to the earlier characterizations. The ultimate acceptance of the framing is a result of timing and the psychological readiness of the parties to accept the definition of the situation. This psychological shift often occurs after dialogue or when the neutral intervenor states the framing.

There is research evidence that parties are often willing and able to hear and accept statements worded by the mediator when they are not able to hear or accept an identical statement from another disputant (Rubin and Brown, 1975).

Appropriate Language

One remaining point needs to be covered regarding the framing of issues: the mediator's language. Disputants often use language that is judgmental, positional, and biased toward their subjective view. In joint session, mediators usually try to translate the language of the disputants into more neutral terms to remove bias, positions, and judgment. Thus, when one party says, "That fat slob hasn't paid his rent money for the past two months," the mediator may translate this as "You are upset that you have not received money that you feel is due to you according to the terms of your rental agreement with Mr. Brown." In this case, the judgmental statement that Brown is a slob is dropped, and the implicit demand on Brown is turned into a statement about the landlord's feelings of deprivation and his need for reimbursement. This, after all, is what concerns the landlord. Reframing the problem in this way also makes Brown feel more comfortable with the issue. The focus is no longer on his character but on the landlord's need to be paid.

In identifying and framing issues, mediators should be careful to state the problem clearly, and in a manner that neither favors one side nor makes one party blameworthy. Ideally, the mediator should depersonalize issues and put them outside the relationship between the disputants. The parties can then focus on the topic in a more objective manner (Filley, 1975). Stulberg (1981a) notes that mediators should take great care to avoid "trigger" words or statements that parties may interpret as mediator bias or preconceived judgments as to who is wrong. Many mediators avoid adversarial language, referring to conflicts as *situations* or *problems,* positions as *viewpoints,* parties as *your group,* and negotiations as *discussions* in order to depolarize and neutralize value-laden and conflict-oriented terminology.

There are times, however, when entirely neutral terminology may not be as effective as more partisan language. If, for example, the parties cannot reach an agreement on issues in joint session, the mediator may call a caucus to discuss the problem of issue identification. The mediator may use language more biased toward the interests or values of the particular party in the caucus to influence that party's decision making. He or she may use the same terminology, syntax, and emotion as the party to promote identification between party and mediator, thereby easing the way to agreement on disputed issues. However, mediators should take care that the way they speak in a caucus is not drastically different from the way they speak in joint session. Otherwise, parties may be confused or feel double-crossed by the shift to more neutral language when they return to joint session.

DETERMINING AN AGENDA

The agenda the mediator designs before negotiations, as discussed in Chapter Six, is a rough draft to which new information is added from the opening statements of the parties. The negotiating agenda that disputants ultimately follow should be developed and approved by the parties alone, by the parties in conjunction with the mediator, or by the mediator alone (with the consent of the parties). Once issues have been identified, they must be placed in an order for discussion.

There are at least eight approaches to agenda development in negotiations: (1) ad hoc, (2) simple agenda, (3) alternation of issues, (4) ranking by importance, (5) principled agenda, (6) "easier items first," (7) building-block or contingent agenda, and (8) trade-offs or packaging.

Ad Hoc Development

With ad hoc sequencing, one party proposes that the negotiators discuss an item, the other party or parties concur, and the item is discussed in its entirety until a conclusion has been reached. The parties then mutually agree on another item, and the process is repeated. The parties move through all items in this manner. This model allows flexibility but also permits and opens the possibility of manipulation by parties for placement of agenda items at particularly opportune moments that are in one or another's favor.

Simple Agenda

In the simple-agenda method, issues for negotiation are taken one at a time, in an order prescribed by one or more parties. (Generally, the party proposing the agenda has sequenced the items in a manner that will be advantageous to achieving benefits for himself or herself.) Typically, each issue is addressed and settled separately.

Gulliver (1979) notes that although this may commonly succeed for decision making in committees and conferences, it can rarely work in negotiations. The chief reason is that it attempts to ignore the essential problems of multiple criteria: that issues are often interconnected in the social life of negotiations and that, in any event, they are necessarily interconnected within the specific context of the negotiations in progress. Parties are aware of this and are unwilling to forfeit advantages that might be gained by getting better terms on one issue through concession (or refusal of it) on another. They wish to explore interconnections without the rigidity of a fixed agenda order.

The simple agenda approach encourages stalling and manipulative tactics in order to gain leverage on items that will come up later on the agenda. Gulliver notes that this procedure tends to subvert the ordering almost immediately.

Alternation of Issues

A third model for agenda construction is the alternating-issue approach. In this method, the parties alternate in choosing the topic of discussion. This structural solution allows the parties to proceed and often inhibits development of deadlocks. Gulliver (1979) says that this process rarely works for long, however, because one or more parties invariably insist on breaking the order.

Ranking by Importance

A fourth model of agenda design is for the parties to pick the one or two items that both consider of greatest importance and place them at the head of the agenda (Gulliver, 1979). The assumption is that if they can agree on these items, the less important items will follow suit. This procedure depends, of course, on the ability of the parties to agree on the most important issues and the order in which they will be addressed. There is evidence that this approach is best used when no claims or counterclaims are made or no offense has been alleged, as when parties are attempting to establish a new relationship where only a limited one has existed before.

Principled Agenda

A fifth approach is to define issues in terms of principles or general levels of agreement that will guide the decisions on specific items. The parties jointly establish the principles and then work out in detail how these principles will be applied on specific agenda items (Fisher and Ury, 1981). For example, in negotiations between telephone companies, a public utilities commission, and consumer groups over access charges on interstate phone lines, all parties agreed that the universal telephone service, which would provide access to telephone service to all people regardless of their income, should be maintained. This agreement in principle became the basis for an agenda item in which the negotiators would discuss how universal service could be financed.

The procedure works only under conditions in which the parties are willing and able to negotiate at a high level of generalization or abstraction, and in which they are willing to defer decision making on minor issues until later. This process of approaching a negotiation agenda will be discussed in more detail in Chapter Eleven.

"Easier Items First"

A sixth method of agenda formation is to identify issues on which the parties will most likely reach agreement and that will probably not take long to discuss and settle. These issues are often small, self-contained, less emotion-laden, and not symbolic in comparison with other topics that might be discussed. Some of these simple items may be placed at the beginning of the agenda and others alternated with more difficult items to (1) ensure agreement on some issues early in negotiations; (2) promote a habit of agreement; (3) create a number of agreements that the parties will be reluctant to lose as the result of an impasse later on; and (4) produce agenda items that can be deferred, traded, or dropped, after they have been discussed, as a demonstration of good faith.

Naturally, this strategy is contingent on the ability of the parties to mutually identify simple issues. This is usually accomplished by trial and error, or the mediator may ask parties to identify issues on which they feel ready agreement may be achieved with little effort.

Building-Block or Contingent Agenda

A seventh method of agenda construction is the building-block approach. In this process, a party or parties identify which agreements must be made first because the issues involved lay the groundwork or foundation for later decisions. Agenda sequencing depends on which agreements are contingent on previous ones. Contingency may be based on principles, time, payment schedules, and so on. This approach, although fairly complicated and dependent on a high degree of party coordination, does prevent deadlocks that would be due to incorrect sequencing of issues. It will be discussed in more detail in Chapter Eleven.

Trade-Offs or Packaging

The final approach to agenda formation is issue trading or packaging. Parties in dispute are sometimes reluctant to settle agenda items one at a time for fear that they will lose leverage on one item if they have settled another one earlier. To avoid this problem, parties may want to link and formulate combinations of issues for discussion. This means that they negotiate a number of issues simultaneously. Satisfaction of interests may later be traded in such a way that equivalence of exchange is attained.

Packaging a proposal containing multiple-issue solutions has advantages as an agenda-forming tool: it demonstrates a willingness to trade satisfaction of issues and interests and meet the other party's needs; it may induce an opponent to generate alternative packages; it demonstrates that some concessions are possible if they are linked with specific gains; and it can eliminate some of the difficulty, at least for one party, of producing settlement options for individual or a combination of issues. However, a package does have drawbacks. It may be seen as a way of forcing an unfavorable settlement or denying a party the chance to participate in consensus or settlement building. A way to circumvent these drawbacks is to present a series of small packages for consideration that are not as comprehensive and are less likely to produce resistance.

PROCEDURAL ASSISTANCE FROM THE MEDIATOR

All of these agenda development tasks can be initiated by one or more disputing parties or the mediator. Because reaching an agreement on an agenda requires coordination between parties that they may not be able to achieve on their own, the mediator may need to suggest a procedure that in his or her judgment will best facilitate resolution of disagreement over topics to be discussed, framing, or sequencing.

If the parties are moving toward a procedure for agenda formation that the mediator feels will be unproductive, he or she should either suggest an alternative method, outlining the basis of its superiority over the one chosen by the parties; or remain quiet, allowing the parties to negotiate and reach an impasse, and then intervene when they are more motivated to accept the mediator's advice. Selecting the latter strategy must be carefully weighed against the potential damage to the parties' relationship from failure to reach procedural agreement on the agenda.

It is important that the mediator, in making suggestions about the agenda, avoid being perceived as forcing a specific process or sequence on the parties (Fisch, Weakland, and Segal, 1982). This situation can only result in loss of credibility, decreased acceptability, more disputant resistance, and less effective later interventions.

CULTURAL APPROACHES

The prevailing culture may significantly influence the process of defining issues and setting an agenda; it is important for an intermediary to develop procedures in these two areas that will be both culturally appropriate and acceptable to the parties. In one case I mediated, a rapid shift in process was necessary to adapt to the specific professional culture of the parties.

I was asked to intervene in a university graduate department of psychology that was experiencing significant turmoil. The chair of the department had been removed after a conflict between faculty members, and now factions within the department were sabotaging each other and rendering decision making impossible. Tasks and assignments would be delegated to a faculty member, and when he or she did what was assigned the results would be rejected, passively resisted, or publicly criticized by other department members.

I was asked by the acting chair and a number of his colleagues to conduct interviews with all key parties, assess their willingness to talk about departmental problems, develop a proposed agenda, and convene a meeting to address identified problems. After holding numerous individual sessions with the parties, I convened a meeting. I began by reporting back on the interviews and proposing an agenda that incorporated the topics that the parties had specifically identified as needing to be discussed. The group immediately balked at the proposal and announced that they were not ready to talk about these issues, even though they themselves had suggested the issues and had individually approved the agenda. I thought I recognized a pattern that many people identified in the interviews, but I decided not to oppose their resistance. I chose instead to ride the horse in the direction that it was going and asked them what they wanted to do.

Finally, one person said that she would like to spend the next hour just "talking about our feelings." Although this approach could have represented avoidance of issues, I recognized that many of the department's members were clinical psychologists, and what they wanted, at least initially, was an approach to agenda development that was probably more akin to a group therapy session than a problem solving mediation—that is, they wanted to be "in their culture" with their dispute, working on feelings first and insights or issues later. I agreed to facilitate the meeting but suggested that they might follow some ground rules, such as talking only about their own feelings and not attributing motives or attacking others. They agreed, and we proceeded.

During the hour that they talked, I recorded some of their feelings and related issues and interests on a flipchart, and at the conclusion of this phase of the meeting they asked me to summarize. I related the history of the conflict as a group story and outlined how it made different people feel, the issues that it raised, and some of the interests that would have to be addressed to resolve past hurts and move ahead to future tasks and better relationships. The group affirmed the summary and agreed to move ahead to problem solving on the issues.

By settling into the group's culture and using its familiar norms and procedures, we were able to develop a more acceptable agenda, define issues out of a discussion of past pain, and jointly move forward to both problem solving and clearing the air for potentially more positive relationships.

There are a number of cultural variations in issue identification and agenda development. Some cultures—such as a number of traditional Native American, First Nations, New Zealand Maori, and other aboriginal tribes or bands—often identify issues through storytelling: a respected party tells the history of the problem and of the people involved almost in the manner of relating a legend or odyssey. The issues and interests are encapsulated in the tale being told.

Members of indirect-dealing cultures, or those that try to avoid overt disagreement or conflict, identify issues and set agendas in a variety of ways. Some Asian cultures that are not direct-dealing do not want to identify conflict issues at all but will talk very obliquely and in a circular manner about "difficulties" or "inconveniences." Lederach (1988) also noted this indirectness in Costa Rican disputants; the parties used the words *nails* and *entanglements* to describe issues, problems, or conflicts (the term *conflict* being reserved for violent physical confrontations). Members of other indirect-dealing cultures talk about conflict in terms of metaphors or attempt to distance themselves from the problem by talking about the people involved in the third person. Yet other indirect-dealing parties, who highly value the preservation of relationships and face, prefer to talk first about a variety of issues that are not conflict-related, especially ones that may affirm the parties' past and future relationships, and only gradually approach areas of disagreement. Easy and less contentious issues are dealt with initially; only later, after some good feelings have been created and progress made on simpler problems, are harder issues tackled.

Direct-dealing cultures may identify issues and set agendas in a variety of ways, among them linear and explicit presentations, brainstorming (identifying and listing issues without immediately discussing or evaluating them), enumerating all topics for discussion on a handout distributed to all parties, listing issues on a wallchart, making specific proposals or advocating specific solutions rather than identifying issues, and proposing principles before identifying specific topics for discussion.

Mediators working within one culture need to develop issue-identification and agenda-setting procedures that are culturally acceptable, and when working across cultures should help coordinate different and often somewhat incompatible approaches. There are a number of ways to accomplish this:

- Being familiar with the approaches commonly used in the parties' cultures
- Interpreting and explaining to other parties the rationale for the diverse approaches to agenda development that are being used
- Listening carefully to the parties and articulating issues and concerns in ways that respect sensitivity to overt disagreement and norms regarding explicitness
- Drawing out issues from stories and making them more explicit, and then suggesting ways to discuss them
- Facilitating discussions on how issues will be identified and agendas developed

Chapter Ten

Uncovering Hidden Interests of the Disputing Parties

People negotiate issues because of the underlying interests they want to have addressed and satisfied. The negotiation process may be considered to be a game in which one or more parties engage in an educational process, a decoding process, and a bargaining process over issues to present and discover interests and trade promises to meet those interests (Cross, 1977).

DIFFICULTIES IN IDENTIFYING ISSUES

Parties in dispute rarely identify their interests in a clear or direct fashion. This lack of clarity occurs because parties:

- Often do not know what their genuine interests are
- Are pursuing a strategy of hiding their interests on the assumption that they will gain more from a settlement if their genuine goals are obscured from the scrutiny of other parties
- Have adhered so strongly to a particular position that meets their interests that the interest itself becomes obscured and equated with the position and can no longer be seen as a separate entity
- Are unaware of procedures for exploring interests

I will discuss each of these obstacles to identifying interests.

Lack of Awareness of Interests

Negotiating parties often misperceive what their interests really are. Misperception may result from external factors (such as law, tradition, or advice from friends) describing how the negotiation game is to be played (positional bargaining) and completed, or from internal confusion in the negotiators themselves. In Chapter Nine, I cited a case in which two parents are struggling over the question of who should have legal custody of their child after a divorce. Both parents are excellent child rearers and nurturers, and they are equally qualified to raise the child. They are fighting over a specific solution—sole legal custody—and in the process are damaging their relationship and indirectly harming the child. They each see their interest, and that of the other parent, defined as gaining legal custody of the child. Each parent views settlement outcomes narrowly because of advice from attorneys and relatives and traditional ideas about custody settlement arrangements. In reality, their interests are having time with the child, being involved in decisions about how the child is to be raised, having the chance to go on vacation with the child, and so on. The struggle is over a position—the demand for sole legal custody of the child—not over ways to meet the real substantive, procedural, and psychological interests of each parent. Unless genuine interests are addressed, the parents will remain caught, negotiating over positions that can result only in a win-lose outcome.

In the Singson-Whittamore case, the clinic director may not realize that his interests might be best served by a solution in which the doctor would not leave the clinic until the term of the contract expired, and that such an arrangement could benefit both the clinic and the medical practitioner. Shifting from a focus on compensation for breach of contract and acknowledging the need to satisfy a range of interests—stability at the clinic, cost containment, avoidance of disruptive working relationships, prevention of patient loss, retention of a valued employee, among others—may open new opportunities for problem solving.

Intentional Hiding of Interests

A second reason that interests are difficult to identify is that negotiators often intentionally obscure them. Parties often see interests, and the degree to which they are met, in terms of positions along a continuum of options. Particular outcomes are more satisfactory or meet more needs than others. Therefore, each party inflates his or her demands and obscures his or her real interests on the continuum of possible settlement options as a means of leveraging the greatest number of concessions from an opponent. Neither party wants to publicly present his or her real interests, or the particular point on the bargaining continuum at which he or she is willing to settle, for fear of receiving less than they might if their real needs remained unknown.

In the Singson-Whittamore case, Whittamore may be reluctant to disclose how important his interest in staying in town and being near his children really is. He may fear that an untimely revelation of his true interests may reduce his leverage, which is based on Singson's fear that Whittamore might totally leave the area for practice delimited in the contract and eliminate the clinic's claim to any compensation. Revealing his interests might give Singson undue power to force a high level of compensation.

Equation of Interests with Positions

A third reason interests are difficult to identify is that in heated conflict, parties may begin to gradually equate satisfaction of a specific interest with a particular position, making separation of the interest from the position extremely difficult. This phenomenon poses a serious challenge to negotiators and moderators who are attempting to get another party to back off hard-line positions and seek mutually acceptable solutions.

In the Singson-Whittamore case, the clinic director may see financial compensation for violation of the contract as *the* way to meet his and the clinic's interests, ignoring the possibility of identifying other interests of importance and developing a customized solution to satisfy each of them. Unfortunately, the former approach is commonly found in disputes such as divorces, personal injury cases, insurance claims, and so on, where interests (substantive, procedural, or psychological) are often reified into financial solutions. Although financial settlements may satisfy some interests, they may not address the other procedural or psychological interests of the parties (efficiency, timeliness, respect, an apology, acknowledgment of harm or inconvenience, and so on).

Lack of Awareness of Procedures for Exploring Interests

The final reason parties often do not directly explore interests is that they are more familiar with advocacy positions or solutions to problems; they are not used to thinking in terms of interests and are not aware of procedures for discovering and discussing them. This often proves to be a significant obstacle in high-tension negotiations.

These four factors—lack of awareness of interests, intentional hiding of interests, equation of interests with positions, and lack of awareness of procedural approaches to interest discovery—can be major blocks to progress in negotiations and may produce deadlock.

PROCEDURES FOR IDENTIFYING INTERESTS

Negotiators (and, if necessary, mediators) use two general types of procedures to identify the interests of disputing parties: indirect, low-profile procedures; and direct, high-profile procedures.

Indirect procedures, such as questioning a party about his or her underlying interests once a position has been advocated, are used when parties take a positional bargaining approach to negotiations or try to obscure interests by adhering to rigid positions. Such procedures are also employed when parties seem unsure of their interests, and the trust level is not high enough to merit direct exploration of their needs.

Mediators use *direct procedures* to preempt (Saposnek, 1983) parties from engaging in positional bargaining or to move them toward interest-based bargaining once positional negotiations have begun. Direct procedures are used when parties:

- Are not locked into the process of positional bargaining
- Are not committed to absolute positions
- Are aware of the need to separate identifying interests from adhering to particular positions
- Are willing to examine their interests explicitly because the trust level is high enough for mutual exploration
- Have delegated to the mediator the authority to design a structured procedure for interest exploration and identification

If parties are already engaged in positional bargaining, direct procedures may be used to identify interests when less direct methods (such as open-ended questioning about interests) have failed, to prevent parties from hardening their adherence to positions, or to manage a large number of parties or issues that are making negotiations cumbersome.

Before exploring direct and indirect moves to identify and explore interests, it is important to note attitudes that lead to productive exploration of interests.

POSITIVE ATTITUDES TOWARD INTEREST EXPLORATION

Regardless of whether positional or interest-based bargaining is being used, an understanding of interests on the part of negotiators can promote more productive and satisfying outcomes. Identification of interests is facilitated by an awareness of what an interest is, the types of interests that need to be addressed, and an open attitude toward interest exploration. The investigation of interests is facilitated by parties' beliefs that:

- All parties have interests and needs that are important and valid to them
- A solution to the problem should meet the maximum number of interests of each party
- Interests can be traded to achieve a satisfactory combination
- There is undoubtedly more than one acceptable solution to a problem
- Any conflict involves compatible interests as well as conflicting ones

Negotiators who hold such attitudes or beliefs about negotiation will be able to make the transition to a focus on interests more easily than disputants who take a narrow view of bargaining.

The critical task facing negotiators at this stage is to gain an understanding of each other's interests. The first step toward doing so is developing an awareness that interests are important. Most negotiators do not distinguish between a solution or position and the specific interest it is designed to satisfy. This linkage prevents creative problem solving. A mediator may assist parties in overcoming this perceptual block.

Before beginning actual interest exploration, mediators can work with parties to change their attitudes and awareness of what interests are and to encourage consideration of their diverse interests and those of others. This can be accomplished through a variety of indirect and direct moves. Indirect moves include modeling behavior that promotes desired attitude change. To increase awareness of the importance of interests, a mediator may state, "All needs and interests of parties are important and valid to them," "We are looking for a solution that allows everyone to have as many needs met as possible," or "There is probably more than one solution that will meet the needs of all parties." Mediators may intervene at even subtler levels by modeling an attitude of expectancy and hope (Freire, 1970). The mediator's expressed attitude often encourages a more conciliatory climate.

Mediators can also confront the need for attitude change more directly. They may explicitly spell out the differences between issues, positions, interests, and settlement options. Or they may state that if a solution cannot be found that meets at least some of the interests of all parties, there will be no settlement. Usually, the more explicit the mediator is about the need for attitudinal change or increase in awareness, the greater the possibility of confrontation between intervenor and disputants. At this point, most mediators prefer low-level, indirect interventions to explicit and direct confrontation over entrenched attitudes.

INDIRECT PROCEDURES FOR DISCOVERING INTERESTS

I have identified several indirect and direct moves to induce change in negotiators' attitudes toward interest identification and exploration. I now turn to a more detailed examination of some additional procedures for discovering interests.

Mediators may use many of the communication tools outlined in Chapters Seven, Eight, and Nine to identify interests. Particularly helpful tools are active listening (to identify psychological interests or needs), restatement, paraphrase, summarization, generalization, fractionation, and reframing to clarify substantive and procedural needs. When used alone or in combination, these tools help disputants and the mediator decode and uncover interests that are intentionally or unintentionally obscured by negotiators.

One common combination of these tools is the process of *testing* (Moore, 1982b). Testing requires a negotiator or mediator to listen carefully to another negotiator's statements and then to feed back the interest that he or she hears expressed. Through trial and error, the listener can gradually gain an understanding of the negotiator's needs.

Another method of identifying interests is *hypothetical modeling* (Pruitt and Lewis, 1977), in which the negotiator or mediator presents a series of hypothetical settlement options or proposals to another negotiator. The questioner does not ask for commitment to, or acceptance of, any of the proposals, but merely an indication of whether the proposal is more or less satisfactory than others under consideration and which better meets a party's interests. Repeated proposals that contain a variety of solutions to satisfy interests can increase a mediator's or negotiator's understanding of the needs to be met without ever having to confront the articulation of interests directly. This approach is often used when a party is hiding interests or when there is not enough trust to explicitly reveal interests.

DIRECT PROCEDURES FOR DISCOVERING INTERESTS

Fisher and Ury (1981) advocate direct *questioning* about interests. They suggest that when a disputant presents a position to another party, the recipient or the mediator should directly ask the presenting party why this position is important or what interests are met by a specific solution. Carefully worded questions that demonstrate genuine concern for understanding the other party's perception of the situation can be used to encourage revelation of important interests.

Because the intervenor has credibility as an impartial party, disputants may be more open to directly identifying and discussing their interests with him or her than with another party who is perceived to be an opponent. The mediator plays a valuable role in this situation because he or she can help the parties explore the substance and salience of each other's interests while minimizing the risks of full disclosure to an adversary. These conversations are often held during a caucus.

Another common procedure is conducting an *interest-oriented discussion.* In this process, the mediator requests that disputants refrain from discussing issues or positions and focus instead on articulating general interests or elements that would make a settlement more satisfactory for each of them. Through careful questioning by both the intermediary and other parties, the mediator moves the parties from a discussion of general interests to a greater understanding of more concrete and explicit interests.

A variation of an interest-oriented discussion is to ask parties to speculate about and articulate what they perceive to be *others'* interests. Recently, in a contentious multiparty negotiation over water development and protection of environmental quality between parties from Northern and Southern California, I asked all the parties to identify and record on flipcharts what they believed were the interests of the other involved parties. After going around the room and each party having an opportunity to identify what they perceived others' interests to be, each party was asked to correct and fill in any gaps in the articulation of their interests as identified by others. This exercise concluded with a question-and-answer session in which all parties could ask questions of clarification about others' interests and gain a greater, in-depth understanding of what they and the others hoped to achieve and needed from participation in negotiations.

Brainstorming is a process in which a group rapidly generates a list of items, such as issues or interests to be addressed. Brainstorming separates generation of items from evaluation, giving the group multiple options to consider before eliminating any of them. (See Chapter Eleven for instructions on how to conduct a brainstorming session.) Negotiators can conduct brainstorming in a joint session or in caucus. The procedure is one of the most common direct procedures to identify interests.

Brainstorming was used to identify the interests of parties in a complicated dispute in Nebraska over the allocation of surface- and groundwater to various users. The mediators carefully divided the forty-nine negotiators into groups of eight. Each group had members who represented diverse views on the questions of water supply: at least two agricultural surface-or groundwater users and one representative of municipalities, recreational interests, environmentalists, and power generators. The groups were instructed to list without evaluation the various interests that would have to be met if an agreement were to be reached. A mediator and a recorder worked with each small group to record the interests on a wallchart that everyone could see. These lists were then presented to the entire group to educate all negotiators about the general interests that would have to be addressed.

POSITIONS, INTERESTS, AND BLUFFS

A mediator's involvement does not mean that parties will be candid about their interests. Parties may engage in bluffing activity. "A party to negotiation is engaged in bluff when he asserts or implies that he will do what he does not intend to do at the time the assertion is made" (Stevens, 1963). Bluffs may also involve a party's misrepresentation of interests to convince another disputant that only a settlement with certain criteria will meet the party's needs. In ideal negotiation situations, bluffing is not possible because all disputants have accurate knowledge of the interests, settlement options, power, and preferences for behavior of the other parties. In reality, however, these variables are not known (or not completely known), and bluffing is common. This seems to be the case especially when there is no external deadline or factors that force the parties to be candid and come to terms with their differences.

To work, bluffs must be credible. One party must be perceived by another to have the authority, capacity, and will to carry out a threatened action in order to satisfy a particular interest. Mediators should probe and question parties in joint session, but more often in a caucus, to determine if a threat or a position is a genuine stance that represents the party's true intentions or is a bluff to mislead an opponent. If the latter is true, the mediator should assess with the bluffing party (1) the long-term effect a bluff will have on the relationship of the parties and (2) the potential cost to the negotiators of letting the bluff go unchallenged by the mediator. This last outcome can have drastic effects on negotiations if the parties reach an impasse based on a false claim.

If in the process of position and interest exploration a mediator discovers that a party has been bluffing and sending inaccurate messages about his or her interests, and this appears to be having detrimental effects on the negotiation process, the mediator may decide to help the bluffing party shift from the artificial posture toward a more accurate presentation of his or her interests. Procedures used by mediators for this purpose are persuasion and rationalization (Stevens, 1963), which refer to activities designed to influence or control the course of actions or operations of another negotiator, alter a party's preferences, or change how a party perceives the negotiation environment. A rationalization is a logical and plausible argument for a shift in position or approach. A rationalization for a change of position may be presented to a negotiator engaged in bluffing, to other concerned parties, to observers, or to a negotiator's constituency as a means of explaining a shift in position or to stress the importance of heretofore undisclosed interests. The rationalization may be presented to other parties by either the negotiator or the mediator. Ideally, the negotiator explains his or her shift in view, because it will increase his or her commitment to the move. However, in some disputes, the negotiator may need to save face (Brown, 1977). In such a situation, the mediator may want to present the newly identified position, interest, or option to help explain or share the responsibility for the shift.

A dispute in the context of regulatory negotiations between industry groups, a public utility commission, and consumer advocates provides an example of how mediators use persuasion and rationalization to help bargainers identify genuine interests and avoid impasse. One issue facing the negotiators was how they were going to pay for mediation. Industry representatives believed that all participants in the negotiations should "pay to play." They took a hardline position that if public interest groups did not financially contribute toward the costs of mediation, then they should not be participants. The public consumer advocates indicated that they could not afford to contribute and intimated that if they were required to pay, they would boycott the negotiations and legally challenge the proposed settlement later when it was presented to the public utility commission for consideration.

The mediators saw that each interest group was escalating its threats (and bluffs) to push the other party to accept its position. The mediators, in reflecting on the industry group's interests, asked its representatives whether they equated financial contributions to pay for the process as a party's indication of commitment to the negotiation and assurance that the party would not later sabotage or delay settlement. The industry representatives replied that they did. The mediator asked the consumers why they believed they need not pay. The consumer advocates replied that because theirs was a nonprofit group, it did not have assets to fund the process, and that in principle advocacy groups should not have to fund alternative regulatory negotiations when they would normally have free access to the regulatory hearing process.

The mediators asked the industry group if it was reasonable or fair to insist that groups lacking funds pay to participate. They also asked the consumer groups if they could find means other than a financial contribution to indicate that they were committed to the process and were bargaining in good faith. The consumer group representative made a public statement that she was committed to the process and asked if, in return, the industry groups would allow a nonprofit group to have a place at the table. The rationalization that made it possible to disconnect financial contributions from good-faith bargaining enabled the parties to reach agreement.

INTEREST IDENTIFICATION, ACCEPTANCE, AND AGREEMENT

Once the mediator and the negotiators have identified the interests of the parties, they will confront one or more situations. Interests may be (1) *mutually exclusive* in that satisfaction of one party's needs precludes satisfaction of another's interests, (2) *mixed* in that the parties have some compatible and some competing needs, or (3) *compatible* in that they have similar and nonexclusive needs.

A particular case illustrates how the division of interests applies.

An author was working on the staff of a research organization, preparing a book that would describe state-of-the-art practice in a human relations field. He had worked for many months on the project and was pleased with the product. As the book neared completion, the organization's director issued a memorandum informing the staff that in the future, no individual authors' names would appear on publications produced by the organization. The author responded with a countermemorandum that argued in favor of having the author's name on the book, citing the precedent of other organizational publications.

In this dispute, it appeared that the positions of the parties were mutually exclusive. A careful examination of the interests, however, indicated room for cooperation. Both parties had *compatible interests* in that they wanted to see the book published and distributed. Publication would financially and professionally benefit both. The parties also had *mixed interests*. The research organization was opposed to the author taking all the credit for the work; the director sought to build his organization's credibility and wanted the book to be seen as a company product. He was not willing to give away all the credit to the author but was willing to share it. He also wanted the staff to enjoy working for the agency. The author, meanwhile, wanted to take credit but was not willing to push the issue so far that he risked losing his job.

There was clearly a mixed set of interests that supported both competition and cooperation, but both parties believed that incompatible or exclusive interests predominated in the dispute. The director wanted the organization's name on the cover and sought to have the work identified as a team project. The author wanted only his name on the cover. It seemed like a win-lose dispute.

The parties agreed to negotiate on the issue of identification of authorship. They acknowledged that they had a common interest in publishing and distributing the book as soon as possible. The author accepted that the organization should get credit for sponsoring the research as long as he was given credit for producing it. The director conceded that the author was the primary researcher for the book, but he wanted the team that had performed some of the preliminary work to be given credit also. The author agreed that this was fair and suggested that he include this point in an acknowledgments section at the beginning of the book. His proposal was accepted.

The process of deciding what was to go on the cover was more difficult. Both parties acknowledged that they wanted a particular name on the cover. A variety of options were explored. The final decision was that both the agency and the author would be credited on the cover. The organization's name was to be in larger type, and the author was to be identified by his title. The two parties agreed that their interests were satisfied by this solution.

This case study illustrates several approaches that mediators can use to work with the interests of disputing parties. First, the mediator should work with the parties to jointly identify interests. A party's willingness to identify and explore his or her interests and those of others does not necessarily mean that he or she agrees with the needs of other disputants. Creighton (1972, p. II–8) makes explicit the difference between acceptance of information and agreement. "You express acceptance when you say: 'I understand that you feel such-and-such a way about this topic.' You express agreement when you say: 'You couldn't be more right, I feel that way too.' In the first you accept that the other person feels the way he does, but in agreement you *ally* yourself with the other person."

At this stage, the mediator should be more concerned with negotiators accepting information about interests than with obtaining agreement. Although agreement with the interests of other parties greatly facilitates a party's progress through later negotiation stages, agreement at this point is not mandatory. Parties can accept that others have interests that are different from theirs and still search for mutually acceptable solutions.

Next, the mediator should identify and make explicit compatible or complementary interests. This enables the parties to change their assumptions about the conflict's purity, builds a habit of agreement, and promotes cooperation. Finally, the mediator should focus on mixed and mutually exclusive interests. I will discuss measures to handle such interests in later chapters. Using a process of interest-based bargaining, trade-offs, and compromise, the mediator can often help parties progress and agree on even the most incompatible interests.

FRAMING JOINT PROBLEM STATEMENTS IN TERMS OF INTERESTS

During the process of discussing parties' issues, an individual party's interests will often be revealed, identified, or defined. Mediators generally restate for each party the interests that they have heard and then proceed to the next task of problem solving: framing joint problem statements. This is another way of defining an issue, but in a manner that incorporates both the individual and joint interests that the parties want to be addressed.

Joint problem statements include the interests of both or all parties in one comprehensive statement. For example, the mediator in the Singson-Whittamore case, after having both parties articulate their interests and restating them back, might encourage the parties to reframe those interests as a new issue in this manner: "How could we state this problem in a way that identifies both of the sets of interests that you want to satisfy?" After further discussion, the doctors might arrive at the following framing: "How can Dr. Whittamore remain in town, maintain his relationship with his children, *and* continue to practice medicine, while at the same time the clinic minimizes staff disruptions due to strained relations between the spouses, continues to have Whittamore provide medical services to its patients, and preserves the terms of the contract that were designed to protect the clinic from patient loss, unexpected staff recruitment costs, unpredictable employment conditions, and competition from doctors that it had helped to establish in the community?"

As can be seen, joint framing includes all parties' interests and often enables negotiators to commit to work on a common problem because they believe that their needs will be respected (if not met) by the solutions that will be developed. The steps for a mediator to frame joint problem-solving statements are to:

1. Clearly identify in your own mind the interests for all parties
2. Restate each party's interests and get confirmation that you are correct in your understanding
3. Publicly restate the interests of both parties in a joint-problem statement ("We are looking for a mutually acceptable solution that does X for party A, and Y for party B")
4. Ask the parties if this description of the problem and the parties' interests is accurate; if not, ask them to modify or restate it until it is mutually acceptable

Once agreement is reached on the joint problem statement, the parties can proceed to explore the issue and interests in more detail; look for objective standards, criteria, or principles that could create a framework for a solution; generate specific settlement options; or construct a package agreement. More will be said about these activities in subsequent chapters.

CULTURAL APPROACHES

Parties and intermediaries' approaches to how they identify, express, articulate, and respond to interests vary significantly with the culture. Members of cultures that are comfortable with direct face-to-face dealing and overt disagreements are generally more at ease with both directly identifying and verbally articulating their interests. People may boldly ask others "what they really want" and what their interests are, or make their own very explicit. They may also, on occasion, practically ignore them. For example, in direct-dealing cultures where face-to-face haggling, argumentation, and positional bargaining are the common or preferred way to handle a variety of transactions, overt awareness of or direct articulation of interests may neither be very high nor common. Parties may put forth positions and counterpositions until they either reach an acceptable compromise or by trial-and-error arrive at an agreement that satisfies their individual or joint unarticulated interests.

Indirect-dealing cultures, those whose members are uncomfortable with direct conflict, confrontations, demands, or specific articulation of interests, often identify and express their needs or wants in roundabout ways. Members of these cultures spend significant amounts of time circuitously and indirectly articulating what is important for them, and indirectly probing and testing for what is significant for others. Negotiators may carefully read body language, ask subtle and indirect questions about wants and needs, or explore with another which of several options or objects they like or prefer as means of identifying interests. They may also engage in extended, sequential, and seemingly social conversations that are really part of substantive negotiations, where they can conduct indirect "informal sounding" to identify what is important to another negotiator, express their needs, and see if the other understands at a gut level what is important. Graham and Sano (1984) note that this is a common practice in Japan.

Direct and indirect identification and articulation of interests are but one important cultural variable related to expressing this kind of needs. Another is the importance of and value placed on *kinds* of interests. For example, many cultures place a high value on establishing, building, and preserving relationships; they see this as the most important set of interests to be addressed and attained. This may be the case for new or older long-term relationships. Members of these cultures assume that if a good relationship characterized by trust and respect can be established, agreements on other substantial or procedural issues and successful implementation will follow.

Although the value of relationships may not be directly verbally articulated in cultures that have relationships as a high priority, it may be expressed by a variety of actions. For example, prior to or during the interest-identification phase of negotiations parties may emphasize hospitality and try to develop reciprocal exchanges of goodwill through drinking tea or coffee or alcoholic beverages together. "Please have some tea or arak before we talk," says a Turkish merchant. In many cultures, eating, conducting small talk, or making each other comfortable are oriented toward creating bridging interests of mutual comfort, harmony, goodwill, and reciprocation that initiators hope will continue in the substantive negotiations that follow. These interests are not directly verbally articulated; they are expressed through actions.

In some cultures, following the correct negotiation ritual (a procedural interest) is critical. When I was negotiating in Indonesia with the local government in the former city-state of Yogyakarta, we had to recognize the importance of the king and show proper respect and deference in a presubstantive negotiation meeting, before we could proceed to discuss procedural and substantive issues and interests.

Mediators working with cultures with differing orientations toward the identification of and degree of explicitness regarding articulation of interests face a number of challenges. A direct-dealing party who is overt in his or her questioning or articulation of interests may affront indirect-dealing parties or intermediaries. The former may believe or feel that the direct dealer lacks subtlety and finesse and is unduly probing into matters that should be explored slowly and uncovered only after safety or relationships have been established. Conversely, direct-dealing parties and intermediaries may believe that an indirect-dealing party is holding out, being inscrutable, or not negotiating in good faith because of a failure to clearly articulate what is important to them. A mediator often has to coordinate direct and indirect dealers' orientations toward interests, in spite of the fact that he or she may hold one of these orientations.

Coordination can be enhanced in a number of ways. First, mediators can help parties with divergent approaches to interests by educating them about preferred approaches and styles of the other culture for exploring interests. This is often done in caucus. Second, enough trust safety and openness can be created that indirect dealers will feel more comfortable talking more explicitly about their interests and gradually making what is important to them clearer. Third, they can also slow down the negotiations for the indirect dealers, while at the same time help them reveal and articulate their interests in a way that feels congruent with their values and norms. Fourth, direct dealers can be educated to understand that gradual or indirect revelation of interests does not mean that indirect dealers are holding out on them, being manipulative, or bargaining in bad faith. Finally, mediators may help direct dealers learn and use more indirect methods of uncovering interests such as asking indirect questions or asking for indications of preferences when discussing issues. They can do this by modeling the desired behavior or coaching them on the process in private meetings.

Chapter Eleven

Generating Options for Settlement

So far, the parties have defined the parameters of their dispute, clarified issues, developed an agenda, and (through joint education and questioning) identified common and conflicting interests. Now, the central task of the negotiators and the mediator is to develop mutually acceptable options for agreement and settlement.

A mediator and parties are required to generate settlement options either because the positions put forth in opening statements are unacceptable to one or more parties or because the parties have focused only on identifying issues and interests and have not yet explored any concrete settlement possibilities.

To develop options, the parties must understand the need for a range of alternatives from which to choose, be flexible enough in their stated positions to disengage from unacceptable proposals if necessary, and be aware of option-generation procedures. In this chapter, I will discuss:

- Development of an awareness of the need for multiple options to consider
- Detachment of parties from unacceptable positions
- Strategies of option generation
- Procedures for developing options
- Types of settlement options

DEVELOPMENT OF AN AWARENESS OF THE NEED FOR OPTIONS

Awareness of the need for multiple settlement options is not an inherent characteristic of negotiators engaged in intense disputes. Disputants often enter negotiations with the belief that they have already discovered the best solution for all concerned, and all that remains is to persuade—or if necessary, coerce—the other party into agreement or submission. For another negotiator or the mediator even to suggest that alternative solutions that might also meet a party's interests are available or desirable may be abhorrent to a negotiator committed to a particular solution. Only after persuasion and pressure fail to convince other parties of the merits of the position being advocated will an entrenched negotiator consider other options.

Negotiators and mediators begin their search for settlement options by developing awareness that multiple choices are needed from which to select the ultimate solution. The mediator may elicit this awareness, or it may develop through the process of the negotiators' interactions. In the latter case, awareness of the need for alternatives may result from a strong negative response to an opening statement or position.

Opening statements are often an expression of a party's maximal position and frequently do not take others' needs and interests into consideration. They are designed to educate parties about how strongly the disputant feels about an issue or solution or to express how far the party wants an opponent to yield. For these reasons, opening statements and positions are rarely accepted by other disputants as final representations of ways to satisfy genuine interests. It is generally expected that parties will adhere to the practice of making a large initial demand (or conversely, a low initial offer). Once a proposal is rejected, one or more parties usually propose another solution or state a counterposition.

Occasionally, however, the party who put forward a proposal or position does not recognize its categorical rejection and doggedly adheres to it. The party ignores the need for alternative proposals, assuming that if the right persuasive techniques are used or the proper influence exerted, the other party will concede. Such a posture often results in a deadlock.

At this point, other negotiators or the mediator must convince the intransigent negotiator that his or her belief that the other parties will eventually accept the current position is inaccurate, and that there is a need for alternatives.

DETACHMENT OF PARTIES FROM UNACCEPTABLE POSITIONS

Parties commit themselves to a specific position for a variety of reasons:

- It meets intangible psychological needs.
- They feel it is the best solution.
- They believe other parties do not know what is best for them.
- They believe they can weaken resistance if they continue to argue their position.
- They believe they have the power or influence to force their solution on the other parties.

Negotiators and mediators faced with an intransigent party need to assess why that party adheres so strongly to his or her position. They must then determine how they might encourage the party to explore other options. Negotiators and mediators use a variety of strategies to persuade a party to reverse commitment to a stated position.

Psychological Means of Reducing Commitment

Most psychological approaches to reducing *positional* commitment begin with identifying the psychological needs of a party through active listening, restatement, and summarization. This can be done by either a disputant or the mediator.

The second step is to gain a commitment from all parties to explore settlement options that will attempt to meet the identified needs. This does not imply agreement that the need will be satisfied in the way demanded; the parties are simply expressing a willingness to examine other solutions that will meet the need. If a disputant can be convinced that his or her need has been heard and will at least be considered in alternative solutions, he or she will often agree to suspend advocacy of an unacceptable position.

It is often the mediator's task to persuade other parties to consider the needs of a recalcitrant negotiator. Parties are often very reluctant to respect and consider a psychological need that they believe to be irrationally founded. Mediators may have to assist parties in assessing the costs of not considering another's need, in determining if the parties actually have a choice, and in deciding what the risks of impasse will be.

Procedural Means of Reducing Commitment

Procedural methods for reducing commitment are actions that increase the likelihood of finding a solution that meets needs and satisfies interests. Parties often adhere to positions because they see no other way to develop new ones. Introducing a logical or acceptable problem-solving process can often allow a disputant to abandon a position in favor of another option. A party may do so because he or she likes the proposed process and considers it fair. I will examine procedural means of reducing commitment later in this chapter.

Leverage to Reduce Commitment

Parties do not always respond to psychological moves or procedural proposals to satisfy needs. Negotiators may have to resort to leverage or means of influence to shift an intransigent party from a hard-line position. There are four ways to reduce commitment to an unacceptable position:

1. One negotiator can convince another that the latter has overestimated the cost to the first party of maintaining a position. For example, an employee who has been dismissed by a former employer might say: "I know that you think the cost of going to court will deter me from filing this wrongful termination suit. Well, it won't. In fact, I've asked my brother who is a lawyer to represent me and he said he would do it for free. It won't cost me anything but time to fight this, and I've got a lot of that these days!"

2. One negotiator can convince another that the latter has underestimated the costs involved in maintaining a position. Thus, the representative of a public interest group might say to a devel-

oper: "Look, if you won't put up a larger performance bond that will assure us that the mined land will be reclaimed as you promised, we will oppose your permit. We are prepared to go to court if necessary, and will even use direct action. Are you prepared for a delay of several years while we fight this out in the legal system? If time is money to you, it will cost you a lot more if you don't settle soon."

3. One negotiator can convince another that the former's position or interests are more important than the latter had initially realized. For example, the seller of a home might say to a prospective buyer: "I realize that when you look at this home, what you see is an old, slightly rundown Victorian house. To me, it's much more than that. It's my family legacy. It was built by my grandfather and willed to me. That is why I'm unwilling to change the terms of the sale."

4. One negotiator can convince another that the latter's interest or position is not as important as he or she originally believed, and that his or her needs can be met satisfactorily in another way. For example, a wife might say to her husband in child custody negotiations: "You say you want legal custody of Jamie so that you can be involved in decisions about his religious upbringing. What happens if I agree that the religious arena of his life is for you to decide? Isn't the religious training issue more important to you than legal custody?"

The mediator can aid parties in exerting any of these means of leverage. In addition, he or she may use other motivational tactics that will be discussed in detail in Chapter Fifteen.

STRATEGIES FOR OPTION GENERATION

Once parties are aware of the need for a range of settlement options from which to choose, they must select a specific issue to discuss and a strategy for generating possible solutions.

The focus of the option-generation procedure depends on the scope of the issue, the type of solution desired, and the way option generation fits into the overall strategy of reaching an agreement. Settlement options can be generated more narrowly to a specific issue that is merely a component of a larger issue or in respect to a general principle. These two basic strategies are similar to the building-block approach and the agreement-in-principle (or formula) approach to agenda formation discussed in Chapter Nine (Fisher and Ury, 1981; Zartman and Berman, 1982). The approaches can be used in combination within any given negotiation session or on a particular issue. I will discuss these two overall strategies and then proceed to explore specific activities mediators and negotiators use to develop settlement options.

Building-Block Approach to Settlement

The building-block approach requires disputants to divide an issue into subissues or component parts. Fisher (1964) refers to this procedure as fractionation. Usually, these smaller components are more manageable tasks for problem solving. Options are generated to address each subissue. Solutions for each subissue are then combined with those of previous issues to form a total solution or settlement. Parties may accept as final their agreements on subissues or may delay final settlement until a comprehensive agreement can be reached on all the issues in dispute.

Issues are divided into smaller components because (1) disputants may see and understand smaller issues more easily than those that are complex and many-faceted; (2) dividing issues into components unlinks them and prevents moves to join unrelated subjects, which may block agreement; and (3) dividing issues into components may depoliticize or isolate specific issues that prevent settlement.

There are two ways to divide issues into smaller components. The first is for the mediator to suggest that the definition of what is being discussed be narrowed. The second is for the mediator or a negotiator to ask parties to look at an issue and split it into component subissues. Obtaining the involvement of the parties in subissue definition can create greater commitment to the process.

Fractionation and the building-block approach are illustrated in a negotiation over how privacy could be maintained for single-family homeowners if condominiums were built close to their residences. The mediator and the parties divided the problem of privacy into several subissues: visual privacy, auditory privacy, and congestion. To achieve visual privacy, the parties generated solutions that (1) reduced building height so that second-floor dwellers in the condominiums could not see into the backyards or windows of the single-family homes; (2) constructed berms and fences to shield single-family homes from the sight of the condominiums; (3) graduated building heights so that condominiums closest to single-family homes were one story in height and those further away were two and three stories high; and (4) shielded lights in the condominium parking lot to prevent them from shining into the windows of the single-family homes. Similar solutions were generated to handle auditory and congestion problems. By dividing the issue into smaller pieces and solving the component parts, the parties were ultimately able to forge a comprehensive settlement.

Agreement-in-Principle Approach to Settlement

The second major strategy for defining options and progressing toward a settlement is the agreement-in-principle or formula approach. This procedure requires negotiators to create or identify a bargaining formula or set of general principles that will guide the shape of the final settlement. This approach is the polar opposite of the building-block approach in that it requires negotiators to reach a general level of agreement and then initiate steps to define specific details. The approach is often appropriate when underlying values of the disputants are similar or when superordinate goals can be identified.

The agreement-in-principle or formula approach to settlement is often not as familiar to disputants as the building-block approach. The mediator may have to be more directive in educating the parties about the procedure. He or she may directly reframe the central issue in broader terms and then encourage the parties to generate general principles of agreement, or explain the philosophy behind the strategic approach and turn the implementation over to the negotiators.

An example of the agreement-in-principle approach is the Metropolitan Water Roundtable negotiations in Denver among water suppliers, environmentalists, ranchers, and recreation interests. The parties were initially stalled over whether additional water was needed in the Denver area and over a proposal to construct a dam at a particular site.

After an intensive educational process, all the parties agreed that the water was needed, that some of it could be obtained through conservation, and that a dam or dams were probably required somewhere on the eastern side of the Rocky Mountains. After agreeing on these three principles, the parties began to investigate how the water needs could be met through a variety of sources (conservation, groundwater, transbasin exchanges), where a dam might be sited, and how large it should be. By reaching a series of agreements in principle on several levels, the parties were able to progress toward agreement.

GENERAL PROCEDURES FOR GENERATING OPTIONS

Once parties have decided on the level of settlement option— general or specific—that is desired, mediators or negotiators need to devise a procedure to generate the options. There are two general approaches: (1) bargaining based on positions and counterpositions and (2) a collaborative search for options—that is, interest-based bargaining.

Positional Bargaining

In positional bargaining, the parties assume that the way to present settlement options is to exchange proposals and counterproposals. If there are two parties to the dispute, the normal dynamic is for them to alternately offer proposals and counterproposals so that no more than two proposals to resolve a given issue are considered at any given time. Ideally, each proposal brings the parties closer to a settlement or settlement range because of increased satisfaction of interests for both sides (Stevens, 1963). The settlement range refers to a number of possible solutions, any one of which is regarded by both parties as preferable to a stalemate.

There are several limiting characteristics to positional bargaining. First, only two proposals or positions are generally examined at one time. This two-sided view tends to limit the number of options explored by the parties and inhibits development of multiple solutions to meet specific needs.

Second, the two-sided view discourages integration of ideas and encourages negotiators to view proposals as total packages requiring a yes-or-no response. Parties often fail to realize that proposals can be combined or recombined to create new options.

Third, two-sided negotiations, with only two possible proposals, tend to produce win-lose or right-and-wrong attitudes toward concessions or counterproposals; a win for one party is viewed as a loss by the other. Parties conducting positional bargaining often commit themselves psychologically to their proposal and view acceptance of another's position as an abandonment of principles.

Fourth, positional bargaining encourages evaluation of the proposals at the same time that options are generated. Simultaneous generation and evaluation of only two options tends to lock the parties into mutually exclusive positions and mitigate against thoughtful consideration of new ideas.

Because the proposal-counterproposal procedure places limits on the negotiating process, negotiators may wish to shift to an interest-based bargaining strategy. Such a shift, though more difficult to accomplish in negotiations in which parties have already used positional bargaining, is nevertheless not impossible. The transition from positional bargaining to interest-based bargaining can be greatly facilitated by the presence and intervention of a mediator.

Interest-Based Bargaining

Interest-based negotiation, a procedure that promotes integrative bargaining in which the interests of all parties are combined and addressed in jointly developed solutions, is often superior to positional bargaining in generating settlement options. Interest-based bargaining works most effectively under certain specific conditions: (1) the resource or interests over which the parties are negotiating must be divisible or negotiable in such a way that a gain for one party does not necessarily mean a loss for another; (2) there must be enough trust and spirit of cooperation to enable the parties to develop a joint solution; (3) one party must not have, exhibit, or be willing to exercise overwhelming power or influence to force a decision in his or her favor; and (4) the parties must be aware of a procedure to develop options that all perceive as equitable and fair. I will examine each of these points in turn.

Many negotiators, when entering a dispute, assume that the parties have entirely conflicting interests and that the outcome will yield more benefits to one party than to another. They are prepared to play a win-lose game.

Most conflicts, however, are not pure; the relationship of the parties is not purely conflictual, and all interests are not mutually exclusive. This mixed characteristic applies even to such apparently finite commodities as money. Some negotiators assume that money is finite and that an increase for one side inevitably means a loss for another. The assumption means that a compromise in which each party receives some but not all of what he or she desires is the only possible option. This type of dispute is often referred to as a *half-a-loaf dispute* (Warren, 1978). However, people may have multiple interests in financial disputes besides a particular sum of money. Monetary disputes can be subdivided into issues of the timing, rate, and form of payment so that a win-win outcome that satisfies many interests is possible.

Seemingly pure conflicts can in many cases be transformed into disputes in which all parties can win more than if they had merely divided available resources in some sort of compromise. Negotiators can accomplish this shift themselves, but they are often locked into the perception of a pure conflict. At this point, the mediator can intervene and reframe the issue so that the parties can see it in a new way.

Mediators use several techniques to produce win-win options. One important technique is *expansion of the resource* (Pruitt and Lewis, 1977). Union-management negotiations, for example, have a history of deadlock when the parties negotiate solely on the issue of a wage increase. However, by adding issues such as cost-of-living benefits, insurance options, goodwill, working conditions, or increased productivity, the mediator may change a win-lose negotiation into a situation in which a mutually satisfactory outcome is a possibility.

Mediators also assist parties in *logrolling* (Pruitt and Lewis, 1977): trading items that are valued differently by the parties. Logrolling allows each party to offer components that are valued less than those offered by the other party. The difference in items to be exchanged and their desirability to the recipients makes agreement possible. Logrolling was used in a case in which an employer hired a consultant but was not explicit about the terms for contract termination. The consultant, who was working in good faith, put in more time than the employer wished to pay for. The consultant felt that the employer owed additional pay, but the employer refused because she was not satisfied with the work. The consultant then hired a collection agency, which contacted the employer and demanded payment.

By this time, the parties had developed an extremely antagonistic relationship and could not talk to one another. Not wanting to deal with the collection agency, the employer contacted a mediator. The employer realized that she would probably have to pay something to settle the dispute, but she did not want to pay the consultant for unsatisfactory work. The mediator discovered that the consultant was more concerned with the principle that the employer should pay her debts than with receiving the small sum due to him.

The mediator, operating on the principle that honoring the debt was the important issue, asked the consultant whether having the employer pay the disputed amount to another party, such as a charity, might meet his needs. The consultant agreed. The mediator then discussed this solution with the employer, who was willing to pay as long as she could choose the charity. The parties ultimately agreed on this solution. By logrolling, trading components of differing importance to the negotiators, the mediator was able to assist the parties in meeting each other's strongest interest without compromising on principles.

A further technique is *alternation.* When there is no way to expand resources, the parties may alternate between the options each of them favors. In an alternating scheme, neither side forsakes his or her *preferred option,* but each is allowed to enjoy it at a different time. For example, to settle a domestic conflict over where to vacation, a couple might go to the mountains this year and to the seashore next year, thus meeting the husband's interest in mountain climbing and the wife's interest in beachcombing. Alternating schemes will be more integrative than simple compromise when the resource that is sought cannot be divided into parts without excessive loss of value to the negotiators.

A final procedure for interest-based bargaining is *designing new and specifically integrative interest-based solutions.* Such solutions meet the needs of each party, but not at the expense of another's needs. The classic illustration of this type of solution, related by many mediators, is the conflict between two children who are fighting over the last orange left in the fruit bowl. Each child adamantly demands that he or she get the orange. The wise mother intervenes and offers to help the children decide who should get it. At first examination, it appears that each child has equal claim to the orange. What should the mother do? She could halve the orange and give each child a piece. She could even alternate who slices and who chooses which piece goes to whom to increase the children's perception of procedural fairness. However, the mother is dissatisfied with these solutions and pursues the exploration of each child's interests in more depth. After several minutes of discussion, she discovers that one child wants to eat the fruit and the other wants the rind to prepare a cake icing. She helps the children agree to split the orange and satisfy all of their needs.

Mediation, through careful data collection and option generation, can often help parties build solutions of this type. It challenges disputants to overcome apparent barriers to settlement that would require them to settle for less than they could attain if they produced a truly integrative solution.

Several other factors can help promote interest-based negotiations: buildup of trust and the judicious use of negotiator power and influence. Trust has already been discussed in Chapter Seven. Interest-based bargaining requires developing at least a minimal level of trust. To accomplish this end, mediators should use techniques described in the earlier chapter.

Parties must have some means of influencing each other if they are even to begin formal negotiations. The threat or exercise of power may, however, inhibit interest-based bargaining.

The mediator can reduce or prevent the effects of threats or exercises of power by (1) ignoring them and persuading the other parties to do the same; (2) minimizing them by translating the threat into nondetrimental terms; (3) educating the parties about the cost of making perceived or actual threats; or (4) in extreme cases, helping another party realize and exercise its power to counter the threat or display. This last strategy tends to maintain polarization and competition rather than promote cooperation. I will discuss contingent moves mediators can initiate to respond to power problems in Chapter Fifteen.

Parties often remain locked in positional bargaining merely because they are not aware of alternative means of negotiating. Mediators can often assist people to shift from positional to interest-based bargaining by suggesting alternative procedures to accomplish co-operative option generation.

A mediator's procedural suggestions for achieving this transition may have several advantages over unilateral moves initiated by disputants themselves. First, research shows that suggestions by an impartial third party may be more readily trusted and accepted by disputants than those suggested by a party with substantive concerns in the conflict's outcome (Rubin and Brown, 1975).

Second, the mediator's suggestions may, because of his or her professional stature and experience, be accorded more credibility. The parties may be more willing to try a more collaborative procedure because they believe the mediator would not suggest an unwise or unworkable procedure (Rubin and Brown, 1975; Brookmire and Sistrunk, 1980).

Third, the mediator can take some responsibility for the success or failure of a negotiation procedure (Stevens, 1963). Parties are often reluctant to initiate new methods because they might have to bear the ill will of other parties or their constituents if the procedure fails. The mediator, by sharing responsibility for the new procedure, takes the burden on himself or herself and removes the party from the risk of blame.

Finally, a mediator may be of assistance because he or she can minimize the time and energy required of the parties to identify the appropriate procedure. Parties can often develop a process that suits their needs if given the adequate time and resources, but they are not always available. Mediators can accelerate the transition and avoid the accumulation of additional negative experiences that may result from a struggle over procedure by presenting a viable process for option generation.

SPECIFIC OPTION-GENERATION PROCEDURES

Parties in mediation using an interest-based approach may employ numerous processes to generate settlement options. These procedures have a number of characteristics in common. First, they attempt to generate several options so that the parties can move from a bipolar view of solutions to a multipolar view (Maier and Hoffman, 1960). Second, they attempt to separate the stage of generating options from the later evaluation or assessment stage. This separation ensures that the search process will be more comprehensive and complete and not inhibited by premature judgments or rejections of potentially viable options. Third, they focus the effort of the negotiators on the issue or problem to be solved and not on the other party. The dispute is depersonalized so that the parties aim their attacks not at the people in the negotiations but at the issues that divide them (Chandler, 1945; Fisher and Ury, 1981; Walton and McKersie, 1965; Filley, 1975). I will now discuss twelve common procedures mediators or negotiators can use to generate settlement options.

Ratification of the Status Quo

Ratification of the status quo is one of the simplest and easiest procedures to begin to develop options and reach an early agreement on selected issues. It is commonly used by parties who have a past or current relationship in which they have established patterns of interaction or developed solutions to problems that they would like to formalize and keep in a future relationship. To initiate this option, the mediator asks the parties to identify what agreements they have reached previously, or what is working in the current relationship that they want to continue and include in their final agreement. The parties will often name a number of things, and the mediator will then work with them to develop acceptable wording that can be incorporated into a new settlement agreement.

Development of Objective Standards for an Acceptable Agreement

Although this procedure does not result in a specific option or options, developing standards for an agreement establishes the parameters for later option generation. To initiate this process, the parties or mediator propose to identify criteria or objective standards that could be used to shape a final agreement. These criteria should be ones that are widely seen to be fair, that are based on historical precedent or tradition, or that are commonly used to establish value. Once a list is generated and discussed, the mediator helps the parties reach a consensus on the criteria to be adopted. This procedure was used to help resolve a dispute over thermal impact on fish of solar-heated water released from a hydropower dam. The parties—state and federal agencies and the private power producer—identified a number of criteria that they would use to shape the final agreement. The criteria included absence of significant impact on other agreements reached regarding operation of the dam, maximization of the number of recreational fishing days downstream, calculation of the impact on fish in specific sections of the stream, and compensation of the state for fish lost because of temperature increases specifically attributable to the dam.

Open Discussion

Open discussion is one of the best means of developing options. However, for free and creative discussions to occur, parties need to feel that they can share ideas without prematurely committing themselves to them. Mediators can assist in this regard by setting ground rules that allow parties to propose and explore ideas without any expectation of later commitment. The mediator may also facilitate discussions to keep the parties on track, focus them on specific topics, summarize the conversation, and test for and identify areas of consensus.

Brainstorming

Brainstorming is a procedure in which two or more people generate a variety of ideas or options for consideration. The mediator or a negotiator begins the process by framing an issue as a "problem." A problem is often stated as a *how* question. How can enough resources be found to send a wife to school so that she can be self-supporting? How can a company pay an outstanding bill with limited assets? How can a popular recreation area be maintained while still allowing companies to explore for minerals?

The parties are then instructed to speak one at a time and suggest as rapidly as possible a number of solutions that might meet the needs of the parties. The mediator should instruct them to avoid stating purely self-serving options and should caution them against making verbal or nonverbal judgments of practicality or acceptability during the session. He or she should inform them that assessment and evaluation of the options will be initiated only after they have generated a substantial number of solutions and should encourage them to build and modify each other's ideas as long as the results move them toward an option that might meet more of their interests. The mediator should record suggestions on a pad or wallchart, taking care to record accurately and keep the session going. Once the parties have generated a satisfactory number of options or have exhausted their ideas, they may shift to an evaluation procedure.

Brainstorming can be done (1) by all disputants together, (2) by individuals or teams from a particular party, (3) by subgroups within a team, or (4) by subgroups composed of delegates or representatives of each of the parties. Brainstorming as individuals, teams, or team subgroups may be used when disputants do not trust other parties and are uncomfortable disclosing options publicly but want to expand their range of settlement possibilities. Conversely, the mediator may randomly assign members of opposing parties to subgroups when he or she or a negotiator wants to maximize participation and increase personal contact between disputants by using small groups. Brainstorming in a subgroup with specifically assigned membership may be used to group or more evenly distribute moderates from opposing negotiating teams. Moderate team members are more likely than hard-line negotiators to come up with integrative solutions that will meet the needs of all parties.

Nominal Group Process

Building on the basic concept of small-group process that individuals invent and groups evaluate, the nominal group process seeks to maximize individual creativity to help a group solve a problem (Delbecq, Vandeven, and Gustafson, 1975). In this process, the issue is stated as a *how* problem, and individuals make their own lists, within a specific time limit, of all the possible solutions they can imagine. They then form small subgroups of about five members each, where ideas are shared one at a time and recorded. These ideas are then elaborated on, discussed, and assessed for merit in the small groups. Potential options that are mutually acceptable are then brought to the larger group for discussion and consideration.

Plausible Hypothetical Scenarios

Parties may occasionally be encouraged to generate settlement options by engaging in hypothetical scenario development. The mediator states the issue as a *how* problem and then charges individuals or small groups to develop hypothetical scenarios, in narrative form, in which the problem is overcome. Scenarios should describe how procedural, substantive, and psychological interests would be met. This approach, when used in small groups composed of disputants from all parties, often produces greater commitment to cooperative solutions. Once the scenarios are developed, the groups may present each one until the negotiators have heard all the possibilities. The parties then assess whole scenarios and individual components for their relevance as solutions to the dispute.

Vision Building

Vision building involves parties in individual and joint construction of an ideal vision of what a workable solution or relationship might look like in the long run. Parties are asked to think separately about the best vision they could develop that would meet each of their respective interests. The present their vision to each other and attempt to reach agreement. If there are some points in common, they are noted. A discussion follows on differences, with an effort to resolve them. Once an agreement is reached on a common vision, parties are asked to identify problems that are inhibiting or will inhibit them from attaining it. Follow-up discussions are conducted to identify and agree upon how these problems can be resolved and barriers overcome.

Model Agreements

This procedure identifies and uses experience, options, or agreements reached in other similar disputes as catalysts for developing now mutually acceptable solutions. Models or agreements reached by other parties who are not involved in the current conflict are explored and modified to meet the needs of the situation. The procedure is often employed in business disputes in which past contract language can be used as a basis for developing a customized agreement in the new situation.

Linked Trades

The linked-trades procedure involves identifying potential linkages of issues and trading specific items that each party values differently. The mediator asks the parties to identify interests that they would trade for specific desired benefits that would be given by another party. By generating such possible trades, the mediator and the parties may be able to develop potential deals that can then be modified to better meet each party's interests.

Single-Text Negotiating Document

Plausible hypothetical scenarios can often be developed into a single-text negotiating document (Fisher and Ury, 1981). Either a party or the mediator may initiate this procedure. The first step is to identify the interests of all parties. The initiator then develops a text or proposal that might satisfy the majority of the interests and resolve the dispute. This document becomes a draft settlement text that is circulated among the parties for comments and revision. Each party should have an opportunity to modify the text to better meet his or her needs. Gradual revision often results in a single text that is acceptable to all disputants.

President Carter used this procedure in 1978 to negotiate the Camp David accords between Israel and Egypt. A similar procedure was used in the Law of the Seas negotiations. The single-text approach is helpful for two-party disputes and almost a necessity for a multiparty dispute.

Procedural Solutions to Reach Substantive Agreements

Options may be generated through procedural solutions when parties perceive different probabilities or risks attached to the outcome of a dispute or when the future is not entirely unpredictable. The parties work to develop a fair procedure that can be implemented at either the present time or in the future to arrive at an acceptable answer. For example, neighbors who oppose the opening of a mine because they fear it will lower their property values or adversely affect the environment may be able to support the development if the mine operator puts up a large enough performance bond to compensate them for any potential losses. Naturally, this process has to specify the time when the evaluation will be made, how the baseline data for property values is established, how differences in projected and actual values are determined, and how funds are allocated.

Package Agreements

The solution of a dispute sometimes lies in constructing a total comprehensive agreement that addresses all parties' key issues and interests. This procedure is generally used only when parties have exchanged enough information to develop mutually acceptable packages. Packages generally strive to balance gains and losses for all parties so that the settlement in its totality is jointly acceptable. Packages can be constructed in joint session; in caucuses; or in smaller, mixed-interest groups. The procedure was applied in 1993–94, in EPA reg-negs on the control of emissions from the manufacturing of wood furniture. The parties first compiled a list of all their interests. They then developed a matrix showing how well various options met those interests. Finally, the parties negotiated a combination of options that was acceptable to all.

Use of Outside Experts or Resources

Parties are often frustrated by a myopic view of the conflict when attempting to generate viable options. This condition may result from their proximity to, or lack of objectivity toward, issues in dispute. Disputants may also be limited by their own experience or may possess inadequate data. Use of outside resources, initiated by either the parties or the mediator, may be of great assistance to the negotiations. Often the mediator, because of his or her perceived neutrality, can increase the acceptability of such a move.

Outside resources may take the form of written material or experts in the topic under discussion. For example, in child custody disputes, mediators may want the couple to read *Mom's House, Dad's House* (Ricci, 1980) or *Joint Custody and Co-Parenting* (Galper, 1980) so that they obtain ideas outside of mediation on how to establish a new parenting relationship. For companies trying to negotiate the structure of a new employee-management grievance procedure, representatives may want to consult books on organizational dispute resolution to broaden the range of options to consider.

Outside resource persons may be substantive or procedural experts on the issue. Among those who may data to contribute are lawyers, assessors, and accountants; parties who have had similar conflicts and have resolved them, such as government officials, managers, or parents; and individuals from other disciplines or backgrounds.

Mediator Suggestions

In spite of the best option-generation processes, developed by the parties or the mediator, disputants can still get stuck and be unable to develop mutually acceptable settlement options. In this event, a mediator may want to try out some of his or her own ideas, become a catalyst, and help parties expand their thinking about what is possible (Wade, 1998; Fisher, 2001).

Mediators who have been listening to parties discussing their issues and interests often develop significant insights regarding what might constitute or go into an acceptable agreement. Mediator suggestions are often helpful to parties, especially late in the option-generation process. Mediator suggestions can open doors to new ideas that may merit further consideration; bring a more objective outsider's view on what is possible, fair, or reasonable; devise a new rationale that allows disputants to agree to terms that they might not have considered; propose options that parties are reluctant to raise themselves; or offer a scapegoat for reaching an agreement that parties know is a good one but are reluctant to publicly consider. Sometimes, parties want to be able to say, "I didn't really like the option, but the mediator said it was fair and reasonable. And the other side could live with it. So I decided to bite the bullet and agree with the mediator and accept the option."

Generally, intermediaries should hold off making suggestions early in the option-generation process so that parties can develop solutions and come to a settlement on their own. However, if a mediator does decide to make suggestions regarding possible components of an agreement, there are some considerations that should be kept in mind.

First, the mediator should be sure that the parties have really had an opportunity to exhaust their own thinking. Premature suggestions from an intermediary can short-circuit option generation by the parties; be perceived by disputants as the mediator taking sides; push parties toward the mediator's preferred option, which might not be as appropriate a solution as they could generate on their own; or lead to rejection of the intermediary's suggestion and potentially a loss of his or her future influence.

Second, it is often wise to suggest more than one way that an issue or set of interests can be addressed and satisfied. Suggesting two or more options can act as a catalyst to parties' thinking, and it is less likely to be seen as the mediator pushing his or her own preferred solution.

Third, the mediator may want to add a caveat prior to proposing some options, to protect himself or herself from being seen as an advocate for a specific solution. The mediator might say, "I have some ideas that I would like to have you consider, but they may not be either the perfect solution or the right thing for both of you. I'd like you to consider them, and take what is useful, but you should feel totally free to reject what is not."

FORUMS FOR OPTION GENERATION

Options can generally be developed in joint session, in caucuses (private meetings), or in subgroups composed of representatives of the major parties.

Joint sessions are generally used when the whole group is somewhat comfortable working together, when the knowledge or expertise of many people is needed to develop multiple options, or when the parties are uncomfortable delegating option generation to a smaller or mixed-interest group.

Caucuses are used when parties are not comfortable exploring options in front of each other; when suggesting options with a contending party present may be perceived as risking a premature commitment; when a party needs privacy to figure out what options he or she wants to explore in joint session; or when mutual option generation may reveal information that a party wants to remain confidential.

People in conflict are often hindered from generating options because groups are too large to be conducive to problem solving, high-level interaction, or candor. This may be especially true for multiparty public disputes. Small, informal discussion groups are often helpful for option generation. In disputes with multiple parties, the entire group may delegate subissues or problems to small working groups or committees, charging them to propose an integrative solution that can be referred back to the main group for final decision. Generally, these subgroups are composed of representatives of the major interest groups. This approach was used by provincial labor negotiators in Saskatchewan, Canada, as a means of developing options in collective bargaining negotiations. Subgroups composed of key negotiators from each side and some of each party's constituents developed some very creative options that were later accepted by both labor and management.

The approach has also been used in international negotiations, such as those to implement the Guatemalan Peace Accords that ended the thirty-six-year civil war in that country. "*Espacios informales,*" or spaces for informal meetings, were created by the intermediaries so that negotiators from each side could discuss and explore options without having to prematurely commit to discussion of a solution in a more public forum.

TYPES OF SETTLEMENT OPTIONS

Settlement options must satisfy the substantive, procedural, and psychological interests of the parties if they are to be considered as acceptable solutions to the conflict. The degree to which interests are met determines how strong the agreement will be. Negotiators and mediators formulate settlement options by varying a number of factors. The goal is to create a package that meets the needs of all parties at an acceptable level.

Fisher (1978) identified some of the variables that determine how strong an agreement will be:

Stronger Agreements Are:	*Weaker Agreements Are:*
Substantive. They define specific tangible exchanges (money, services, labor, and so on) that will result from negotiations.	*Procedural.* They define the way or process by which a decision is to be made.

Comprehensive. They include a resolution of all issues in dispute.

Partial. They do not include a resolution of all issues in dispute.

Permanent. They resolve for all time the issues in dispute.

Provisional. They may be temporary or trial decisions subject to change in the future.

Final. They include all the details in their final form.

In-principle. They include general agreements, but the details remain to be worked out.

Nonconditional. They arrange for termination of the dispute without the requirement of future conditional performance.

Contingent. They state that the conclusion of the dispute is contingent on additional information or future performance by one or more parties.

Binding. They are formal contracts that bind the parties to certain actions. (People often agree to be bound and adhere to the terms of a settlement if they can identify consequences of nonperformance.)

Nonbinding. They make recommendations or requests only; the parties are not legally obliged to comply.

Mediators generally want to help the parties reach the strongest agreement possible, but it may not always be feasible to develop a settlement with all the characteristics listed in the left-hand column. For example, a mediator may not be able to obtain a substantive agreement on the value of a piece of property but may be able to establish a procedure for assessing the land's value that all parties will accept. The mediator in another case may not be able to obtain a permanent decision about where a child will live after his parents' divorce but be able to reach settlement on a trial solution that will be periodically evaluated and changed if necessary.

A procedural solution that partially settles issues, that is provisional, that is contingent on future performance, that elaborates general principles, and that is nonbinding may be the strongest agreement possible and preferable to no solution at all. By experimenting with the form of settlement options, the mediator can assist the parties in negotiating the strongest agreement possible, while tailoring it to their specific needs and interests.

OPTION GENERATION IN THE SINGSON-WHITTAMORE CASE

In the Singson-Whittamore mediation that we have been following in previous chapters, the disputing doctors worked in earlier stages of the process to gain a common understanding of the issues, explore their interests, and agree on a joint problem statement. But after further discussion, the mediator discovered that Singson was not totally confident that a solution could be found in which Whittamore stayed in town and continued to practice medicine and the clinic's interests would be satisfied. The mediator acknowledged this concern and suggested that they explore developing three possible settlement frameworks: (1) Whittamore stays in town, practicing medicine and maintaining a connection with the clinic that would not violate the terms of the contract; (2) Whittamore stays in town, opening his own practice and compensating the clinic for ending his employment prior to the contracted date; and (3) Whittamore moves out of town (beyond the minimum distance specified in the contract), practicing medicine and maintaining contact with his children. All parties agreed to this approach for developing multiple options for their consideration.

In addressing the first framework, the mediator asked the parties to generate some options that would address the issue of limiting the Whittamores' contact with each other and yet allowing Andrew to continue to practice with clinic staff. The processes that they used to develop options included brainstorming and, later, discussion to refine the possible solutions that had been proposed.

To address the second framework, the mediator asked the parties to identify some of the elements that would need to be taken into consideration when calculating the amount of compensation to be paid to the clinic. Through listing, discussion, and the building-block approach, these factors were identified:

- Potential patient loss
- Costs of recruiting a new doctor

- Coverage of medical services between the time that Whittamore left the clinic and the time that a new doctor's services could be procured
- Adverse precedent costs to the clinic if other doctors would follow Whittamore's example and leave the clinic before their contract was fulfilled
- Costs of setting up a new practice
- Timing of compensation payments

Both doctors agreed that these components needed to be discussed further and proceeded to talk about each one in detail. On the issue of recruitment, they agreed that advertising costs, several recruitment trips (air fare and per diem payments), and site visits by at least two prospective candidates would have to be paid for. The doctors reached a deadlock on the amount of advertising costs to be included in the financial settlement and agreed to have a mutually respected staff member at the clinic compile some realistic figures. They also disagreed over how many site visits would be necessary. After caucuses with the mediator, they finally agreed that there could be up to three, but if there were fewer the costs would be prorated. They then developed some numbers to cover each of these costs.

Regarding the costs of potential patient loss, the disputants agreed to explore two potential procedural solutions. The first would have Whittamore continue to serve the clinic's patients in his new practice but pay the clinic a percentage of fees collected from those clinic patients until the end of the contract period. This would compensate the group practice for patient recruitment costs and for helping to establish the doctor's new practice. The second option was a flat fee based on data and a formula from other medical clinics that had lost patients to doctors who left the group practice.

After addressing each of the issues listed earlier and developing cost figures, Singson and Whittamore put together a total financial package that they continued to discuss and fine-tune.

With the first two frameworks discussed, there was little interest in pursuing the third—(Whittamore leaving the area altogether). The doctors agreed to take a break in negotiations so that they could consider and evaluate the options, and to meet again the following week, when they would try to reach a conclusion.

CULTURAL APPROACHES

Option generation is one of the stages of the mediation process that is most strongly influenced by culture. Professional culture (legal, business, education); organizational culture (corporate, governmental agency, nongovernmental organization); or ethnic, regional, national, or class culture often influences parties' preferences and comfort in using different methods, as well as their skills in doing so.

For example, in the past, American legal culture has been strongly oriented toward positional bargaining as a procedure for developing options. In another arena, international studies have identified national preferences for particular approaches in specific settings. Negotiators from the People's Republic of China (Pye, 1982; Seligman, 1989) and the former Soviet Union and Russia (Smith, 1989; Schecter, 1998) often seem to prefer positional bargaining for resolving both political and economic disputes.

Many European or European-derivative cultures like to generate options jointly in a give-and-take process at the negotiation table. In contrast, Japanese in commercial situations frequently prefer informal discussions away from joint sessions as means of developing settlement options, with formal meetings used primarily to ratify agreements reached in earlier dialogues (Graham and Sano, 1984).

North American and German businesspeople often like brainstorming or highly linear and systematic option-generation approaches. Other cultures such as more traditional societies, where option generation may be less formal, prefer extended linear, looping, or circular conversations, which include lots of social asides, by which potential solutions evolve and are elaborated until they are mutually acceptable.

Mediators working across cultures should take time to explore with the parties their familiarity with and preferences for various option-generation procedures and then develop approaches that will be culturally acceptable. In some cases, a different approach will have to be used with each party in caucus to accommodate cultural diversity.

Part Four

Reaching a Settlement

Chapter Twelve

Assessing Options for Settlement

The stage of assessing options is procedurally similar to the prenegotiation stage of searching for a dispute resolution approach and arena, which was discussed in Chapter Four.

Parties are engaged in:

1. Reviewing their interests
2. Assessing how these interests can be met by solutions developed through positional or interest-based generation procedures
3. Determining the costs and benefits of selecting or not selecting one of the solutions
4. Assessing whether there is a better alternative to the proposed negotiated settlement
5. Beginning the process of modifying, integrating, combining, dropping, and trading options to reach a final agreement

The major differences between the assessment process and the earlier stage are that (1) the amount of time that has already been invested in negotiation often encourages parties to reach a negotiated agreement, (2) the parties may jointly assess options rather than conduct their evaluation in isolation from each other, and (3) the focus of the parties is primarily on the substantive content of the negotiations rather than the future mediation procedure.

The central task of the parties at this stage is to assess how well their interests will be satisfied by any one option or combination of options that have been generated collaboratively or offered unilaterally by one of the disputants. The mediator's task is to help the parties evaluate the options and assist them in determining the costs and benefits of their acceptance or rejection (Gibson, Thompson, and Bozerman, 1996; Gibson, 1999).

Because assessment procedures have already been discussed in detail in Chapter Four, they will not be reexamined here. However, two concepts and related series of activities need to be explored further: establishing a positive settlement or bargaining range, and considering the best alternative to a negotiated agreement, or "BATNA"(Fisher and Ury, 1981).

THE SETTLEMENT RANGE

A positive *settlement range* is a sequence of acceptable options any one of which the disputants would prefer to embrace rather than accept the consequences of a breakdown of negotiations. The settlement range is often referred to as the *bargaining range* when applied to options generated by positional bargaining. I will now examine how parties recognize when they have produced, by means of positional bargaining or cooperative problem solving, options that fall within a positive settlement range.

Creating and Identifying a Bargaining Range

Positional bargainers generally assume that they are negotiating about a finite or fixed-sum resource (money, time, tangible objects). Thus the total value available to all parties cannot be increased. This assumption is not always valid, but I will consider it here as a hypothetical given. If parties are negotiating for fixed shares of a finite resource, a gain for one party must mean a loss for another. If parties are to reach an agreement on dividing the resource, they must reach a compromise position that shares gains and losses in a mutually acceptable manner.

Possible outcomes in fixed-sum negotiations are plotted in Figure 12.1. In this figure, the vertical axis represents gains for Party A and the horizontal axis represents equivalent gains for Party B. If the parties are to divide a fixed-sum resource, the division will have to occur at some point along the diagonal line *xy*. Some of the settlement options are identified at points along the line, with point 5.5 considered an equal distribution of the resource. On this con-

Figure 12.1. Possible Outcomes in Fixed-Sum Negotiations.

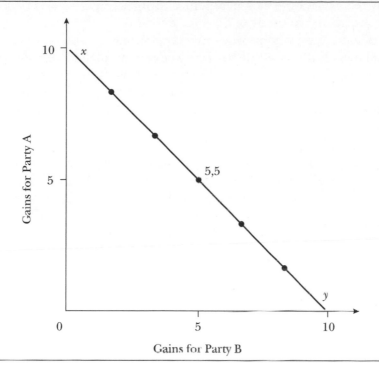

tinuum of distribution, parties usually identify a point that is a preferred solution or target. This point becomes their goal in subsequent negotiations.

The *target point* is *the* preferred distribution of resources, in which the party's compensation is considered to be the best that can be obtained under the circumstances. It is also a point of aspiration. Targets may be developed on the basis of the gut-level feelings or high aspirations of a party, or they may be the result of highly sophisticated calculations and analysis.

In addition to target points, negotiators may have upper or lower limits, often called *resistance points*. The upper limit indicates the maximum that a party will pay or give in settlement. The lower limit is the minimum that a party will accept and still reach an agreement.

Between the target point and the resistance point is the settlement or bargaining range: a field of options that, although satisfactory, afford degrees of benefits or losses for each negotiator. Because each party generally has a range of acceptable options, the goal of each disputant is to (1) discover the other party's settlement range, (2) determine if there is an overlap with his or her own settlement range, and (3) maximize his or her own gains within the range of possible outcomes if there is an overlap of ranges.

In the best possible case, the disputing parties will have overlapping settlement ranges so that there are mutually satisfactory solutions or divisions of resources. Figure 12.2 illustrates how the options of two parties may be compatible. Parties in positional bargaining, with or without the assistance of the mediator, will ideally be able to identify a mutually acceptable settlement range and

Figure 12.2. Positive Settlement Range.

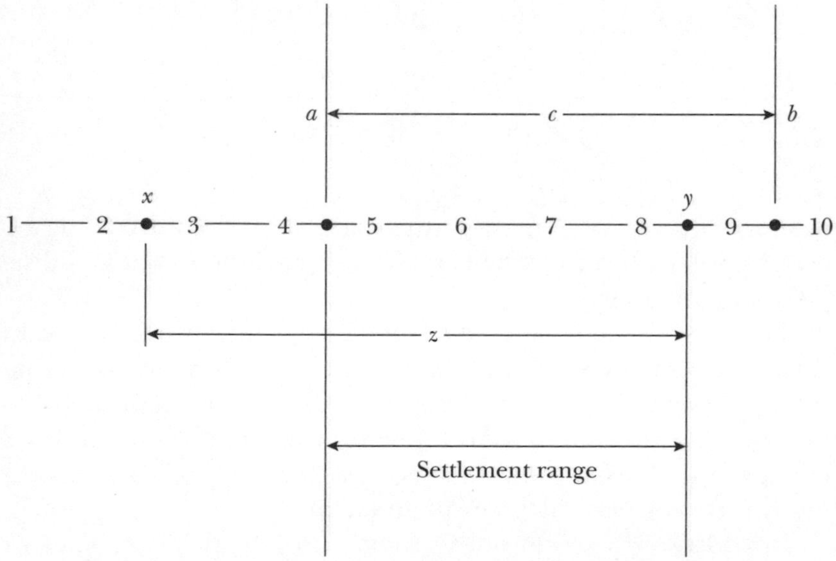

a = Party A's resistance point   x = Party B's target
b = Party A's target   y = Party B's resistance point
c = Acceptable options for Party A   z = Acceptable options for Party B

make proposals between the boundaries established by their resistance points. When settlement ranges overlap, parties must decide how they will make a final decision on the distribution of the resource within the positive range of agreement.

Occasionally, parties reach the assessment stage and discover that their settlement ranges do not overlap (see Figure 12.3). This condition is known as a *negative settlement range.*

When a party discovers that a negative settlement range exists, he or she has several procedural options:

- Continue to negotiate and make subsequent proposals in the hope that the other party or parties will shift their target and resistance points so that a positive settlement range is created.
- Change his or her own target point and resistance point and continue to offer new proposals that demand fewer concessions from other negotiators.

Figure 12.3. Negative Settlement Range.

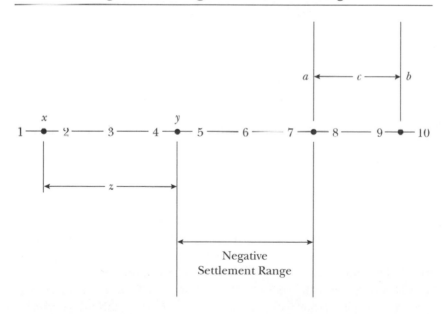

a = Party A's resistance point x = Party B's target
b = Party A's target y = Party B's resistance point
c = Acceptable options for Party A z = Acceptable options for Party B

- Expand the number of issues to allow trade-offs on other interests that will compensate for losses on the fixed-sum issue.
- Cease negotiations.

The mediator can assist the party in assessing the feasibility and desirability of pursuing any or all of these four options.

Settlement Ranges and Cooperative Problem Solving

Reaching a positive settlement range when parties are engaged in interest-based bargaining involves a somewhat different procedure from the one used in positional bargaining. Although the concept of the settlement range remains valid, options that the parties consider do not necessarily fall along a continuum in which one party gains value at the expense of another. The outcome in interest-based bargaining represents a compromise only in a worst-case scenario. The norm appears to be solutions that, in the long run, are more satisfactory than a compromise for all parties concerned. Figure 12.4 identifies the field in which this type of outcome can be found.

In Figure 12.4, the diagonal line *xy* represents a division of values in which parties reach some compromise in an apparently fixed-sum negotiation. Point 5.5 represents an equal division of the contested resources. The solutions sought by interest-based bargaining are those found in quadrant C, which represent greater joint satisfaction of interests by settlement than any distribution of benefits along the *xy* range.

RECOGNITION OF THE SETTLEMENT RANGE

In some negotiations, parties have little difficulty recognizing their arrival at an acceptable settlement range. Either through prenegotiation planning in which a range was established or in the process of negotiations, all parties may recognize that they have developed options any one of which is preferable to no agreement.

Occasionally, however, parties have perceptual difficulties in recognizing a positive settlement range. This condition may be due to misperceptions about what is an acceptable option for settlement

Figure 12.4. Cooperative Problem-Solving Settlement Range.

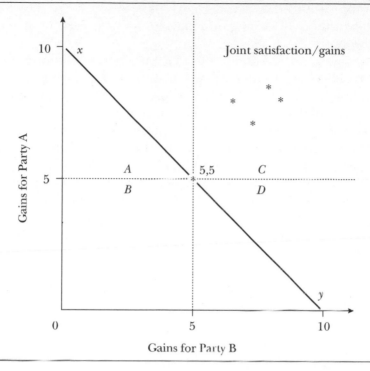

or to the existence of a negative settlement range. The mediator's intervention to prevent an impasse at this stage of negotiations may be crucial. I will discuss here how mediators respond to the first problem.

Identification of the Acceptable Field of Settlement

The problem of identification here is similar to perceptual or attitudinal problems identified earlier in negotiations. For example, it is necessary to be aware of the importance of interests and to recognize when a party should shift from an initial position to a new one that still meets his or her needs. The mediator, through public and private discussions with the disputing parties, often has the most accurate perception of what an acceptable settlement range will be for all the negotiators. The problem for the intervenor is to communicate to disputants that a bargaining range has been reached without disclosing or determining the precise outcome of the dispute.

Mediators should attempt to make the parties aware that they have reached a settlement range by indirectly questioning them about how well their interests or needs can be met by the available options. Mediators can also ask in caucus whether a party is willing to risk losing one of the available options as the result of an impasse. If the party responds that he or she is not willing to risk the impasse, the mediator knows that the party has reached a point equal to or better than his or her resistance point. The party has moved into an acceptable range of options. The same procedure is then repeated with the other parties, generally in caucuses.

Once the mediator identifies that a settlement range acceptable to all parties has been reached, he or she may privately—or on occasion, publicly—announce to the parties that the conditions for agreement exist. Perhaps more commonly, the mediator may quietly lead the parties into the settlement procedures that will be described in Chapter Thirteen.

Moderation of Inflated Expectations

Most of the discussion so far has concerned disputes in which the parties have been willing to acknowledge that they have moved into a positive settlement range. In some disputes, however, parties have inflated expectations, unrealistically have their hopes raised, and subsequently make unreasonable demands. Such behavior may prevent disputants from progressing into an acceptable settlement range. In order to avoid this situation, mediators should try to persuade the party with inflated expectations either that his or her demand is out of line with what is attainable in reality or that the other party has reached his or her resistance point or bottom line and cannot offer any more. Both strategies are designed to raise the specter of impasse—a specter that will dissipate only if the unrealistic party modifies his or her position.

The mediator often accomplishes the first strategy—convincing a party that his or her demands are unrealistic—by asking one or more of these questions:

- If you were in the other party's situation, would you accept the proposals that you are making now, or would you expect that more should be offered in exchange for an agreement?
- Is the offer fair? Will those whom you respect—the community, the public, your family—perceive it as such?
- Is the offer in line with community, legal, or other norms?
- Is the demand that you are making in line with other negotiated settlements or court decisions on similar issues or under similar conditions?
- Do you have the influence or power to force agreement on the issue?
- What are the benefits to you of pursuing your present course? Are there any risks?

If the mediator cannot, by careful questioning, induce the party to decide to moderate inflated hopes or positions, he or she may have to use information about the other side as a lever of influence. Transmitting specific information about one party's position or means of influence is always problematic for mediators. The mediator may not have an accurate assessment of a party's position or influence or may be the victim of a party's bluffing tactics. Before telling one party that another has reached his or her bottom line and cannot offer any more, the mediator should be certain that there are no additional offers to be made. The party to whom the request is being directed should generally be given an opportunity to make additional offers before the mediator transmits any messages regarding lack of flexibility to the other party. Generally, most of this activity occurs within a caucus. Once a mediator has gained permission to transmit a final offer, he or she may convey it to the party who has inflated expectations. The form in which a final offer is transmitted may vary according to specificity, timing (when it must be accepted), and implications for rejection (Fisher, 1978; Walton and McKersie, 1965).

Mediators should be cautious and use this tactic only as a last resort. If the party with inflated expectations does not shift position, an impasse is likely to occur. Mediators should usually try to keep parties uncommitted to particular solutions for as long as possible so that the parties do not become entrenched in an untenable position. However, if disclosure of a party's bottom line is successful, the intransigent party may revise his or her demands and shift toward a mutually acceptable settlement range.

Negative Settlement Range

Unfortunately, negotiations do not always result in a positive settlement range. I have discussed the interventions that a mediator makes when there is a perceptual problem in recognizing an existent settlement range. I now turn to strategies when the problem is not perceptual—when the differences are real and there are no mutually acceptable options.

The major strategic intervention mediators make when a negative settlement range is present is to assist the parties in determining their Best Alternative to a Negotiated Agreement (BATNA; Fisher and Ury, 1981). In defining the BATNA, the mediator returns to the process of selecting an approach and arena of conflict as outlined in Chapter Four. Separately or jointly, the mediator and the parties should discuss procedural options available to them should negotiations fail, and potential substantive and psychological outcomes that might result from a fallback to these approaches. Parties may at this time decide either to terminate negotiations and move to other resolution approaches or reassess their positions and proposals and move toward an acceptable negotiated settlement. Often, a careful and realistic assessment of each party's BATNA brings all the disputants back to negotiation with a renewed commitment to reaching a mutually acceptable agreement (Lax and Sebenius, 1985).

OPTION EVALUATION IN THE
SINGSON-WHITTAMORE CASE

In the Singson-Whittamore dispute, the parties developed a range of settlement options, including one with and one without compensation. As both of these options were generated primarily in joint session, the parties also began the evaluation process together. They discussed which option would best preserve their relationships with each other and with the clinic and staff, which would be most cost-effective for each of the parties, which would address concerns about precedent, and so on. In the end, they tentatively agreed on the option of Whittamore continuing to practice with the clinic, but at a satellite office, until the contract expired. But they both needed to explore this solution with other concerned parties before a final agreement could be reached. Singson wanted to confer with his board, legal counsel, and other physicians; and Whittamore with the mediator, his lawyer, and his soon-to-be ex-wife. Whittamore's meeting with the mediator was brief and focused primarily on how he might approach his estranged wife to discuss the potential settlement option.

CULTURAL APPROACHES

Culture is often a critical factor in how parties assess settlement options, because it usually shapes the standards and criteria that parties use to define fairness, justice, efficiency, or implementability. Some cultures that are dominated by the rule of law, such as mainstream North American culture, often use legal standards—that is, calculations of what one might gain in court—to determine the acceptability or fairness of an outcome. In such contexts, parties are bargaining in the shadow of the law.

Other cultures might use traditional law or customary practices to evaluate outcomes. For example, parties may want to determine how close the agreement comes to the way the problem was handled in the past or the way similar disputes have been handled. In traditional or indigenous societies, age-old standards are often invoked when decisions are made.

Some cultures use a person's rank or status to determine what would be a fair distribution of resources or benefits, with higher rank carrying a greater entitlement. This was the case in a number of Tswana disputes in Southern Africa (Comaroff and Roberts, 1981) where nobles or chiefs were able to voluntarily gain larger settlements than peasants because of the former party's rank and status.

Finally, parties may use standards and criteria that are particular to their ethnic group or religion. A few years ago, while working in Sri Lanka, I observed a mediation in which the parties settled after the mediator explored with one of them the "merit" that he would accrue if he reached a negotiated settlement. The mediator later explained to me that among Sri Lankan Buddhists, storing up merit by doing good deeds was seen as desirable because it enabled one to get off the wheel of life and reach nirvana more rapidly.

These examples illustrate how important it is for mediators to explore with parties the specific standards and criteria they are using when determining the acceptability of an agreement. Understanding their conceptual framework may help the intervenor work successfully within their worldview, interpret one party's logic and rationale to others, and ultimately facilitate agreement.

Chapter Thirteen

Conducting Final Bargaining and Reaching Closure

Final bargaining involves activities initiated by both the parties and the mediator late in negotiations to reduce the scope and number of substantive and procedural differences between negotiators; move toward a formal agreement and terminate conflict; and assist disputants to reach the greatest psychological closure regarding the people involved, issues in question, and the substantive terms of the settlement.

FINAL BARGAINING ON SUBSTANTIVE AND PROCEDURAL ISSUES

Gulliver (1979, pp. 161–162) identifies four situations in which negotiators find themselves in the final bargaining stage:

1. The bargaining range may have been so narrow that the advantages to be gained from bargaining have become small, even trifling, given the agreement already achieved. . . . What remains to be done is a clearing up of minor details and make a joint commitment to the culminating outcome.

2. The bargaining range may have been narrowed, or the bargaining formula may have already established a number of agreements in principle, but the details of terms need to be worked out.

3. In a third bargaining situation, although something like a viable bargaining range has been discovered, albeit roughly and with unclear limits, considerable differences may remain between the parties. In principle, any point within the range is mutually

preferable to no agreement, yet considerable gain or loss of advantage can still result from final agreement on a particular point.

    4. No viable range has been discovered, and it may well not exist. Here, although the parties are deliberately working toward agreement and are making "real" proposals for an outcome, their preference sets and expectations are still not altogether clear.

Parties who find themselves in the first situation usually reach agreement easily. Their relationship is cordial, the acceptable options are clear, and the procedural route to completion of the negotiations is uncomplicated and direct. The remaining situations, however, are more problematic for negotiations, and a mediator's intervention may be needed to prevent deadlock. I will focus the discussion in this chapter on procedures negotiators and mediators can use to accomplish final bargaining in the last three situations.

    There appear to be four major patterns of moves negotiators use during the final stage of bargaining: (1) incremental convergence (Gulliver, 1979; Walton and McKersie, 1965); (2) a delay of agreement and then a final leap to a package settlement (Zartman and Berman, 1982); (3) development of a consensual formula; and (4) procedural means to reach agreements (Fisher, 1978; Zartman and Berman, 1982). I will first explore these approaches to final settlement and then examine the crucial factor of timing to see how the mediator uses deadlines to bring negotiations to a conclusion.

INCREMENTAL CONVERGENCE

In incremental convergence, the parties make gradual concessions within a positive bargaining range until they reach a mutually satisfactory compromise position. Parties may isolate concessions to offers on a single issue or link issues to balance losses and benefits.

    If the disputants have adhered to positional bargaining, the mediator's main task is to assist them in making offers that will be acceptable to the other party, and to prevent them from prematurely committing to a position that will be difficult to back away from later in negotiations.

    Offers are the specific terms of a position that a party presents as a possible solution to an issue. Especially in positional bargaining, an offer frequently implies some form of concession or trade a party is willing to make in exchange for an acceptable reciprocal offer or agreement. Parties engaged in positional bargaining face several problems that may inhibit them from making offers.

Reluctance to Overconcede or Reveal Bargaining Positions

At this point in negotiations, parties may be reluctant to make offers that go beyond their opening positions, even if they have discovered an opponent's settlement range. They do not want to concede more than is necessary, nor do they want to indicate the bargaining positions within their own settlement range. This situation can result in endless avoidance behavior and a lack of commitment to a specific proposal.

In this situation, mediators should assist parties in developing tentative or hypothetical offers that can be used to test for potential agreement while not formally committing a party to a specific solution. A negotiator, the mediator, or both can design tentative or probing offers. Such offers can vary in degree of specificity, resources exchanged, time of performance, and implications if the offer is accepted in a timely manner. This allows a party more flexibility in exploring the settlement range without prematurely committing to a position. The mediator might say, "I'd like to try out a possible settlement option. If you find it to be reasonable, I will explore its acceptability with the other party." Tentative offers can often be explored with the other party by having the mediator shuttle between the parties, testing areas of agreement without formally committing a party to a specific solution.

Fear of Being Perceived as Weak

A second factor that inhibits parties in initiating offers is the fear of being perceived as weak (Rubin and Brown, 1975). People in conflict often do not want others to see them being "forced" to make a concession. They fear that concession making will become—or will be perceived to be—a pattern, and that the opponent will hold out on later issues expecting similar compliant behavior. There is evidence in pure game theory that concession making may be perceived as a sign of weakness (Deutsch, 1974); however, in actual negotiations in which there is personal interaction, making the first offer or concession can be turned into an asset rather than a liability. The classic case is Anwar Sadat's initiative in proposing to Menachem Begin that they begin discussions on a Middle East peace plan. Sadat's proposal to travel to Israel to talk was a potent first offer, and a definite sign of strength.

Mediators can aid a party in making a first offer by helping to frame the offer in such a way that the concession becomes an initiative of strength, not weakness. Through framing, the party can make explicit the fact that he or she is making an offer or concession to demonstrate good faith, show a willingness to take the other's needs into consideration, encourage the other party or parties to make similar moves, or establish a trading arrangement in which a concession is made on one issue in exchange for a concession on another. The mediator may coach and assist the party in framing the offer so that the other party will perceive it favorably. The mediator may also prime the recipient so that the offer will be accepted or reciprocated.

Negative Transference

Parties often reject an offer not because of its substantive content but because of their attitude toward its initiator. The mediator can help negotiators avoid this pitfall by proposing one party's ideas to the other as if they were his or her own. This eliminates the possibility that the other party will perceive offers as "partial, biased, or tainted more because of their source than because of their substantive content" (Young, 1972).

Fear of Rejection and Impasse

Parties are often discouraged from making offers because they fear rejection and stalemate. They may prefer to continue discussion rather than reach an impasse. Mediators can assist parties in overcoming this obstacle by testing the ideas of the parties in private and bringing to the joint session only those points on which the parties can agree. The mediator can encourage the parties to make the offers, or make the offers that they agree to for them. It is generally preferable for the parties themselves to make the offers as this increases their commitment to proposals and maintains the mediator's impartiality toward the substance of the negotiations.

Public Pressure on Negotiators

In cases in which negotiators represent a constituency, the parties may be constrained from making public offers because of possible personal repercussions from unpopular concessions. This is often the case in labor-management negotiations when a union team feels constrained by the union membership from making an offer that the team may feel is reasonable and acceptable. Here, the mediator can make a proposal and become a negotiator's scapegoat. Negotiators can agree to the concession and later claim that they agreed because the mediator requested concurrence, not because they initiated it or the other party forced them to agree.

Closely related to the scapegoat function of the mediator is the role of mediator or coalition former. The mediator's presence and his or her suggestions of offers can cause the disputants to reevaluate their relationship to each other and the issues that divide them: "One possibility is, of course, that the two original contestants both become antagonistic towards the third person and decide to agree so as not to let the newcomer influence the settlement" (Aubert, 1963, p. 35). The mediator can induce this situation by proposing one or more solutions that are more extreme than either party is willing to accept. In this situation, they may be forced into a coalition to moderate the mediator's exaggerated position.

Loss of Face

Another block to parties initiating offers is the issue of losing or saving face (Brown, 1977). Mediators can assist parties in making new offers by giving them rationalizations for shifts in positions and by reframing the situation so that an offer does not result in a loss of dignity. This strategy also aids parties in abandoning untenable positions.

The six blocks described here can all be impediments to initiating offers that can lead to an incremental convergence of positions or selection of an interest-based settlement option. Appropriate mediator intervention, however, can minimize the negative effects and ease the decision-making process.

LEAP TO AGREEMENT

The leap-to-agreement approach to final bargaining is characterized by a strategy of opening with a high demand, offering few concessions, and then making a final leap toward a package that meets the negotiators' demands toward the end of negotiations (Zartman and Berman, 1982). Leaps to agreement usually occur when (1) negotiators consciously pursue a hard-line strategy to educate an opponent about a principle; (2) negotiators want to use deadline pressure to force an agreement; or (3) all options are equally acceptable (or unacceptable) and no one proposal has superior merit.

The leap-to-agreement process of negotiation is often characterized by a package deal or "yes-able proposal" that attempts to incorporate the needs of all parties into one acceptable linked package (Fisher, 1969). Advantages to this approach are that:

- It prevents incremental concession making that may result in expectations of more concessions
- It allows a party to make a point about the strength of his or her commitment to an issue or principle
- By turning the task of developing a comprehensive solution over to one party, it attempts to eliminate part of the difficult task of jointly drafting an agreement
- It demonstrates that acceptable trade-offs are possible
- It may incline a party toward agreement when a deadline is close and there is no time to develop a counterproposal

This approach does, however, have some drawbacks. Intransigence on a position and lack of progress early in a negotiation may cause the other party to adhere to its initial position and may also foster increasing hostility over any procedure used to resolve the dispute rather than over the issues themselves. Presenting a package late in negotiations may also cause problems because the opposing party may believe that he or she has not had an opportunity to participate in formulating the terms for settlement. Rejection thus may be based on procedural participatory factors rather than the proposal's substantive content.

The leap-to-agreement approach may have both positive and negative impact for negotiators, as described previously. Mediators can either promote or inhibit the use of this procedure, depending on the dynamics of the negotiation session. If the procedure is being used by a party in final bargaining and is causing damage to negotiations, the mediator can notify the party in caucus of the potential detrimental effect on the other party. If, on the other hand, the hard-line procedure of delaying commitment is serving to educate the other party on a particular principle or point, and if the mediator has learned that the other party is progressing toward agreement, the process can be encouraged.

The mediator can also use the leap-to-agreement tactic by delaying a party's presentation of a solution until the mediator is certain that the other party will agree to a particular proposal. At that time, the mediator can ask one of the parties to make the proposal, or he or she may make it. With agreement ensured, the parties can leap to a one-step settlement.

FORMULAS AND AGREEMENTS IN PRINCIPLE

I have already discussed at some length the procedures used to reach a bargaining formula or an agreement in principle. This strategy is one of progressing from the most general level of agreement to more specific details of a settlement. The mediator may initiate this approach early in negotiations, even as early as the stage of defining dispute parameters, or it may appear as late as final bargaining, after more specific options have been generated and assessed.

The procedures for reaching a formula settlement are somewhat like those used in constructing a puzzle. First, the outside boundary— the general agreement—is constructed. The outside pieces determine the overall boundaries of the settlement. The negotiators then construct various packages that will fit into this framework. The formula-development process is conducted by consensus and usually entails modification, refinement, and synthesis of proposals, or occasionally exchange of small incremental pieces. The process often involves creating multiple levels of agreements with increasing specificity.

Parties often begin building a formula or attempt to develop agreements in principle early in negotiations. This process usually starts during the stage of defining dispute parameters, when the parties attempt to outline the boundaries, both conceptual and substantive, within which they will negotiate. Development of a formula or agreement in principle may later become much more explicit during the process of defining issues and interests.

In final bargaining, formula development or agreements in principle are primarily useful in preventing deadlocks. Formulas may be designed to define principles by which a limited resource within a bargaining range can be divided or to set forth procedures for combining solutions that meet the needs of all parties. Mutual decision about a formula or agreement in principle "is desirable . . . because a formula or framework of principles helps give structure and coherence to an agreement on details, helps facilitate the search for solutions on component items, and helps create a positive, creative image of negotiation rather than an image of concession and compromise" (Zartman and Berman, 1982, p. 93).

Parties with extensive experience with or bias toward positional bargaining are often not aware of the merits of establishing a bargaining formula or agreements in principle to reach final settlement. Mediators can often assist parties by educating them about the approach and by identifying such a formula in much the same manner as an intervenor is able to help identify interests.

Zartman and Berman (1982) maintain that recognition of a common formula depends on three elements: (1) a shared perception or definition of the conflict, (2) an understanding of the primary and underlying values or interests that give meaning to the issues under discussion, and (3) an applicable criterion of justice. By the final bargaining stage, it is hoped that the parties have developed a shared perception or definition of the conflict. If they have not, the mediator should refer them back to the previous stages of issue and interest identification. Interests and underlying values must be satisfied or be met by a settlement. The formula must contain provisions for responding to both the primary and secondary interests of the disputants, or it will be unacceptable.

The third component of a formula is a mutually accepted standard of justice. Zartman and Berman (1982) identify five types of justice: substantive, procedural, equitable, compensatory, and subtractive. *Substantive justice* refers to a concrete objective outcome that the parties believe is fair. *Procedural justice* refers to the process by which a solution is reached and the settlement is carried out. Most disputants expect the same procedure to be in effect for both parties; if the procedure is to be different, the reasons for the difference should be mutually acceptable. *Equitable justice* refers to the "apportionment of shares on the basis of each party's particular characteristics" (p. 104). The basis of equity will vary from dispute to dispute; it may be based on need, power, historic precedent, or the size or amount of resources available for division.

Compensatory justice refers to payments that remedy an unequal distribution of resources. Compensatory justice is usually an issue when one party has been deprived as a result of a previous relationship with the other. For example, a husband may agree to pay spousal support and fund his ex-wife's school expenses so that she can earn an income and attain a standard of living equal to what she was accustomed to in the marriage. A developer may monetarily compensate the immediate neighbors for potential damages to their lifestyle due to the siting of an unpopular new facility needed by the community (O'Hare, Bacow, and Sanderson, 1983). *Subtractive justice* refers to equal denial to all parties of a resource, so that no one wins. This component of a formula is used when parties attach a higher priority to denying the other parties access to a resource than to possessing it themselves. For example, if in a divorce property settlement the couple cannot decide which of them should have their antique marital brass bed, both may agree to sell it and deny possession to each other rather than agree that one of them should have it.

PROCEDURAL MEANS OF REACHING SUBSTANTIVE DECISIONS

Occasionally, negotiators are unable to make a decision on a particular substantive issue, and the impasse delays the settlement of the entire conflict. Inability to agree may be based on psychological unwillingness to settle a dispute, reluctance to agree to a point for fear of constituency disapproval, multiple solutions that are equally acceptable (or undesirable), and so on. Regardless of the reason agreement cannot be reached, the parties may still be under pressure to find some solution to their impasse. To break the deadlock, they may turn to a procedural solution to resolve the substantive problem. This process was discussed briefly in Chapter Eleven, on option generation, but it should now be explored in more detail.

Procedural solutions are process decisions that parties make to resolve disputes without directly deciding an issue. Generally, the process selected results in a substantive answer. There are four common types of procedural approaches to resolving substantive impasse: the procedural time line, third-party decision makers, arbitrary decision-making procedures, and postponement or avoidance.

Procedural-Time-Line Approach

The procedural-time-line approach requires negotiators to develop a process and time line for particular substantive agreements and to define specific advantages, consequences, or penalties for parties meeting or failing to meet the agreed deadlines. Time determines the substantive outcome. For example, if parties are negotiating payment, they may agree that if payment is received before a specific date it will be of a certain amount. If payment is received after that date, a penalty charge will be imposed. A party then has a choice about when to pay. The procedural time line approach allows the parties to avoid reaching a specific substantive decision on issues and creates instead a procedural formula governing how the decision will be made.

Third-Party Decision Makers

Parties who reach an impasse on a substantive question can turn the problem over to a third party other than the mediator. The most common form of third-party decision making is performed by a judge or jury; disputants generally agree to be legally bound by the decision of the impartial third party. Another third-party structure is arbitration, which was defined in Chapter One. Mediators often suggest referral to an arbiter or judge of issues over which parties are deadlocked.

Other third-party decision makers who can assist parties in breaking deadlocks are property appraisers, custody evaluators, and similar technical experts. Parties can agree to engage the assistance of third parties and to abide by their recommendations. In one business dispute over the division of common property, the parties disagreed about what the property was worth. They decided to submit the problem to two appraisers who were mutually acceptable and to average the answers received. Thus a mutually acceptable and fair process produced a substantive answer that both parties could accept.

Mechanical Decision-Making Procedures

Parties often wish to make a decision on issues in which there is an equal chance of winning or losing or in which the outcome is of little consequence to the disputants. Negotiators or mediators frequently resort to procedural mechanisms that automatically result in a decision.

Mechanical decision making is appropriate when the difference between the parties is not large, and therefore the loss for either would not be great, or when the probability of reaching a decision by another means has an equal chance of loss or gain for one of the parties. Parties split the *difference* in order to maximize their rewards and minimize their losses.

Negotiators may also choose to take turns in satisfying their interests—for example, by alternating the selection of items to be inherited from an estate—or to use games of chance such as flipping coins or drawing lots or straws. These procedures give each disputant an equal chance to win rewards. The process, not the disputants, decides the outcome. The mediator may impartially supervise the process to ensure fairness.

Postponement, Avoidance, and Issue Abandonment

Parties may also break a deadlock by postponing or avoiding a decision or by abandoning an issue. Postponement may mean delaying a decision until the other party is more psychologically disposed toward an issue or is represented by a different person. Postponement may also be used to allow time for developing new proposals or arguments, mobilizing power or resources, or reconfiguring external structural variables or influences on the conflict. In one public policy dispute, the parties decided to hold off on making an agreement until an election had occurred and the disposition of the newly elected officials could be determined.

Postponement may be used in conjunction with third-party decision making. In cases in which parties cannot reach agreement on a particular issue and in which failure to agree on that issue might result in total impasse, negotiators may decide to forge a general agreement and defer decision making on the particular issue until the specific conflict arises at a later date. They may designate one component of a dispute for referral to an arbiter or judge for final resolution. This approach avoids total deadlock and allows agreement to be reached in the absence of a full consensus agreement on all issues.

At the start of negotiations, parties raise a number of issues or demands that they want addressed. Each issue can be ranked according to its importance in terms of the overall settlement. It is not unusual for negotiators to include one or more bogus or throwaway issues that are made to appear important so that they can be used for educational or trading purposes. A party uses throwaway issues as part of an initial large demand to educate his or her opponents about how many concessions will have to be made for a settlement to be reached. Throwaway issues are used in final bargaining as chips that are traded for desirable concessions. However, they are useful only if the other party believes that they are genuine and valuable. If this illusion can be maintained throughout negotiations, a bargainer may truly have a tradable commodity.

The manner in which throwaway issues are used varies. They may be used as an early concession to demonstrate goodwill; they may be offered later in exchange for the withdrawal of another negotiator's demand; or they may be deployed as positive tradable items. Negotiators will often mutually agree to abandon issues in an "I'll get rid of mine if you'll get rid of yours" manner.

On occasion, the mediator is in the best position to manage the dropping of issues. He or she should determine with the parties in caucus whether they require acknowledgment in joint session that they have abandoned the demands or issues or whether they prefer merely not to mention them. If they prefer acknowledgment, the mediator can help establish the conditions for abandoning issues or demands.

POSSIBLE SUBSTANTIVE AND PROCEDURAL OUTCOMES TO A CONFLICT

I have listed a range of procedures that can be used to arrive at substantive or procedural agreements, but not every conflict ends with a comprehensive agreement or total satisfaction of all parties' substantive procedural or psychological interests. I now present a range of possible outcomes to conflict. Ideally, the mediator will want to work toward the most comprehensive agreement possible, but for the involved parties even partial settlements may be preferable to no settlement at all (Gibson, 1999).

Spectrum of Possible Negotiated Outcomes to a Conflict

- *The 100 percent solution.* Parties have all substantive, procedural, and psychological interests satisfied.
- *The acceptable-settlement package.* Parties trade satisfaction of interests of different strengths, and the total package is mutually acceptable.
- *Compromise.* Parties share gains and losses in order to reach agreement. Compromise can occur on specific issues or in the negotiations as a whole.
- *Experimental or trial decisions.* Parties are unable to reach a permanent decision and agree on a temporary settlement that will be tested and evaluated at a later date.
- *Creation of spheres of influence.* Parties have defined arenas or issues about which each party has exclusive decision-making authority.
- *Alternate satisfaction.* Parties agree to alternate when they have their interests met so that they can have a high level of satisfaction, but not at the same time.
- *Splitting the difference.* Parties mechanically share equally the gains and losses to reach settlement. This strategy generally occurs when the distance between the parties' positions is slight.
- *Procedural solutions to substantive problems.* Parties devise a *process* by which they can obtain an answer to a substantive issue in dispute. The process mechanically results in an answer to the problem.

- *Mechanical means of deciding.* Parties use mechanical and arbitrary means, such as drawing straws or flipping coins, to reach a decision.
- *Deferred decisions.* Parties decide, either unilaterally or jointly, to delay decision making until a more auspicious time when either additional facts, a more favorable external environment, more power, wider constituent support, and so forth, are available.
- *Partial settlement.* Parties agree on many issues but continue to disagree on others.
- *Agreement to disagree.* Parties mutually agree to disagree. The contested issue is not dropped but is no longer pursued at this time.
- *Mutual dropping of issues.* Parties implicitly or explicitly agree to drop an issue in dispute.
- *Nonbinding decision.* Parties make a nonbinding request of each other for cooperation, but compliance is not promised or guaranteed.
- *Issue avoidance.* One or more parties refuse to join others in negotiating a solution to an issue.
- *Development of multiple choices that are referred to a third-party decision maker.* Parties turn to a judge or arbiter for a decision between two or more settlement options that they have generated.
- *Development of a list of interests or objective criteria that are referred to third-party decision maker.* Parties refer contested interests to a judge or arbiter who is asked to use parties' individual or joint interests or criteria to formulate a decision.
- *Decision referred to a third-party decision maker.* Parties cannot decide, and they defer the decision to a third party for a binding or nonbinding decision.
- *Impasse or stalemate.* Parties cannot decide, and negotiations stall or break down. Neither party has the power to force the issue in his or her favor or to develop a mutually acceptable solution.
- *Continued negotiations.* Parties cannot agree, so they do agree to continue negotiating.
- *Shift to another approach of conflict resolution.* The parties are unable to reach an acceptable negotiated settlement and move to another approach—voting, nonviolent action, violence, and so on—to resolve their differences.

DEADLINES

Timing is a critical component in final bargaining and settlement. Cross (1969, p. 13) notes, "If it did not matter *when* the parties agreed, it would not matter whether they agreed at all." Time is both an important motivational factor for negotiators and a variable that helps determine how well their interests will be met. In final bargaining, time may be managed for the purpose of inducing a settlement. The most common form of time management at this stage is the deadline.

Deadlines are limits that delineate the period of time in which an agreement must be reached. Deadlines perform an important function in settling a variety of issues. For example, lawyers often settle legal cases in the days or hours before trial date. Much of the impetus for out-of-court settlement comes from the unpredictable outcome of court proceedings and the potential for negative consequences if the parties engage in direct litigation. The deadline of a court date motivates parties to settle.

Deadlines play an equally important function in prompting the settlement of labor-management disputes. The eleventh-hour settlement before a strike deadline is well known. The same dynamics are common in nearly all other types of negotiations. Stevens (1963, p. 200) argues: "An approaching deadline puts pressure on the parties to state their true positions and thus does much to squeeze elements of bluff out of the later steps of negotiation. However, an approaching deadline does much more. It brings pressures to bear which actually change the least favorable terms upon which each party is willing to settle; thus, it operates as a force tending to bring about conditions necessary for agreement."

An understanding of deadlines and how they can be used is an invaluable tool for negotiators and mediators. It is beneficial to discuss several characteristics and variables of deadlines that affect their utility in negotiations.

Internally and Externally Established Deadlines

A party can establish his or her own deadline, or outside forces may determine when negotiation ceases. A contract deadline, an ultimatum imposed by an outside agency, and an impending court date are examples of externally imposed constraints.

External deadlines are often important to negotiation strategies. Shapiro (1970, p. 44), in referring to negotiations in which one party represents a constituent group, observes that "any settlement made without the pressure of a last minute crisis leaves the negotiators open to attack by the people they represent, who may feel that they could have gotten a more favorable contract if only their negotiators had bluffed the other side right down to the final moment."

Coordinated and Uncoordinated Deadlines

Deadlines can be symmetrical or asymmetrical in that the parties may have either the same time limits or different ones. For some parties, a delay in decision making may result in increased benefits, whereas for others a rapid decision may be essential (Lake, 1980).

Actual and Artificial Deadlines

Parties may be constrained by deadlines that correspond to particular events beyond which they have little control, or they may be influenced by artificial time constraints that are almost arbitrarily established by one or more parties.

An artificial deadline was created during negotiations between environmentalists, industry representatives, and two U.S. governmental agencies over restrictions on oil and gas development on federal lands. The environmentalists stated that if they did not see progress in the talks within six weeks, they would cease negotiating. They arbitrarily set a deadline in order to encourage industry and government representatives to reach an agreement.

Rigid and Flexible Deadlines

The rigidity-flexibility variable is closely related to the distinction between actual and artificial deadlines. Although rigid deadlines are usually viewed as the stronger impetus for settlement because they set fixed time boundaries that the parties dare not overstep, more flexible deadlines, at least at the eleventh hour, may allow the parties necessary latitude to reach a decision. Parties often need additional time to reconsider a last-minute proposal or to gain constituent or bureaucratic approval to reach a final accord. Mutually determined extensions of deadlines may be a prerequisite for a settlement.

Deadlines with and Without Consequences

Deadlines promote settlements primarily because they usually imply negative consequences if the time limit is transgressed. Possible consequences include termination of negotiations, stalemate, loss of gains already achieved, withdrawal of an offer, acceptance of another party's offer, a court suit, a strike, and other undesirable outcomes. Although a deadline does not have to imply dire consequences such as threat or actual imposition of negative sanctions, it must present the possibility of a worse option than if settlement were reached. Negotiators and mediators often manipulate the explicit or implicit consequences of not settling before a deadline because known or unknown consequences may incline another party toward agreement.

Explicit or Vague Deadlines

Deadlines may be explicitly defined, or they may remain vague. The appropriate strategy depends on the particular negotiation. Explicit deadlines create a definite point at which settlement must be reached. Though involving a positive benefit in creating motivation for settlement, explicit deadlines may also create resistance because of a perceived threat of negative consequences; they may promote unwise decisions because there is not enough time to consider all options; and they may encourage an excessive willingness to settle at the sacrifice of an important principle. Negotiators usually argue for explicit deadlines only when all parties will bear the negative consequences of a failure to reach agreement within the prescribed time. An example of this situation is a strike in which both labor and management stand to lose if a new contract is not negotiated.

Nonexplicit deadlines, on the other hand, may be used to imply that the negotiator is willing to talk as long as necessary to reach an acceptable settlement. Such deadlines can be used to the advantage of negotiators who know that an opponent is under pressure to settle by a certain time. The appearance of unlimited time for discussion may motivate an opponent to settle early in order to curtail rising costs that result from delay. However, even if time is an important factor for negotiators, a party may gain more in the end by concealing his or her deadline. Cohen (1980), a business negotiator, describes a case in which he lost thousands of dollars because he discussed his time constraints too openly and his opponent discovered his settlement deadline. His opponent was willing to talk for a longer period of time than was available to Cohen, and thus forced him to make concessions and reach an agreement just before his deadline—the departure of his plane.

MEDIATORS AND DEADLINE MANAGEMENT

Mediators can significantly assist negotiators in managing deadlines by making them aware of internal or external deadlines or assisting them in setting artificial deadlines when none exist. When appropriate, mediators may also make rigid deadlines more flexible, assist the parties in avoiding negative moves related to time, and enhance the usefulness of deadlines.

Making Parties Aware of Deadlines

Parties are often not aware of the existence or consequences of deadlines. This is especially the case when the deadlines are externally imposed or implicitly assumed. In final bargaining, mediators often remind negotiators that a deadline is approaching and that positive benefits may be lost or negative consequences incurred from a failure to reach an agreement. This function should not be construed to mean that the mediator should reveal a hidden deadline that is crucial for another party to meet his or her interests. Mediators should take great care not to reveal confidential information about a party's time constraints lest they unduly influence the settlement and create a mediator-induced imbalance in the power relationship between the parties. The mediator should, however, bring to the consciousness of the negotiators the explicit time parameters that affect final bargaining.

Assisting Parties in Establishing a Deadline

The presence of a deadline often enhances a negotiation's outcome. Parties who have the capacity to reward or punish other disputants for their performance with respect to time parameters can create deadlines. They can also be established by external constituencies—bureaucratic authorities or collectives of interested parties—or by external events. Finally, the mediator's moves can create deadlines. I will examine each of these means of defining time boundaries for negotiation and the mediator's role in influencing them.

The mediator, if he or she deems it advisable or necessary, may encourage one or more parties in a dispute to establish a deadline. This move may be made in caucus or in joint session and may be developed unilaterally or multilaterally. There are some situations in which it is appropriate for the mediator to suggest that only one party set a deadline, whereas in others a cooperatively established time limit may be necessary to motivate all disputants to reach agreement. However, a mediator's suggestion in a caucus that only one party set a deadline may be seen as undue manipulation of the negotiation process and may represent a loss of neutrality; it may also carry the risk of exposure in joint session. Mediator advice to only one party should be taken with great care.

If a jointly established deadline is desirable, the mediator can assist the parties in deciding the criteria to be used in determining the deadline. Relevant factors may include time needed to learn about or study the issue; time for ratification of an agreement by a constituency; availability of necessary data; and structural constraints such as court dates, business schedules, and even changes of season.

Persons or events external to negotiations may also establish deadlines. Mediators often help parties negotiate with superiors or constituencies not directly involved in the mediation regarding the establishment of time parameters. However, such externally imposed boundaries are often beyond the direct control of negotiators but may be needed to motivate other parties to settle.

Although mediators rarely control external events that impose deadlines on negotiations, they can translate the consequences of these events to the parties to encourage them to settle within an agreed period of time. For example, if economic forces allow an offer to be made for only a limited period, the mediator may inform the parties of this fact. Raising awareness about an imminent court date that cannot be changed is another means of deadline leverage.

The mediator can also create his or her own deadline if such a move appears to be the only means of settlement. This can be done in several ways. First, the mediator can make all parties aware that a settlement is possible and that he or she thinks it can be accomplished within a specific period of time. The mediator can request that parties reach agreement within these time parameters. Deadlines imposed by the mediator may encourage the parties to negotiate more expeditiously; for example, some commercial mediators structure a limited number of sessions within which the parties must agree or cease mediation.

Second, the mediator can announce that he or she will make a public statement after a certain date that the parties are not negotiating in a timely and serious manner. Third, a mediator may threaten to leave the negotiations at a certain time unless the parties agree to honor a deadline (Kolb, 1983). This threat creates a functional deadline to which the parties must respond if they want to retain the mediator's services.

Mediators can impose deadlines on parties only if (1) the mediator's threat is credible, (2) the parties are willing to agree to the mediator's request or demand, and (3) the services of the mediator are genuinely needed or desired. The mediator's expendability or his or her failure to carry out a threat may lead to either a loss of credibility or the mediator's departure.

Lack of a deadline may not be the problem in a dispute. Deadlines themselves can cause impasse. Parties may believe they face a rigid deadline, and the lack of adequate time to negotiate an acceptable agreement may create a deadlock. The mediator's task in this situation is to create a more flexible time frame, which can be accomplished by several methods.

First, the mediator may find ways to actually extend the time available for negotiation. Specific procedural agreements may be proposed to postpone the deadline so that parties have more time to make a decision. A suggestion to this effect by the mediator rather than by one of the parties often makes the proposal more palatable to the disputants and also avoids the appearance that if the deadline is extended one party will make a concession. Another mediator tactic, which is often used in labor negotiations, is to "stop the clock." In this maneuver, the mediator obtains agreement to continue negotiations and to temporarily ignore the passage of time and the consequences of exceeding the deadline. Negotiation is extended without publicly disavowing that a deadline exists. This approach works as long as progress toward agreement is being made. If not, a party may unilaterally terminate negotiations after the deadline has passed and thus incur the consequences of deadlocked negotiations. A third strategy mediators can use to create more flexibility in deadlines is to delay the time or date by which a specific component of a decision is to be made or is to go into effect. This allows the parties more time to work out controversial details of a particular problem and still reach general agreement.

Avoiding Deadline Dangers

There are several dangerous but common moves that negotiators may make in conjunction with deadlines. Among them are exposure of another party's deadline, games of "chicken," threats of dire consequences if agreement is not reached before the deadline, unrealistically quick agreements because of false momentum toward the deadline, and manipulation of embarrassment to force an agreement. Mediators can help parties avoid pitfalls in each of these situations.

Chicken is a strategy in which each party delays making concessions until the deadline is imminent. The tension of intransigence will supposedly test another negotiator's will to the extent that he or she will give up and make concessions rather than risk deadlock or negative costs if the deadline passes. Unfortunately, no party may be willing to break the cycle of resistance, and then all parties are forced to carry out threats and endure consequences that no one wanted. Mediators may help parties avoid playing chicken with deadlines by (1) publicly labeling the strategy, (2) privately working with each party to assess the costs of pursuing such a tactic, and (3) figuring out ways that parties can abandon extreme positions and make offers that will allow them to maintain their dignity.

Threats made close to deadlines seem to be especially common when parties experience intransigence from other negotiators and impasse is looming. Generally, mediators discourage parties from making threats and encourage them to make positive offers to induce agreement. This is both a more constructive and a less risky tactic.

The presence of a deadline occasionally forces parties to reach unrealistic and unimplementable agreements. Parties begin a process of agreeing and become so involved in the excitement and dynamics of settlement that they formulate impracticable agreements. When a mediator recognizes this pattern, he or she should temper the enthusiasm of the disputants by using reality testing, asking questions that raise doubts about the viability of an option or settlement, encouraging the parties to seek more information, or physically separating parties into caucuses so that they can more realistically assess the settlement without the stress of the presence of other negotiators.

Kheel, a labor mediator, has used this delaying tactic both to avoid untenable agreements and to psychologically encourage settlement (Shapiro, 1970). Kheel separates parties, assuring them that they are "not ready to settle," until they virtually demand to return to joint session to make an agreement. After the delay, in which the real merits of the settlement are analyzed, the parties are ready to make a solid and realistic agreement.

Parties are often embarrassed if they ask to delay settlement until they can be more certain of a proposal's merits. Other negotiators can manipulate such embarrassment to force an untimely agreement. Mediators can legitimize delay and prevent manipulation of embarrassment by publicly calling for more time to reasonably consider a proposal. As an impartial intervenor, the mediator may even claim a personal lack of understanding of the settlement in order to delay a decision and give the parties more time to educate the mediator or for deliberation.

Enhancing the Usefulness of Deadlines

Mediators can assist parties in enhancing positive use of deadlines in several ways. First, they can help parties to design offers that contain fading opportunities. They can also create artificial mileposts by which to measure progress before the ultimate deadline is reached. Each milepost marks a certain number of benefits that an opponent will receive if he or she settles at that time. The longer the settlement is delayed, the fewer benefits are offered.

An example of the first strategy occurred at a dinner party I attended one winter. Parents of several children attending the function told them that they had had enough hors d'oeuvres for the evening, but the children wanted more. At a certain point, more firewood was needed to heat the room. The children were offered the option of having more hors d'oeuvres if they would each bring in one log. They protested, started delaying tactics, and said they really didn't want to go out into the cold and get the wood. One of the guests changed the terms of the bargaining by saying that if the children did not bring in the wood in five minutes, he would do so; thus the offer of more food would no longer be available. The children decided that the proposed exchange was worthwhile and carried in the wood before the adult could do so.

CULTURE, TIME, AND DEADLINES

Culture often significantly influences how parties view time, and consequently deadlines. Generally, people from cultures that see time as a limited commodity and an item to be saved or spent sparingly value efficiency, rapid agreement, and timeliness. Such cultures frequently expect and allocate shorter periods of time for negotiations and often set hard and fast deadlines.

Many other cultures see time as an unlimited resource; they believe that problem solving should not be rushed and will occur all in good time. It is not that these cultures do not have deadlines; their deadlines are more distant than is common in speedier cultures.

When disputants are out of sync in their sense of time and timeliness, additional conflicts may result. For example, North Americans often complain of the time it takes to reach an agreement in many Latin American and Asian countries and grouse that if deadlines are set, they are ignored. This cultural problem is generally due to differing expectations regarding the meaning, value, and use of time.

When working in intercultural disputes, mediators need to become aware of the expectations that parties may have for the use of time and deadlines (to say nothing of clashes with mediators' own expectations in this regard). Mediators may need to act as cultural interpreters of time and timing to coordinate parties' activities in the context of time.

PSYCHOLOGICAL CLOSURE AND THE REDEFINITION OF PARTIES' RELATIONSHIPS

Often closure on substantive issues and implementation procedures is not enough to ensure final agreement, compliance, or termination of a conflict. In addition, parties often need a significant degree of psychological closure with the other people who have been involved, the process process itself, and the terms of substantive agreements that have been reached. This psychological aspect of agreement making is often necessary and critical to help disputants end or let go of a dispute.

Psychological closure means that parties to a conflict have gained enough emotional satisfaction as a result of participation in the dispute resolution process that they are willing to emotionally disconnect themselves from the historic antecedents and actions that provoked the dispute, the conflict itself, contested issues, and former opponents. Lack of psychological closure can be caused by any number of factors. Antagonistic or derogatory statements or actions conducted before or during negotiations, perceptions of lack of good-faith bargaining, past efforts by other negotiators to take advantage of a party, lack of being listened to or respected prior to or during negotiations, or feelings that an agreement is being pushed down the throat of a disputant are all grounds for lack of psychological closure.

Psychological closure can be achieved by building increased feelings of comfort on the part of parties with the substantive agreement and implementation process, having them feel that they have been respectfully listened to and accurately heard by other disputants and the mediator, receiving acceptable levels of acknowledgment or ownership by other parties of their role in or consequences of the conflict, allowing participants to hear and accept genuine and meaningful apologies, or increasing levels of trust and respect for the "other side" from productive and meaningful engagement in negotiations and mediation. When there will be a continuation or termination of a relationship, albeit in a new form, psychological closure helps clarify what future interactions the parties expect or desire.

Hopefully, movement toward psychological closure has been happening throughout the mediation process, and communication enhancement and emotional processing procedures (active listening, open-ended questioning, reframing) have helped parties become more comfortable with the other people who have been involved and the terms of the settlement. I examine the issue of psychological and emotional closure here and in detail because it is at this time that it is most crucial for the termination of a conflict. Often, parties may be able to reach acceptable substantive and procedural agreements but without psychological closure will be unable to implement them or end their dispute.

Although a total or high level of psychological closure may not be absolutely necessary to resolve or terminate many disputes—in that people can reach workable agreements without having to trust, respect, like, or love their former opponents—emotional closure often helps people detach from conflict and can help create the conditions for more postive future interactions between former disputants or other uninvolved parties. Psychological closure can also create some degree of inner peace for former disputants and help prevent continued feelings of uneasiness, frustration, hurt, lack of respect, mistrust, animosity, anger, hate, guilt, unfairness, or the desire for revenge.

Psychological closure often requires mental recognition, verbal expression, or specific actions to address the damage done by a conflict to the parties' relationships. This form of closure can be enhanced by direct or indirect, or unilateral or multilateral statements or actions by the involved partes. It can also be encouraged by mediator interventions.

Psychological closure can often be enhanced by action from one or more parties: (1) acknowledgment of what happened; (2) ownership of roles played, actions that occurred, and negative or positive consequences that resulted: (3) affirmation of, or expectations for, a more positive or productive relationship in the future: (4) acceptable and genuine apologies; (5) requests for, or acts of, forgiveness; and (6) reconciliation. Some disputants require only acknowledgment to achieve psychological closure; others require more from another party.

Acknowledgment means that a person recognizes and can accurately describe what has occurred. Acknowledgment often indicates a greater (or even a common) understanding of past events, issues, interests, or actions, but not necessarily total agreement with the perceptions of other parties. For example, in a mediation between two co-workers that involved one of them sending "flaming" e-mails (abusive messages transmitted by computer), one party said, "I acknowledge that I did send an inordinate number of very direct e-mails during a short period of time. Both the number and tone of the messages caused and exacerbated problems between us."

Acknowledgments may be initiated unilaterally and unconditionally by a party, or with the expectation of reciprocation by another disputant. If either initial or reciprocal acknowledgments are not forthcoming, and it appears to the mediator that they will be necessary to make progress toward psychological closure, the intermediary may encourage one or more people in the dispute to make them. This encouragement may occur either in private or joint sessions. For example, in a caucus the intermediary might say, "After listening to the other people involved, I believe that it would be very helpful for them to hear from you, that you acknowledge what has happened and the consequences that have occurred. Hearing this directly from you may enable them to let go of their hurt and anger and help them to move forward with the substantive agreement that you want."

Ownership is a step beyond acknowledgment. Ownership means that a person acknowledges what happened, recognizes his or her role, *and* takes responsibility for the potential or actual consequences. For example, in the flaming case, the party who sent the problematic e-mails went on to say: "I recognize that I am a very direct person, and that I often do not stop to think about the possible impacts that the frequency or tone of my messages may have on their recipients. I recognize that the form my e-mails took not only hindered getting our work done, but also damaged our relationship and ability to communicate in a productive manner."

Affirmation refers to positive statements concerning possible or actual future relationship between disputing parties. Affirmation confirms or reconfirms connections, or potentially positive disconnections between people, and helps create an encouraging tone and constructive interaction between them. For example, in the event that a mediation terminates a relationship, one or more parties might say, or be encouraged by the mediator to say: "The medition process has certainly been a less painful way for us to resolve our strong differences and dissolve our business partnership, and the agreements that we have reached seem to me to be fair and reasonable for both of us. During our discussions, I believe that we have come to understand each other in ways we never did in the past, and learned that we could both be right and not have to be in agreement. My expectation is that although we will not continue to be business partners, and will not be interacting in any way in the future, both of us will be able to put these differences behind us and pursue to the best of our abilities our important work."

If the relationship is continuing, albeit in a different form, an affirmation might sound like this: "This divorce has been tough on both of us, but the process of discussing our concerns about our two children has enabled us to come together on this one aspect of our life—parenting—that we have done well . . . even when we were in conflict. Although we will not continue to be spouses, I have every reason to believe that we will continue to be good parents, and will be able to co-parent effectively with trust and respect for each other."

Apologies are very powerful actions that can significantly help to achieve psychological closure (Schneider, 2000). They are the next level of ownership for what has happened to the people in a conflict. Apologies not only involve ownership for what has happened, roles played, and consequences but are also expressions of regret or remorse. On occasion they may include requests for acceptance of the apology or petitions for forgiveness.

In general, apologies are only effective and accepted when they are (1) given sincerely, (2) voluntary and without coercion, (3) expressed in language that is acceptable to the person to whom they are addressed, (4) made at an appropriate time when the receiver is likely to be most receptive, and (5) are specific about what is being apologized for. Apologies may be given without expectation of acknowledgment, acceptance, or reciprocation. They also may be initiated in the hope that they will be either indirectly or directly accepted, or be reciprocated by a responsive statement of ownership or counterapology from another party.

Apologies involve saying in one form or another "I'm sorry." Ability to acknowledge ownership and make apologies varies tremendously between people, genders, and across cultures. Members of some cultures, such as many Japanese, find acknowledging fault or inconvenience relatively easy. Japanese often apologize for asking a question or putting another party to even a minor inconvenience. Individuals from other cultures, or those in high-conflict situations where the stakes are high, may find it very difficult to make apologies because of fear of being in the wrong, loss of status, or anxiety about the possibility of shifting power relationships. For example, in personal injury lawsuits over medical malpractice in the United States, defense lawyers often advise their clients not to say "I'm sorry for what has happened," for fear that it will be construed as accepting legal liability.

If a party can say "I'm sorry that this happened," or the even stronger "I'm sorry that *my* actions [with a specific description] contributed to this situation, and caused you harm," the parties may be on the road to making reciprocal exchanges, which may help one or more of them reach psychological closure. The latter statement is much stronger than the former because it involves personal ownership of the situation, problem, or dispute; the consequences that occurred; and expression of *personal regret*.

In general, there are at least four possible responses to an apology. The recipient can acknowledge the apology and directly accept it, acknowledge and indirectly accept it, acknowledge but not accept it, or outright reject it. Progress may be made toward psychological closure from the first two responses. If a party says either "I accept your apology" or "If that is really what you truly mean, I can probably live with it," a step has been taken toward a viable psychological exchange. Sometimes receipt of an apology is all that can be expected. In very tense or hurtful situations, the recipient may say, "I've heard what you said, and I will consider it." Often the fact that an apology has been made, even if it is not immediately accepted, helps the recipient move toward more closure.

Outright rejection of an apology is a difficult situation for either the party who has made it or the mediator to manage. Mediators may want to coach parties in caucus on how and when to make, or not make, an apology. If a party or a meditor does not believe that an apology will be accepted by an injured party, it may be better not to make it all rather than risk the backlash, frustration, hurt, or anger that might occur if it is rejected. In this instance, a party or a mediator may make more progress toward psychological closure by exploring statements of acknowledgment and ownership.

If, however, a party has made an apology and it is rejected, the mediator may decide to intervene to help minimize the negative impact of the rebuff. The intermediary may decide to pursue one or more strategies. First, he or she may initially ignore, and help the other initiating party ignore, the rejection and move on to clarification of other issues involved in finalizing the settlement. Or the mediator may finesse the rejection, by saying something like "Mr. X has made an apology for what has happened, but the timing may not be right for its immediate acceptance. Sometimes it is valuable to take some time to think about what has been said before dismissing it. Perhaps you can consider what has been said, and come back to it later." Or the mediator may restate the apology in the same words used by the giver, or perhaps with only slight modification, to explore whether changing the messenger who gives the apology will help the recipient better hear, understand, and accept it.

If an intermediary believes that an apology is genuine and really should be considered by the party who rejected it, he or she may try to figure out why it was dismissed and develop appropriate strategies to address the specific barriers to acceptance. For example, was it the content of the apology that was unacceptable? Was it not to the point, vague, or too general? Did it not go far enough to meet the recipient's psychologial need, or perhaps it was too extreme to be believable? Were the specific words, wording, or syntax the problem? Was the difficulty the tone or perceived insincerity of the initiator? Was the kind and degree of emotional expression appropriate for the situation, in that it articulated the right level of regret, remorse, or contrition? Was the timing wrong? Was the apology made too early or too late in the mediation process? If it was a group dispute, was the apology given by the wrong person? If the person giving it is changed, would it be more likely to be accepted?

On the basis of a hypothesis for the probable cause of rejection, the mediator may be able to coach either the giver or receiver of the apology to make it in another way or perhaps hear it differently. An intermediary may reframe an apology in different words to make it more explicit, remove value-laden language, and reframe it to express a more acceptable emotional content. For example, a disputant has said in a rather frustrated and reluctant tone: "Okay, okay, so I'm sorry for bungling the books, and causing you an accounting nightmare. I've said it over and over again. What more do you want? You can't wring water from a stone!" Although this is an apology, it is not likely to be accepted. The mediator might reframe it this way: "You are really sorry that the accounting procedures that you used to report the company's income did not accurately reflect its financial position, and that your method and behavior has caused Steven a number of legal, public relations, and personal problems and stress. If you had known what you know today, this wouldn't have happened, and you strongly regret that you have put Steven and the company in this position. At this time, you are not sure what more you can say to indicate how much you regret your actions, and if you knew what to say, you would say it." If the giver of the apology affirms the mediator's restatement, the recipient may be much more likely to accept it than if it was phrased in the earlier manner. The reframed statement is explicit, takes ownership, shows an appropriate level of emotion and contrition, and opens the door for further conversation.

Forgiveness, whether in interpersonal, intergroup, or international relations, and whether requested or unilaterally given, goes beyond ownership or acknowledgment. It involves one party absolving another for statements, actions, or situations that occurred in the past. Forgiveness is not social amnesia, in that an offended party forgets what went before. It is a way of acknowledging the past and past harms, and "walling off history," so that the forgiver and the forgiven can move on with their lives (Blake and Mouton, 1984).

Forgiveness is often intimately related to reconciliation. However, the two concepts will be discussed seperately because the latter often goes beyond an act of individual forgiveness. Forgiveness has been examined by psychologists, sociologists, theologians, politicians, and a variety of conflict managers. The context for work on forgiveness has been interpersonal and family, victim-offender, organizational, intergroup, political, ethnic, and international relations (Henderson, 1996, 1999; Minow, 1998; Müller-Fahrenholz, 1997; Tutu, 1999; Umbreit, 1985, 1994, and 2000). It can involve, but is not limited to, forgiveness between divorcing spouses, former business partners, patients and doctors, victims and offenders in criminal cases, political rivals, or victims of abuse and torture in intraethnic conflicts, and victors and vanquished in wars.

Forgiveness, even though it may involve apologies, generally moves far beyond them. Forgiveness involves a party in really letting go of a conflict and the resentment, animosity, or anger that has been held toward others. Forgiveness also often includes recognition of the common humanity of the other party, identifies and strengthens commonality of interests, reconnects former adversaries, establishes or renews relationships, lowers anger and heals grief, contributes to the construction of new positive alliances, and breaks the cycle of conflict (Hunter, 1965; Müller-Fahrenholz, 1997).

Forgiveness does not mean or require that there should not be consequences for harmful words or actions in the past. It means a change of feelings by one person or group toward another. The philosopher Jeffrey Murphy explains it this way: "[Because] I have ceased to hate the person who has wronged me it does not follow that I act inconsistently if I still advocate his being forced to pay compensation for the harm he has done or his being forced to undergo punishment for his wrongdoing—that he, in short, gets his just deserts" (Murphy, 1988). But forgiveness does not always require compensation or punishment. Individuals or institutions can forgive a person or group and not require any further negative consequences.

At this time, two questions need to be asked about forgiveness and its relationship to mediation. First, what role should mediators play in trying to promote forgiveness? Second, if forgiveness is an important or desirable goal, how can intermediaries help parties move toward it?

It is clear that achieving substantive and procedural settlement is not necessarily dependent upon one or more parties forgiving each other or achieving a high level of psychological closure. People reach negotiated or mediated agreements every day with others whom they do not trust or who have done them harm. They reach these agreements without forgiveness ever entering into the equation. But it is also true that mediators want to help parties achieve settlements that are sustainable and do not result in the conflict reemerging later or in another form. Intermediaries also generally desire to assist parties whenever possible, to mend, repair, redefine, or end conflicting relationships in such a manner that the parties retain their emotional balance, self-respect, dignity, and feelings of worth. An even broader concern of third parties may be the desire to improve broader social relationships and society by promoting and achieving the deeper resolution of specific disputes. Many intermediaries see people as being connected in a web of interlocking and interdependent relationships. Successful, positive, and comprehensive settlement of a dispute in one area will inevitably have beneficial ramifications or repercussions in others. Conversely, an incomplete settlement, one that does not address psychological closure or perhaps involve forgiveness, may result in a continuation of negative dynamics or behaviors on the part of one or more parties in interactions with others who are not parties to the current conflict. All of these concerns may lead mediators to consider forgiveness as a valid aspect of mediation.

So, how important is it for a mediator to work with parties toward achieving forgiveness as a factor of psychological closure? Mediators differ widely regarding how critical forgiveness or reestablishment of positive social relationships is when seeking and building durable agreements. They also differ regarding whether mediators should work toward these goals at all, and if so, what priority it should take. Intervenors also have different views on the level or depth of intervention they decide to initiate and the magnitude of change they hope the parties will achieve.

Some mediators, who practice a more therapeutic or transformational approach to mediation, often have as one of their primary goals forgiveness and reconciliation between parties. For example, in the early days of court-based mediation between potentially divorcing spouses, some intermediaries wanted to help the partners forgive each other, reconcile, and continue to be married. Other transformational mediators are more concerned with acknowledgment, empowerment, and recognition (Bush and Folger, 1994).

I believe there are two guidelines that should be applied when deciding how far a mediator should go to encourage or help parties forgive one another. First, if it appears that forgiveness is the only way, or a key, to an acceptable and durable agreement, the mediator should discuss with the parties how work on the issues that will allow the emergence of this goal. Second, the mediator should work toward the goal of forgiveness *only* if the parties desire it. "Forgiveness is a power of the victimized, not a right to be claimed by another [such as a mediator or a government entity such as a Truth Commission designed to address past violent interactions between parties]. The ability to dispense, but also withhold, forgiveness is an ennobling capacity and part of the dignity to be reclaimed by those who survive the wrongdoing" (Minow, 1998, p. 17). Consideration of forgiveness may be raised by the mediator, but he or she can only open the door; the parties must choose to walk through it. Pushing for forgiveness or reconciliation when parties do not desire it violates one of the basic tenets of mediation: that the parties define and set their own goals.

So, how can a mediator help explore with parties whether forgiveness is desirable or possible? First, the intermediary can discuss and educate them about desirability, or the need for (or possible value of) forgiveness as an aspect of settling the conflict and moving forward with their lives.

Second, the mediator can explore whether there are any conditions that might merit consideration for forgiveness to occur. Forgiveness can, and probably should, occur only when it is merited—that is, there should be one or more good reasons for a person to forgive another. (The obvious exception to this view may be held by adherents of religions that value forgiveness in and of itself, or who believe that forgiveness will transform the wrongdoer as well as the forgiver.) In reviewing conditions for forgiveness, the intermediary can help parties consider whether one or more actions have occurred that would merit a pardon:

- Acknowledgment and ownership by the perpetrator of the specific wrong that he or she has done, his or her role in what happened, and the negative consequences or harm that has resulted
- A direct request for forgiveness, and possibly an explanation for why it is desired
- Voluntary statements or acts that help make the aggrieved party psychologically whole

- Voluntary and appropriate levels of efforts to materially compensate the aggrieved party for inconvenience, losses, or harm, or acts to make the party whole (restitution)
- Voluntary self-denial of something that is valuable to the person asking for forgiveness, as an indication of his or her willingness to take responsibility for the harm done to the other party
- Willingness to accept a consequence imposed by the aggrieved party
- Tangible demonstrations that the offending party really has changed and will not act in the unacceptable manner again

Third, the mediator can note some of the possible benefits that may be gained by asking for and giving forgiveness. For the person requesting forgiveness, the act itself may be liberating. It acknowledges ownership for a wrong that has been done, involves an apology, requests forgiveness, and may also include a verbal or tangible way to right the wrong (such as compensation). Making a request for forgiveness often helps the wrongdoer feel that he or she has done his or her best to right a wrong, and that it is now in the other parties' hands to decide what is to be done.

Benefits to those doing the forgiving can be both therapeutic and tangible. Forgiving another person can prevent one from becoming a "bitter or resentful person" (Kushner, 1996). The release of anger, which may result during the process of discussing painful issues and moving toward forgiveness, may also be therapeutic and physiologically beneficial. Parties granting forgiveness may also find some comfort in having told their story of what happened; knowing that the truth is finally out, expressed, and known; and having the perpetrator hear about and acknowledge the pain that was caused. Forgivers may also find new freedom to move on with their lives, and not remain caught in the past.

Fourth, the mediator can explore with the parties individually or together whether conditional or unconditional forgiveness is the goal. Conditional forgiveness means a pardon is contingent on the requesting party saying or doing something prior to a pardon being granted—that is, the forgiving party must receive something in exchange for the absolution. If forgiveness is conditional, the intermediary can help the parties identify what actions or exchanges will be necessary to achieve this level of forgiveness. For example, a customer in a small-claims mediation has been in conflict with the owner of an auto repair shop. The customer claims that he was the victim of abusive language and behavior by the shop's owner, inconvenienced by the firm keeping his car for a week and not completing the job on time, and charged $200 more for the job than it was projected to cost. The owner of the shop has been going through some hard times—a declining number of customers, a high turnover of mechanics, and a number of other complaints to the consumer protection unit of the district attorney's office. He really wants to keep the customer's business, preserve the good name of his shop, avoid future consumer complaints, and not have to deal with the DA's office ever again. He proposes to drop $200 dollars off the expected bill, agrees to lower the total price for the work to compensate the car owner for lost time, and promises to provide certificates for a free oil change and tune-up in the future—all this in return for forgiveness and an agreement by the customer not to bad-mouth his business. The car owner rejects the offer as being inadequate and says that a substantive deal and forgiveness is only possible after an apology for the abusive language and a promise that the shop owner will try to treat future customers with more respect and contact them if their bill is to be more than $50 dollars over the projected cost for the repairs. The mediator seizes on the apology that is needed regarding the language and the promise of changed behavior, and works in caucus for how these will be stated to the customer. The right statement at the right time leads to a statement of forgiveness.

Reconciliation is often a confusing and contradictory term. Reconciliation can mean coming to terms with or accepting a less-than-desirable situation, as in "I understand what happened and hate it, but now I will just have to reconcile myself to live with the consequences." Reconciliation can also mean a positive change in disputing parties' relationships so that they can interact positively and productively, and with trust and respect in the future.

Both forms of reconciliation can be important in achieving psychological closure in mediation. There are some instances where an intermediary may have to work with a party to accept and live with a less-than-desirable outcome, or acknowledge that what has happened in the past cannot be changed, no matter how hard the party might try. Talking through issues, interests, and perceptions, and feelings of guilt, frustration, or anger, can often help a party reconcile themselves and help them accept their circumstances. Mediators can also help parties discover an acceptable explanation or rationale for what has happened that will give them some peace of mind. Although not the most desirable psychological outcome of a dispute, this form of reconciliation is sometimes the best that can be achieved.

It is important to examine reconciliation in the second sense, that of changed relationships, in more detail. It should be noted that reconciliation is more of a process than a definable end state. As Lederach (1997, 1999) noted, reconciliation involves an *encounter* between conflicting individuals or groups to address the past and share their trauma, grief, and anger, without getting mired in what has occurred before. It is a process of *knowing, acknowledging,* and *validating* the experiences and feelings of others. The focused encounter is the first step in the process of reconciliation.

In addition to examining and addressing the past, disputants need to develop a positive joint vision for their relationships in the future. This involves envisoning new or redefined relationships, different and more positive forms of and forums for interaction, reciprocal and jointly beneficial exchanges, and development of common and mutually acceptable expectations.

Closing the door on old conflict-ridden relationships and opening the door to future positive ones is not easy; it requires parties to carefully balance and reconcile four interrelated components or goals, which operate in tension with each other and upon which reconcilaition is dependent: (1) truth, which requires revelation, transparency, acknowledgment, and clarity of what has happened in the past; (2) mercy, which entails "acceptance forgiveness, support, compassion and healing"; (3) justice, which requires "equality, right relationships, making things right, and restitution"; and (4) peace, which is characterized by "harmony, unity, well being, security and respect" (Lederach, 1977, p. 30).

Reconciliation requires balancing the needs of conflicting parties for the satisfaction of each of these four components, and addressing the inherent contradictions of achieving one at the expense of another. For example, in a dispute between members of different ethnic groups and races, where the minorty group has undergone years of discrimination, the current conflict over equal opportunity to advance in an organiztion is only the most current manifestation of ongoing differences. The minority grievants and the majority parties have to value and reconcile tensions between goals or desired outcomes of truth, mercy, justice, and the desire for peace. How much truth and acknowledgment of wrongs do they want to come out about the less-than-complementary behavior of both their side and the other, versus showing mercy and asking for support to spare the feelings of all concerned and begin relationships anew? How much justice, equality, and restitution do they want, if it comes at the expense of peace, respect, and harmony in ongoing relations or the perpetuation of adversarial relationships? How is telling the truth and achieving justice related to the long-term goal of showing mercy and achieving peace?

Developing practical procedures for addressing and resolving tensions between these four elements of reconciliation is on the cutting edge of dispute resolution practice, and it is critical to helping parties achieve psychological closure. Several authors have developed more elaborate and lengthy processes to begin to address these tensions (Blake and Mouton, 1984; Kelman, 1991; Lederach, 1997; Rothman, 1992, 1997), but our concern here is what a mediator can do in the short period of time that he or she works with disputing parties to begin the process of reconciliation. There are a number of brief intervention strategies that can help promote reconciliation, some of which have already been described. Others include creating:

- A safe forum and envrionment where parties feel free to talk about their feelings, views, perceptions, and opinions on what has happened in the past, and openly describe the impact that events have had on them, their friends, colleagues, or identity group members
- Opportunities for acknowledgment and demonstrated understanding by other parties that they have accurately heard the experiences, feelings, and impact the conflict has had on others
- Mutual ownership of roles and responsibility for what has happened
- Time to identify and discuss cross-cutting experiences, interests, activities, relationships, or affiliations that parties share in common

- Opportunities to discuss individual and shared successes in reconciling differences that each side is proud of
- Positive vision(s) for new relationships and new ways of interacting
- Time to identify and discuss what each "side" has done right in their prior relationship, as well as what they have done that is problematic
- Opportunities to identify what has happened in the past, or what is currently happening, that gets in the way or blocks achieving the positive joint vision(s)
- Confidence-building statements, actions, or measures that indicate that the current negative situation can and will change
- Group social activities that create opportunities for positive interactions between contending parties and that minimize possibilities of negative encounters
- Common tasks, the completion of which requires cooperation

Many of these activities can be or are incorporated into stages of the mediation processes. Others may require more structured or extended time to execute but may well contribute substantially to the process of reconciliation.

CULTURAL APPROACHES

Diverse cultures have differences about what constitutes psychological closure, the degree to which it is desirable or needed at the conclusion of a conflict resolution initiative, and how to achieve it. Different kinds of conflicts and relationships between disputants too may require more or less psychological closure. For example, in many legal cultures and lawsuits, lawyers place little or no value on psychological closure; they focus almost exclusively on procedural fairness and mutually acceptable substantive settlements. For other cultures, such as in a village society—especially where disputing parties have to continue to interact, live, or work together—psychological closure may be critical for those involved in a conflict.

Some general cultural and situational considerations can help intermediaries decide how important psychological closure is likely to be for disputants. If certain conditions exist, more emphasis may need to be placed on psychological closure:

- If the parties have no choice but to continue to interact or relate, and there is a low likelihood that they can be permanently separated (as in a traditional family, marriage, or village; inmates in prison; in workplaces where there is not an opportunity to transfer or leave the job; or ex-spouses who may need to continue to co-parent minor children for a number of years, and so on)
- If the culture of the disputants is more collectively oriented than individually oriented (as in many Asian, African, Latin American, and indigenous societies and communities)
- If the harmony of the group and smooth interpersonal relationships take precedence over individual needs or interests (as in many Asian cultures or church communities of believers)
- If the culture of the parties or the parties themselves inherently value forgiveness or reconciliation (as with followers of some religions)

If one or more of these conditions are present, how can a mediator respond in a culturally sensitive or appropriate way? To this question there are no easy answers. A first step is to talk with the parties about how psychological closure happens in their cultures. Getting disputants to tell stories of how others, or they themselves, have been able to let go of a conflict can point the way to both individual and cultural paths of reconciliation. Another approach is for mediators to tell stories (real ones or fables) that illustrate psychological closure, and use them to engage parties in dialogue about how they might begin to move in this direction.

Chapter Fourteen

Achieving Formal Agreement or Settlement

The final stage of mediation involves disputants in reaching procedural closure, designing and implementing monitoring mechanisms, identifying and developing dispute resolution procedures to handle future differences or conflicts that may arise, and formally implementing the substantive agreement or settlement.

PROCEDURAL CLOSURE AND IMPLEMENTATION AND MONITORING

Implementation refers to *procedural* steps that disputants or mediators take to operationalize a substantive agreement and terminate a dispute (Coser, 1967). These steps involve helping parties achieve substantive, procedural, and psychological or relationship closure. Depending on the situation and the culture, formalization of the agreement may occur before or after development of the implementation and monitoring plan.

Implementation is discussed here as a specific phase of negotiation and a separate set of mediator interventions because it poses critical problems that must be overcome if the agreement is to be executed and, if necessary, endure over time. The success of a *substantive* agreement frequently depends on the strength of the implementation plan or *process* that is put in place to operationalize tangible exchanges or behaviors.

On occasion, parties may fail to reach substantive agreement because they cannot conceive of how it will be implemented. Parties may also later fail to adhere to a poorly conceived implementation plan. Insufficient consideration to implementation may result in settlements that create devastating precedents, which can result in a party's reluctance to negotiate or deal with the other party in the future. Other possible results are damaged interpersonal relationships and losses in money, time, or resources. For these reasons, mediators may need to carefully assist parties in devising reasonable, efficient, and effective implementation procedures.

There are two types of procedures for executing substantive agreements: "A self-executing agreement is one which is either: (1) carried out in its entirety at the time it is accepted, or (2) formulated in such a way that the extent to which the players adhere to its terms will be self-evident. A nonself-executing agreement, on the other hand, is one which requires continuing performance which may be difficult to measure in the absence of special monitoring arrangements" (Young, 1972, p. 58).

An example of a self-executing agreement is the mediated settlement of a dispute over the amount of legal fees a client was to pay a lawyer. Once the parties agreed on the amount, the client wrote the lawyer a check for the agreed-on amount. The payment immediately terminated the dispute.

The negotiated settlement of visitation terms for the child of a divorcing couple illustrates a non–self-executing agreement. Because visitation will occur over many years, the agreement will not be carried out in its entirety when the negotiation terminates. The parents will need to cooperate over time to ensure that both the spirit and the specific terms of the agreement are fulfilled. Frequent conflicts over visitation rights illustrate the difficulties of interpreting and complying with non–self-executing agreements.

A self-executing agreement is clearly a stronger and more effective means of ensuring that a settlement will be managed according to the negotiated terms. Compliance is tangible and immediate, and chances of violation are minimized. Mediators can often assist parties in designing self-executing implementation plans so that the conflict can be terminated rapidly and there is no need for compliance with the terms of the settlement over time.

However, not all conflicts can be settled or executed in a self-executing manner. Certain agreements—regarding child or spousal support payments, house or car payments, monitoring of ongoing environmental mitigation measures, and continuing work relationships—may inherently or structurally require performance over a long period of time.

Compliance is often difficult to measure in non–self-executing agreements; this type of accord can often result in later discord due to differing interpretations of terms agreed on in the past. For this reason, in some disputes in which a self-enforcing agreement cannot be reached, the parties may prefer not to settle at all or to use other settlement procedures rather than negotiate an agreement that may be difficult or may not be implemented or in which it is difficult to determine compliance. In such cases, disputants may fail to agree not because they are unable to reach a substantive settlement on issues in dispute, but because they do not trust each other to perform according to the implementation plan or follow the agreed-on procedure over time (Schelling, 1956).

Mediators and negotiators should consider eight factors that are important for the successful implementation of a settlement:

1. A consensual agreement about the criteria used to measure successful compliance
2. The general and specific steps required to implement the decision
3. Identification of the people who have the power to influence the necessary changes
4. An organizational structure (if applicable) to implement the agreement
5. Provisions that will accommodate both future changes in the terms of the agreement and changes in the disputing parties themselves
6. Procedures to manage unintended or unexpected problems that may arise after the settlement or violations of the settlement that may arise during implementation
7. Methods to monitor compliance, as well as the identity of the monitor(s)
8. Determination of the monitor's role (for example, whistleblower or enforcer)

CRITERIA FOR COMPLIANCE AND IMPLEMENTATION STEPS

The probability of noncompliance by one or more parties increases in rough proportion to (1) the number and complexity of issues in dispute, (2) the number of parties involved, (3) the degree of psychological tension and distrust, and (4) the length of time during which the obligations of the agreement must be performed. This does not mean that parties will intentionally violate the agreement, but that structural variables can make violation more likely. Negotiated or mediated agreements are not inherently more prone to noncompliance than other forms of dispute resolution processes. In fact, research indicates that mediated agreements have a high compliance rate (Cook, Rochl, and Shepard, 1980; Pearson, 1984; Bingham, 1984). However, because negotiated settlements are often conducted on an ad hoc basis, they are more susceptible to violation than conflict resolution approaches with strictly defined implementation procedures, such as a judicial or legislative decision.

To mitigate this inherent weakness, mediators generally encourage disputants to carefully define both the criteria and the steps to be used to implement their decisions. Mediators generally believe that the degree to which compliance criteria and steps are defined significantly determines how well substantive or procedural disputes due to misinterpretation of agreements can be avoided. Of course, implementation steps can also be so strictly defined that they hinder more than help, and parties can use highly defined agreements to create problems for each other. Minor infractions can escalate into another full-scale conflict or to claims of lack of compliance. However, this does not appear to be the norm.

Criteria for evaluating implementation steps are similar to those used to evaluate the effectiveness of a substantive settlement. Implementation steps should be (1) cost-efficient; (2) simple enough to be easily understood, yet detailed enough to prevent loopholes that cause later procedural disputes; (3) realistic in their demands on or expectations of parties; and (4) if necessary, able to withstand public scrutiny of standards of fairness.

MONITORING THE PERFORMANCE
OF AGREEMENTS

Agreements that must be performed over time frequently require self-contained evaluation procedures and structures. Parties often strictly define standards and schedules of performance, and periodic meetings are held to review compliance. The performance agreement may be monitored by the parties themselves, by a joint committee composed of party representatives (in complex multiparty disputes), or by a third party who is usually not the mediator—for example, a governmental agency, a respected third party, a court, or an independent monitoring committee (Straus, Clark, and Susskind, n.d.).

In one complex dispute involving seventy city government employees, the parties established an ongoing monitoring committee to ensure that all participants complied with tasks, responsibilities, and a work schedule that had been established. An annual meeting was set up, in which all the parties were to report on their progress and reach additional decisions as new issues developed.

If an independent third party is to effectively conduct monitoring, the monitoring body must be an individual or group that the disputants respect and trust. Its membership may vary according to the type of dispute. Community disputes may call for a large committee. Straus, Clark, and Susskind (n.d.) urge that "a committee of this type should include prominent community leaders, agency representatives, and technical advisors committed to the consensus that has been reached and to implementing the terms of the bargain. The membership of such a committee should be approved by all parties to the negotiation (and might include some of them)" (p. V–55).

In small interpersonal disputes or in intraorganizational conflicts, the monitor may be one or two individuals who are trusted by the disputing parties. For example, a divorcing couple may designate mutually respected relatives to monitor compliance with visitation terms.

If monitoring is to be effective, parties must clearly define the performance standards by which compliance will be measured, the role of the monitors, and the limits of the third party's authority.

Careful definition of these variables minimizes problems at a later time with the monitoring committee's or individual's functioning.

The degree of responsibility given to monitoring committees or individuals assigned to oversee implementation varies from one case to another. Monitors may merely review progress and confirm or deny that compliance has occurred, or they may actually oversee implementation of the agreement.

Another role for monitors is to activate or participate in a future dispute resolution process or grievance procedure conducted by the parties themselves or by a third party. A grievance procedure is a process disputants resort to when disagreements arise during or as a result of settlement implementation. Establishing an acceptable, fair, and efficient grievance procedure is often a functional prerequisite for initial settlement. Parties often believe that having a grievance procedure in place gives them a way to redress new problems, to modify an agreement if necessary, or to avoid abandoning the entire settlement because of difficulty in implementing a small component of the accord.

CULTURAL APPROACHES AND MONITORING

In many North American mediations between members of dominant ethnic groups, implementation and monitoring procedures are considered to be part of the immediate negotiations, and agreements reached about these issues are incorporated into the final settlement agreement. In other cultures, implementation and monitoring may be seen as yet another negotiation or as an ongoing process of bargaining that follows formalization of an initial substantive, procedural, or psychological agreement. For example, in many Asian countries, or in negotiations involving Asian nationals (Japanese or Chinese in particular), negotiation of specific types of agreements may occur in phases. A first phase may conclude with an affirmation by all parties that a positive relationship exists and with an agreement that the parties will pursue further discussions. A ritual ceremonial meeting or meal often marks this phase and all subsequent phases. A second phase of negotiations may conclude with a set of agreements in principle that will guide the parties' future relationship. The third phase may result in significant substantive agreements, but with few details about how they will be implemented. This phase is generally celebrated with an "official" social occasion and meal that involves the key spokespersons or dignitaries from the various sides. The final phase is often a series of ongoing negotiations to work out the details and modify the existing agreement to meet unforeseen changing circumstances. This phase of negotiations may not have a formal ending, as the working out of the relationship between the parties is considered to be part of ongoing relationships and day-to-day activities.

As these descriptions indicate, cultural expectations are crucial elements in implementation. For example, if Western and Asian negotiators are not familiar with each other's expectations for the content and phasing of implementation activities, extreme frustration or additional conflict may arise. The Westerner will be striving for a highly defined agreement that includes a detailed implementation plan. After the agreement is formally recognized, negotiations are considered to be over. The Asian party may be expecting a series of negotiations, with each phase recognized by a ritual meeting; the final agreement will be only generally defined because the details will be worked out during the life of the agreement. Such differences in expectations have resulted in serious tensions between parties in a number of international joint ventures. For example, in the automobile industry, Mazda and the United Automobile Workers (UAW) encountered problems in implementing new labor-management relations because of different expectations about the schedule for working out details of the labor contract and because of the Japanese orientation toward informally modifying agreements to meet changing circumstances (Fucini and Fucini, 1990). Chrysler also had difficulties in China with the phasing and timing of negotiations; the company lacked understanding of the role of ritual occasions that recognized establishment of a relationship, affirmation of general principles, substantive agreement, and ongoing mini-negotiations to address day-to-day problems (Mann, 1989).

Needless to say, a mediator working in intercultural negotiations needs to understand parties' expectations and procedures for implementation. In many cases, the mediator may have to act as a cultural interpreter between the parties, explain their differing assumptions and approaches, and assist them in working together to implement the agreement.

PROVISIONS AND PROCEDURES FOR RESOLVING FUTURE DISPUTES

Agreements or settlements that are not self-executing—where performance will happen over an extended period of time; where parties will continue in close living or working relationships; or where unanticipated issues, problems, or conflicts may develop in the future—are often best served if there is a process put in place at the end of a current dispute that provides for how issues that emerge in the future will be handled and resolved.

The procedure for resolving future conflicts may be no more than a general agreement or clause in the settlement agreement to reopen negotiations or return to mediation before pursuing other options such as litigation, or it may specifically define the method, sequence of dispute resolution processes, or a comprehensive system with multiple steps and procedures to be used to settle new tensions. Here are two sample mediation and dispute resolution clauses:

> In the event that a future dispute arises between the designated parties, they agree to submit the issue to mediation prior to resorting to arbitration, litigation, or other dispute resolution procedures. [The firm that will conduct the mediation and the rules that will apply may also be specified in the clause.]

> In the event that a future dispute arises between the designated parties, they commit to making a good-faith effort to resolve it by unassisted and direct negotiations. If negotiations fail to develop a mutually satisfactory solution, the parties agree to submit their dispute to mediation. If mediation is unsuccessful, the parties agree to refer their dispute to arbitration for a binding [or nonbinding] decision.

Many labor-management, commercial, environmental, and interpersonal contracts provide for renegotiation, mediation, or binding arbitration to resolve future disputes. A number of organizations have gone beyond dispute resolution clauses and specification of procedures for resolving specific disputes, and developed comprehensive systems that include mediation and subsequent forms of third-party decision making, to resolve internal disputes, those with other organizations, and altercations with members of the public. These systems help ensure that if there are future problems with relationships or agreements are not complied with, parties have an alternative means to enforce them rather than returning to overt conflict (Ury, Brett, and Goldberg, 1988; Constantino and Merchant, 1995; Slaiku, 1989; Moore and Woodrow, 1999; Lynch, 2001).

For example, Levi Strauss, the international manufacturer of denim clothing, developed a four-step employee dispute resolution procedure (Moore and Woodrow, 1999). The first step involved unassisted problem solving or direct negotiations between disputing parties. Step two added the assistance of a coach for one or both sides to improve the parties' abilities to conduct problem solving in an unassisted manner. The third step was mediation, made available by either an internal third party selected from a roster of trained mediators drawn from both labor and management's ranks or mediation by an external neutral. The final step was binding arbitration using an external third party.

Courts too, are including or requiring similar dispute resolution procedures to address compliance problems in a variety of cases. Some family courts look very favorably on mediated settlements that include procedures for resolving future disputes that may arise between divorcing spouses who are continuing to co-parent. This may involve including a clause to return to meditation or referral to a neutral third-party decision maker, such as an arbitrator. In an interstate water compact conflict between the states of Colorado, Kansas, and Nebraska that was under the jurisdiction of the U.S. Supreme Court, the parties developed a multistep dispute resolution process, which included mediation as a means of resolving future disputes. This procedure afforded them a timely means for the resolution of future differences and the ability to meet immediate water needs, and it provided a mechanism that did not require the parties to return to the Supreme Court for decisions on operational issues. This dispute resolution process was part of the states' stipulated agreement presented to the court.

In cases such as the Singson-Whittamore dispute, the parties will need to work to develop a detailed agreement with a time line for implementation. They probably will also want to include a dispute resolution mechanism with an option to return to mediation if the settlement is found to be unsatisfactory or if modifications are needed to achieve implementation.

REACHING SUBSTANTIVE CLOSURE AND FORMALIZING THE AGREEMENT

By this point in mediation, parties have usually reached agreement on the substantive terms for settlement. What remains to be done to achieve substantive closure is to fine-tune the substantive settlement by developing an accurate final description of what has been agreed upon, and putting it into a mutually acceptable form that will induce compliance and ensure that issues are really settled and not likely to resurface at a later time.

If either the parties or the mediator has been keeping records of agreed-upon terms throughout the mediation process, and confirming agreements as the parties have reached them, this final step to formalize substantive settlement should be relatively easy. However, if accurate records of previous decisions made during negotiations have not been kept, the parties and/or intermediary may have to reconstruct agreements, and combine them into a package that will be acceptable to all. Described next are two common ways of formalizing agreements: informal or formal (legal) written documents.

SUBSTANTIVE AGREEMENT AND COMMITMENT-INDUCING PROCEDURES

Negotiated settlements endure not only because implementation plans are effectively structured and meet the interests of the parties but because parties are psychologically and structurally committed to the agreement. Negotiators and mediators should be particularly concerned in this last phase of negotiations with building in psychological and structural factors that will bind the parties to comply with the terms of the negotiated settlement. Commitment-inducing procedures can be voluntary and implemented unilaterally by the parties, or they can be involuntary measures executed by an external party.

Voluntary Commitment Procedures

Voluntary commitment procedures are activities initiated by the mediator or the negotiators that enhance the probability that disputants will voluntarily comply with the settlement. Here are some specific measures:

- Private oral exchange of promises between disputants made in the presence of the mediators
- Private oral exchange of promises between disputants in the presence of authority figures or parties whose disapproval the disputants would be reluctant to incur should they violate the agreement (relatives, workplace superiors, mentors, religious leaders, and so on)
- Public oral exchange of promises (press release or press conference)
- Symbolic exchange of gifts, tokens of affection, first payments, early payment (Fisher, 1969), and so on, as an indication of bargaining in good faith and willingness to fulfill commitments
- Symbolic gestures of friendship that demonstrate a willingness to take personal risk in order to implement the negotiated settlement
- Informal written agreements or memorandums of understanding (MOUs)
- Formal written agreements (contracts, covenants, MOUs, and so on)

Voluntary agreements and commitment-inducing activities should not be underestimated as means of ensuring compliance. In a 1980 study measuring agreement compliance in mediated cases at neighborhood justice centers with informal or unenforced commitment procedures, between 81 and 95 percent of respondents stated that they had honored all the terms of their agreement. (A total of 315 respondents from the various centers answered this question.) In response to another question answered by a total of 286 people, between 52.4 and 74.1 percent of respondents agreed that the other party or parties had honored all the terms of their agreement (Cook, Rochl, and Shepard, 1980). Labor-management settlements have much higher rates of compliance. These studies indicate that there is significant voluntary adherence to the terms of negotiated settlements.

A review of fifty-one studies of the process and outcome of family mediation found that the parties reached complete agreement in between 40 percent and 60 percent of the cases and partial agreement in 10 to 20 percent of the conflicts. "These overall agreement rates varied between 50 percent and 80 percent, with most studies closer to the higher than the lower figure" (Benjamin and Irving, 1995, p. 57). These rates tended to be consistent regardless of whether the services were provided by a court-based or private program, whether participation was mandatory or voluntary, or whether little or intense family conflict was involved. A handful of the studies looked at satisfaction compliance and postmediation reescalation of family disputes from four months to two years after the last session was held. Forty to sixty percent of the parties remained satisfied with both the process and the outcome of mediation, and all of the studies found higher rates of satisfaction than in control groups that used litigation as a means of settling their differences.

Satisfaction can generally be correlated with compliance: "In addition several studies noted that a substantial portion of clients, in the 40 percent–65 percent range, had made changes to the terms of their agreement by mutual consent" (Benjamin and Irving, 1995, p. 63). The authors of the report also found that relitigation rates among couples who participated in mediation were extremely low, and much lower than among families that used litigation to resolve their initial conflicts. Benjamin and Irving conclude that "mediated agreements tend to endure and their terms and conditions are typically complied with" (p. 64).

Externally Executed Commitment Procedures

On occasion, there can be problems with voluntary compliance. Negotiators and mediators often attempt to overcome these weaknesses with structural and external enforcement provisions that enhance the probability of or require compliance.

Parties may initiate mutually binding commitment procedures that, once established, are structural assurances that the settlement will be complied with. These structural assurances determine that performance of settlements will be enforced, and that the parties will not have to rely exclusively on promises of good faith or the unpredictable pressures of public opinion. There are a variety of structural means of inducing commitment.

Let us for the moment assume that there is agreement between or among the parties on the substantive terms of settlement, and examine in more detail the implementation and psychological aspects of closure.

Legal contracts are the most common way of ensuring commitment to an agreement in many situations and cultures. A legal contract is an agreement between two or more parties that is judicially enforceable. Contracts are characterized by an exchange of consideration, a promise, or an act that one party agrees to perform in return for promises or acts from another. For example, several professionals wanted to establish a private group practice. One of their prospective partners was better known and earned a larger income. They wanted to resolve how they were to invest capital in the practice and the terms for payment of each partner. They hired a mediator to help resolve their differences over financial arrangements and to draft a memorandum of understanding that they would later ask a lawyer to formalize as a contract. All parties wanted to have their financial rights protected by a formal and legal agreement.

Legal contracts generally permit parties a judicial recourse should one or more parties fail to honor promises. Parties who have suffered what they consider a breach of contract can sue another party for redress of grievances. If the suit is successful, the plaintiff or party initiating the suit can receive one of three possible remedies (Straus, Clark, and Susskind, n.d., pp. V–58–59):

- Damages: financial compensation for the consequences of the defendant's breach
- Recision of the contract: the court voids the contract and releases the plaintiff from his or her contractual obligations
- Specific performance: the court orders the defendant to comply with the terms of the contract

Negotiated agreements do not automatically become contracts enforceable under law. The enforceability of contracts depends both on the laws and rules of the legal jurisdiction in which they are promulgated and the forms that the contracts take.

Although a verbal agreement may be considered a legal contract, especially if made in the presence of witnesses, a written document is more predictable. Written documents that are to become contracts must contain at minimum (1) the *name* (or kind of contract); (2) the *parties,* including date and place of agreement; (3) *recitals* that detail the relationship of the parties and describe the contract's function; (4) the *promise clause,* which describes the exchanges the parties are to make; and (5) *closing* and *signatures* (Brown, 1955).

In addition to the contents of the agreement, the way the settlement is written can make a difference in its acceptability and later compliance. Saposnek (1983) identifies four additional factors to consider in drafting agreements: (1) the clarity of the clauses, (2) the degree of detail in the clauses, (3) the balance of concessions, and (4) "the attitude and perspective connoted."

Clarity of clauses refers to writing that precludes the possibility of diverse interpretations or misinterpretations. Mediators should work with the parties to clarify their intentions and then—either alone or in collaboration with the parties—draft a memorandum of understanding, which may later become a contract, so that loopholes are eliminated. The mediator should ask himself or herself and the parties where later interpretation problems might exist and try to eliminate them in the initial draft (Salacuse, 1989).

Degree of detail in the clauses refers to the specificity of the agreement. Usually, the more precise the terms of settlement, the less likely that interpretation conflicts will arise. In disputes in which the parties are highly emotional and in which there is little trust, strictly worded agreements that specify all details may be crucial in terminating the dispute.

In disputes in which the parties have a positive relationship, however, detail can sometimes be viewed as a disadvantage. A detailed agreement may suggest lack of trust or inability to solve new problems that arise in the future. One party may also use a detailed agreement to harass the other so that the terms are honored to an excessive degree. On occasion, fanatical adherence to an agreement's details can cause another party to resist compliance and thus promote additional discord.

The mediator, in drafting an agreement, must clearly consider the abilities of the parties to negotiate later details if they are needed, the degree of trust of the parties, and the tendency of the parties to use an agreement as a weapon against their opponents. Specificity may either encourage or discourage future conflict.

Balance of concessions refers to the equity of the exchanges made by the parties. The written agreement should clearly identify what is to be exchanged, and it should be written so that the settlement does not appear one-sided. The document may alternate parties from one exchange clause to the next to maintain the perception of balance. The exchanges need not be equal in number, but the importance of the interests satisfied must be equivalent if renewed conflict is to be avoided. The mediator will often have to search for the terms that will facilitate exchange.

On occasion, a psychological concession such as "John acknowledges that Philip was proceeding in good faith" can be traded for a specific substantive exchange. Equality of exchange can also be maintained by mentioning both parties in the clause— for example, "Neither Paul nor Mary will make disparaging remarks about the other parent in the presence of the children." With equal treatment for the two parties, an acceptable exchange may be made.

A positive attitude and perspective are the final consideration in drafting an agreement. A settlement document is an affirmation of the willingness and ability of the parties to cooperate. The document should note and encourage cooperative attitudes and behaviors. In the recitals—the preamble to the section that details precise exchanges—the mediator may include a statement about the willingness of the parties to end the dispute, their commitment to bargaining in good faith, their dedication to complying with the agreement, and their commitment to cooperative problem solving.

In a business relationship, the statement may read, "After a period of bargaining in good faith, labor and management have agreed to the following terms that both expect to result in mutual benefit." In a custody case, the parents may affirm, "Both of us love our children very much and want to arrange for a living situation that will provide them with stability and continuity of relationships with both parents, their extended families, their neighborhood, and friends. We make the following agreements because we believe that they are the best possible arrangements for the children and for each of us."

It should be noted that specific kinds of disputes and particular cultures may merit different kinds of written documents. In some cases, informal minutes or a memorandum of understanding may be all that is expected or needed by the parties. In other situations, a more formal document may be needed, both to detail the terms of the settlement and for ritual purposes. Elaborate settlement documents, on high-quality paper with the parties' signatures or seals, may serve to induce commitment. Settlement agreements in some of the phases that were described under "Culture, Implementation, and Monitoring" may also be expected.

It has already been noted that cultures may differ in their expectations concerning the levels of detail and closure on issues described in a written settlement document. The mediator may have to work with the parties to coordinate their expectations and to develop a document that is mutually acceptable in these respects. The mediator may also have to work with translators to ensure that versions of the document, if written in more than one language, are congruent and have the same meanings to all parties.

Judicial supervision is a second structural means to bind parties to agreements. If disputing parties reach a negotiated settlement while awaiting a court hearing, they may stipulate to the court the terms of their agreement, and the court will then include these terms in a final decree. This is common practice in many countries—for example, in mediated business disputes or divorce settlements. Generally, the parties take their agreement to their respective lawyers, who may change the wording to comply with legal standards and practice and then submit the document to the court as a stipulated settlement.

A second example of judicial supervision of negotiated settlements is the process used in selecting representatives to negotiations that will affect classes of people in a complex dispute. Straus, Clark, and Susskind (n.d., pp. V–61–62) suggest that legislation could be passed that would establish "a process whereby a court supervises the selection of representatives to act as agents of recognized diffuse interests. This is precisely the procedure currently employed to appoint representatives in class action suits." A similar procedure has been used to appoint the guardian *ad litem* to represent a child's interests in mediated disputes involving termination of parental rights (Mayer, 1985).

Administrative or legislative action sometimes follows from negotiated settlements and serves to enforce compliance. (Many administrative and legislative bodies commonly use negotiation procedures in their daily operations, but here I refer to extraparliamentary negotiations.) Negotiated settlements that involve regulatory or policy content have routinely been recommended for inclusion in new agency policies or regulations or in legislative bills. A negotiated settlement that is drafted into a bill or regulation and becomes law can be enforced by appointed officials.

Executive action is also used in some instances to formalize negotiated settlements and bind the parties to adhere to them. This is especially the case when an elected or appointed executive sponsors negotiations. The settlement of conditions for issuing general dredge and fill permits on Sanibel Island in Florida was negotiated under the supervision of the U.S. Army Corps of Engineers and was subsequently approved and implemented by that agency.

Economic incentives or constraints are another structural device that encourages adherence to the terms of a settlement. Two economic approaches are common: agreement on indemnification and performance bonds (Straus, Clark, and Susskind, n.d.).

Agreement on indemnification refers to a commitment by the parties to the amount and form of compensation if one or more parties fail to comply with the terms of the agreement. Agreement on indemnification pressures the parties to adhere to the agreement because the costs of not doing so are specified before the breach of contract occurs. However, this succeeds only when conditions of violation are easily identified or measured. An example of agreement on indemnification can be found in the terms of settlement between the developer of a new shopping center and residents of the surrounding neighborhood, who argued that they would be adversely affected by the mall's presence. The developer agreed to protect land values of residential property owners by guaranteeing a sale of the property at a fair market price to be determined by an appraisal before the mall's construction. The developer agreed to buy the properties or pay the difference between the actual selling price and the appraised value if the former price was lower. This offer was to be in effect for five years after the mall's construction (Baldwin, 1978).

Performance bonds are one step beyond agreements on indemnification in that they require a party to post a bond or reserve a specific sum of money to ensure that assets are available to pay for noncompliance. The use of performance bonds is an ancient method of ensuring adherence to agreements. Fifteenth- and sixteenth-century Japanese warlords required performance bonds in the form of relatives of their subordinates. The warlords would hold these relatives captive in their capital cities; if a functionary did not perform his contractual duties, his relatives would be put to death.

Performance bonds today are usually funds held in escrow by a financial institution. An appointed neutral party who establishes that the terms of the settlement have been violated effects the release of the bond. This third party may be a monitoring committee established by the parties themselves or an independent, publicly recognized authority.

In the case of the shopping center, the developer agreed to construct a fourteen-foot-high landscaped berm as a boundary between the development and the residential neighborhood. A $100,000 letter of credit was deposited at a local bank to guarantee construction funds.

CLOSURE, RITUAL, AND SYMBOLIC CONFLICT TERMINATION ACTIVITIES

Whereas some social processes have definite beginnings and endings, others have no precise points at which they may be said to have started or terminated. Coser (1967, p. 47) observes that social conflicts "follow a law of social inertia insofar as they continue to operate if no explicit provision for stopping their course is made by the participants. Whereas in a game, for example, the rules for the process include rules for its ending, in social conflict explicit provisions for its termination must be made by the contenders."

Unlike lower animals, human beings have not devised totally routinized communication patterns to symbolize when a conflict should or has in fact ceased. Failure to define when a dispute has ended or when a negotiated settlement has been reached can result in unnecessary extended conflict. The forms that symbolic conflict termination activities take clearly depend on the context in which the dispute occurs and the degree of common acceptance of the symbols.

Negotiators and mediators often try to create activities that symbolically indicate termination of a conflict. Handshaking, formal signing procedures, toasts, and celebratory meals are common ways of jointly affirming the termination of a dispute. One mediator gave a divorcing couple a bottle of champagne to acknowledge the end of a successful child custody negotiation. In a large community dispute over county land use, the participants celebrated successful completion of negotiations with a banquet that all parties attended.

In the Singson-Whittamore dispute, the parties would normally opt either to develop a new written contract or modify the old one, detailing the new terms of the agreement and the steps of implementation. This document would probably be drafted by the attorneys of one or both parties and couched in legal language based on the memorandum of understanding reached by the parties in mediation and drawn up by the mediator. There could be a joint signing ceremony in which the agreement would be sealed by a handshake between the parties. There might also be some witnesses present, to confirm that a settlement has been reached.

Although negotiators themselves may identify and initiate some ritual acts or behaviors that they believe will terminate a conflict or negotiation, lack of common perceptions as to the meaning of the act, or persisting antagonism on the part of the other side may inhibit its acceptance. Mediators can often help the parties plan or structure termination signals, rituals, or ceremonies that will be mutually acceptable and meaningful. Naturally, the type of initiative that a mediator takes will depend on the situation, the relationship of the parties, and the authority the parties have vested in him or her to design such activities.

CULTURAL APPROACHES

Culture is often a significant factor when considering approaches for substantive, procedural, and psychological closure, for each culture usually has norms, rules, and rituals that will be expected or needed to terminate a conflict. Ritual meals, with special menus, symbolic speeches, blessings by priests, prayers, or other symbolic acts may be appropriate if participating parties attach importance to them. An interesting ritual closure occurred in a recent case in

Thailand, in which two families had fought a long and lethal feud over land rights and timber sales. After concluding substantive negotiations, the mediator, a Buddhist priest, invited the parties to attend a ritual ceremony to end the conflict. He asked them to bring a dysfunctional weapon that they would surrender at the ceremony to symbolize the giving up of violent means of resolving differences. At the gathering, the weapons were placed in a box, and sacred water was poured on them. All parties were asked to drink from the box to symbolize the end of the dispute and their mutual bond. The priest knew that this ritual—which had been performed in times past by a Thai king—would have meaning to the parties and would act on them as a strong inducement to keep their commitments.

Chapter Fifteen

Strategies for Dealing with Special Situations

The previous chapters have focused for the most part on noncontingent mediator strategies. These interactions between the mediator and a single party or between the mediator and multiple disputants are generally performed regardless of the type of dispute, the number or variety of issues, or the number of parties.

I now turn to contingent strategies and activities—interventions a mediator makes to respond to specific or unusual problems posed by disputants or to conditions that are not present in every negotiation (Smart, 1987). In examining contingent activities, I will discuss interventions that are applicable to two-party and multiparty disputes, negotiation teams, and relations with constituents and secondary parties.

It is impossible to identify and describe all contingent strategies and activities mediators initiate to respond to specific situations. Some of the most comprehensive listings of contingent strategies were developed by Fisher (1978), Maggiolo (1972), and Wall (1981). However, five categories of contingent strategies and activities are particularly common:

1. The caucus technique
2. Techniques for exerting mediator influence
3. Techniques for managing the power relations between parties
4. Grand strategies for responding to past, present, and future causes of conflicts
5. Approaches for mediating disputes involving strong values

CAUCUSES

In a caucus, the disputants are physically separated from each other and direct communication between parties is intentionally restricted (Moore, 1987; Bethel, 1986). Caucuses are initiated in response either to external forces that affect the negotiators and the general conflict situation or to problems arising from issues, events, or dynamics in the joint session.

Factors That May Necessitate a Caucus

External forces—political, economic, and social and cultural pressures—can all create changes during negotiations. More easily catalogued are the internal dynamics between negotiators that may require a caucus. There are three general categories of internal dynamics: (1) problems with the *relationships* between the parties or within a team, (2) problems with the *negotiation process,* and (3) problems with *substantive issues* under discussion.

Numerous problems in the relationships between team members or opponents may lead to initiating a caucus. The parties or the mediator may call for a caucus for various reasons: to allow intense emotions to be vented without escalating differences between the parties, clarify perceptions or misperceptions, change unproductive or repetitive negative behavior, or diminish and limit unhelpful communications.

Procedural problems may also call for a caucus. The parties or the mediator may hold a private meeting to clarify or assess the negotiation procedure used by one or all parties; to design new procedures, either for negotiations within a group or team or for joint negotiations; or to break a pattern of negative procedures. Caucuses can also be called by parties or the mediator to explore substantive issues such as definition of interests, clarification of positions, identification of new offers, or weighing of another party's proposals.

In addition, mediators can use a caucus to:

- Allow the parties (or the mediator) a pause if the pressure to progress in joint session is too intense and is not promoting productive exchange

- Refocus the motivation of the parties on why a settlement is important and what alternatives to negotiated settlement exist
- Conduct reality testing of a party's proposals
- Encourage a party who is in doubt about whether his or her interests can be satisfied by pursuing present unsatisfactory tactics to persevere or try a new negotiation approach
- Act as a sounding board for a party
- Uncover confidential information that may not be revealed in joint session
- Control communication between parties so that they focus exclusively on substance and eliminate all emotional communication as conveyed by speech or nonverbal signals
- Educate an inexperienced disputant about negotiation procedures or dynamics
- Prevent a party from making premature concessions or a premature commitment in joint session, or from adhering to an untenable or hard-line position
- Develop a single-text negotiating document when parties are too numerous, issues too complex, or emotions too heated for face-to-face encounters
- Develop settlement alternatives in an environment that separates the process of option generation from that of evaluation
- Determine if an acceptable bargaining range has been established (or create one)
- Design proposals or offers that will later be brought to joint session
- Test the acceptability of one party's proposal by presenting the offer to another party as an option the mediator himself or herself has generated
- Make appeals to common principles or superordinate goals
- Express their own perceptions of the situation and possibly make suggestions for settlement options

Timing

Caucuses can be held at almost any time in negotiations. If they are initiated early, it is usually for the purpose of venting emotions, designing negotiating procedures, or identifying issues. Caucuses held in the middle of negotiations typically focus on preventing premature commitment to a position, identifying interests, generating alternatives, and testing bargaining ranges. Those held at the end of negotiations usually are designed to break deadlocks, develop or assess proposals, develop a settlement formula, or achieve a psychological settlement. Clearly, there is no correct time to call a caucus because its necessity is highly dependent on the needs and skills of the individual negotiators and mediator. In some disputes, there may be numerous caucuses, whereas in others caucuses may not be used at all.

Mediators should take care not to schedule caucuses prematurely (when parties are still capable of working productively in joint session) nor too late (after unproductive hostile exchanges or actions have hardened positions).

Location

For caucuses to be most effective, they need to genuinely separate the parties. This usually means separate rooms where parties neither see nor hear each other, and where they feel safe to discuss issues or problems candidly. Mediators responsible for selecting the negotiation site should choose facilities that have spaces for caucuses. Inadequate sites may necessitate returning to a party's headquarters or to neutral ground where confidentiality can be ensured.

Protocol

Although the caucus is a technique commonly used to facilitate productive negotiations, there are few standards for implementation that apply to all situations. These tasks must be undertaken by mediators who initiate a caucus:

- Educating the parties about the technique before it is used
- Overcoming resistance of the parties to separate meetings
- Making the transition to the caucus
- Deciding which party to caucus with first
- Determining the duration of the caucus
- Determining what is said in the caucus
- Facilitating the return to joint session

Although the caucus is familiar to experienced negotiators, novices may not be aware of its usefulness. Mediators should explain at the start of negotiation and in their opening statements that caucuses may be held at some time during mediation, and that either the parties or the mediator may initiate them.

Parties occasionally resist caucusing with a mediator. This resistance may be associated with concerns about confidentiality, fear of coalition formation between the mediator and the other party (Simmel, 1955), or political problems with constituencies that can result from private meetings (Maggiolo, 1972). The mediator does not want to create unnecessary barriers between himself or herself and one or more parties by pushing disputants to use an unacceptable technique. For this reason, mediators should explain the general reasons for the caucus before using the technique and should allow disputants to make an independent decision about whether to meet in private at the specific time that a caucus might be needed. If the parties do not consider a caucus necessary, the mediator should accede to their decision. However, if the mediator believes that failure to caucus will eventually lead to a breakdown in negotiations, he or she may push the parties to meet separately.

Progress from joint session to caucus must be conducted smoothly so that the flow of negotiations is not interrupted. Parties may initiate caucuses by formally calling for a time to meet privately or by asking for informal breaks. Mediators use the same procedures. When caucuses are formally called, a specific duration for the separate meetings is often jointly agreed on or proposed by the mediator. To make this transition, the mediator can say, "You have been discussing this issue together for quite a while. I believe that it might be helpful to take a break so that you can reflect on the available options in private. During this time, I would like to speak to each of you privately and explore whether there is any additional room for movement. I estimate that I will talk to each of you for about ten minutes."

Mediators can use several informal guidelines to determine which party to meet first. In early caucuses, the mediator usually meets first with either the initiator of the dispute or the party that called for the caucus. Caucuses held later in negotiations follow a different rule: "If neither side has indicated any flexibility in their bargaining position, the first caucus should be held with the party appearing most inflexible. In such situations, some movement is necessary if negotiations are to proceed along fruitful lines" (Maggiolo, 1972, p. 53). If, however, the mediator perceives that one of the parties is extremely upset or is exhibiting emotional distance from or hostility toward the mediator, the intervenor may choose to caucus with that party first.

There is no general rule for duration of a caucus. Some mediators argue that private meetings should be held for as long as necessary to accomplish a desired purpose (Maggiolo, 1972), whereas others argue for brief, time-specific meetings. Common practice and courtesy dictate that if a caucus is to take more than an hour, a formal break should be called in negotiations so that the party with whom the caucus is not being held is not kept waiting.

Regardless of how long a caucus with one party lasts, the mediator should confer with the other party before reconvening joint sessions. Meeting with the other party demonstrates equitable and impartial behavior and may also be an occasion to test options that have developed in the first caucus. Meeting with the other party can alleviate curiosity about what has occurred in the first caucus, maintain the trust relationship between the intervenor and the parties, and help educate disputants about what will transpire when they return to joint session.

Unless specified otherwise, conversations held between the mediator and disputants in caucus are considered confidential. Confidentiality generally encourages parties to be more candid in conversations with the mediator and enables them to explore options that entail more risk.

In caucus, mediators can play stronger roles as allies to parties and can be more supportive than is acceptable in joint session. This often enables parties to progress and to find acceptable options that they resisted in joint session. Care must be taken, however, not to form so close a relationship with a party that impartiality is lost. Similarly, the mediator must not lose the capacity to separate from the party and play a multi-partial role in the following joint session.

Mediators can also be firmer and more direct and exert more influence on a party in caucus than they can in joint session. They can undertake reality testing, propose hypothetical options, and question a party's judgment in caucus, which they cannot do in joint session. They can protect the negotiator's integrity while asking probing questions and creating doubt about the viability of adhering to hard-line positions.

Information shared with mediators in caucus is often crucial to reaching agreements. However, the confidentiality barrier may inhibit such information from being used to its best effect. The mediator can pursue several strategies to overcome this barrier. First, he or she may directly obtain the party's permission to disclose information to the other side by explaining how it will be used and what benefits could result.

Second, the mediator may explain that he or she would like to talk with the other party about information discussed in the caucus and ask, "Is there anything that we have talked about that you would not like me to disclose?" This process allows the party to specifically identify what he or she wishes to remain confidential and gives the mediator the authority to disclose other information as he or she sees fit.

Third, the mediator may take an idea generated with one disputant and claim it as his or her own when talking with another disputant. This conceals the proposal's connection with the originating party—making it perhaps more acceptable—and enables the mediator to test a possible settlement without committing any of the parties to it. If both parties agree to a solution but do not realize that the other is in agreement, the mediator must then decide who is to propose the solution, and how it is to be framed.

It is crucial that the party who proposes a solution developed in caucus assume ownership of it and not present it simply in order to please the mediator. Furthermore, the party must be able to defend the offer in joint session. This is true whether or not the mediator knows that the proposal is acceptable to the other side. The mediator may otherwise be accused of forcing his or her own preferences on the disputants.

During caucuses with the parties, the mediator should determine how the parties will be brought together again in joint session. Factors to consider are how to (1) explain the purpose and results of the caucus, (2) determine which party speaks first after the caucus, and (3) decide how information generated or offers developed will be shown or made after the caucus. Many of these strategic questions must be answered while the caucuses are in session so that the mediator can prepare the parties for their next moves.

Although there are no firm rules for mediator and negotiator activities that result from a caucus, there are some general guidelines. Parties with greater power are often able to make the first move or offer after a caucus without losing integrity or advantage. They may have greater resources and therefore can be magnanimous, or they may have sufficient self-confidence or sufficient respect from other parties that they will not lose face or status by making the first move. Parties with offers contingent on another party's offer should speak only after the opponent's offer has been made. Simultaneous offers (with both parties putting written offers on the table at the same time) or incremental alternating offers, in which the parties alternate the provision of benefits to each other, may also be used. Mediators should take care to sequence speakers to ensure that the order of presentation does not prejudice a party's interests, and that a party does not inadvertently offer premature concessions.

Caucuses and Manipulation

Although the caucus is one of the most common and effective contingent strategies, it is not without its problems. Caucuses give mediators the greatest opportunity to manipulate parties into an agreement because disputants do not have the advantage of face-to-face communication to test the accuracy of information exchanged.

Keltner (1965, pp. 74–75) notes:

> In separating the parties during negotiations the mediator establishes himself as the main channel of communication between the parties. For example, in a separate session with the company the mediator expresses doubts that the offer that he is asked to carry to the union will be accepted, thereby *minimizing* the possibility of acceptance. Shortly thereafter he will meet the union and will *maximize* the desirability of acceptance of the proposal. This control and manipulation of the channel of communication and the introduction into it, thereby, of evaluative material provides him with some strength in bringing the parties closer together toward an area of agreement.

The ability to control, suppress, or enhance data, or to introduce entirely new information, gives the mediator an inordinate amount of influence over the parties. The ethics of such control and the proper role of the intermediary are hotly debated topics among mediators (Stevens, 1963). Young (1972, p. 57) observes that "it is difficult for an intermediary to engage in such manipulative activities without exhibiting some degree of partiality among the original players, either explicitly or implicitly. This raises a variety of problems concerning the acceptability of partial behavior on the part of intermediaries. And it may generate additional tactical rigidities in the interactions among the original players if they become concerned with actual or perceived partiality on the part of an intermediary."

An additional problem in caucuses arises with tensions between pushing for disclosure and encouraging retention of information. The majority of mediators treat communications in the caucus as confidential. Parties occasionally reveal information to the mediator that may place him or her in a potentially compromising position. For example, a husband may tell a mediator that he has a hidden bank account that his wife does not know about and that he does not want to include in the financial settlement. Or a party may acknowledge to a mediator that he or she has lied or made a false claim in the joint session that will adversely affect the outcome for the other party. These examples illustrate how the mediator, by using a caucus and ensuring confidentiality, may place himself or herself in an ethical bind. Should confidentiality be the mediator's highest value, or should full disclosure of information relative to a fair settlement of the dispute have primacy? There is probably no single right answer to this question, but because of problems created by the commitment to confidentiality, many mediators take great care when using the caucus. Some mediators tell the parties what they are willing or not willing to hear, and where the limits of confidentiality end. Several ethical codes or model standards require that the mediator disclose the limits of confidentiality at the beginning of the mediation session and carefully describe when mediators will not be bound by confidentiality. Lack of full financial disclosure, child abuse, or imminent physical danger, for example, are legitimate grounds for breaking confidentiality, according to the *Model Standards of the Association of Family and Conciliation Courts* (1984).

Other mediators refuse to ensure confidentiality in caucuses and use them merely to discuss issues without the tension induced by the physical presence of the other party. Although this procedure is an exception, not the rule, it does protect the mediator from being placed in the bind described above.

Regardless of its susceptibility to confidentiality problems and manipulation, the caucus remains one of the major contingent mediator strategies. In many disputes, settlement would be impossible if separate meetings were not conducted.

EXERTING MEDIATOR INFLUENCE

Ideally, conflicts should be resolved by rational dialogue and good-faith efforts by parties to reach mutually acceptable and beneficial agreements. However, mistrust, exercise of destructive forms of power and influence, and power imbalances often prevent productive dialogue in a significant number of disputes. Parties frequently resort to exercise of power, especially coercive power, to determine the outcome of negotiations, without considering possible rights and interests that may be involved (Ury, Brett, and Goldberg, 1988). These decisions and outcomes are often to their detriment.

Power or *influence* is the capability of a person or group to modify the outcome of a situation—that is, the benefits received by another and the costs inflicted, in the context of a relationship (Thibaut and Kelly, 1959). The capacity to influence the outcome for another party depends on the exercise of various means of pressure, persuasion, or coercion that either discourage or encourage the possibility of various options.

Influence is usually designed to change the viewpoint or condition of another. Means of influence can be placed on a continuum that indicates the amount of leverage or pressure being applied to encourage change and the degree of directiveness of the initiator. Usually, directiveness and pressure are directly correlated. Thus, at one end of the continuum the means of influence exert low pressure toward change, and the person using the leverage is not very directive. At the other end, the pressure is intense, and the initiator is extremely directive.

Parties use a range of means to influence each other (Mayer, 1987, 2000). Some of them are the exercise of:

- *Formal authority:* legal or widely recognized responsibility that is given to an organization or individual to act
- *Legal prerogative:* laws, rules, regulations, or customary law that furthers a widely recognized and legitimate mandate for an action, or specific process, decision, or outcome
- *Information:* adequate, accurate, applicable, and often widely acceptable data concerning the issues in question, or possibly experts who can provide this information
- *Associational influence:* formal or informal connections with people who, because of their authority, status, reputation, or influence, can enhance the power or influence of a disputant or put pressure on an opponent to change
- *Resources:* such factors as time, money, and labor
- *Rewards and sanctions:* the ability of a party to award benefits for cooperation or compliance, or harm or losses for non-cooperation
- *Nuisance:* ability to irritate another
- *Procedural power:* the ability to influence or control deliberative or decision-making processes
- *Habitual power:* parties' orientations toward maintaining the *status quo,* or inability to overcome inertia
- *Moral power:* an appeal to strong beliefs, values, or what is considered to be "right" by another party
- *Personal power:* traits of a negotiator that make him or her influential, such as "intelligence, communication skills, physical stamina and strength; concentration, wit, perceptiveness, determination, empathy and courage" (Mayer, 2000, p. 57).
- *Perception of power:* the ability of a party to influence the views of others regarding the amount of influence that he or she potentially has and the willingness to exercise it
- *Definitional power:* the ability to define the situation, issue, problem, or conflict in a way that is favorable to a party

Needless to say, these diverse forms of power and influence are used, either independently or in combination by parties in conflict, depending upon the kinds of issues, problems, or disputes in question; the parties involved in the altercation; the emotional charge or dynamics in play; and the disputants' orientations toward and perceptions about the utility of each strategy to achieve their desired goals.

Mediators are often directly involved with disputants in identifying, managing, and helping parties select and implement the most effective influence strategies that will enable them to reach beneficial decisions and mutually acceptable agreements. Mediators use various means of influence to change the dynamics of negotiations and the exercise of power and influence: (1) management of how parties exercise power and influence on each other; (2) means used by the intermediary to directly or indirectly influence one or more disputing parties; and (3) utilization of the input, interests, concerns, or pressure of external parties, who may not be directly involved in the conflict, to influence disputants. For mediators to be effective, they must know how to manage these three broad means of influence and power. In the sections below, I will examine how mediators work with each of these means of influence, as well as discuss how intermediaries work when there is a significant imbalance of power between parties.

Coordinating the Parties' Means of Influence

The first means of mediator influence is to help parties identify means that they can use to effectively promote agreement with others, and if necessary to change an "opponent's" mind. This task also includes identifying means of influence that have been, are being, or will be used by the parties, identifying means that may not be effective in modifying others' views or behaviors, and assisting parties to avoid or prevent their use.

Early in mediation, perhaps as early premeeting interviews and data gathering, the intermediary can often begin to get a feel for the strategies and tactics that will be (or are being) used by a party to influence others. For example, a party may say "If they don't agree, I'll see them in court," or "They need to do what is morally right!" Statements such as these are a clue as to what the party considers to be influential or persuasive. This is the case because parties usually pick influence procedures that they believe would modify *their* views if they were in a situation similar to that of the other side. But this is not always the case. For example, parties often decide to stress sanctions, harm, or incurred costs as a primary lever on an opponent, either to coerce them into an agreement or as an act of revenge. Unless coercive power is overwhelming, is believable, and cannot be resisted, this means of influence often creates more resistance than positive change, as people usually resent being coerced into agreements.

Mediators generally want to be as helpful as possible in assisting parties to present the best case for their interests and needs, and to help them avoid unnecessary resistance from other parties to either hearing about their concerns or positively responding. By helping parties to identify, choose, and decide how to exercise the best means of influence, the intermediary can significantly contribute to their reaching agreement. Mediators can do this by observing behavior, listening, and asking parties questions regarding their preferred or chosen means of influence. This is typically done either in premediation meetings or in caucuses. Here are some questions to ask before a specific means of influence is used:

- How do you plan to educate and persuade the other person or party regarding the merits of your views on the issues in question?
- Do you believe that this means of influence is the best one? If so, why?
- What means of influence have you used with this person or party in the past that has worked? Why?
- What means of influence have you used with this party in the past that has not worked? Why?
- On the basis of your experience with the other person or party, how can you avoid influence strategies that have not worked and use the ones that will be best received?
- What might be causes of resistance?
- If you encounter resistance, what other means of influence might you try?
- Where might you need help from me or others to influence the other person or party?
- How can I help?

Once parties are in joint session and have begun to exercise power and influence on each other, one of the mediator's tasks is to help them avoid initiating or continuing influence strategies that are not effective or are creating resistance. Intermediaries should also be on the lookout for ways to coordinate parties' persuasion approaches so that they can move toward agreement. It should be noted that parties may each respond better or worse to different influence strategies, and that the means used to achieve change in one party may not be the same as that preferred or needed by another. Mediators can help parties exercise effective influence and inhibit resistance to agreement by a number of approaches and questioning strategies:

• Call for a caucus to reassess the impact and effectiveness of specific influence strategies and to select others that may be more productive.

• Reframe an influence tactic used by a party to lower the threat level or resistance, such as changing "If you do not agree to our demands, we will mount demonstrations and shut your business down" to "If a reasonable agreement that meets your interests cannot be reached, you will have to reconsider what other options you have to achieve the desired change."

• Ask one or more parties either in caucus or joint session, "Is the current discussion and ways that you are using to influence each other working? Do you feel that the other person (or party) is listening, can hear, and is responding in the way that you want?" or "What impacts do you think your persuasion strategy is having on the others who are involved? Can you try another way to influence each other?"

• Ask the recipient of the persuasion tactic, either in caucus or joint session, "What are you feeling right now? Is the way that you are being persuaded or treated effective? If not, what would be persuasive to you and might make you change your mind?"

• Acknowledge that people or parties may have different expectations, needs, or preferences for means by which they are persuaded or influenced. Ask each party, "How would you like to be treated in these negotiations and what would you consider persuasive? An apology? More data? An agreement on fair and objective criteria that can be used to help make a decision? An agreement not to use threats?"

Initiating Mediator Strategies to Directly or Indirectly Influence Parties

I have just described strategies to coordinate the parties' means of influencing each other. I now turn to mediator strategies of influence. Intermediaries use a number of forms of influence to move parties toward agreement.

MANAGEMENT OF THE NEGOTIATION PROCESS

In every dispute, the mediator exerts a specific degree of control over the sequence of negotiation and problem-solving steps and the management of individual agenda items. He or she must choose—on the basis of the situation, the parties, and the issues in dispute—whether to have limited influence and make few procedural suggestions (general or specific); to be moderately influential and provide some structure; or to be highly influential and provide a highly detailed procedure over which parties have a low degree of control. Kolb (1983) notes this continuum in her description of labor-management mediators. She found some to be orchestrators (recall the discussion in Chapter Two) who made less directive procedural interventions; and others to be deal makers, who were highly directive and controlled both the process and substance under discussion. A similar continuum is common in family disputes. Coogler's work (1978) illustrates the more directive end of the continuum, and Stulberg's discussion (1981a) is probably at the other end.

Communication Between and Within Parties

The mediator can manage both communication behavior and structure in negotiations. Communication behavior can be managed by using techniques of active listening and reframing for the purpose of clarification and problem definition. The structure of communication may be modified by asking the parties to meet together, talk directly to each other, talk only to the mediator in each other's presence, or caucus and communicate only through the intervenor. In caucus, the mediator has extensive control over what will or will not be communicated and can frame information exchange so that it is more likely to be accepted. The mediator can exert great influence by being very directive about acceptable communicative behavior or structures, or play a much less directive role and still be effective.

Physical Setting and Negotiations

Mediators may modify the physical setting to encourage parties to settle. Seating arrangements, table shape, room size, availability of caucusing space, and removal of the negotiations from the scene of conflict can all affect outcomes. Highly directive intervenors may use one or many of these activities to influence settlement.

Timing in Negotiations

Decisions on timing govern the start of negotiations and their duration, the imposition or removal of deadlines for settlement, and the issuing of specific communications and offers. Mediators can be directive or nondirective in their control of timing, depending on their assessment of the parties and the situation.

Information Exchanged Between Parties

Negotiation involves a constant flow of information among the parties and the mediator. However, the content and form of that information vary with the situation. Fisher (1978, pp. 141–142) developed an "asking ladder" that depicts how information is given or received in terms of the initiator's degree of directiveness. The ladder ranges from requests for information to general suggestions, specific suggestions, concrete proposals, and demands. Mediators usually make less directive moves with respect to information; they usually ask questions and make suggestions rather than issue demands or force parties toward specific substantive conclusions. They may, however, play more directive roles in helping parties identify what information needs to be exchanged, what form it should take, and how it will best be heard or received by other parties. Mediators may also occasionally refer parties to sources of needed information.

Authority

Authority refers to a widely recognized right or legitimate power to exercise influence or make a decision. Authority can be vested in an institution or in a person's formal role. Mediators may exercise authority as a result of their affiliation with a mediation agency or, occasionally, a governmental body. Because of the prestige of their institutional connections, mediators who work for the Federal Mediation and Conciliation Service or those who are connected with a court or district attorney's office may be able to exercise more influence than the independent mediator without such affiliation. Parties may defer to the mediator on procedural and sometimes substantive issues because they acknowledge his or her skill, knowledge, and legitimate authority to be involved in a dispute.

Mediators may also call on other authorities to influence negotiators. They may appeal to a party's constituencies, superiors, judges, creditors, custody evaluators, or others to exert pressure on parties to settle. When a mediator enlists outside authorities, he or she is generally being highly directive. Although the mediator's goal may be gentle persuasion of a difficult party, an external authority's pressure is often almost tantamount to coercion. Mediators should take extreme care when involving external authority figures directly in negotiations.

Habits of Disputants

Many people in conflict have long-standing relationships in which routine patterns of behavior have been established. Business colleagues, lawyers, teachers, students, and spouses all develop relational routines that, for better or worse, are accepted as normal.

Mediators can often appeal to personal habits to reach settlement. For example, business disputants may be open to continuing established accounting practices; divorcing spouses may readily agree that both should continue to make proportional financial contributions toward child support. Agreement to ratify some element of the status quo is often the first decision that parties may reach.

Parties' Doubts

Probably no negotiated agreement is ever reached without some doubt on the part of the parties that a better settlement might have been obtained if they had been firmer, bargained longer, or pursued another means of dispute resolution. Doubt, however, was generally their rationale for pursuing a negotiated settlement. If they had been certain that they could have reached a more satisfactory agreement by negotiating in a different way or pursuing another approach to dispute resolution, they probably would have done so.

Mediators often use doubt to influence parties toward settlement. Doubt about the viability of a position or settlement option can be raised or explored in joint session, where both parties must bear the potential negative consequences; but more often, the mediator instills doubt in one or more parties in a caucus. By raising questions about potential outcomes that the party may not like, the mediator can often moderate a party's position and incline him or her toward mutually acceptable settlement possibilities. For example, a mediator might ask:

- Do you think you can win in court (or other public setting, such as before a commission or in the legislature)?
- How certain are you? Ninety percent? Seventy-five percent? Fifty percent?
- What risk are you willing to take?
- What if you lose?
- What will your life be like then?
- What impact do you think your victory in court (or other arena) will have on your ongoing relationship with the other party?
- Will you ever be able to work together again?
- Who else might be affected?
- What would they think of your position?
- Would you be proud to publicly announce this stance?
- Would others whom you respect feel it is reasonable?
- If you were in the other party's place and this proposal were made to you, would you accept it?
- Could you accept it over the long run?

Through careful questioning that may vary in degree of directiveness, the mediator may begin to create doubt in a party's mind about the feasibility of his or her adherence to an option. If misused, this technique obviously approaches manipulation and raises questions about the ethics of mediator influence.

Appeals to Moral Arguments or Values

Mediators can often help parties reach agreements by appealing to their sense of fairness, morality, or common values. These may be individual, group, organizational, or societal values that the parties may hold in common, or that they perceive to be fair. More will be said about this approach to influence in the section later in this chapter on approaches for mediating disputes that involve strong values.

Rewards or Benefits

Generally, mediators only indirectly influence the rewards that a party receives as a result of negotiation. The other party or parties to the dispute are usually the grantor of those benefits. The major exception to this rule is in international disputes in which the mediator is a representative of a powerful interest or nation and has resources at his or her command to bestow, such as foreign aid, military assistance, or recognition if the parties settle.

Mediators do, however, have some indirect rewards to offer as inducements to settlement. The mediator's friendship, respect for a person or point of view, interest in a party's personal well-being, or affirmation of how a point was settled can all induce a disputant to agree. The mediator's relationship with the parties is often the only positive reward that he or she can offer in negotiations. If the disputants value this, they may behave in ways that will encourage the mediator to continue his or her positive responses.

Another indirect means of rewarding a party is to identify the benefits that the disputant could receive as a result of a settlement and to help him or her visualize what it would be like to have that settlement. Mediators can verbally project the beneficial outcome. If the disputants perceive the mediator's vision of rewards as adequate for settlement, they may move toward agreement.

Coercive Influence

Coercive influence refers to the use of force to change another's opinion or behavior against his or her will. Coercive influence depends on decreasing a party's choices for settlement and then increasing the damage that the party will incur if he or she does not accept the proposed designated outcome. Because mediation is voluntary and the mediator serves the will of the parties, he or she usually has few direct coercive techniques available to influence disputants. Exceptions include some court-related mediators who are on occasion empowered by statute to make recommendations to a judge if the parties cannot settle; international mediators with powerful superiors who can damage recalcitrant parties; and intervenors practicing "med-arb," a mediation-arbitration hybrid in which the parties agree to allow the intervenor to mediate until an impasse occurs, at which time the mediator becomes an arbiter and decides the conflict's outcome.

There are, however, several indirect coercive techniques that can be used by mediators and may incline the parties to move toward settlement. A mediator's display of impatience or displeasure, as indicated by nonverbal communication or verbal statements, may coerce a party to move toward agreement. This may be especially true when a party wants the intervenor's respect or wants to maintain the respect of his or her group, and when this respect may be eroded by continuing an unpopular course of action. Mediator or peer approval—or its withdrawal—can be very important in moderating hard-line positions.

The mediator's most direct and coercive means of influencing parties is to threaten to withdraw from negotiations, or to actually do so. This is the ultimate act of disapproval and denial of service to the parties. In one case, a mediator believed that the parties were not negotiating in good faith and were delaying settlement. He announced that he wanted to terminate his participation because the parties did not seem to be making progress. He offered the parties his business card, told them to call him when they were ready to talk, and walked toward the door. He never reached it. The parties called him back and settled immediately.

Withdrawal or the threat of withdrawal is risky for the mediator and the parties because it may precipitate a breakdown in negotiations. Threats to withdraw succeed only if the parties consider the mediator unexpendable, and if they believe the threat. If these conditions are not met, the parties may even welcome the mediator's departure. Mediators should exercise care in using this technique because it can backfire and leave them out of the negotiations. Even if it works, the tactic may create resentment or later resistance from the parties.

The Mediator's Personality

Mediators often have significant influence with parties because of who they are, personal traits they exhibit, and the relationships or bonds that have been formed between the intermediary and disputants (Bowling and Hoffman, 2000). Research in persuasion has found that liking and desiring to be positively associated with a person or organization that is liked or respected is a powerful influence (Cialdini, 2001). In general, we like people (1) who like us, (2) who are similar to us, (3) who have cooperated with us to help us achieve our own or common goals, and (4) with whom we have pleasant associations (Oren, 2001). By cultivating genuinely respectful, listening, trustful, concerned, and caring relationships with parties, mediators can develop a significant capacity to influence them. Mediators can use this means of influence to help parties assess the fairness of offers or agreements from or with other parties, do reality testing and if necessary deflate unrealistic expectations, explore BATNAs, or encourage greater efforts to reach agreement.

Using External Parties to Influence Disputants

Conflicts do not occur in a vacuum. There are always other parties who know about or are concerned with the outcome, or whose influence can be brought in and mobilized to influence disputants. Certain people wield *associational influence* on disputants to the extent that their opinions or actions affect the parties' attitudes or behavior. Associates include friends, colleagues, family members, other members of a disputing group, and constituents. Mediators should assess when these associates might be included or excluded from the negotiations in order to induce settlement. The trusted words of a professional colleague, a supportive peer or therapist, the involvement of a stepparent or grandparent in family negotiations, the view of a member of the clergy, or the opinion of a governor or senior official may be all that is needed to change the dynamics of the dispute and incline the parties toward settlement. The mediator can often manage the form and effect of associational influence, and help the parties decide if and when to involve other parties.

Experts

Mediators can often influence the parties to settle by involving people with particular expertise or areas of knowledge in negotiations. The mediator can play a more directive or less directive role in identifying the need for substantive, procedural, or psychological experts; in encouraging their use; and in proposing procedures for selecting them. Parties often want to jointly select experts so as to avid the dynamic of battling experts selected by each party.

POWER BALANCE BETWEEN PARTIES

Power is not a characteristic of an organization or person but is an attribute of a relationship. A party's power is directly related to the power of an opponent. Power relations generally occur in two forms: *symmetrical*, or equal; and *asymmetrical*, or unequal, levels of influence (Bagozzi and Dholakia, 1977).

Symmetrical Power Relations

Practical experience and social psychological experimentation indicate that when negotiators have an equal or symmetrical power relationship, they favor cooperation, function more effectively, and behave in a less exploitative or manipulative manner than when there is an asymmetrical power relationship (Rubin and Brown, 1975). Disputes in which parties have roughly equal power tend to be the most amenable to mediation.

Mediators working with parties of equal power usually attempt to improve the cooperative behavior of the parties, enhance the perception of equal power in the relationship, and limit the expression of coercive power in negotiations. The most common influence problems that disputants with equal power encounter are perceptual difficulties between the parties with respect to symmetry and the presence of a negative residue of emotions resulting from past exercise of coercive power within the relationship.

Perception of power symmetry is usually dependent on the ability to measure or project the potential outcome of a dispute if one or more parties decide to exercise their power. For example, if two people contest a piece of property and both know that the other has unlimited funds, equally qualified lawyers, and case law to back up their arguments, the perception of each other's power may be relatively easy to determine. This is true because the variables by which power is measured—capital, personnel, and case law—are the same for each party and are known.

However, what if the sources of power are different such that the types of power and even the standards of measurement are not the same and are not known by each party? For example, in some labor-management negotiations, labor must assess management's ability to carry on production in the event of a strike, management's staffing capabilities, product stockpiles, and public demand for the product. The employer must assess the number of employees who are willing to strike, the assets available to the union and its allies to sustain an industrial action, the climate of public opinion regarding the merits of the dispute, and so on. In this instance, the basis of power differs for the two parties, as do the variables used to measure that power.

When parties have differing bases of influence, a power assessment problem often develops. This can result in a breakdown in negotiations. Parties may return to negotiations only after they have exercised and tested their power and have developed a more accurate assessment of the leverage of the other parties. For example, many divorcing spouses attempt to negotiate issues, fail, and hire lawyers. A large proportion of these cases settle before the case actually goes to trial. The act of testing the strength and will of an opponent to go to court may be an important step in developing an accurate perception of another disputant's power and willingness to use it.

Unfortunately, testing power often involves exercising coercion, which tends to produce negative effects on the ability of the parties to work together cooperatively. Even in symmetrical relations, exercise of power—especially coercive power—may lead to increased resistance to settle or an irreversible breakdown of negotiations.

Mediators in disputes in which symmetry is hard to determine because of differing power bases or measures should attempt to help the parties assess each other's power without encouraging the parties to resort to coercion.

Changing perceptions about power, especially when the parties have symmetrical relationships, is usually accomplished by developing an accurate power assessment mechanism or by changing conditions so that power is irrelevant. In the first method, mediators can privately encourage a party to list his or her own sources or bases of power and then identify the costs and benefits of exercising them (Fisher, 1969; Bellows and Moulton, 1981). The party can then be encouraged to use the same procedure to assess their opponent's power. The process may be repeated, if necessary, with the other side. A cross-reference of costs and potential outcomes in symmetrical power relationships will frequently induce parties to recognize similarities in their abilities to influence each other.

The second technique requires parties to shift their focus from power relationships to interests. By calling attention to the process of how needs can be satisfied, the mediator often can persuade the parties to avoid emphasis on how they can force the opposing party into submission.

Asymmetrical Power Relations

Although symmetrical power relations seem to be the optimal relationship for effective bargaining, this type of relationship is not the norm. Parties generally differ in the form or amount of power or influence they possess in relation to one another.

Mediators in disputes in which parties have asymmetrical or unequal power relationships face two kinds of problems: (1) perceptual problems (situations in which the stronger party believes that the weaker party has equal power, or in which the weaker party has an inflated view of his or her strength) and (2) extremely asymmetrical relationships (situations in which a party is in a much weaker position, and both parties know it).

Mediators can work with both weaker and stronger parties to minimize the negative effects of unequal power (Kelly, 1995; Roubana and Korper, 1996; Gewurz, 2001). In a situation of unequal balance of power where the weaker party bluffs about his or her power and the stronger party accepts the bluff, the mediator should usually meet with the bluffing party to educate him or her about the potential costs of being found out or called on to carry out the bluff. The other party's discovery of the deception can lead to deterioration in relationships and may lead to retaliation if the victim of the bluff is the stronger party.

If the party can be convinced that the costs of bluffing are too high, the mediator and the party should jointly search for a way to retreat from the bluff or minimize the importance of power dynamics in the context of the negotiations. Retreating from a bluff or minimizing the effects of bluff can often be achieved by ceasing to make threatening statements or false promises and by giving a plausible rationalization for the change in stance or position.

In power situations in which parties appear to have an asymmetrical relationship and the bases of power differ, the mediator may attempt to obscure the strength or influence of both parties. He or she can pursue this strategy to create doubt about the actual power of the parties by questioning the accuracy of data, the infallibility of experts, the capability or costs of mobilizing coercive power, or the degree of support from authority figures. These techniques can prevent the parties from ascertaining the balance of power. If a party cannot determine absolutely that he or she has more power than another, he or she usually does not feel free to manipulate or exploit an opponent without restraint.

By far the most difficult problem mediators face regarding power relationships is a huge discrepancy in strength of parties' means of influence (Kelly, 1995). The independent mediator, because of his or her commitment to impartiality, is generally ethically barred from direct advocacy for the weaker party yet is also ethically obligated to assist the parties in reaching an acceptable and durable agreement.

Wall (1981) argues that the mediator's primary task is to manage the power relationship of the disputants. In unequal power relationships, the mediator may attempt to balance power: "To strike the balance, the mediator provides the necessary power underpinnings to the weaker negotiator—information, advice, friendship— or reduces those of the stronger" (p. 164).

If this strategy is adopted, the mediator may undertake moves to assist the weaker party to recognize and mobilize the power he or she possesses. The mediator should not, however, directly act as an organizer to mobilize or develop new power for the weaker disputant unless the mediator has gained the stronger party's approval. To act as a secret advocate puts the mediator's impartiality and effectiveness as a process intervenor at risk.

Empowering moves may include:

- Assisting the weaker party in obtaining, organizing, and analyzing data and identifying and mobilizing his or her means of influence

- Assisting and educating the party in planning an effective negotiation strategy
- Aiding the party in developing financial resources so that he or she can continue to participate in negotiations
- Referring the party to a lawyer or other resource person
- Encouraging the party to make realistic concessions

Wall (1981) notes that stronger parties often welcome a mediator's involvement in power balancing. The mediator can assist a weaker party who is unorganized and unable to negotiate in preparing for a productive exchange that will benefit both parties. This role of the mediator as organizer has been practiced in husband-wife disputes (Haynes, 1981), labor-management conflicts (Perez, 1959), community disputes (Lincoln, 1976), large-scale environmental contests (Dembart and Kwartler, 1980), and interracial disputes (Kwartler, 1980).

GRAND STRATEGIES FOR RESPONDING TO TEMPORAL SOURCES OF CONFLICTS

Much of current mediation thinking, and the views of many practitioners, posit that mediation is a forward-looking process, one that does not strive to place blame for past negative or harmful events, and one that strives to solve immediate problems so that parties' interests and future relationships are positively met and redefined. However, in reality mediators and parties have to respond to incidents, events, and conflicts that have happened, are happening, or will happen at three temporal periods: the past, present, and future (Lederach, 1999).

Grand strategies refer to decisions made by parties or an intermediary concerning the approach, emphasis, and sequencing of responses to the causes of conflicts that have occurred at different times. Let's look at the three times in more detail and then examine how they might be sequenced in dispute resolution initiatives.

The *past* can either be the near present, or it may go back in time many years or even generations. On occasion, issues that have developed in the past are so dominant in the life of one or more parties that no progress toward agreements in the present can be made, or development of alternative visions for the future achieved until past problems have been acknowledged, discussed, or addressed.

The *present* refers to events that are currently occurring. The immediacy of events may result in feelings that are both strong and high. Often parties believe that this immediacy forces them to address pressing issues and redefine their relationships.

The *future* is an upcoming time when parties will, or may have to, unilaterally or jointly address new issues, problems, or conflicts. Development of both a positive future vision and ways to manage difference is often critical for parties to reach agreements on either current issues or those in the past.

Sequence refers to the order in which past, present, or future issues are or will be addressed by parties during the mediation process. The order of discussion of these issues is a strategic question. Certain issues, interests, relationships, or psychological states of the parties may dictate the order in which the past, present, and future are addressed, and one sequence may be more effective than another. Some possible sequences for working on issues are:

• *Present, with no past or future relationships.* For example, a victim-offender mediation, in which the parties have not had any past relationship, the current conflict is over recent property damage, and there is no desire or opportunity for future interactions or relationships between the parties. The mediator focuses only on resolution of the immediate conflict issues and feelings.

• *Present, with a past and no future relationships.* For example, a couple in a five-year, very stormy marriage with no children are separating. They each want psychological closure and a divorce and never plan to see each other again. The mediator helps the parties process the past, explores acknowledgments and potential apologies, and then works with the parties on current separation issues.

• *Present with no past, and potential for actual future relationships.* For example, new petless neighbors have moved into a house in a suburban neighborhood. They have had no conflicts with past neighbors but have one now with their current neighbors over a dog that barks at all hours of the night. The new neighbors have never had a problem with a barking dog before. They want to resolve the current issue and build a positive relationship with their dog-owning neighbors. No one plans to move. The mediator focuses on addressing current issues (the barking dog), explores what issues might emerge in the future, helps develop effective dispute resolution procedures for them, and assists the parties in developing more positive communication and mending neighborly relationships.

• *Present with a past, and future relationships.* For example, former adversaries in a civil war have had a long, stormy, and bloody relationship. All parties need to address the past, deal with present and ongoing conflicts, and devise ways to manage interracial differences in the future. Local intermediaries help address immediate and current problems relating to housing, jobs, and how people can live together peacefully on a day-to day basis, and so on; help to establish a Truth and Reconciliation Commission and restitution mechanism to address past wrongs; and design effective collaborative decision-making and conflict management procedures to handle future issues.

• *Past, with no present relationship, but the potential for a future one.* For example, the children of refugees of an internal displacement that occurred thirty years ago are returning home and want to regain property that has been lost. They have a conflict with the people who did their parents harm in the past, but do not have a conflict with the current government of the country to which they are returning or directly with the people who are living in the property in question. How they regain their property may affect their relationship with the current occupants of the property, or others in the neighborhood. The mediator helps parties understand and work through the past, and develop a procedure to resolve the issue of home ownership, and what happens depending on whether the family currently residing in the house leaves or stays.

• *Future with present or current conflictual relationship.* For example, two businesses are merging. They do not have a past relationship, or a current conflictual one. However, the chief executives are uncomfortable about the future provisions to keep on existing staff. The deal for the future cannot go through until the executives feel comfortable about what will happen to their people. The mediator focuses with the parties on how future employment and possible termination might be handled in a fair, just, and mutually acceptable way.

Given these patterns of disputes, and possible sequences for addressing the past, present, and future, how can a mediator determine a grand strategy? Here are several guidelines that may be helpful in making this determination.

Start with Past Issues and Relationships

A number of authors and practitioners, especially advocates of what is termed "problem solving workshops," encourage intervenors to start with the past, or significantly explore the underlying needs and past and current relationships that are at the basis of deep rooted conflicts, and then move the parties toward addressing the present or future (Fisher, 1997; Kelman, 1991, 2001; Saunders, 1999; and Rothman, 1992, 1997). The rationale that supports this sequencing is based on an analysis that:

- Parties are so enmeshed in feelings about the past that they cannot discuss the current situation or envision any positive future relationships
- The issues regarding what happened in the past are the basis or cause for the current conflict
- Parties hold diverse views or interpretations of what happened in the past—views that they believe others need to hear and understand before addressing present issues
- How issues of the past are addressed and handled will seriously affect how current or future issues will be managed or resolved
- Addressing or resolving a key issue in the past will create an opening for addressing current or future issues
- One or more parties need acknowledgment, ownership, or apologies from another for past wrongs, as a prerequisite for negotiations over current or future issues

Work on the Past and Then Go to the Present

After working on the past, go to present issues and relationships if:

- Current issues in dispute also seem to be the parties major focus

- Resolution of current issues will open doors to address possible future ones or enhance future relationships

Work on the Past and Then Go to the Future

After working on the past, go directly to potential or actual future issues or relationships if:

- The parties do not have much of a current relationship and few if any current issues exist
- Parties are trying to reconcile after a long hiatus in the relationship
- Resolving potential future problems or relationship issues will make it easier to return and handle any present issues that exist

Do Not Start with the Past

Do not start working on the past if:

- Discussion is likely to lead to immediate deadlock because of strong emotions or totally polarized views
- The parties are not ready or willing to talk about the past, because it is too painful or they have more important immediate needs that need to be addressed
- Parties believe that the past is over and done with and cannot be changed, and they want to focus on current or future issues or relationships

Start with Current or Present Issues and Relationships

Probably the majority of mediation practitioners in North America, Europe, and the Pacific region (Australia and New Zealand) subscribe to an approach and sequencing that starts with current or present issues and relationships. The exception may be some therapeutic or transformational mediators who subscribe to a past-future-present or past-present-future sequences. The logic for starting in the present and trying to resolve current conflicts first applies when:

- Current issues and relationships are perceived by the parties to be the most important ones to address
- Resolution of current issues and relationships is easier than addressing those in the past
- Resolution of current issues will establish a firm basis for positive future relationship
- Parties do not have much of a negative past history
- Resolution of current issues will help prepare for discussion of past issues and relationships, by establishing a level of trust, respect, understanding, or tangible agreements

After working on the present, go to past issues and relationships if:

- Parties are open, are willing, and want to talk about the past
- Addressing the past is a prerequisite for addressing future issues and relationships
- Failure to address the past is likely to result in a reopening of current issues in the future, because the past has not been dealt with

After working on the present, go to future issues and relationships if:

- There is not much of a negative past relationship between the parties
- Development of a future positive relationship and procedures to handle future differences will help solidify agreements on current issues and make parties more comfortable with a prospective future relationship
- Addressing future issues or relationships will make it easier to eventually respond to the past

Start with Future Issues and Relationships

The approach of starting with future issues and relationships also has its adherents among mediators and practitioners of problem-solving workshops (Blake and Mouton, 1984). Proponents of future sequencing assert that if the parties develop a positive future vision of where they want to go, and which sets up affirmative standards and criteria for interactions, later problem solving on current issues will become much easier. They suggest that the future should be addressed first when:

- Parties do not have serious current or past conflicts, are very uneasy about an unpredictable future, and need agreements for this time in order to form positive and predictable future relationships
- Success and progress is more likely on future issues and relationships than trying to handle current or past ones first
- Development of a positive vision of the future (one that details where parties want to go regarding their issues and relationships) and reaching mutual agreement on the vision and future interactions will positively condition and help them return at a later time to address and resolve present and past issues and relationships
- Development of a potential positive future relationship with both individual and joint benefits is likely to outweigh the costs and problems associated with the present conflict

Work on the Future and Then Go to the Present or Past

After working on the future, go to the present or past issues and relationships if:

- The present or past need to be addressed or "cleaned-up" before moving into the new future relationships as defined by the parties
- Implementation of future agreements is contingent or conditional on an acceptable resolution of current or past issues or relationships

Start with One Temporal Orientation and Switch to Another

Yet another approach to grand strategies for responding to past, present, and future issues and relationships is to start with one temporal period and move between one or more other times and issues depending on the issues and willingness of the parties. For example, in some disputes it is possible to settle a current issue, jump to the future and address how conflicts that may arise will be handled, skip to the past for an apology, and return to the present and address another current issue. Using this approach, mediators can develop integrated agreements or packages, albeit in a highly nonlinear way. This approach is very common among mediators, and in fact it may be the norm in cultures that do not compartmentalize issue processing according to the time when the conflict developed, or cultures that engage in a circular or looping (discussion of an issue with multiple diversions to explore other topics) rather than a linear approach to processing issues.

Develop Integrated Grand Strategies

From the approaches and sequences that have been described, it is clear that there is no one grand strategy or sequence that will always be appropriate or successful for responding to conflicting parties' issues and relationships. Mediators, through discussions with parties and using their own best judgment regarding which approaches are likely to be most successful, should determine a sequence and try it out. If it is successful in helping parties address issues, so much the better. If not, the mediator might say, "Let's put the past on hold for a while, and look at some of the present issues that concern you. We will return to the past later, once you have addressed some of your immediate needs" or "You presently have a number of current issues that we have begun to discuss. But I wonder if it might be helpful to take a jump into the future, and have you talk about what your future relationship might look like if everything is going well. This view might help inform or even establish some standards and criteria for how you resolve current issues."

APPROACHES FOR MEDIATING DISPUTES INVOLVING STRONG VALUES

Values disputes, which are sometimes referred to as moral conflict (Pearce and Littlejohn, 1997) or one form of intractable conflict (Kriesberg, Northrup, and Thorson, 1989), are quite common in interpersonal and wider social relationships. It is well known that conflicts over values, or disputes in which strong beliefs play a significant role, are very difficult to resolve. Some authors have gone so far as to say that strong differences over values cannot be reconciled, and the most that disputing parties or an intermediary can do toward addressing these differences is to encourage an exchange of information about the differing beliefs, foster understanding and tolerance, and acknowledge that no agreement is possible (Gordon, 1978). However, this advice offers little assistance to parties or intermediaries who are enmeshed in efforts to manage deep differences, reach agreements, and end contentious and often costly altercations. There is a need for a range of possible approaches and strategies that both parties and mediators can try to respond to disputes with strong value components. Before examining them, it is important to have a firm understanding of what values are.

Values

Values are freely chosen internal standards or beliefs that people use to judge whether issues, behaviors, or events are good-bad, right-wrong, moral-immoral, fair-unfair, just-unjust. People use values as both standards and maps to guide their behavior in social interactions. The development of values is the result of a complex socialization process in which parents, siblings, peers, education, religion, work, associations, and ethnic and national affiliation all play a part. The end result, the value system of an individual or group, is an elaborate set of beliefs that have developed over a long period of time. These basic values rarely change dramatically during the life of an individual or group, and if so they usually shift only after an extended period of time, in-depth introspection, a significant life-changing critical incident or event, or dramatic pressure from external sources. The relatively permanent and stable nature of values means that disputes involving clashes of strong belief systems may require months or years to reconcile, if they are resolved at all.

However, any specific value may not be held with equal fervor or be equally important when compared to another value. Most people have a hierarchy of values, with some beliefs or standards being more important than others. In general, people have three levels of values: self-definition, terminal, and operational values.

Self-definition or moral values are the deepest and most basic form of individual or group beliefs. They define how a person or group believes they really are or present their core self or selves to others. Values about gender (what it means to be a man or woman), integrity (what this term means in all aspects of one's life), honesty and truthfulness (how important truth telling is and how one sees oneself as living up to this value), candor (directness), fairness (what constitutes fair treatment), equality (what it means to be equal or be treated equally), openness (how much personal disclosure is acceptable), love and lovability (what constitutes this emotion or relationship, and what is needed or expected to be given), emotions (ways of expression to self and others), and safety (what level is needed to ensure security or an acceptable level of comfort) are examples of self-definition values.

Terminal values are the next level of values. These strong and deep beliefs guide the behavior of an individual or groups in most areas of their lives. Here are examples of statements that illustrate terminal values:

- Lifestyle: "My family settled on this ranch in Kansas in the 1890s, and it's been in my family and blood ever since. It's my identity. I was born a rancher and I'll die a rancher."
- Class: "My father was a member of the working class, as was his father. I am too. With us, it's union all the way!"
- Sexuality: "I'm gay and proud of it!"
- Nature: "Wilderness is my church and cannot be replaced. Allowing the cutting of forests is totally incompatible with preserving wilderness and the spirit of this place!"
- Political beliefs: "I participated in the civil rights movement for racial equality, and I'll be damned if I'm going to let them treat me that way just because of my color!"
- Ethnicity: "My Indian people have hunted and fished in these lands and waters from time immemorial. Who are you to tell us how to live and that we cannot trap, hunt, or forage for food?"
- Nationality: "I'm French; need I say more?"
- Religion: "There is that of God and good in every person, to harm someone diminishes the individual, the community at large, and the deity."

Operational values are strong beliefs, attitudes, or preferences that guide day-to-day activities and interactions of individuals and groups. They are very different from the likes or whims that a person desires but can live without. Operational values are the standards and norms that people use to guide everyday life; people use them to judge the attitudes and behaviors of others. Examples of this kind of values are individual or group standards regarding how people expect each other to act:

- Expectations for proper behavior when eating with others: "Don't eat with your mouth open or with your hands."
- Cleanliness: "Cleanliness is next to godliness."
- Acceptable levels and kinds of noise or music: "I can't stand rock music, especially at that volume."
- Expectations for what it means to be on time for meetings, delivery of reports, or arriving at work: "Eight o'clock means eight o'clock."
- Beliefs about obligations to pay-back debts: "One should always pay back one's debts, in full and on time."
- What does and does not constitute offensive language: "Do you always have to use profanity every other word?"
- Thrift: "A penny saved is a penny earned."
- Promises: "A promise is a promise."
- General norms about truth telling: "Always tell the truth; not even white lies are acceptable."
- Quality-of-life preferences: "I could never drive a car like that; it doesn't fit my lifestyle and would never hold all my camping gear."
- Aesthetics: "That color is ugly!"

When an operational value is violated by someone who does not conform to another's value or expectation, the latter is likely to say, "He just wasn't brought up right," "She doesn't understand how we do things around here," "That language is offensive," "They're snobs," or "You have no taste."

It should be noted that a hierarchy may also exist within each of these value categories (operational, terminal, or self-defined) so that if forced to make a choice an individual may choose to satisfy one value at the expense of another, with the more important outweighing the less important. For example, an elderly retiree may have operational values about living independently in his or her own large house that was purchased shortly after retirement, and having all of his or her collector's items and family heirlooms prominently displayed. However, age, mobility, the increased cost of living, upkeep of the property, and having to clean all the collector's items may shift his or her operational value and accept that living in a smaller retirement home, where there will be some assistance in taking care of his or her daily needs, will be easier, less expensive, and more comfortable. In this situation, the values of ease, assistance, comfort, and cost may be more important and trump the value of the large house or having personal property on display.

Why Are Values Conflicts So Difficult to Resolve?

As can be seen, individual and group values differ as to importance and how strongly they are held. Self-definition and terminal values are generally much more important than operational values. Conflicts that involve operational values are typically much more easily resolved, or differences accepted, than those that involve terminal or self-definition values.

So why are these latter so difficult to resolve? Three possible reasons are that these kinds of value conflicts often challenge the identity of individuals or groups and predictability about how the world should be ordered, and they frequently trigger significant fears concerning change.

"Identity is defined as an abiding sense of the self and of the relationship of the self to the world. It is a system of beliefs or a way of construing the world that makes life predictable rather than random" (Northrup, 1989, p. 55). When a dispute involves a clash of self-identity or terminal values, it challenges who an individual or group is, both in terms of how they see themselves and in relation to others, and it threatens to destabilize the predictability of life and raise fears of change.

Because of the deep-rooted nature of conflicts that involve identity or terminal values, parties are often unable to acknowledge the importance or validity of values held by others. Conflicts of this type are also not as amenable to trading and compromises to satisfy interests as is common in other kinds of disputes. Compromise is seen as invalidating one's identity or the loss of self or group image; a sacrifice of enduring and unchangeable principles; and a loss of self-respect, way of life, or worldview. With uncompromisable values at stake, escalation is very likely to occur.

Recognizing Values and Values Disputes

In some disputes, parties' values are clearly articulated and can be explored and addressed directly. In others, because values are often highly individualized or personal and are carried internally by individuals or group members, they may not be directly articulated. What other parties or a mediator hear or sees are verbal comments or behavior, which are driven by but do not necessarily clearly articulate or demonstrate the underlying values that motivate them. If values are not clearly and directly stated by parties to a dispute, how can people identify the roles they are playing in a conflict? Creighton (1983) identified three behavioral indicators that often point to the presence of strong values in a dispute, and I have added a fourth: (1) the significant presence and use of value-laden language, (2) predictions of dire consequences, (3) quotation of venerable sources, and (4) characterization of other involved individuals or parties.

Value-laden language involves the presence or use of words that express values or judgments (unfair, unjust, unreasonable, bad) or strong feeling words (outraged, frustrated, incredulous, hurt). Statements of values usually imply a judgment about the attitudes and behavior of one party by another ("That kind of division of property is horrendous . . . it's just not fair").

Predictions of dire consequences refer to potential or feared outcomes if a particular strategy or solution to a problem is pursued. Examples can be seen in a divorce ("That solution will leave me in abject poverty!"), in a natural resource conflict ("It will be centuries before we ever have another tree grow on that hill"), in an employer-employee altercation ("If we grant this employee that privilege, we'll have every other person in the plant making the same claim!"), and in a commercial or insurance lawsuit ("That type of claim would break the company!").

Quotations of venerable sources are appeals to documents or people whom the claimant believes to be trustworthy, credible, and unquestionable, and that he or she will use to try to convince another party of the "truth" of his or her position. "The Bible, Koran, or Talmud says . . .," "The Constitution grants . . . ," "Public Law 404 provides that . . . ," "As Abraham Lincoln used to say. . . ," and "Our boss believes . . ." are all examples of appeals to a venerable source to bolster a position.

Characterization refers to judgments about the views, values, or capabilities of another person or group: "Why, he's irrational" (or incompetent, or not wrapped right, or out of touch with reality) or "She's a "right-winger" (or a crazy environmentalist, or a rape-and-plunder developer, or an irresponsible parent, or a dictatorial manager, and so forth).

The presence of one or more of these indicators gives notice to other parties or the mediator that there are values in play, and that there are strong beliefs underlying a party's words and non-verbal and verbal behavior.

Before looking at ways of responding to and managing differences in disputes that involve strong values, it is important to note that not all value disputes can, should, or have to be resolved. For example, in a dispute involving significant religious differences, if one person is a fundamentalist Christian, his or her counterpart is a fundamentalist Muslim, and each wants the other to convert, there is a very low probability that either will significantly alter their basic religious beliefs. (The exception might be if they want to marry, and their love for each other or family pressure or desires are stronger than either of the parties' adherence to specific religious beliefs or practices.)

In other cases, it's important not to try to reconcile values. For example, there are some values that are incompatible with the preservation or enhancement of human dignity, personal security, or life. A wife's need and value for safety should always outweigh an abusive husband's belief and value that his wife is his personal property and that he should be able to treat her in any way he pleases. In this type of case, it may be important that one value—safety—prevail over the other—the personal freedom of doing what one wants.

Finally, it is important to remember that people do not have to hold the same values to live together in relative harmony and happiness. Husbands and wives frequently live together in long and happy marriages yet do not hold the same values in every area of their lives. Interreligious communities can live together in peace, as during Spain's golden age of 750–1100 A.D., when Muslims, Christians, and Jews shared much of a common culture and lived together side-by-side without killing each other (Menocal, 2002).

Conflicts involving strong values, especially self-definition and terminal values, become most difficult or intractable when one or more parties see their values as being mutually exclusive; insist that only theirs can be right; feel that their value-based individual or collective identity is threatened; believe that people who hold different strong beliefs are entirely wrong; or think that opponents should be converted, neutralized, isolated, or marginalized, or even totally eliminated. This is the kind of dispute where parties need help to manage their value differences and minimize the harm or pain they may cause each other.

General Approaches for Responding to Value Differences

The more a dispute or conflict involves an individual's or group's identity and is related to deeply held terminal or operational values and beliefs, the more a party is likely to feel threatened if their values are challenged or if they are asked to change in any significant way. So, what can be done to address, defuse, and deescalate conflicts that involve differences in identity, terminal, or operational values?

There a number of approaches for responding to value disputes (which will be explored next). Each approach requires a varying level of change in the identities and values of those involved. Some approaches seek to address components of the conflict without addressing tensions related to underlying values. Others require shifts in beliefs.

Any one of these approaches may or may not be appropriate for a given conflict. They may be effective when used alone or in combination with another approach. Parties and intermediaries may need to experiment and try one or more approaches before finding one or more that will help disputants effectively manage or address their differences.

Timing of the introduction or trial of approaches is also an important question. Some of the first approaches that will be presented may be appropriate for cases where there has been either very little interaction or a high level of conflict between parties, and where trust, positive communication, cognitive mutual understanding, or emotional empathy is minimal or nonexistent. Other approaches may be more appropriate once some elements of a positive relationship have been established, communication has been enhanced, and a greater openness to exploring differences in values is present among the parties. With these caveats in mind, let us now examine some possible approaches to handling values differences and conflicts.

APPROACHES FOR RESPONDING TO VALUE DIFFERENCES WITHOUT CHANGING A PARTY'S BELIEFS

These approaches focus on increasing understanding of diverse beliefs, not value shifts. Although they do not resolve disputes, they can help parties move forward with agreement making.

Address or Resolve Peripheral Conflict Elements or Issues

The first approach involves helping parties in conflict reach agreements on peripheral issues or levels of change, agreements that will help lower tensions and hostilities but do not alleviate specific or underlying value related issues or problems (Susskind and Field, 1996, p. 158). These issues are often peripheral to the central dispute, but their successful resolution can help lower negative or unproductive interactions and lay the foundation for other approaches to address value differences.

For example, during the 1980s, when anti-apartheid activists were aggressively challenging, both nonviolently and violently, the racially discriminatory apartheid government of South Africa, a mediator, H. V. van de Merwe, was called in to defuse and try to reach a settlement of a highly volatile interracial and political conflict. Capetown activists with weapons had taken over a religious building to protest unfair repressive actions by the regime and the violation of human rights. A few shots had been exchanged with police, and the situation promised to escalate if nothing was done.

When van de Merwe first contacted the activists and offered his services, they initially declined. They said that they wanted the conflict to continue—a common strategy in confrontation politics—so that the world would know how oppressive the regime was. Van de Merwe acknowledged the genuine value conflict that existed for raising public awareness, but he asked whether their cause would be furthered by a confrontation with police in which either the activists or police officers might be killed. Was it possible to continue the conflict, put pressure on the regime, and gain the public awareness that they desired, and at the same time lower the level of probable violence? After a number of long interchanges, the activists agreed that it would be better to continue their value conflict by less violent means and lower the risk of a violent confrontation in which all of them and police would be killed. They agreed to give up the building and relinquish their guns, if they were allowed to leave, were guaranteed safe conduct, and would not be followed or prosecuted by the police. Van de Merwe took this offer to the government. Since no one had been physically harmed during the confrontation, it was accepted.

This case illustrates the utility of negotiating peripheral issues while refraining from or delaying addressing or resolving strong value differences. There are a number of strategies that can help people reach agreements on some issues without having to change their basic values. One is to *avoid talk about identity or values.* If a party or mediator knows or learns that there are strong identity and value differences between disputants, and he or she believes that discussion of the strong beliefs is either not imperative for resolution of at least some of the contested issues or may block any agreement, he or she may refrain from or discourage any discussion of values. A mediator may meet with each party in a caucus before a joint meeting, or after values have been mentioned in a joint session, and explore whether further discussion of values will be productive and whether it is really necessary for another party to understand the values in play. He or she may also help the parties assess if discussion of values is likely to cause further intransigence or will result in conversion. By discussing these merits or possible outcomes, the mediator may be able to help the parties decide whether or not to discuss their values in the context of the mediation.

On some occasions, the mediator may unilaterally decide to restrict the discussion of values between the parties. Such was the case in the South African conflict.

A second strategy is to *avoid framing issues or problems in terms of identity or value differences.* Many negotiators and mediators, when faced with a party who describes a conflict in terms of polarizing values, will often ignore or finesse addressing the value component of the party's position. They do this to avoid escalation or framing the dispute in terms of irreconcilable differences. For example, in an Equal Employment Opportunity (EEO) dispute over job reclassification, an African American employee claimed that she was discriminated against by her white supervisor because of her race; she charged him and the institution in which they worked with racism. The supervisor vehemently denied the accusation and levied a counterclaim that the employee was "playing the race card" to gain unfair advantage over other job applicants.

The mediator chose not to confront the charges of racism head on. Heated discussions between the employee and the supervisor about racism would probably not have gotten anywhere. The third party reframed the problem away from racism to the need for a fair and joint examination of the written standards or criteria that the organization uses to reclassify employees, and to explore how these criteria were applied to the employee's application for reclassification. After a joint examination of the standards and criteria and the process used for reclassification, the parties determined that the employee was not eligible for the new position and that other applicants were better qualified; the complainant was encouraged by the mediator to drop her claim.

Change the Relationships of the Parties, Not Their Values

Another level of change involves altering some aspects of the ongoing relationship between conflicting parties, but not challenging or seeking to transform their fundamental values (Susskind and Field, 1996). The assumption behind this strategy is that if the relationship is improved between parties—in that liking, respect, or tolerance is enhanced by either behavioral or attitudinal changes—parties may be able to interact, work, or live together in reasonable proximity without having to hold the same values (Cialdini, 2001). Here are three strategies and case examples that illustrate them.

1. *Change the parties' behaviors, not their values.* In the employment discrimination case, or in disputes that involve strong values about sexual harassment or expectations for equal treatment, parties or mediators can sidestep direct confrontation of clashing values issues, and focus instead on changing the behaviors of disputing parties. For example, on the interpersonal level the mediator in the reclassification case could have asked each of the parties, either separately or jointly, to identify statements or behaviors of the other party that they perceived to indicate or express racist attitudes or behaviors. These statements could be shared and discussed by the parties, and each could agree to refrain from saying or doing them in the future. This change in behavior may (but does not necessarily) result in a change in values. However, it may prevent statements or behavior from occurring in the future that result in a direct clash of strong beliefs.

2. *Change the parties' attitudes toward each other, not their values.* Attitudes are beliefs, but they are not as deep or as important as fundamental values. Attitudes are often related to liking or not liking someone or something (Cialdini, 2001). They are also related to preferences.

A strategy that parties or mediators can use for responding to value differences but not attempting to change them is to improve parties' relationships with each other and increase liking. For example, a socially conservative couple found out that their unmarried daughter was living with her male "significant other." The parents were shocked when they first found out. Cohabitation out of marriage violated the parents' values, and they stated this fact quite clearly when they saw their daughter on a visit to their home. The parents decided to give their daughter and "son-out-law" somewhat of a cold shoulder. They declined to visit the couple in their apartment in another town, and when the parents called on the phone they would only speak with their daughter. After a year or so, during which the daughter and her man friend continued to live together, the daughter invited her mother to come for a visit. After a great deal of soul searching, she agreed. She came to visit for a week and during that time got to know her son-out-law. Surprisingly, she found him to be a friendly, considerate, and responsible fellow who treated her daughter very well. She began to like him. When she returned home, she conveyed her feelings to her husband. Ultimately, the parents reciprocated the invitation for a visit of the daughter and her friend. A month or so later, the couple flew to the parents' hometown and stayed at their house. (Not in the same room or bed, of course!) After several subsequent visits, the parents finally consented to let the couple stay together in one room. They continued to hold significantly different values from their daughter and her male friend, and still would prefer that the couple were married before living together, but they were willing to tolerate the living arrangement because they liked the son-out-law and loved their daughter.

Similar dynamics have been found to occur in highly conflicted interventions. For example, in the mid-1990s a dialogue intervention was initiated by U.S. and Russian intermediaries to assist diverse political factions involved in the civil war in Tajikistan to build more positive working relationships and develop possible solutions to end the conflict (Saunders, 1999). The parties were secondary leaders of the various factions, many of whom had lost family members as a result of the conflict.

The formal dialogue began the process of building interpersonal relationships between adversaries. Early sessions included opportunities for participants to talk about the sources and development of the conflict, and how it had personally affected them and their families. Increased conversations, both at and away from the formal problem-solving table, enhanced personal relationships. A structured cocktail time before dinner and informal drinks afterwards offered additional time for informal conversations, which gradually increased the bonds between the members of the dialogue group. After a number of sessions, personal bonds of respect and trust developed. It should be noted that the process did not necessarily change parties' basic identities or the values that they advocated. It did enable them to focus on some issues that they could resolve; clarify interests; and develop some operational suggestions to deescalate the conflict, move toward peace, and promote reconciliation between the involved parties.

3. *Change the structural relationship within which parties interact, but do not seek to directly change values.* Changing the rules under

which people associate or modifying structural opportunities for them to meet, socialize, and have positive interactions can often change disputing relationships for the positive. Interactions of this kind can help lower or minimize tensions between diverse identities and values.

Rules generally refer to specific laws, regulations, standardized procedures, or operational norms that define what is and is not acceptable behavior. These may be rules in the home, the community, the organization, or the nation. For example, the passage of civil rights laws in the United States that forced integration of schools, other public facilities, and means of interstate commerce prescribed new norms and behaviors for interracial (and thus identity-group) relationships. Prescribed norms for respectful and equal treatment created new frameworks for interactions between people from diverse ethnic and racial backgrounds. The umbrella of laws that prohibited discriminatory behavior encouraged positive social interactions while not directly challenging the identity values of either African Americans or whites, or whatever values each group had about race. Similar approaches can be used in the workplace. Rules and norms for behavior can be established, which set out a new framework for developing mediated agreements concerning expected behavior. Although modifying structures does not directly shift values, it may over time create new behavioral norms and ways of interacting that can ultimately change beliefs.

Changing structures can also mean changing the forums and activities in which diverse parties with differing values engage each other. Structural change can involve separating negatively enmeshed parties, limiting their joint interactions, and creating spheres of interest in which each one's values are dominant. More on this approach will be elaborated later. It can also mean creating forums where positive interactions and relationship building and enhancement are more likely to occur.

Increase Understanding and Tolerance for Diverse Values

The next group of five approaches focus on increasing cognitive or intellectual or emotional understanding by conflicting parties of diverse identity, terminal, and operational values, but they do not try to directly change underlying beliefs.

1. *Encourage parties to educate each other about their values, but stress that neither will be expected to change their beliefs.* This approach strives to increase awareness of differing beliefs, and at the same time take all pressure off parties to change them. Greater understanding of what a parties' values are, the importance they attach to them, how they affect his or her life, and how they influence motivation can often create greater tolerance and acceptance of diverse beliefs.

A first step in responding to values clashes is typically to create a safe forum and process for expressing, explaining, and exploring strong beliefs. Each party is given an opportunity to express and explain their values, and then an intermediary or opposing party is asked to accurately restate the beliefs.

Sometimes an articulation of values is as far as parties are willing to go in examining individual or group beliefs. For example, in an environmental fight over species protection, which involved animal rights activists who did not want any animals killed, the leading spokesperson for the activist group stated that she was willing to present her values, beliefs, and positions but was unwilling to have them probed, questioned, or directly challenged. If these procedural ground rules were followed, she was reluctantly willing to listen to a presentation on the values and views of others.

2. *Acknowledge values, but do not require agreement with them.* This approach moves beyond the process just described, in that it involves parties in a mutual education process about their values *and* it requests that each of them directly acknowledge the importance of the values expressed by the other. Acknowledgment does not mean that a party agrees with the opposing values, but merely that they have been heard and are recognized as being valuable to the other party.

3. *Create cognitive understanding of and emotional empathy toward another's values, but do not push for agreement.* This approach moves beyond acknowledgment of another's values and asks one or more negotiators to recognize that he or she understands the other's values, and why they are intellectually or emotionally important to the other party. It does not require acceptance of these values.

For example, in a species protection dispute between an animal rights activist and a Native American in Alaska over the selective management (killing) of wolves to protect moose and caribou populations from extermination, the animal rights activist acknowledged that she understood the need for the indigenous people to have food, and that predation by wolves lowered the number of animals available for them to take by hunting. She also expressed that she could *feel* how important protecting game was to the tribes, and that it felt like a survival issue for them.

A step beyond cognitive or emotional empathy is legitimization of another's values. Legitimization involves recognizing that the values of another are reasonable, justifiable, and valid for the party that holds them (and possibly for the party to whom they have been presented). For example, in a hotly contested water dispute in the western United States that was referred to mediation by the U.S. Supreme Court, one of the parties, a downstream state, articulated values that included "fair and equitable treatment under the terms of the interstate water compact between the three involved states," and a requirement that "the state be made whole for water that was denied to it in past years." The representative of an opposing upstream state accurately restated the other's values and related interests; he demonstrated, by his articulation of the problem, understanding of the beliefs and strong feeling involved, and he recognized that at least the first one, fair and equitable treatment under the terms of the conflict, was both legitimate and one that he could agree to. He noted that if he were in the other's shoes and believed he was being treated unfairly, he would feel the same way. However, he strongly denied that the other state had been shorted in past years.

Acknowledgment is usually easier to achieve than legitimization. However, once acknowledgment has occurred, it is often not too difficult for a mediator to say and get agreement to a statement such as: "From what we have heard and you have said, you recognize that the values and beliefs of this group are important to them, and have guided their interactions with your organization. All of us need to acknowledge that you are not in exactly the same position as they are. But if you were, would these values be reasonable to try to achieve? Would you consider their beliefs to be valid, legitimate, and worth striving for?"

4. *Clarify values, and agree to disagree.* This approach is an explicit effort to get parties to clarify their values and develop some cognitive and emotional understanding and empathy about them, but then put them aside and attempt to resolve the dispute with-

out putting further effort into changing the opposing strong beliefs. After parties have articulated and explored their values and why they believe they are important, it often becomes clear that they will not be able to convert the other side. The mediator might acknowledge the situation and ask the parties to agree-to-disagree on their strong values and move forward to see if the dispute can be addressed and resolved in other ways.

5. *Create spheres of interest.* When parties cannot agree over values, they sometimes agree on realms of influence where each party's values will predominate. This approach does not eliminate a conflict, but it can reduce the issues over which parties will conflict in the future, because each has been assigned a sphere in which the other agrees not to meddle. U.S.-Soviet relations in Eastern Europe were relatively stable after the Berlin blockade and the Cuban missile crisis, because the spheres of influence and values of the Soviet Union in Eastern Europe and the U.S. in the Western Hemisphere were fairly well defined.

In divorce cases, separating partners can agree on different spheres of influence and rules, which are often related to values, when a child is at mom's house or at dad's house. In disputes between two managers who work on shifts, they can each exercise their own management style but at different times.

APPROACHES FOR RESPONDING TO VALUES THAT STRIVE TO SATISFY INTERESTS

Values are beliefs that generally require actions to be actualized. A focus on actions can often enable parties to shift from a focus on values to an emphasis on interests—the interests that need to be addressed or met to operationalize a value.

1. *Translate values into interests, and operationalize their satisfaction.* Values are mental constructs or ideas that define identity and guide speech or behavior. Operationalizing values generally requires developing opportunities and forums for people to act on their identity and strong beliefs. Operationalization also involves identifying options or ways for living out values, and how these options can best be implemented. This leads to an intimate connection between values and interests.

Interests are the substantive, procedural, and psychological or relationship needs that must be satisfied for an individual to feel good about the results of a negotiation or resolution of a conflict. For an individual or a group to feel their values are legitimate and have been respected, and that they have a chance to act on them, they must be able to satisfy certain interests. For example, changes in the values of the labor force in North America and Western Europe over the last fifteen to twenty years have led to greater expectations on the part of employees for increased participation in organizational decision making. The employees' operational (and possibly their terminal) values are greater participation in the workplace and having more influence over decisions that affect their lives. Advocates of this view say, "We live in a democratic society where we can elect our leaders and vote on key decisions, so why can't we have greater say in the workplace?" Some managers shudder when they hear these values advocated by employees because they hold strong countervailing beliefs. The managers often think that management has and should have major prerogatives regarding organizational decision making. The boss knows best; employees are to be led and not be leaders.

If the values and associated interests of those who advocate more participation are examined, several questions emerge. Are they interested in direct participation, or representative participation? Does participation mean input into decisions, or direct involvement in decision making? Is the level of participation to be focused on the particular task or job, or on policy formation for the organization? Depending upon the particular interests of the employees and managers, the values of employee involvement in decision making and management prerogatives may not be mutually exclusive.

For example, in mediation between a teachers' union and a large urban school board, the educators' association demanded the right of consultation and involvement in the financial management of the district. The union representatives said that it was a basic principle and value of the organization and of its leadership that they should be involved in decisions that affected members' salaries and working conditions. The board said that these decisions were management prerogatives. After a long discussion, management agreed in principle to greater involvement on the part of the union in financial matters but specified that involvement was conditional upon the union being willing to engage with management when making hard decisions such as addressing projected budget shortfalls and potential layoffs of teachers. Management's operational value was that if pain were to result from shared decision making about financial issues, responsibility for the pain should be shared.

Upon reflection, the union representatives were not so sure they wanted to take responsibility for decisions that might lead to layoffs. Being involved with management in making unpopular decisions would make them directly responsible for the loss of jobs, and it could undermine the their position in the union. Consequently, they began to look more closely at the values of the union and the interests they wanted to achieve. They agreed that they wanted input on some of these difficult financial decisions but did not want to be responsible for all them. After further discussions, management and labor found financial areas where both the union and management could be involved in shared decision making as well as protecting and promoting their seemingly incompatible values.

2. *Clarify values, identify what is most important, and set priorities.* As mentioned earlier, individuals and groups have hierarchies of values; some values are more important than others. It often occurs that after parties have articulated their values, understood them, and shown empathy with each other they may have to choose which beliefs will be given a higher priority. For example, in a child custody case, the mother and father were arguing over what kind of extracurricular activities should be provided for their children and who should pay for them. The mother, who had strong artistic values, wanted their daughter and son to have several dance and art lessons per week. The father, even though he supported the artistic development of his daughter, felt that his wife was going overboard on after-school activities, wanted the children to have some free and unstructured time, and was also concerned about who would pay for all the lessons. He had a low-paying job and could not contribute the same amount as his wife. He did not want the children to feel that his wife gave the children more opportunities for growth than he could.

After an extended discussion, the couple agreed that it was important for their children to have both after-school lessons and unstructured time. Because of the age and talent in dance exhibited by their daughter, they decided that she should receive more lessons; they agreed to pay half of the costs. Because their son was younger, the father and mother agreed to spend more quality time at home with him or allow him to have more unstructured activities. The parents decided that they could hold different values regarding how each child spent his or her time and that the value of each paying for a reasonable amount of lessons was more important than the children's perceiving one parent as wealthier or more giving or caring than the other.

3. *Create cognitive dissonance between the values held by one or more parties to encourage a prioritization or shift in values.* Individuals typically hold multiple values at the same time, some of which may be in conflict with each other. For example, an individual may value thriftiness and savings for a rainy day while holding competing values related to spending money for a car that demonstrates status and offers comfortable transportation. In deciding whether to save money or purchase the car, the individual must resolve his or her internal value dispute and determine which value is superior or subordinate.

The negotiation or mediation strategy of creating cognitive dissonance (Festinger, 1962), or tension between two conflicting beliefs (and related actions), is premised upon the assumption that people generally strive (or can be induced) to make their beliefs or actions congruent, and that people are uncomfortable when their values or beliefs contradict each other. The negotiator or mediator pursuing this approach designs a situation in which a party is placed in a position of choosing a superior or more important value over another that is less significant.

A case involving negotiations over access in a child custody case illustrates this approach. A father was very badly hurt as a result of separation from his wife. The wife had an affair at the end of the marriage (the trigger event that initiated the separation). Because of the affair, the father wanted custody of the child and considered the mother to be "unfit," "immoral," and "unsuitable" as a parent. The father, who had temporary custody, would allow the mother to visit with the child but not permit their son to stay overnight for fear that he would be exposed to "illicit sex." The mediator decided to explore the husband's values in a caucus to identify what his value priorities were. Through private discussions, the mediator discovered that the husband placed a very high value on autonomy and freedom of individual action. He did not want to be controlled by his wife. The mediator decided to explore the husband's values to see whether his value for autonomy and independence might outweigh his values about sexual morals. The dialogue proceeded:

Mediator: It sounds to me like you really value being able to make free choices and don't want to be restricted by someone else's demands; especially those of Bobbie [his soon-to-be-ex-wife].

Husband: Yes, that's true.

Mediator: And you feel that once you are legally separated, your wife shouldn't make the kinds of demands on you that might normally be expected in a marriage.

Husband: Of course not. I should be able to run my own life and make decisions independent of her.

Mediator: Let me raise a hypothetical question. Is it possible that in the future, you might find another person who you care deeply about and with whom you want to spend a lot of time?

Husband: Yes. Although it's hard to imagine now, it is possible in the future. I do want to marry again and have another child.

Mediator: If this new person was important to you, would you want that person to meet and get to know your son?

Husband: Sure, that would be important.

Mediator: Is it possible, since your son is quite young and probably does not understand or know about the dynamics of intimate relationships, that this new person might spend the night at your house, while your son was there?

Husband: Well, I think it's not the best idea, but if it was someone I really cared about and she was to be part of my family, it might be OK.

Mediator: So she might stay overnight?

Husband: Yes.

Mediator: What would happen if your ex-wife said that was unacceptable and you didn't have a right to do that?

Husband: Why, I'd say that was an invasion of my privacy. Once we are divorced, she doesn't have a right to control my life . . . sex life or otherwise.

Mediator: So as a general principle, people who are no longer married shouldn't have a right to control the lives of their ex-spouse, and you would not want to have limits placed on you by Bobbie.

Husband: No.

Mediator: This looks to be a very important value to you, one that should be a strong guide to your future relationship with Bobbie. I know you are concerned about your son being at Bobbie's house when she has male friends over.

Husband: Yes.

Mediator: Isn't it important that the same principle that you would want applied to you—freedom and independence of action—should be applied to both of you so that there is one fair standard that is universal?

Husband: Well, yes, but what about his exposure to all her affairs?

Mediator: Well, it seems like what you want is limited exposure to casual relationships, but if there was a particularly important person in Bobbie's life that would be OK.

Husband: Well, it's not entirely comfortable, but I guess I could live with that.

Mediator: Let's go and meet with Bobbie again. Perhaps you can propose your new idea emphasizing that you want to maximize independence and freedom in decision making and personal lifestyle to each of you, but minimize your son's contact with any potential casual sexual relationship that either you or Bobbie might have.

Husband: OK.

As can be seen, the mediator identified two competing values—belief in the right of people to make independent decisions and sexual morality—held by the husband. The mediator explored which one might be more important and then went further to create a universal principle that might be applied to both parties.

4. *Assist parties in reaching an agreement to respect each other's values, and try to develop solutions that meet each one's basic values and needs to the greatest extent possible.* This approach is a version of a procedural agreement to a substantive problem. The substantive problem is a clash in apparently irreconcilable values. The procedural solution is a commitment by all parties to seek solutions that address the differing values to the greatest extent possible.

Let's examine a real situation and some of the possible solutions that might be developed. In Canada, there has been an ongoing dispute over a requirement that bicycle riders have to wear helmets. Government agencies, police forces, and insurance companies are all strong advocates of helmets. However, some riders strenuously object to the requirement for headgear. At first blush, this looks like a value dispute over safety and freedom of choice or expression. But the Canadian dispute has an extra twist. Some of the major opponents of the helmet law are Sikhs, a religious group founded and primarily based in northern India and Pakistan, in which the men and boys are required to wear turbans. The Sikhs have argued that the helmet law violates their religious rights. Men and boys have either refused to wear helmets or forgone bicycle riding. What might be done?

First, each party might agree to respect each other's values: the goal of promoting safety for bicycle riders and automobile drivers who could potentially harm them, and freedom of religion and expression. Second, the parties might generate a range of options that satisfy the competing values: designing larger helmets that will fit over turbans, developing a turban that also works as a helmet, recognition by the government that the multiple wraps of cloth that make up a turban are the functional equivalent of the helmet, possibly (the most extreme) legal release from liability of drivers who injure an unhelmeted rider, and so forth.

5. *Compensate for lost values.* People have hierarchies of values; on occasion they may be willing to trade satisfaction of one value for another, similarly to the way that interests may be satisfied. For example, citizens who live adjacent to a proposed gravel pit oppose the development and operation of a three-year mining project because it violates deeply held values concerning peace and quiet and

quality of life. On the other hand, the company and its officials value prosperity and economic development and (although not eschewing quality of life) place the neighbors' values lower on their hierarchy of priorities.

At first glance, this dispute appears to be based on totally incompatible values: peace and quiet and quality life, versus individual financial advancement and economic development. However, if the company acknowledges the values of the homeowners who live adjacent to the proposed mine and recognizes that they might suffer some negative impact on their quality of life during the three years of operation, they might be able to help identify what would be acceptable compensation for the lost values. For example, if the company offered to mitigate potential adverse impact through a noise abatement plan, rerouting of truck traffic, provision of buffer landscaping, and reclamation of the pit and construction of a lake and park at the end of the mining operation, then the homeowners might consider the long-term compensation for loss of short-term quality-of-life values enough to sacrifice their immediate needs for a long-term gain.

Compensation for lost values can take a variety of forms (Pruitt, 1981):

- *An equal trade of the same item.* For example, in an environmental dispute where wetlands that are important for water quality and habitat are lost to construction of new developments, the state may be compensated for the loss by a wetlands replacement or enhancement program in another area. In fact, more wetlands may be built than have been lost, thus enhancing the satisfaction of an environmental value.
- *Trade of an item in the same realm but different form.* For example, two sisters and one brother are dividing up the estate of a deceased parent. They all value having a specific family heirloom, a grandfather clock; their mother owned the timepiece. It has strong sentimental value because of its connection to her and had always been in a prominent place in the family home. It is a permanent link with the family's past and is financially worth a lot. After a discussion about why each one values the clock and what it means to them (sense of family, continuity, love of their mother, the safety of their home growing up), they agree that one of the daughters

should receive it. They also agree that if there is another item that belonged to their mother that more than one sibling values, the sister who got the clock will step aside and allow one of the other children to receive it.

• *A trade or compensation for a lost value but in another currency.* For example, in mediation of a personal injury lawsuit where the plaintiff has lost the use of his legs in an automobile accident that was due to the negligence of another driver, the plaintiff might be compensated for his lost value (peace of mind, mobility, independence, ability to care for himself) by a large monetary settlement from the defendant's insurance company. The financial settlement can never replace in the same form what has been lost, but it can present a way to help address the replacement of these values.

APPROACHES TO CREATING NEW COMMONLY HELD VALUES

The final pair of approach helps parties integrate or reconcile diverse values or develop new ones that all can support.

1. *Search for superordinate values.* Superordinate values are beliefs jointly shared by people in a conflict. Parties in a dispute often view their values, interests, and needs as being mutually exclusive. Kriesberg (1973) labels this type of dispute as being pure conflict. However, pure conflicts are relatively rare. In many conflicts, parties share one or more overarching values that bridge their differences. By emphasizing superordinate values or principles, parties can be encouraged to work together to resolve their differences. The risk of sacrificing their superordinate value to attain lesser values may force the parties to initiate cooperative problem solving.

An example of this strategy occurred in a large urban local of a teachers association. The local was at odds with the state organization over the kinds and amounts of services that were provided by the central office to the local association. They valued equity of exchange—dues from the local for a commensurate amount of service services. The local threatened to leave the association if the exchange relationship of dues for services was not modified so that the local received more benefits for its contribution. The mediator explored with both parties their overarching values. Both organizations wanted to better the working conditions of teachers, neither group wanted to unnecessarily divide the profession, and both groups could benefit tremendously from the skills and resources of the members of the other group. After identifying these superordinate values in private meetings with the parties, the mediator brought them together in joint session to discuss their beliefs. The larger superordinate values moderated the parties' positions on other less important issues and enabled them to make the compromises necessary for the groups to remain part of one association. The local accepted fewer direct services in exchange for better statewide services that would benefit all of the union's locals. A lower set of values held by both parties was sacrificed for a larger common good or belief system.

2. *Create new commonly held values.* Parties who hold differing values are often required to work together and can achieve their common goals only if they find a way to either reconcile their beliefs or create commonly held new ones. Strong adherence to one value system at the expense of another can be debilitating for the parties involved.

This situation is regularly faced by international corporations that link many companies or parts of companies across the globe. Members of various cultural or national groups have culture-specific values that may be in tension with or incompatible with those held by managers and employees in other countries or cultures. How can these differences be reconciled? An effort by Levi Strauss demonstrates one approach. Levi convened a representative intercultural task force to identify the values that should guide the work of the corporation across the globe. While being sensitive to and highly valuing diversity, the company sought to develop superordinate values that would be cultivated throughout the corporation. These values would guide the overall activities of the company and at the same time allow local values, which did not conflict with the bridging ones, to coexist and be dominant in different countries. For example, one of the key values that the corporation sought to enhance was respect for and professional development of all employees. But how this value would be achieved and implemented was left up to the management and employees in the national and cultural locales.

REFER VALUE CONFLICTS TO A
THIRD-PARTY DECISION MAKER

In some disputes over values—especially those where requiring creation of a universal precedent, or where living with competing value systems is socially unacceptable, or where another means of reconciling values has not worked—submitting the value component to an impartial and mutually acceptable decision maker to break the deadlock may be a desirable way to overcome an impasse, and possibly be the only way.

Frequently, values-related issues, or issues that revolve around a legal principle, are only part of the dispute. Once a third party has issued a decision on the value-based issue, the parties may be able to negotiate the details about how the decision will be implemented.

Chapter Sixteen

Strategies for Multiparty Mediation

Multiparty negotiations and mediations take place in a variety of contexts. International negotiations may be bilateral agreements between teams representing two nations over trade, human rights, or defense issues; or multilateral team interactions as occurred in the development of the Law of the Seas or in Rio de Janeiro and Capetown over international environmental issues. This bilateral and multilateral distinction is found in public disputes, organizational and corporate conflicts, legal suits, and community altercations. Even an apparent two-person dispute between an ex-husband and ex-wife renegotiating child support can become a multiparty dispute if the children, new spouses, or extended family become involved in the conflict.

When negotiations are between more than two people, interpersonal and group dynamics become exponentially more complex (Cormick, 1989). This section will detail three contexts for involving mediators in multiparty conflicts: working with negotiation teams, coordinating multiparty conferences or interteam negotiations, and working with parties' constituents.

NEGOTIATIONS AND TEAMS

A negotiation team is a group composed of two or more people who share similar experiences, interests, likes, dislikes, or sentiments. People form teams to negotiate issues of concern for a variety of reasons. A team may be a coalition of weaker parties who are trying to increase their influence. A team may be a group of people who want to verbally represent a broader viewpoint or include more diversity of opinion or expertise than is the case with a sole negotiator. Finally, a team may also be selected for negotiation because the members do not trust one person to negotiate on behalf of their interests.

By the time a mediator is asked to assist in a dispute, the parties have usually already formed teams. The mediator must work with the people whom the parties have selected. Occasionally, however, a mediator may enter a dispute before team formation has occurred, as a when a procedure for resolving a public dispute is being developed or a team to solve an organizational problem is being convened. In this case, the mediator may significantly assist disputants in forming effective negotiation teams.

Although the mediator cannot and should not select the negotiating team's members, he or she may suggest criteria for selection. A team member should understand the various issues in the dispute, be able to identify and articulate his or her own interests and those of other team members, and represent the concerns of his or her constituency, if one exists. Other team members and the wider constituency should have confidence in each team member so that agreements reached at the negotiating table will be credible and acceptable to those represented by the team (McSurely, 1967). Rapport, credibility, and the capacity to deal with people who are on an opposing team are also possible criteria. A team composed of people who cannot negotiate or who will be unacceptable to the other side is useless. It makes no sense for negotiations to break down over a question of who is involved if competing interests are the principal issues that divide the parties.

In addition to suggesting general criteria for selecting team members, the mediator may also help directly with team formation. This function is often carried out in the context of conducting a situation assessment or convening services for an entity that is sponsoring negotiations.

Although most mediators do not play this level of catalytic role, they can make significant procedural suggestions. Mediators can often suggest the number of representatives appropriate to participate in the dispute resolution process, the type of expertise that would be beneficial, and a decision-making process for selecting team members. One mediator was called into a complex housing dispute by a large group of disgruntled apartment renters as they were about to meet with their landlord. The intermediary decided that this huge number of people would not be able to bargain effectively with the landlord and also saw that the tenants' disorganized state and raucous manner might provoke even more resistance from their opponent. She refused to mediate the case until the tenants had organized themselves and selected a bargaining team. After indicating possible criteria for team membership (including some of those listed earlier), she suggested a specific number of representatives and a process for deciding whom to appoint.

Team Dynamics and Mediation Strategies

Once the disputants have selected a team, the mediator should carefully analyze and assess the group's crucial dynamics, individual and group interests, the personal behavior patterns of individual members (including the way they interact with people on their own and the opposing team), and the team decision-making structure (Anacona, Friedman, and Kolb, 1991).

A negotiating team, when viewed by an opponent, may appear monolithic, unified, and unshakable in its commitment to a stated position or option. Usually, however, this is not the case. Negotiation teams are composed of individuals with varying interests. The members may vary in their strength of commitment to their own needs, those of other team members, or group interests as a whole. Mediators should carefully assess the spectrum of interests within a team to determine the potential for noncompetitive interests, both within each team and between the teams.

Negotiation styles of team members are often closely related to how they believe their interests can best be achieved (Frost and Wilmot, 1978; Rubin and Brown, 1985). Mediators should assess the relative degrees of collaborative and competitive behavior within the team. Colosi and Berkeley (1980) identify three types of team members: stabilizers, nonstabilizers, and quasi-mediators. Stabilizers are those committed to negotiations and a settlement, often at any cost. Nonstabilizers may not be committed to negotiations, may be disruptive, and may be unwilling to settle regardless of the offer. The quasi-mediator wants to build a realistic and workable settlement that meets as many needs as possible for all concerned parties

(Kriesberg, 1998). The quasi-mediator will be the mediator's ally and will work with him or her to forge an agreement. A mediator should look for quasi-mediators with moderate interests and collaborative styles within a team because he or she will need their assistance in moving the team toward agreement. They may alternately support each other to bolster their respective proposals or activities.

Negotiating team members also have diverse means of influence or power that they bring to the negotiation table. Mediators should assess the influence relationships that exist between team members in an effort to understand internal team dynamics.

A group's decision-making methods are often closely related to its power relationships (Brett, 1991). In general, negotiation teams tend to make decisions by *fiat, hierarchical decision making, consensus,* or *voting.*

Decision by fiat is a command decision by an individual or group in a position of power. Fiat decisions, whether within a team or between teams, are generally unilateral in nature and often involve minimal or no consultation with other team members or people on the other side of the table. In working with this form of decision making, the mediator usually focuses a significant amount of effort on the one or two individual leaders with the authority to make decisions by fiat. Mediators often work with them to explore possible consequences of their action and the desirability of including more people, for both their team and the team on the other side of the table, in decision making.

Hierarchical decision making occurs when one or more team members make a decision that is accepted, supported, or deferred to by others on a team on the basis of the decision maker's legitimate authority or ability to coerce or grant benefits to other members. This decision-making model is characteristic of bureaucratically organized institutions (government agencies, businesses, churches). The process works well only when adherence of team members to the decision maker's choices can be ensured by the means of influence just described. If allegiances cannot be ensured, the team's cohesion will suffer greatly under the stress of joint sessions.

The third method of decision making within a team is consensus. Consensus involves a synthesis of the ideas and interests of all team members, leading to a broad, general agreement on issues. Consensus may be used because team members hold a philosophical commitment to the process, or it may be the only functional way that a group can reach agreement. In negotiations in which team members are representatives of independent groups, or in which no one group is either dominant in terms of power or recognized as the central decision maker, consensus may be the only means for a group to develop a coalition with a common purpose.

The final process, voting, is generally not an effective procedure for decision making within teams. A vote taken within a team may cause irreparable divisions resulting in decreased team cooperation in joint sessions, direct collaboration with an opponent, or rejection of the negotiation process itself. Divisions caused by voting and majority rule can be avoided only if the team makes decisions by consensus or if one or more team members have the authority to make binding decisions for the team.

Negotiators are often unfamiliar with appropriate internal decision-making procedures. Mediators may be called on as process advisers to in-team negotiations, and they may even mediate disputes within a team. The inability of a negotiation team to manage internal conflict and make group decisions can be as detrimental to successful negotiations as an impasse in a joint session.

The mediator's role in helping negotiation teams make decisions can vary significantly, from an educator who informs the parties about appropriate decision-making procedures to a process observer who makes an occasional procedural suggestion to assist parties in bargaining more effectively, to an actual facilitator of team meetings (Kolb, 1983). The role of the mediator in in-team meetings often depends on the team's knowledge of, and sophistication in, internal negotiation processes, the amount of commonality of interest between team members, and the facilitative skills of individual team members. In community disputes in which negotiators are appointed informally, have little experience in working together, and have little or no experience in in-team or joint-session negotiations, the mediator may play a significant role in internal team bargaining. He or she may educate the team members about how to negotiate and how to facilitate meetings (Doyle and Straus, 1976; Coover, Deacon, Esser, and Moore, 1977).

Types of Team Negotiations

The addition of multiple negotiators to a dispute not only increases the complexity of in-team negotiation but also widens the range of possible interactions between people on two or more opposing teams. In two-person negotiations, the two central actors are the primary channels through which communications flow. Additional participants increase both the amount and the complexity of the communications and raise the problem of coordinating communication.

Lincoln identifies three types of negotiation that occur at meetings of disputants in which each party has multiple representatives (Lincoln, n.d.). *Bilateral bargaining* takes place when there are two sides and communication occurs primarily between the spokespersons of the two groups. Bilateral bargaining is often considered "official" communication between the teams, as it is most likely to express either the consensus of the teams or the team position as expressed by the hierarchical decision maker.

Alongside the official communications that pass between the teams may be two types of unilateral bargaining. *Unilateral conciliatory bargaining* is commonly initiated by a quasi-mediator or by a member of a team who has some common interest or bond with a member of another. Conciliatory bargaining is usually conducted (publicly or privately) with the negotiating team's explicit or implicit consent. The goal of conciliatory bargaining is to find a formula or option that will satisfy both parties. The conciliatory bargainer is not primarily motivated by personal gain.

In contrast to conciliatory bargaining, *unilateral vested-interest bargaining,* or under-the-table bargaining, is almost invariably motivated by a particular negotiator's drive for personal gain. This objective may even be sought at the expense of the interests of fellow team members. Vested-interest bargaining is nearly always conducted covertly, although occasionally there may be a public sellout by one member of a team.

Mediators can play an important role in facilitating bilateral bargaining and conciliatory bargaining, as well as in inhibiting unilateral vested-interest bargaining. They can influence effective bilateral negotiations by assisting and supporting the major spokespersons for each side. Kolb (1983) notes that in disputes in which the spokespersons are skilled in negotiation, the mediator need only affirm and support them in the activities they are pursuing. In doing so, the mediator conveys to the team that their leader is on the right track. In cases in which the spokespersons are not expert negotiators, the mediator may have to coach them on how to carry out their roles. Such coaching may include process suggestions, education about specific tactics, and questions to help clarify interests and goals.

Mediators also help team members communicate to the other team more clearly. By using some of the communication skills mentioned in earlier chapters, mediators can assist teams conducting conciliatory bargaining. They can also aid quasi-mediators to develop internal team agreement. Quasi-mediators may be encouraged to communicate to the other team messages that promote positive relationships, as well as moderate proposals that meet the interests of all parties.

SPOKESPERSON MODELS

Negotiations that have two or more teams often structure their cross-table communications through a spokesperson. Spokespeople are individuals who formally represent and advocate for their team's interests in negotiations with another party.

In general, there are two kinds of formal spokespersons. The first involves an individual who is the sole voice for his or her team. This person starts negotiations, builds rapport with the other side, presents issues and interests, and bargains to close. Other team members engage in the negotiations, but they do so by participating in in-team bargaining. They generally do not talk across the table to the "other side." Strengths of this model are that a team speaks with one voice, the team is likely to send fewer confused messages, and the other side knows who to talk with. Some of the weaknesses of this model are that the spokesperson may not be able to build positive rapport or is mistrusted by the other side; personality traits or idiosyncrasies may hinder productive negotiations; the spokesperson may not be adequately knowledgeable or articulate on all issues in question; he or she may not go as far as (or go beyond) what the team has agreed to; and the spokesperson may unilaterally make process decisions, substantive offers, or concessions for which there is little team support.

The second spokesperson model is that of the *facilitative* spokesperson. Facilitative spokespersons are advocates for their team's views, but they do this by including and coordinating multiple team members' involvement in negotiations across the table with the other side. A facilitative spokesperson coordinates with team members as to who will speak on what issue, what they will say, and how much authority the individual member has to reach agreement or closure on any given issue. In some cases, total authority will be delegated to an individual or several team members. In other situations, the authority to close returns to and rests with the facilitative spokesperson. The strengths of this model include increased involvement of team members in negotiations and decision making, possible better use of knowledge and expertise on the team, and a higher probability of team support and ownership of decisions that are reached. Some of the weaknesses of this model are problems of in-team coordination, the possibility of sending mixed or confusing messages across the table, unclarity on the part of the other team about who to talk to on a given issue (or about who has the authority to decide), and members who may go beyond what their team has agreed to.

On occasion, mediators may be involved with parties in selecting an appropriate spokesperson model. In these situations, the intermediary should discuss the two models, help parties assess the strengths and weaknesses of each as applied to the dispute in question, and assist them to decide upon and implement the preferred approach. If parities select the facilitative spokesperson model, mediators often work with these individuals to help design the best cross-table procedures possible.

MULTIPARTY NEGOTIATIONS

Multiparty negotiations can take a number of forms and follow diverse formats. They can be between two teams, among multiple teams, or among a group of individuals who represent diverse interests.

The mediator's role and function in team negotiations is to help coordinate communication and problem solving across the table between teams, and if necessary within a team. In multiparty negotiations without teams, the mediator's role is to design and facilitate a process that allows involved individuals to identify and focus on problem solving as a whole group. Mediators can help parties achieve their goals by proposing and implementing appropriate forums for problem solving and negotiations. In many of these venues, the intermediary will play a prominent and direct process facilitation role. Here are some of these negotiation forums and formats:

• *Formal forums for across-the-table negotiations among spokespersons, teams, or multiple individuals.* When many people are involved in negotiations, this format is appropriate for introductions, opening statements, scoping issues to be discussed, possibly identifying interests or generating a laundry list of options to be considered, and formalizing final agreements. This format is not as effective as small groups for deeply probing issues, identifying interests, saving face of disputing parties, developing tentative agreements, refining proposals for consideration by a whole group at a later time, or drafting the language of a final agreement. These tasks are better accomplished in small working groups. More will be said about this later.

• *Informal conciliatory bargaining.* This approach involves an individual making an informal approach to a member of another team, with the full knowledge of his or her own team, to explore informally how issues, interests, concerns, options, or deadlocks can best be addressed. The mediator often encourages these informal contacts or may actually be present when they occur.

• *Caucuses.* Caucuses are one of the major forums where teams can work out differences between members and develop options to bring to the table. Mediators often call and participate in parties' caucuses, when they believe that process assistance, reality testing, or substantive advice might be helpful.

• *Mixed-team or mixed-interest working group.* The number of participants in a multiparty negotiation is often too large for the group to engage in refined problem solving. Too many people want to speak; multiple ill-defined or unconnected ideas are on the table; or the large group is unable to focus on, generate, or refine mutually acceptable solutions. Appointing a smaller working group with representatives of all teams or interests can help larger groups achieve a breakthrough. It should be noted that if small groups are used, they need to have a clear mandate and defined limits concerning their authority to make decisions. If they are authorized to make final decisions, all parties should agree that this is the case before the small group meets. If they are to bring proposals back for the whole group to decide, this too should be clear. Mediators on occasion may facilitate these small groups.

• *"Sidebars."* Sidebars are private meetings between team leaders or principals. These meetings are held to build rapport, explore options, and break deadlocks. Sidebars remove audiences, other team members, or wider observers of negotiations and create opportunities for greater candor and frank conversations between leaders. Mediators are often involved in initiating and facilitating sidebar negotiations. A colleague and I used this format quite effectively in a four-team, twenty-person negotiation over water allocation. We pulled the three state water engineers aside, took them to a private nook in the lobby of the hotel where negotiations were occurring, and helped them discuss and develop options that broke the deadlock.

• *Small-group-to-large.* This format alternates use of small and large groups to move parties toward agreement. For example, a large group may define the problem, identify the range of the interests to be addressed, and mandate a small working group or groups to address specific aspects of the conflict or generate a range of options for the whole group to consider. After completing their task, the small group (or groups) will present the options that have been developed to the whole group for consideration. The latter narrows the options down to just a few that will be considered in more detail by the smaller working group, which is charged with refining one or more of the options for the whole group's approval at a later time. The small group picks what it believes to be the best and most viable option, refines it, and then presents it again to the whole group for consideration. Mediators often manage both the small and large group processes and offer facilitation services in each forum.

- *Sequential small group negotiations.* Some individuals and groups do not like to reach agreement in large formal multiparty sessions. Reasons for this preference are many: dislike of large group problem solving, discomfort in multiparty groups, reluctance to speak or engage in public debates, a desire to make negotiations less formal, and so on. It should be noted that members of a number of cultures, such as Japanese and Indonesians from Java, often prefer sequential small group meetings because they help avoid confrontations and enable parties to save face when there are disagreements. When appropriate, mediators can help parties set up the appropriate sequence for conversations and decision making so that a final agreement evolves. Once an agreement has been reached through sequential individual and small-group discussion, a mediated formal session may be held to acknowledge and ratify the agreement that has been developed.

- *Separate forums and activities to build relationship.* When relationships are problematic, intermediaries may want to provide and promote separate times and opportunities to build relationships between parties. These meetings may be sharply separated from problem solving or substantive negotiation sessions. Meals, cocktail parties, site visits or "walking the land" of the locale where a dispute is occurring, joint sightseeing, and sports activities have all been used to establish forums for relationship building. If a mediator believes that strengthening positive interpersonal relationships may be necessary for agreements to be reached or implemented, he or she may consciously build or present forums where this can occur.

- *Informal issue exploration and option generation forums.* Formal negotiations, especially if they involve large numbers of people or are public, seem to provoke posturing and presentation of hardline positions. Wise negotiating and decision making often requires opportunities for parties to explore possible options without having to prematurely commit to them. Colleagues working in the Organization of American States' PROPAZ program, which was mandated to assist the Guatemalan government and former insurgents in negotiating detailed terms of peace agreements to end that nation's thirty-six-year civil war, used informal option-generation meetings to great effect. They hosted small, informal, and off-the-record discussions among negotiators, which were held between formal negotiation sessions, to explore in a more open and explicitly noncommittal atmosphere possible options to resolve their differences.

TEAMS WITH CONSTITUENTS

Members of negotiating teams often do not make the final decision in a dispute. Teams are frequently responsible to other parties who have not been present at negotiations. Typically, the individuals or groups that have final authority to ratify a decision reached through negotiation form a "bureaucratic constituency," or a "horizontal constituency."

A *bureaucratic constituency* consists of a hierarchy of decision makers who may or may not be present at negotiations and who must sign an agreement or signify final approval before it is considered valid. Bureaucratic constituencies are most common when one party is a governmental agency, a hierarchically organized company or industry, or a bureaucratically organized institution such as a hospital.

Final approval of a settlement by persons not present may be a formal or legal requirement—or a negotiating tactic a team employs to weaken an opponent's direct influence (Cohen, 1980; Stevens, 1963). A negotiator's argument that he or she is not empowered to make the final decision may give that team additional leverage. For example, a team may be able to claim that a higher authority does not approve of a proposed settlement and thus eke out additional concessions from the other side. A further advantage may be gained from the additional time that is required for bureaucratic review or approval; this time may be used to bolster a negotiating position. Not having an authoritative decision maker at the table may also alleviate pressure on a negotiator to produce a final decision at the table; in addition, it may hinder the development of trust between teams.

A *horizontal constituency* is a group of decision makers that is not organized in a hierarchical manner. Relatives, coworkers, public interest groups, tenants, unions, prisoners, and members of industry associations and coalitions may be considered horizontal decision makers. Negotiating teams that are responsible to horizontal constituencies usually must gain approval of a negotiated settlement through some form of ratification process. Voting is probably the most common procedure used, although consensus may also be employed. For voting or consensus to work, however, the members of the constituency must all accept it as the process for settlement approval. The absence of an acceptable ratification and commitment-ensuring procedure is one of the principal causes of breakdown in negotiations in which one of the teams is both horizontally organized and responsible to a horizontal constituency.

The lack of procedure for constituent approval can end in disaster. One of the many reasons negotiations between inmates and correctional authorities at Attica Prison and New York State failed in the late 1960s was the absence of a procedure by which inmates could ratify any agreements that were reached (New York State Special Commission on Attica, 1972; Wicker, 1975). This problem is often common among public interest groups, when they do not have institutional means for ratifying negotiated settlements or when ratification does not bind and commit all members to adhere to an agreement. Constituency ratification problems, however, are not confined to public interest groups. In mediated negotiations over information exchange and stipulations pertaining to oil and gas drilling in federal wilderness study areas, environmentalists challenged the Independent Petroleum Association of the Mountain States and Rocky Mountain Oil and Gas Association, the two industry associations involved, to explain how they would gain individual company ratification and commitment to any agreement. Both trade associations, although maintaining a hierarchically organized staff, had horizontally organized constituent companies. Neither organization had a formal method for obtaining binding constituency approval of, or commitment to, negotiated settlements. Ironically, the environmental groups had decision-making structures that were similar to those of the industry organizations and encountered the same problems.

The mediator's primary role is generally not to work with the constituents of a negotiator or negotiating team. However, some efforts in this area may be necessary to attain a settlement's approval.

First, mediators may assist negotiating teams in identifying and organizing their constituents. They may aid teams in defining to whom they are responsible and who should ultimately be involved in final ratification and decision making (Straus, Clark, and Susskind, n.d.). This task may be relatively easy when teams are hierarchically organized or responsible to a bureaucratic constituency, and extremely difficult when the team and constituency are horizontally organized. The task may be especially complex when a negotiating organization has elements of both models. In some unions, for example, the executive committee, the union president, and union members must approve all agreements reached in negotiation at large.

Second, mediators may assist negotiators in explaining to each other the constraints imposed by their various bureaucratic or horizontal constituencies and the ratification procedures that will be used at the time of settlement. Early notification of both the procedures to be used for approval of a settlement and the time necessary to achieve ratification can reduce unnecessary conflicts that may arise from false procedural expectations.

Third, mediators may work with negotiators or negotiating teams to develop specific procedures for notifying constituent groups about ongoing developments in negotiations. Constituent groups often expect their representatives or negotiation teams to bring back for their approval a settlement that resembles the team's opening position. This is usually an unrealistic expectation. If constituents are not kept informed about changes or options developed during bargaining, they may begin to view their representatives, whom they saw as heroes at the opening of negotiations, as traitors.

Constituencies, like negotiators, must be educated about the composition of a realistic and probable settlement. Constituent education must occur throughout the negotiation process so that the final proposed settlement that reaches the constituency is not a surprise, and so that the constituency has an opportunity to contribute ideas and comments during bargaining. For the constituency to reach substantive, procedural, and psychological closure on any given issue or package of issues, it must believe that the substantive deal is the best that could have been negotiated given the options available, the power constellations of the parties, and external social forces. The constituency must also feel that its negotiators used the best process at their disposal and that constituents had adequate opportunity to contribute to the negotiations. It must also trust its representatives and believe that they have bargained in good faith to obtain the optimal solutions.

In some disputes, the negotiators take full and adequate responsibility for educating and obtaining input from their constituency. In other conflicts, lack of negotiating experience, failure to understand the importance of the educational process, poor procedures, or constraints on negotiation privacy result in distance between negotiators and constituents. This distance may have serious effects on the ratification of an agreement.

To avoid settlement rejection, mediators may occasionally assist in talks between negotiators and their constituencies before or after the announcement of the terms of settlement. They may also attempt to convince negotiators that a potential option for settlement is acceptable to their constituency (Stevens, 1963).

Fourth, the mediator may assist the negotiator or negotiating team in convincing a recalcitrant constituency that the negotiator or team has done as much as possible to promote the interests of constituents (Kerr, 1954). This may entail discussing the merits of the substantive proposals and contrasting them with what the opponent originally offered, discussing the effectiveness of negotiation strategies, and verifying the integrity and commitment of the constituency's representatives to find solutions that could meet their interests.

Finally, the mediator may also work with a constituency to modify recalcitrant behavior of a negotiator or negotiating team. A mediator, through public or private statements, may indicate to a constituency that a negotiator is being too obstinate and suggest that the constituents encourage the negotiator to abandon a hard-line position (Shapiro, 1970). The mediator may also appeal directly to the constituents for concessions that will advance negotiations (Douglas, 1962).

Chapter Seventeen

Toward an Excellent Practice of Mediation

As the field of mediation has developed, procedures become more formalized, in some places roles are professionalized, and practitioners take a number of initiatives to promote excellent practice. These include development of:

- Conflict management and mediation associations and organizations, which promote networking and information exchange
- Codes of ethics and model standards of practice, which define ethical behavior and clarify good performance
- Training seminars and educational programs to teach intermediaries relevant conflict resolution approaches and skills
- Qualifications and standards for practice in specific arenas

This chapter details some of these activities as they have occurred in North America, as well as in other countries around the world.

ASSOCIATIONS AND CONFERENCES

The development of associations in the field of voluntary dispute resolution first occurred in North America, in the area of arbitration. In 1947, a group of professional arbiters formed the National Academy of Arbitrators, but this organization failed to meet the needs of a growing number of mediators and other intermediaries who wanted an association that would present an opportunity for their professional development. In 1972, the Society of Professionals in Dispute Resolution (SPIDR) was created to "promote the peaceful resolution of disputes." This membership association, which was originally composed of professional mediators, arbiters, ombudspersons, and others who were working in the field as paid professionals, expanded to include a much broader membership. SPIDR held annual international and regional meetings and spearheaded development of codes of ethics, practice guidelines, qualifications, and competencies, in the field in general and in several practice areas. The organization also established informal mentoring programs at conferences and an ethics committee to address members' ethical concerns.

In 2001, SPIDR formally merged with two other organizations, the Academy of Family Mediators and the Conflict Resolution Education Network (CREnet), to form the Association for Conflict Resolution (ACR), the largest mediation and dispute resolution organization in the United States. ACR currently has commercial, community, consumer, court, criminal justice, education, environmental and public policy, family, health care, international, organizational conflict management, ombudsperson, online dispute, youth, training, and workplace sectors; chapters in twenty-one regions, states, or cities; and more than seven thousand members.

In 1980, a second dispute resolution organization, the National Conference on Peacemaking and Conflict Resolution (NCPCR), was founded, primarily as a forum where public and community sector mediators could share ideas, experience, and skills. Since its founding, membership has expanded to include mediators from all sectors of the field. In the 1990s, the organization changed its name to the Network of Communities for Peacemaking and Conflict Resolution.

In the early 1980s, two organizations for family mediators emerged, primarily oriented around two early practitioners in the field, Jim Coogler and John Haynes. Ultimately, these two organizations merged to form the Academy of Family Mediators (AFM). Initially, membership in this organization was limited to those who had had academic training in the legal, therapeutic, and social work fields; experience or training in mediation was not emphasized. Eventually, the criteria for membership were broadened, so that AFM membership could include intermediaries from a range of backgrounds who handle many types of interpersonal disputes.

In the area of court-based family mediation programs, the Association of Family and Conciliation Courts (AFCC) has offered a significant degree of leadership. AFCC produces a number of publications and holds an annual conference.

Since the founding of these professional associations, a number of specialized organizations have been formed to address particular areas of practice or practitioners with specific foci. In the area of education, the National Association of Mediation in Education (NAME) and the National Institute for Dispute Resolution emerged to meet the needs of dispute resolution practitioners in primary, secondary, and university settings. These organizations eventually merged to become CREnet, which subsequently became part of ACR.

The Section on Alternative Dispute Resolution of the Association of American Law Schools was also established to promote the sharing of information among law professors teaching courses on conflict management and mediation. This association promoted the development and exchange of teaching materials, and the education of legal dispute resolution practitioners. Lawyers have been very active in the field of dispute resolution, and along with active involvement in many of the organizations already mentioned they have formed a number of organizations to meet their specific professional needs. The Section of Dispute Resolution of the American Bar Association (ABA) publishes a newsletter and other literature and has sponsored conferences on targeted topics in the field. The Family Law Section of the ABA serves to link lawyer-mediators who practice in the family arena.

In the early 1980s, public policy and environmental mediators started a very loose association that sponsored invitational conferences; by the 1990s the group had become a sector within SPIDR. This sector has primarily focused on defining the field of environmental and public dispute resolution, sharing strategies and skills, and developing a compendium of competencies and skills that constitute best practice (Society of Professionals in Dispute Resolution, 1995).

In addition to associations of mediation practitioners, an informal network has emerged of universities that have mediation and theory-building programs financially supported by the William and Flora Hewlett Foundation. The Harvard Program on Negotiation and George Mason University have also convened gatherings of university faculty who either coordinate programs or conduct courses at U.S. or international universities. In Canada, the University of Victoria's Institute for Dispute Resolution, as well as Conrad Grebel College and Queens University, have developed courses and other professional programs in the area of dispute resolution and mediation.

Other associations that emerged in the late 1980s are specialized bodies for community mediators (National Association for Community Mediation), victim-offender mediators (Victim Offender Mediation Association), and commercial mediators (the International Academy of Mediation). Also, a large number of state-level mediation associations have formed across the United States.

An association of U.S. organizations focused on the resolution of international disputes was formed in 1999. The Applied Conflict Resolution Organizations Network (ACRON), which changed its name to the Alliance for International Conflict Resolution (AICR) in 2002, is composed of the leading conflict resolution organizations working on intra- and interstate conflicts around the world. Composed predominantly of nongovernmental organizations, the twenty-five members are actively involved in peacebuilding activities, coordinating among members on common initiatives and linking applied and academic organizations in related fields.

Canada has several mediation organizations—including The Network: Interaction for Conflict Resolution and Family Mediation Canada—as well as a cadre of mediators who have handled farmer-lender disputes. A number of mediation associations have also been set up in several Canadian provinces. These associations, which meet the specific needs of Canadian mediators, have constituted a valuable network for sharing information and providing services across the nation.

The emergence of this array of mediation organizations in North America has spurred the founding of a number of international conference-based organizations worldwide. The Asia-Pacific Organization for Mediators (APOM) held its first conference in Manila in 1985. Attended by private mediators, program-based mediators, and program organizers from several Pacific nations, the conference was a forum for the exchange of experiences; it set the stage for development of new mediation programs in the region.

The tradition of this organization/conference was continued by a 1994 conference, Conflict Resolution in the Asia-Pacific Region: Culture, Problem Solving and Peacemaking, held in Penang, Malaysia. The gathering, which was sponsored by the Asia Foundation, Univeristi Sains Malaysia, and the Asia Pacific Peace Research Association, was attended by close to one hundred practitioners from most Asian and Asia Pacific nations.

The first European Conference on Peacemaking and Conflict Resolution was held in Antalya, Turkey, in 1992. Subsequent conferences have been held in several European countries approximately every two years. This conference-based organization has linked Western European conflict management specialists and mediators and has reached out to bring in a number of Eastern European practitioners.

Since the late 1990s, a number of conferences have been held in Latin America. Mediation organizations have been started in Argentina, Brazil, and Colombia. ACR has also developed a special Latin American subcommittee.

In addition to the international and regional associations just described, a number of national associations have been developed in the Asia Pacific region and Western Europe. These organizations focus on either general practice or specialized fields of mediation and dispute resolution. In Australia, the Australian Dispute Resolution Association (ADRA) and the Conflict Resolution Network, and in New Zealand the Arbitrators' Institute of New Zealand have conducted conferences and established networks and are working on development of ethical standards and high-quality performance in delivery of services. Lawyers Engaged in Alternative Dispute Resolution (LEADR), in Australia and New Zealand and many countries in the Asia-Pacific region, is an organization that promotes the use of consensual dispute resolution processes and provides mediations for business, legal, and community dispute resolution. In Europe, there are a number of mediation associations and organizations, including Mediation UK in Great Britain, Centro Italiano per la Promozione della Mediazione in Italy, the Bundesverband für Familienmediation in Germany, the Mediation Network for Northern Ireland, Gernika-Gogoratuz in Spain, and the Umut Foundation in Turkey.

South Africa, too, has developed a national association of conflict managers and mediators: the South African Association for Conflict Intervention. Established in 1989 by intermediaries opposed to the apartheid system, this organization was a forum for the exchange of ideas on successful conflict handling, mediation strategy development, and dispute systems design. Many members of this organization were active in helping parties institute and operate local and regional peace committees that were part of the National Peace Accord between the major conflicting parties in the country.

CODES OF ETHICS AND STANDARDS OF PRACTICE

As the dispute resolution field developed, practitioners, members of the public, other concerned professionals, and government agencies in North America have become interested in formulating clear ethical standards for practice and other means of accountability (Herman, 2002). The motivation for this initiative has been a desire to educate the public and mediation practitioners about ethical practice, to ensure that work with clients is conducted according to the highest ethical standards, and to protect the reputation of the profession from being sullied by less-than-responsible practitioners.

The ethical standards developed in North America and most other societies have been designed to address the roles and responsibilities of independent or professional mediators in relation to their clients and the broader society (Grebe, 1989). It should be noted that ethical standards developed for independent mediators are not always applicable to—and often do not fit—the roles and activities of many social network or authoritative mediators. To date, there are no formal codes of conduct for the latter type of intermediary.

The first codes of ethical standards for intermediaries were developed in the United States and Canada, but a number of other countries and regions have since used the drafting of codes as a way of establishing the profession and defining good practice. This activity has been most common in areas where the independent mediator is the typical practitioner.

The first code of ethics was developed by the Federal Mediation and Conciliation Service of the U.S. government. Among other things, this code covered the responsibilities of the mediator to the disputing parties, to the negotiation process, to other mediators, to his or her agency, to the profession, and to unrepresented third parties.

The first code for general mediation practice at the state level was developed in Colorado (Moore, 1982a). It was rapidly followed by model standards of practice or ethical standards formulated by the American Arbitration Association, the Association of Family and Conciliation Courts, the Academy of Family Mediators, the American Bar Association Family Section, and the Society of Professionals in Dispute Resolution, as well as by a number of state codes.

The Ethical Standards of Professional Responsibility of SPIDR, which were approved in 1986 and are the current standards for ACR, cover the largest number of mediation practitioners in the field and address standards for intermediaries serving in a variety of capacities. The standards state that neutrals have an ethical obligation "to the parties, to the profession and to themselves. They should be honest and unbiased, act in good faith, be diligent, and not seek to advance their own interests at the expense of their parties." Further, "neutrals must act fairly in dealing with the parties, have no personal interest in the terms of the settlement, show no bias toward individuals and institutions involved in the dispute, be reasonably available as requested by the parties, and be certain that the parties are informed of the process in which they are involved." (The full text of the standards appears in Resource A.)

Among the responsibilities that the intermediary has to the parties are:

- An obligation to remain impartial and maintain "freedom from favoritism or bias either by word or by action, and a commitment to serve all parties as opposed to a single party"
- Assurance of informed consent to guarantee that participants understand the "nature of the process, the procedures, the particular role of the neutral, and the parties' relationship to the neutral"

- Disclosure of the limits, if any, of confidentiality, and a commitment to hold confidences once given
- Avoidance of conflict of interest or its appearance
- Implementation of the process in a timely manner
- Assistance in conducting a process and a settlement that they will hold as their own, and in which the neutral "has no vested interest"

In addition to these responsibilities to the parties, neutrals are advised to consider—and where appropriate, raise with the principal parties—the interests of unrepresented parties and to educate the principals about the use and impact of multiple dispute resolution procedures. Intermediaries are advised to accept only those cases where they have sufficient knowledge and expertise, in terms of process and substance, to engage in an ongoing process of professional development, and to assist in developing new practitioners in the field.

Intermediaries are expected to disclose to the parties at the beginning of any intervention the "bases of compensation, fees, and charges." Where appropriate, they should provide *pro bono* services. No commissions are to be paid or received by an intermediary for referring clients.

Where more than one intermediary is working on a case, all have an ethical obligation to inform each other of their involvement and to maintain a cordial and professional relationship.

Finally, advertising is to be accurate with respect to services offered and should not promise a favorable outcome to a particular side.

No code of ethical standards can cover all circumstances, nor will the rules be totally clear when applied to real-life disputes. This is especially the case when there are tensions between different ethical precepts. A commitment to confidentiality may conflict with the risk of adverse impact on unrepresented third parties. The mediator's capacity to remain impartial of neutral may be undermined by past, present, or potential future relations with one or more of the parties. At times, an intervenor may wonder whether his or her assistance, which may be motivated by the desire to produce a settlement, is merging into an unacceptable level of coercive influence.

A mediator who has industriously and in good faith acquired expertise in a new area of practice may wrestle with the question of whether he or she has enough knowledge to begin to offer services in that area. Then there are cases in which the mediator's commitment to impartiality is tested by an agreement that he or she feels is grossly unfair, unconscionable, or lacking in durability.

To assist practitioners who have encountered ethical dilemmas, SPIDR, and later ACR, has established an ethics committee to which questions can be referred for an advisory opinion. Currently, there are no means of securing a binding judgment from the committee that enforces an opinion or imposes sanctions on an errant practitioner. Although it is possible to go to court to seek a judicial decision regarding possible malpractice, there have been very few suits over violations of ethical standards in mediation, and in the few cases that have gone to trial most were either dismissed or decided in favor of the intermediary. Regardless of the fact, many mediation practitioners have obtained malpractice insurance through either legal, psychological, or social work associations or Complete Equity Markets, a liability carrier for mediators.

TRAINING, EDUCATION, AND PROFESSIONAL DEVELOPMENT

A significant component in establishing ethical and excellent practice is the development of high-quality training and professional development programs. Seminars and courses on mediation have been routinely conducted in the United States since the early 1970s. This practice has now expanded to the point that training programs are readily available on a range of topics and practice areas across North America, and increasingly worldwide. As well as general mediation seminars, there are specialized programs on mediation of interpersonal, family, divorce, parent-child, victim-offender, student-student, neighborhood, consumer, commercial, employment, grievance, discrimination, collective bargaining, environmental, and public policy disputes.

As formal educational programs on mediation develop, a number of key issues in training have emerged:

- Criteria for trainee selection

- Forums and formats for training
- Content, methodology, and duration of programs
- Qualifications of trainers and instructors
- Consumer criteria in program selection

Criteria for Trainee Selection

Obviously, anyone should be able to obtain training and education as a mediator. The world needs proficient and effective intermediaries in any number of arenas to help resolve a range of disputes. But the question is often raised: Who will make a good mediator? Simkin (1971) listed eighteen qualities sought in a mediator, among them:

- The patience of Job
- The physical endurance of a marathon runner
- The guile of Machiavelli
- The personality-probing skills of a good psychiatrist
- The hide of a rhinoceros
- Demonstrated integrity and impartiality
- Fundamental belief in human values and potentials tempered by ability to assess personal weaknesses as well as strengths
- Hard-nosed ability to analyze what is available in contrast to what might be desirable
- Sufficient personal drive and ego, qualified by a willingness to be self-effacing

Some mediation organizations, in seeking either potential trainees or staff, try to screen applicants for these and other qualities using interviews, life experiences, questionnaires, requests for case examples where the applicant has helped people in disputes, quick-decision problem-solving exercises, and role-playing. Although these methods may begin the screening process, the best measure is probably performance in simulations during a mediation training seminar or demonstrated proficiency in actual cases after training or apprenticeship. Many organizations train a pool of mediators and make selections for volunteers and staff on the basis of performance in the seminar.

Since the mid-1980s, there has been an ongoing controversy regarding who should receive training and be able to practice as a mediator in professional settings. The crux of this issue is whether previous education and professional training should be used as adequate or relevant criteria for entry into practice as a mediator. The issue has become especially important as other professions and professionals who also see themselves as conflict resolvers seek to stem the loss of their clients to mediation practitioners, limit entry into the mediation field, or capture the mediation profession as their own. Unfortunately, some states have begun to restrict the practice of mediation to those with professional qualifications that have little relationship to knowledge or proficiency in the practice of mediation.

The SPIDR Commission on Qualifications, after careful deliberation on this matter, "found no evidence that formal academic degrees [in fields other than mediation], which obviously limit entry into the dispute resolution field, are necessary to competent performance as a neutral. There is impressive evidence that individuals lacking such credentials make excellent dispute resolvers and that well designed training programs, which stress the specific skills and techniques of mediation and arbitration, are of critical importance in attaining competence. As a consequence, SPIDR recommends qualifications based on performance" (*Qualifying Neutrals,* 1989). The commission also emphasized training by qualified and competent trainers, performance-based testing, and continuing mediation education as means of promoting mediators' competence.

Forums and Formats for Training

Currently, there are six paths that an individual may take to obtain knowledge and skills in mediation theory and practice:

1. Short courses on mediation and other dispute resolution procedures offered by associations and conferences, some in the dispute resolution field and some not
2. Longer training programs (several days to one or more weeks) on general mediation processes or on particular topics, offered by experienced public or private mediation practitioners, organizations, and firms
3. Conflict management certification programs composed of multiple courses, offered by a number of colleges and universities and continuing education programs

4. Courses in professional schools
5. University degree programs in conflict theory, analysis, and practice
6. Mentoring programs in which prospective practitioners learn mediation skills and practice as apprentices to experienced mediators

In general, short courses are appropriate for presenting overviews of the conflict management field and mediation practice, introductions to new areas of practice, and in-depth treatment of advanced topics. They are generally not adequate, in and of themselves, to train participants to be mediators.

Longer programs, lasting approximately forty hours, in mediation process and individual dispute resolution topics are currently the most common vehicle for formal training. Since the mid-1980s, a range of courses has been developed and offered regularly by a number of reputable nonprofit and for-profit organizations. Some of these courses are presented by staff of community mediation programs; others are conducted by professional conflict management and mediation firms. The programs are often combined with internships or volunteer mediation opportunities so that trainees can more easily make the transition into practice. These programs vary significantly in quality and depth and in the experience of trainers. Prospective consumers of such programs should ask, Are the trainers practicing mediators? In general, the higher-quality seminars are taught by individuals who are experienced mediators as well as good educators.

In the late 1980s, several colleges and universities began to offer certificate programs in conflict management and mediation. In this context, *certification* means satisfactory completion of a prescribed number of hours of course work and does not necessarily imply a specific level of competence as a mediator. The faculty in these programs may be practicing mediators from the local community who teach part-time, but as in a number of university-based and professional-school courses described later instructors may be academics with little experience of actual mediation practice.

Professional schools of law, business, social work, and urban planning have also begun to offer courses on mediation and other types of dispute resolution (Savage, 1989). Some of these are overview seminars that educate students about a range of conflict management procedures, whereas others focus specifically on mediation. These academic programs offer an in-depth study of the mediation process. Some schools have instituted mediation clinics or teamed up with local community mediation centers as a way of integrating theory with practice.

A significant number of colleges and universities have begun to offer courses on dispute resolution and mediation, and a small number have specialized degree programs in conflict analysis or conflict management. A study undertaken by George Mason University identified hundreds of institutions of higher learning that offered courses in conflict management, peace studies, and mediation. Most of these courses offer good theoretical information. Generally, more training and practice beyond these seminars is necessary before participants are ready to serve in a professional capacity.

Degree programs, both undergraduate and graduate, that combine theory and practice are growing in number. Most programs teach a variety of dispute resolution procedures, of which mediation is one. The programs that appear to best prepare participants for work in the field are those that have an active clinical practice component. Of note in this area is George Mason University's Institute for Conflict Analysis and Resolution, which offers comprehensive master's and Ph.D. programs, and a consortium of universities in the Boston area, loosely associated with Harvard's Program on Negotiation, that offer a number of cross-registered courses and degree programs in traditional subjects with an emphasis on dispute resolution.

Content, Methodology, and Duration of Programs

Content of training programs and courses is related to the competencies that individuals will need to perform well as intermediaries, to the specific types of disputes or issues they will handle, and to the setting in which they plan to work. Training programs developed in the 1970s tended to focus on general concepts and skills, but more recent educational programs have included both general and issue-specific or context-specific skills and content.

In 1989, the SPIDR Commission on Qualifications prepared a report that identified a number of competencies for intermediaries in general, and mediators in particular:

a. Skills necessary for competent performance as a neutral
    include:
    (1) General
         (a) ability to listen actively;
         (b) ability to analyze problems, identify and separate the
              issues involved, and frame these issues for resolution
              or decision making;
         (c) ability to use clear, neutral language in speaking and
              (if written opinions are required) in writing;
         (d) sensitivity to strongly felt values of the disputants
              including gender, ethnic, and cultural differences;
         (e) ability to deal with complex factual materials;
         (f) presence and persistence, i.e., an overt commitment
              to honesty, dignified behavior, respect for the parties,
              and an ability to create and maintain control of a
              diverse group of disputants;
         (g) ability to identify and to separate the neutral's per-
              sonal values from issues under consideration; and
         (h) ability to understand power imbalances.
    (2) For mediation
         (a) ability to understand the negotiating process and
              role of advocacy;
         (b) ability to earn trust and maintain acceptability;
         (c) ability to convert parties' positions into needs and
              interests
         (d) ability to screen out non-mediable issues;
         (e) ability to help parties to invent creative options;
         (f) ability to help the parties identify principles and cri-
              teria that will guide their decision making;
         (g) ability to help parties assess their non settlement al-
              ternatives;
         (h) ability to help the parties make their own informed
              choices; and
         (i) ability to help parties assess whether their agreement
              can be implemented.
b. Knowledge of the particular dispute resolution process being
    used includes
    (1) familiarity with existing standards of practice covering
         the dispute resolution process; and
    (2) familiarity with commonly encountered ethical dilemmas.

c. Knowledge of the range of available dispute resolution processes, so that, where appropriate, cases can be referred to a more suitable process;

d. Knowledge of the institutional context in which the dispute arose and will be settled;

e. In mediation, knowledge of the process that will be used to resolve the dispute if no agreement is reached, such as judicial or administrative adjudication or arbitration;

f. Where parties' legal rights and remedies are involved, awareness of the legal standards that would be applicable if the case were taken to a court or other legal forum; and

g. Adherence to ethical standards [Society of Professionals in Dispute Resolution, 1989].

Most reputable mediation training programs present content that develops the general competencies—concepts, approaches, procedures, and skills—just described and then supplement this with material on specific issues and contexts.

As the field has grown, there is an increase in the number of specialized mediation training programs that prepare trainees to handle disputes in specific arenas. Of note are child custody and divorce, family, parent-child, neighborhood, victim-offender, consumer, school-based, organizational, personnel grievance, discrimination, labor-management (collective bargaining), commercial, public policy, and environmental mediation seminars. Some of these programs may be taken as free-standing educational programs, whereas others, such as those dealing with environmental and public policy mediation, are advanced programs and should ideally be taken after completion of a basic mediation process seminar.

Procedures used to teach the competencies identified by SPIDR are fairly diverse, but some general conclusions can be drawn about the educational goals embraced by most mediator trainers and mediation training programs. First, prospective mediators need to learn a concrete process that can be used by both the intermediary and the conflicted parties for approaching and resolving disputes. Second, contingent approaches and skills for handling special problems need to be acquired. Third, the process needs to be presented in or embedded in a specific context, and related substantive information also needs to be learned. Finally, ethical dilemmas related to the specific area of practice need to be raised and explored so that new practitioners will be prepared for certain problems that may arise. Most mediator trainers believe that learning all these things can best be accomplished by combining didactic presentations and practice sessions so that trainees have an opportunity to try out and integrate materials presented in the training.

Among the teaching methodologies commonly used in mediation training are:

- Lectures on a variety of topics
- Conflict analysis exercises to develop the ability to understand the causes and dynamics of disputes
- Negotiation simulations to teach the dynamics and procedures of advocacy
- Mediation demonstrations by trainers to model approaches and skills
- Strategy design sessions to show how interventions are planned and implemented
- Demonstrations and practice sessions on the caucus process
- Case study presentations by trainers and trainees to explore the dynamics of conflict escalation and resolution
- Presentations and practice sessions on co-mediation exercises
- Discussions to explore the forms and exercise of parties' and mediators' influence and power
- Quick-decision problems or role-plays to help trainees learn to think on their feet and respond to unanticipated problems
- A number of two-party (and where appropriate, multiparty) simulations
- Discussions and presentation of ethical problems in the prospective field of practice

Qualifications of Trainers and Instructors

As more mediators are trained, and more training programs spring up, a concern has developed—both among consumers and trainers—as to the qualifications, expertise, and experience of individuals offering such programs. Professional associations such as ACR have advocated that instructors should have practical experience in the area that they are teaching, and associations such as the Academy of Family Mediators certified training programs on the basis of both content and the experience of instructors.

Consumer Criteria in Program Selection

The number and variety of training options available to them often confuse potential consumers of mediation training programs. The questions given here are presented as a guide for individuals or organizations seeking to evaluate the quality of the various seminars being offered. Although no individual program will possess all of the qualities outlined here, an acceptable program should meet a significant number of these criteria.

Instructors

1. Are the trainers practicing mediators?
2. How many years have they been in practice?
3. Do the trainers meet the standards established for membership in SPIDR, the international professional association for conflict managers? These standards are that a member must establish qualifications as a neutral or impartial person with a minimum of three years substantial experience:

As an official or professional employee or ombudsperson of a local, state, provincial, or federal governmental or private agency or corporation with the primary purpose of resolving disputes. The conflicts may be in such areas as labor relations, the environment, prisons, or mental health facilities. The work of the applicant may also involve resolution of community, family/interpersonal, homeowners' warranty/ other consumer, intergovernmental, regulatory, educational/ student, and intra-corporate disputes.

As a neutral practitioner engaged primarily in the resolution of disputes.

As a teacher of a curriculum directly related to the negotiation, arbitration, mediation, or conciliation processes.

4. Have the trainers handled cases in the arena (labor, family,

environmental, personnel, insurance claims, farmer-lender, community, and so on) in which they are conducting training or in another arena that is similar in substance or complexity?

5. Do the trainers have substantive knowledge of the arena in which they are training?

6. If the trainers are working in a substantive field that is new to them, do they have adequate access to substantive resource people who can educate them about the new arena for which they are training conflict managers?

7. Have the trainers conducted other dispute resolution training programs in the arena covered by the present course? Where mediation or facilitation is being applied to a new arena, such prior experience may not be possible. In this case, past programs in similar areas are good indicators of trainer performance and seminar quality.

8. Do the trainers have any formal academic training in conflict management procedures? Academic training can indicate a stronger understanding of conflict and conflict management theory.

9. Are the trainers experienced at working as a team so that the program's content has continuity and there is coordinated interaction between the trainers?

Program

1. Does the program present to the participants an overall framework for analyzing the diverse causes of conflict? Conflict is usually caused by multiple factors, and these need to be understood by the prospective mediator.

2. Does the program enable the participants to understand what they bring—past experience, skills, values, and biases—to the conflict situation and the role of the mediator? People are motivated to be mediators or conflict managers by a variety of factors—some good, others not so good. A training program should amount to a forum for exploring trainees' backgrounds, motivations, strengths, and weaknesses as conflict managers.

3. Does the program educate the trainees about theories, dynamics, strategies, and tactics of *negotiation?* Because mediation and facilitation are extensions of the negotiation process, mediators

and facilitators need to understand the dynamics of negotiation. In particular, they should understand positional and interest-based bargaining assumptions and procedures.

4. Does the program offer demonstrations, either live or on video-tape, of conflict management procedures as used by experienced practitioners? Trainees often learn conflict management skills by watching experienced negotiators, mediators, or facilitators resolve a dispute. Demonstrations by trainers are generally a component of high-quality programs.

5. Does the training program present an understandable and practical step-by-step model of dispute resolution? Trainees initially need a simple procedural framework to guide their conflict management efforts.

6. Do trainees have an opportunity to practice individual tasks or stages of the conflict management process? Skills are best learned by isolating specific manageable "pieces" or behaviors and practicing them until proficiency is attained.

7. Do the trainees have an opportunity to engage in role-plays or simulated resolution of disputes? Do they have an opportunity to play the role of negotiator (disputant), mediator, or facilitator for an adequate period of time and become proficient in the requisite skills? One study of mediators found that their success rate drastically increased after they had handled five cases. Most conflict management skills are best learned by hands-on practice. How many simulated cases does each trainee get to participate in, and how much time does he or she spend in the role of the conflict manager? Most high-quality forty-hour programs have five to ten hours of simulations.

8. Do trainees receive one-on-one feedback about their performance from their trainers or coaches? Conflict management procedures and skills are best learned through practice and feedback on performance. The quality of the seminar is greatly enhanced if trainees receive individualized coaching rather than being trained exclusively in a large group.

9. Are trainees taught to use specific conflict management procedures such as active listening, reframing, giving clear and direct messages, procedures for moving disputants from positional to interest-based bargaining, and the caucus technique? Are trainees taught how to overcome substantive, procedural, and psychological

barriers to settlement and how to manage negotiator, mediator, or facilitator power? Knowledge and skill in using these behaviors and procedures makes for more sophisticated and effective conflict managers.

10. Does the training seminar contain substantive presentations relevant to the field for which the trainee is being prepared? In order to help parties resolve their conflicts, mediators and facilitators need some substantive knowledge about the issues in a dispute and possible resolutions. Procedural knowledge alone may not be enough to move the parties toward settlement.

11. Does the training program have a procedure for moving from training to practice? Seminars should teach trainees how to set up a practice, integrate their new skills on the job, or define the way they will work in an established program.

12. Does the training program educate the trainees about the need for ongoing conflict management education and offer some means of supervision or quality control, such as co-mediation, supervision by an experienced practitioner, or group supervision? New mediators and facilitators generally need assistance to effectively practice their newly learned skills. Means to obtain supervision and assistance in intervention strategy design should be addressed in the training program.

13. Does the training program address some of the critical ethical problems, questions, and dilemmas involved in practicing conflict management? Does the seminar familiarize the participants with relevant standards of practice and codes of ethics? The Standards of Practice of the Society of Professionals in Dispute Resolution or ACR, the Code of Ethics for Labor Mediators, the Model Standards of Practice for Family and Divorce Mediation and the Model Standards of Practice for Child Custody Evaluation of the Association of Family and Conciliation Courts, the Standards of Practice of the Academy of Family Mediators, and the American Bar Association's Standards for Divorce Mediators are guidelines for ethical practice.

14. How long is the training seminar? Basic mediation training programs should be thirty-two to forty hours. This standard has been adopted by numerous practitioners, one of the major professional associations, and a large number of state and private mediation programs.

15. What kinds of written materials are given to trainees? Seminar workbooks and handouts should be useful as training aids and be comprehensive enough to serve as "refreshers" after the seminar is finished. Trainees should also be given an up-to-date bibliography that can aid them in conducting further studies of the dispute resolution process.

PROMOTING THE FIELD AND ENSURING COMPETENCE AND QUALITY

As the field of mediation matures, there has been increasing interest, both within the profession and among governmental agencies, in promoting the use of alternative dispute resolution, ensuring that practitioners are competent, and guaranteeing provision of quality services to the public (Gentry, 1994). This concern has led to a significant increase in legislation to promote and regulate the field: "As of 1988, roughly 35 states and the District of Columbia had adopted some type of statutory authority for mediation. At least nine states had adopted comprehensive statutes to define and encourage the development of 'alternative' dispute resolution methods" (*Dispute Resolution Forum*, 1989, p. 5).

In 1990, the U.S. Congress passed the Administrative Dispute Resolution Act, which encouraged use of alternative dispute resolution and mandated each federal agency to "adopt a policy that addresses the use of alternative means of dispute resolution (ADR) and case management" ("Administrative Dispute Resolution Act," 1990). Executive orders encouraging the use of ADR were issued during the first Bush administration, and in 1993 President Clinton issued an executive memorandum directing "each agency to explore and, where appropriate, use consensual mechanisms for developing regulations, including negotiated rulemaking" (President, 1993).

As of the late 1980s, "at least 21 states provide for mediation of labor disputes, usually by state boards of mediation. At least ten states have statutes specifically addressing mediation of family disputes, including issues of divorce, separation, child custody, and visitation rights. Individual states authorize or require the use of mediation in other specific types of dispute—for example, foreclosures by lenders against farm property and the siting of hazardous waste facilities" (*Dispute Resolution Forum*, 1989, p. 5).

Because of the push to use alternative dispute resolution procedures, and especially mediation, there has been a strong need to develop qualifications for mediators. In 1992, SPIDR appointed a new Committee on Qualifications and authorized its members to reexamine emerging qualifications issues. After two-and-a-half years of deliberations, the committee, composed of U.S. and Canadian practitioners and mediation program administrators, issued a report, *Ensuring Competence and Quality in Dispute Resolution Practice,* which was a response to the need of policy makers, governmental agencies, and others to identify qualifications that would "ensure skillful, honorable and effective dispute resolution" (Society of Professionals in Dispute Resolution, 1995). The report recommends a set of guidelines to help organize the discussion of the ingredients of practitioner competence. These guidelines are, in part, that:

1. The formation of standards of competence and qualifications should be undertaken through a process of consultation with all stakeholders and should provide for ongoing review and revision.

2. Programs should clearly state their qualifications and ethical standards, and their goals and values in a manner that can be understood by practitioners, parties, and the public.

3. In a pluralistic society, the development of qualifications standards must reflect an understanding of the context, the diversity of stakeholders, and respect for the variety of values and goals of all parties.

4. The context of the dispute resolution service must be examined and understood because it determines what should be considered competent practice in that context.

5. The multiple paths to becoming a competent practitioner ought to be recognized, maintained, and expanded. Some combination of natural aptitude, skills, knowledge, and attributes acquired through an appropriate combination of dispute resolution training, education, and experience is the best route to ensuring practitioner competence.

6. No one method of assessment should be relied on because it may lead to emphasis of one measure of competence at the expense of other valuable measures. Use of a combination of measures of competence also will reduce the likelihood of inadvertent discrimination.

7. Assessing competence is key to enduring quality service delivery and is a shared responsibility of practitioners, programs, dispute resolution associations, and parties (Society of Professionals in Dispute Resolution, 1995, p. 2).

In addition to these recommendations, the committee developed a seven-step framework of questions to assist the concerned parties that were listed earlier in analyzing, within specific contexts, how high quality and competence can be achieved. Each step requires an answer to a central question and a number of subquestions (Society of Professionals in Dispute Resolution, 1995, pp. 2–4):

1. "What is the context?" (the social and cultural setting, the parties' relationships to each other, the disputants' values, the nature of the dispute, the types of procedures available, and the program context)
2. "Who is responsible for ensuring competence?" (practitioners, consumers, program administrators, associations)
3. "What do practitioners and programs do?" (practitioner tasks to provide procedural, substantive, and relationship-building assistance, and program tasks to provide services, such as case assessment and assignment, training, and monitoring and evaluating practitioners)
4. "What does it mean to be competent?" (knowledge of and ability to effectively apply mediation concepts and skills to assist in the prevention and management of disputes)
5. "How do practitioners and programs become competent?" (identification of a variety of paths including life skills, past experience, formalized training, apprenticeships, group supervision, peer review, and degree programs)
6. "How is competence assessed?" (assessment of practitioners and programs by a variety of concerned parties—practitioners, programs, organizations, and mediation participants—at various times in a practitioner's career or in the life of an organization)
7. "How should assessment tools be used to assure quality?" (use of tools to support program goals, to determine admittance to organizations, to make referrals, to develop rosters, to obtain funding, or to improve practice)

In general, the committee found that certification, which recognizes that a practitioner "has achieved a level of competence and met certain standards of education, training and experience," can help ensure that qualified individuals are providing services to the public and can enhance the stature of the profession (Society of Professionals in Dispute Resolution, 1995). However, the committee was opposed to licensure—"governmental permission to practice based on a prescribed level of education, experience and training"—because of the risk of creating arbitrary standards, the possibility that the field might be dominated by one group or profession, and the danger that standards might inappropriately "freeze" who is allowed to act as a mediator and how the profession is practiced.

In August 2002, the ACR Board of Directors approved the work of the Guidelines Committee of ACR in its *Recommended Guidelines for Effective Conflict Resolution Education Programs in K-12 Classrooms, Schools and School Districts*. The guidelines outline how teachers, administrators, dispute resolution practitioners, and policy makers can assess conflict resolution programs and make decisions regarding resources and strategies for implementation.

Another effort to promote standardization of the field and best practices has been the effort of the National Conference of Commissioners on Uniform State Laws (NCCUSL). In the late 1990s, this group began work on developing a Uniform Mediation Act (UMA) that would present a prototype for legislation that could be adopted by states desiring specific substantive law concerning mediation. The draft act went through several modifications and iterations after consultation with mediators and mediation associations across the country. The board of directors of ACR conditionally approved the act in April 2002, subject to revisions of sections related to confidentiality and child protection mediation privilege.

Challenges for the Growth and Development of Mediation

Conflict is an omnipresent phenomenon in human interaction. Conflicts can lead to productive and positive changes or growth, or to the destruction and degradation of relationships. A significant variable in the outcome of a dispute is the means that the participants use to resolve their differences. Now, more than ever before, there is a need for dispute resolution procedures that assist parties in meeting their needs, satisfying their interests, and reaching voluntary agreements that minimize physical and psychological harm. Mediation is one process that can make an important contribution to peaceful dispute resolution.

The use of mediation has grown tremendously during the seventeen years since this book was first published. Its practice has expanded not only in North America, where the procedure has been highly articulated and applied to diverse problems, but also in Africa, the Asia Pacific region, Latin America, the Middle East, and Western and Eastern Europe. Arenas of practice have grown to encompass all areas of life: interpersonal, family, communal, educational, occupational, medical, commercial, local, urban, regional, national, ethnic, international, and environmental.

For mediation to achieve even broader utilization as a means of voluntary dispute resolution, several developments must occur. First, the public needs more education about the availability of mediation and its ability to help people address and resolve important conflicts. Mediation is currently underused not because of its lack of applicability but because those involved in disputes are not aware of mediation's benefits. Public education about the process should become a priority among mediators and others interested in peaceful dispute resolution.

Second, more research has to be conducted on mediation formats, procedures, strategies, and tactics, and the findings must be disseminated. More information is needed about how mediators enable parties to manage intense emotional multiparty conflicts, imbalances of power, and communication problems. Great progress has been made in this area over the last twenty years, through both practitioner and academic publications, and this work needs to continue.

Third, mediation must become more highly institutionalized. It must be incorporated as a significant component of organizational dispute resolution systems at all levels of society. Mediation has for too long been conducted on an ad hoc basis. Fortunately, in the last decade formalized training has given mediation much wider acceptability, and the increase in the number of organizations that now routinely incorporate services is an indication of this trend.

Fourth, funding must be developed that will promote the growth of mediation organizations and agencies in the private and public sectors. Funding must come from governmental agencies, the business sector, foundations, and individuals who will use mediation on a fee-for-service basis. Only through funded institutionalization will mediation become readily accessible to a broader public.

Finally, participants in conflicts, mediators, and other professionals need to search for new arenas in which mediation can be applied. Following the Gandhian example, we need to conduct "experiments in truth" to discover appropriate new applications for mediation. Although mediation is not a panacea and does not guarantee perfect settlements in all conflicts, it is a tool that has wider application than is currently recognized.

In conclusion, I will identify seven major areas where advancement is needed and where I believe growth will occur in the field of mediation during the next decade:

1. *Ethnic and religious disputes.* The late 1980s and early 1990s have produced some of the most brutal incidents of violence between ethnic and religious groups seen since World War II (Brown, 1993; Horowitz, 1985). Ethnic cleansing in new states carved from the former Yugoslavia; genocidal killings in Rwanda; decades-long guerrilla war between the government and Indians in Guatemala; disputes in India between the government and separatist groups in Kashmir and the Punjab; civil war in Liberia and Somalia; ethnic conflicts in Afghanistan, Tajikistan, and Turkey; and civil war between Sinhalese and Tamils in Sri Lanka are large-scale examples on the international front.

But conflicts with strong ethnic components are not found just in war-torn countries. Ethnic disputes occur on a smaller scale in most multicultural countries: attacks on Turks in Germany and foreigners in France; disputes between members of tribal or ethnic groups in South Africa; violations of the land or water rights of Native American, First Nations, and other aboriginal peoples in a number of countries; beatings of African Americans by members of other races and police in the United States; conflicts between Korean store owners and African American youths in New York or Los Angeles; racial discrimination in the workplace.

Certain conflicts with ethnic components have been handled and resolved creatively. The relatively peaceful transition to democracy in South Africa and innovative mediation work in cases of alleged discrimination in a number of countries exemplify this. However, the field is still in its infancy and desperately needs more research, experimental applications, and aggressive initiatives. Effective use of mediation, especially when combined with procedures to establish and build relationships and to foster interest-based bargaining, offers the promise of helping entrenched parties deal with and manage disputes that include ethnic differences.

2. *Psychological and relationship barriers to agreement making.* Closely related to some of the ethnic disputes just described is resolution of what have come to be called intractable disputes (Kriesberg, Northrup, and Thorson, 1989). These are conflicts where trust, respect, and cognitive empathy or understanding between parties are so lacking that disputants are unable to move toward discussion of, or agreement on, any substantive issues that divide them. They are locked into a cycle of negative intimacy that, without as-

sistance, they appear to be unable to break out of. This dynamic commonly occurs in the context of diplomatic relations, ethnic group interactions, labor-management bargaining, superior-subordinate relationships, community disputes, divorce, and a range of other group and interpersonal confrontations. Until new procedures are developed to break this type and cycle of negative conflict, many disputes will remain both unmanageable and unresolvable. This topic will be a critical research focus and area of experimentation in the future. It is probable that mediation, with a greater emphasis on establishing and building relationships and developing cognitive empathy, will be able to make a greater contribution to unlocking these intractable disputes.

3. *Violent conflict.* Again related to the preceding points is the need to find alternative means of regulating and resolving violent disputes: creative approaches to deescalating potential violence, shifting to nonviolent means once violence has actually occurred, and addressing postviolence trauma and relationships. In the international arena, research and interventions in preventive diplomacy (Evans, 1993) and the development of peace accord systems that use mediation on the ground (Moore, 1993) are significant new steps toward control of violent conflict. On the domestic front, they are matched by initiatives to prevent gang violence, stem spousal and child abuse, and promote reconciliation between victims and offenders. More work needs to be done to explore the roles of third parties and mediation in such contexts.

4. *Education for creative conflict management.* The development of nonviolent cultures will require structured educational initiatives to teach people how to work through their conflicts more effectively, more productively, and with less harm to each other. This effort should start with the youngest of children, but it should be presented in all phases of education and life. Students need to be introduced to mediation principles and procedures early in their education so that they can apply them throughout their lives. Additional formal courses of instruction should be developed for secondary, undergraduate, graduate, and professional schools, and public seminars must be provided for those not in schools.

Teaching people from various cultures how to handle conflict more effectively and nonviolently will also mean further research into how different cultures successfully manage disputes. Sometimes procedures may be borrowed by one culture from another, but rarely can prescriptive solutions from one society be transferred or imposed in their totality in another. More elicitive approaches to research and conflict analysis will have to be used, in which people from diverse cultures are asked to decode their own patterns of dispute escalation and deescalation and their successful management and resolution methods. This will ensure that appropriate, effective, and culturally acceptable procedures are being developed and taught (Lederach, 1995).

5. *Dispute systems design.* The trend of designing dispute resolution systems that incorporate mediation as one of the central procedures is already significantly under way for a variety of disputes and in a number of public and private organizations. Systems that use mediation have been developed to handle large numbers of employment disputes, charges of discrimination, consumer complaints, and environmental controversies. Organizational leaders, personnel, and mediators will increasingly appreciate the multiplier effect of systems that channel disputes to appropriate procedures and intermediaries and facilitate resolution of multiple conflicts, as opposed to mediation of single disputes on an ad hoc basis. In the future, many mediators will be called on to design and implement dispute management and resolution systems as well as being requested to mediate individual cases. Creating such systems can exponentially increase the number of conflicts that are addressed and resolved and can substantially broaden public exposure to, and awareness of, cooperative means of managing differences.

6. *Conflict management and public governance.* Although there appears to be a worldwide trend toward more democratic decision making within organizations and governments (Huntington, 1991), there also seems to be a growing level of dissatisfaction both with the forms of participation that are prescribed or allowed and with the adversarial and often ineffective nature of decision-making processes. Citizens, government officials, coworkers, and managers are increasingly seeking means to build consensus agreements that a broad spectrum of people can support and to move beyond adversary democracy (Mansbridge, 1983). This is an arena where mediation has a lot to offer.

Mediation has been used effectively to build consensual decisions on a range of public policy, regulatory, site-specific, and organizational issues. There is every reason to believe that this trend will continue in this new century, and that the range of applications will become even more diverse. Mediation has the potential to be an alternative to divisive politics in a number of arenas and to help build social consensus on critical issues of concern.

7. *Conflict management and the global environment.* Social conflicts are often played out in the context of a natural environment that sets significant parameters for what is and is not possible. As worldwide awareness of the interlocking relationship between our social and natural worlds increases, there will be a greater impetus to explore how more sustainable societies can be developed, at the local and global levels. Mediation has been an effective procedure for addressing certain critical environmental issues and will increasingly be used to handle major problems such as transboundary air pollution, global warming, and limited water resources. Large environmental issues, more and more of which are cross national boundaries or are regional, will be highly appropriate for mediation because no one international actor has either the authority or the power to impose a unilateral decision.

Today, people around the world are in need of effective means to help manage and resolve conflicts in all aspects of their lives. Mediation has proven itself in the past to be a helpful tool in accomplishing this goal in a variety of situations and cultures. It is my hope that the detailed elaboration of the mediation process found in this book will help both parties and intermediaries to develop better, more creative, and more acceptable solutions to joint problems; promote more positive working relationships between and among the people; and create a deeper peace in all aspects of society.

Professional Practice Guidelines

The Association for Conflict Resolution (ACR)* Ethical Standards of Professional Responsibility

The Society of Professionals in Dispute Resolution (SPIDR) was established in 1973 to promote the peaceful resolution of disputes. Members of the Society believe that resolving disputes through negotiation, mediation, arbitration, and other neutral interventions can be of great benefit to disputing parties and to society. In 1983, the SPIDR Board of Directors charged the SPIDR Ethics Committee with the task of developing ethical standards of professional responsibility. The Committee membership represented all the various sectors and disciplines within SPIDR. This document, adopted by the Board on June 2, 1986, is the result of that charge.

The purpose of this document is to promote among SPIDR Members and Associates ethical conduct and a high level of competency among SPIDR Members, including honesty, integrity, impartiality, and the exercise of good judgment in their dispute resolution efforts. It is hoped that this document also will help to (1) define the profession of dispute resolution, (2) educate the public, and (3) inform users of dispute resolution services.

*Formerly the Society of Professionals in Dispute Resolution (SPIDR)

APPLICATION OF STANDARDS

Adherence to these ethical standards by SPIDR Members and Associates is basic to professional responsibility. SPIDR Members and Associates commit themselves to be guided in their professional conduct by these standards. The SPIDR Board of Directors or its designee is available to advise Members and Associates about the interpretation of these standards. Other neutral practitioners and organizations are welcome to follow these standards.

SCOPE

It is recognized that SPIDR Members and Associates resolve disputes in various sectors within the disciplines of dispute resolution and have their own codes of professional conduct. These standards have been developed as general guidelines of practice for neutral disciplines represented in the SPIDR membership. Ethical considerations relevant to some, but not to all, of these disciplines are not covered by these standards.

GENERAL RESPONSIBILITIES

Neutrals have a duty to the parties, to the profession, and to themselves. They should be honest and unbiased, act in good faith, be diligent, and not seek to advance their own interests at the expense of their parties'.

Neutrals must act fairly in dealing with the parties, have no personal interest in the terms of the settlement, show no bias toward individuals and institutions involved in the dispute, be reasonably available as requested by the parties, and be certain that the parties are informed of the process in which they are involved.

RESPONSIBILITIES TO THE PARTIES

1. *Impartiality.* The neutral must maintain impartiality toward all parties. Impartiality means freedom from favoritism or bias either by word or by action, and a commitment to serve all parties as opposed to a single party.

2. *Informed Consent.* The neutral has an obligation to ensure that all parties understand the nature of the process, the procedures, the

particular role of the neutral, and the parties' relationship to the neutral.

3. *Confidentiality.* Maintaining confidentiality is critical to the dispute resolution process. Confidentiality encourages candor, a full exploration of the issues, and a neutral's acceptability. There may be some types of cases, however, in which confidentiality is not protected. In such cases, the neutral must advise the parties, when appropriate in the dispute resolution process, that the confidentiality of the proceedings cannot necessarily be maintained. Except in such instances, the neutral must resist all attempts to cause him or her to reveal any information outside the process. A commitment by the neutral to hold information in confidence with the process also must be honored.

4. *Conflict of Interest.* The neutral must refrain from entering or continuing in any dispute if he or she believes or perceives that participation as a neutral would be a clear conflict of interest and any circumstances that may reasonably raise a question as to the neutral's impartiality.

The duty to disclose is a continuing obligation throughout the process.

5. *Promptness.* The neutral shall exert every reasonable effort to expedite the process.

6. *The Settlement and Its Consequences.* The dispute resolution process belongs to the parties. The neutral has no vested interest in the terms of a settlement, but must be satisfied that agreements in which he or she has participated will not impugn the integrity of the process. The neutral has a responsibility to see that the parties consider the terms of a settlement. If the neutral is concerned about the possible consequences of a proposed agreement, and the needs of the parties dictate, the neutral must inform the parties of that concern. In adhering to this standard, the neutral may find it advisable to educate the parties, to refer one or more parties for specialized advice, or to withdraw from the case. In no case, however, shall the neutral violate Section 3, Confidentiality, of these standards.

UNREPRESENTED INTERESTS

The neutral must consider circumstances where interests are not represented in the process. The neutral has an obligation, where in his or her judgment the needs of parties dictate, to ensure that such interests have been considered by the principal parties.

USE OF MULTIPLE PROCEDURES

The use of more than one dispute resolution procedure by the same neutral involves additional responsibilities. Where the use of more than one procedure is initially contemplated, the neutral must take care at the outset to advise the parties of the nature of the procedures and the consequences of revealing information during any one procedure which the neutral may later use for decision making or may share with another decision maker. Where the use of more than one procedure is contemplated after the initiation of the dispute resolution process, the neutral must explain the consequences and afford the parties an opportunity to select another neutral for the subsequent procedures. It is also incumbent upon the neutral to advise the parties of the transition from one dispute resolution process to another.

BACKGROUND AND QUALIFICATIONS

A neutral should accept responsibility only in cases where the neutral has sufficient knowledge regarding the appropriate process and subject matter to be effective. A neutral has a responsibility to maintain and improve his or her professional skills.

DISCLOSURE OF FEES

It is the duty of the neutral to explain to the parties at the outset of the process the bases of compensation, fees, and charges, if any.

SUPPORT OF THE PROFESSION

The experienced neutral should participate in the development of new practitioners in the field and engage in efforts to educate the public about the value and use of neutral dispute resolution procedures. The neutral should provide *pro bono* services, where appropriate.

RESPONSIBILITIES OF NEUTRALS
WORKING ON THE SAME CASE

In the event that more than one neutral is involved in the resolution of a dispute, each has an obligation to inform the others regarding his or her entry in the case. Neutrals working with the same parties should maintain an open and professional relationship with each other.

ADVERTISING AND SOLICITATION

A neutral must be aware that some forms of advertising and solicitation are inappropriate and in some conflict resolution disciplines, such as labor arbitration, are impermissible. All advertising must honestly represent the services to be rendered. No claims of specific results or promises which imply favor on one side over another for the purpose of obtaining business should be made. No commissions, rebates, or other similar forms of remuneration should be given or received by a neutral for the referral of clients.

Mediation Services Agreement
Sample Waiver and Consent Form

The purpose of this waiver and consent form is to ensure that you, our client, understand the nature of our service and the responsibilities you have to maintain the confidentiality of the mediation process.

Your Initials

_____   I understand that CDR Associates offers neither legal advice nor legal counsel.

_____   I agree that I will not, at any time (before, during, or after mediation of this dispute), call the mediator as an adversarial witness in any legal or administrative proceeding concerning this dispute.

_____   I agree that I will not subpoena or call for the production of any records, notes, or work product of the mediator in any legal or administrative proceeding that arises before, during, or after the mediation of this dispute. However, any agreement resulting from mediation that is intended by the parties to have legal effect and to be legally enforceable may be subpoenaed, called for, or produced in any proceedings to which it is relevant, unless the agreement specifically provides otherwise.

I have read the above and have no further questions regarding the confidentiality of this process.

Signature _____

Date _____

AGREEMENT TO MEDIATE

This is an agreement between and among _____ and _____ (hereafter referred to as the "parties") and CDR Associates as represented by _____ and _____ (the "mediators"). The parties have entered into mediation with CDR Associates with the intention of reaching a consensual settlement regarding _____. The provisions of this agreement are as follows:

1. The mediators are impartial facilitators who will assist the parties to reach their own settlement. The mediators will not make decisions about "right" or "wrong" or tell the parties what to do.

2. It is understood that open and honest communications are essential if mediation is to work. Because concern for future reprisal or retaliation can interfere with communication and the mediation process, the parties agree not to take such actions.

3. The parties agree to make full and honest disclosure to each other and to the mediators of all relevant information and documents. This includes providing to each other and the mediators all information that would be available through the civil discovery process. Failure to disclose this information may result in this agreement being set aside.

4. The parties and mediators agree that all written and oral communications, negotiations, and statements made in connection with mediation will be treated as privileged settlement discussions and are confidential. Therefore:

   A. The mediators will *not* reveal the names of the parties or matters discussed in the course of mediation unless expressly requested to do so by all parties. It is understood that the mediators are *not* required to maintain confidentiality if there is reason to believe any party is in danger of bodily harm.

B. The parties agree that they will not, at any time before, during, or after mediation, call the mediators or anyone associated with CDR Associates as witnesses in any legal or administrative proceeding concerning this dispute. To the extent that any party may have a right to call the mediators or anyone associated with CDR Associates as witnesses, that right is hereby waived.

C. The parties agree not to subpoena or demand the production of any records, notes, work product, or similar materials from the mediators in any legal or administrative proceeding concerning this dispute. To the extent that any party may have a right to demand these documents, that right is hereby waived.

D. If, at a later time, any party decides to subpoena the mediators, the mediators will move to quash the subpoena. That party will reimburse CDR Associates for the expenses (including attorneys' fees), plus $100 per hour for the mediators' time, associated with responding to that subpoena.

E. The sole exception is that this agreement to mediate and any written agreement made and signed by the parties as a result of mediation may be used in any relevant proceeding, unless the parties make a written agreement not to do so.

5. Although the parties intend to continue with mediation until they reach an agreement, it is understood that any of them may choose to withdraw from mediation at any time. It is agreed that if this occurs, best efforts will be made to discuss this decision in the presence of all parties and the mediators.

6. If the mediators determine that it is not possible to resolve the issues through mediation, the process can be terminated once this determination has been conveyed to the parties and confirmed in writing.

7. The mediators do *not* offer legal advice or provide legal counsel. In the event that legal advice is appropriate, each party is advised to retain his or her own attorney in order to be properly counseled about his or her legal interests, rights, and obligations. This includes, but is not limited to, reviewing any written agreement between the parties that results from the mediation.

8. The parties agree to share the costs of mediation according to the terms of the Fee Agreements that accompany this Agreement to Mediate.

9. Copies of this agreement may be executed separately by the parties and CDR Associates.

I have read, understand and agree to each of the provisions of this agreement.

Signed _____   Signed _____
Date _____   Date _____

For CDR Associates:
Signed _____   Signed _____
Date _____   Date _____

Settlement Documentation Form
Sample Memorandum of Understanding

This is a memorandum of understanding regarding the revision of the contract of employment between Dr. Richard Singson, director of and representative for the Fairview Medical Clinic, 3504 Arizona Avenue, Smithville, Colorado, and Dr. Andrew Whittamore, a physician working at the same clinic.

Because of personal difficulties between Dr. Andrew Whittamore and his wife, Dr. Janelle Whittamore, who also works at Fairview Medical Clinic, it is agreed by Dr. Singson and Dr. Andrew Whittamore that the latter should continue to practice medicine for the Fairview Medical Clinic, but that his principal office should not be at the clinic's address listed above. This arrangement will allow the Whittamores the physical separation that they both desire.

The following points detail the agreements reached by Dr. Andrew Whittamore and the clinic regarding establishment of a separate office:

1. Dr. Andrew Whittamore will remain an employee of the Fairview Medical Clinic for the next two and a half years, although his practice will not be at the clinic's address listed above.
2. Dr. Andrew Whittamore will find new office space on his own time. The time frame for the search is left up to Dr. Whittamore.
3. Dr. Andrew Whittamore's current desk and office furniture will be moved from the clinic to his new office.
4. Dr. Andrew Whittamore will pay one-half of the cost for all new equipment purchased for his new office. The cost of

the equipment will be prorated and deducted from his salary on a monthly basis over the next two and a half years. The furniture will remain the property of the clinic.

5. Moving expenses will be equally borne by the clinic and Dr. Andrew Whittamore.

6. The clinic will continue to provide Dr. Whittamore with a full-time nurse receptionist.

7. Dr. Andrew Whittamore will continue to have full access to the laboratory, staff, and facilities of the clinic.

8. All billing from Dr. Andrew Whittamore's practice will be managed by the bookkeeper for the clinic.

9. Dr. Whittamore will duplicate at his own expense all new patient records developed through his separate practice and file records in the central file of the clinic. Duplicate reports on patient care should be submitted to the clinic by the end of each month.

Both doctors agree to comply fully with this agreement and expect that the arrangement will be mutually beneficial. Should problems arise in the implementation of the agreement, both doctors agree to return to mediation before pursuing another course of dispute resolution.

It is the understanding of Drs. Andrew Whittamore and Singson that this agreement will be reviewed by their respective lawyers before it becomes effective.

In the event any future dispute arises in regard to the provisions of this agreement or otherwise related to our revision of the employee contract which we cannot settle ourselves, we agree to enter into mediation before seeking a solution in court.

Each of us has considered the implications of this agreement, has discussed it with our own legal counsel, and considers it to be a fair and equitable arrangement. We intend for this agreement to be a final settlement of all issues pertaining to the employee contract.

Richard Singson, M.D.	Andrew Whittamore, M.D.
(for Fairview Medical Clinic)	
Date	Date
Attorney/Witness	Attorney/Witness
Date	Date

List of Professional Associations and Organizations, Journals, and Training Resources

INTERNATIONAL

Association for Conflict Resolution
1527 New Hampshire Ave., 3rd Floor
Washington, DC 20036
(202) 667–9700; fax (202) 265–1968
info@acresolution.org
www.acresolution.org

CPR Institute for Dispute Resolution
366 Madison Ave.
New York, NY 10017–3122
(212) 949–6490; fax (212) 949–8859
info@cpradr.org
www.cpradr.org

International Academy of Mediators (IAM)
1807 Jancey St.
Pittsburgh, PA 15206–1065
(412) 362–3470; fax (412) 363–7913
iam@mediate.com
www.iamed.org

International Association of Mediators and Arbitrators (IAMA)
5718 Westheimer, Suite 1430
Houston, TX 77057
(800) 559–5262; fax (800) 455–2834
www.e-iama.com

LEADR National Dispute Resolution Centre
Level 4, 233 Macquarie St.
Sydney, NSW 2000 AUSTRALIA
61–2–9233 2255; fax 61–2–9232 3024
(800) 651–650
leadr@leadr.com.au

Network of Communities for Peacemaking
and Conflict Resolution (NCPCR)
Philadelphia Office
3070 Bristol Pike, Suite 116
Bensalem, PA 19020
(215) 245–6993
ncpcr@apeacemaker.net

World Mediation Forum
13 Royal Terrace West
Dun Laoghaire, Co. Dublin IRELAND
fax 00353 12800259
www.mediate.com/world/pg.7.cfm

NATIONAL

United States

American Arbitration Association, National Office
335 Madison Ave., 10th Floor
New York, NY 10017–4605
(212) 716–5800; fax (212) 716–5905
(800) 778–7879 Customer Service
websitemail@adr.org
www.adr.org

American Bar Association
Section of Dispute Resolution
740 15th St.
Washington, DC 20005–1009
(202) 662–1680; fax (202) 662–1683
dispute@abanet.org
www.abanet.org

American College of Civil Trial Mediators
200 East Robinson St., Suite 500
Orlando, FL 32801
(407) 843–5880; fax (407) 425–7905
www.acctm.org

American Society of Professional Mediators
2140 Professional Dr.
Roseville, CA 95661
(916) 204–2147

Applied Conflict Resolution Organizations Network (ACRON)
1321 Pennsylvania Ave., S.E.
Washington, DC 20003
(202) 544–4141
www.acron.iwa.org

Association of Attorney Mediators (AAM)
P.O. Box 741955
Dallas, TX 75374–1955
(972) 869–1183; fax (972) 669–8180
(800) 280–1368
aam@airmail.net
www.attorney-mediators.org

Association of Family and Conciliation Courts
6515 Grand Teton Plaza, Suite 210
Madison, WI 53719–1048
(608) 664–3750; fax (608) 664–3751
afcc@afccnet.org
www.afccnet.org

Bureau of National Affairs (BNA PLUS)
1231 25th St., N.W.
Washington, DC 20037
(202) 452–4323
(800) 452–7773
bnaplus@bna.com

Conflict Research Consortium
Campus Box 580
University of Colorado
Boulder, CO 80309–0580
(303) 492–1635; fax (303) 492–2154
www.colorado.edu/conflict

Eastern Mennonite University
Conflict Transformation Program
1200 Park Rd.
Harrisonburg, VA 22802–2462
(540) 432–4490; fax (540) 432–4449
ctprogram@emu.edu
www.emu.edu/ctp

Harvard Law School Program on Negotiation
Harvard University
513 Pound Hall
Cambridge, MA 02138
(617) 495–1684; fax (617) 495–7818
pon@law.harvard.cdr
www.pon.harvard.edu

ICAR (Conflict Analysis & Resolution)
George Mason University
4260 Chain Bridge Rd. (Rte. 123)
Fairfax, VA 22030
(703) 993–1300; fax (703) 993–1302
www.gmu.edu/departments/icar

National Association for Community Mediation (NAFCM)
1527 New Hampshire Ave., N.W.
Washington, DC 20036–1206
(202) 667–9700; fax (202) 667–8629
www.nafcm.org

Policy Consensus Initiative (State Agencies)
811 St. Michael's Dr., Suite 103
Santa Fe, NM 87123
fax (505) 820–6836
www.policyconsensus.org

Society of Federal Labor Relations Professionals (SFLRP)
P.O. Box 25112
Arlington, VA 22202
(703) 685–4130; fax (703) 685–1144
info@sflrp.org
www.sflrperp.org

Straus Institute for Dispute Resolution
Pepperdine University School of Law
24255 Pacific Coast Hwy.
Malibu, CA 90263
(310) 506–4655
law-www.pepperdine.edu/straus

Victim Offender Mediation Association
c/o Center for Policy, Planning, and Performance
2344 Nicollet Ave. South, Suite 330
Minneapolis, MN 55404
(612) 874–0570; fax (612) 874–0253
voma@voma.org
www.voma.org

Victim-Offender Reconciliation Program (VORP)
Information and Resource Center
19813 N.E. 13th St.
Camas, WA 98607
(360) 260–1551; fax (360) 260–1563
www.vorp.com

Argentina

Asociación Argentina de Arbitraje y Mediación
Uruguay 390 piso 20 oficinas "B" y "C"
1015 Buenos Aires, ARGENTINA
(54–11) 4373–7800/4372–7117
www.inter-mediacion.com/semed-arg.htm

Fundación Libra
Lavale no. 1125 Piso 7 Of. 16
(1048) Buenos Aires, ARGENTINA
+54 (11) 4312 7414; fax +54 (11) 4312 7415
ombudsnet@fundacionlibra.org.ar
www.fundacionlibra.or.ar/

Australia

Australian Dispute Resolution Association (ADRA)
P.O. Box A2468
Sydney South, NSW 1235 AUSTRALIA
02 9231 5822; fax 02 9231 5833

Conflict Resolution Network
P.O. Box 1016
Chatswood, NSW 2057 AUSTRALIA
+61 (0)2 9419 8500; fax +61 (0)2 9413 1148
crn@crnhq.org
www.crnhq.org

Belgium

Belgian Centre for Arbitration and Mediation
Contact CEPANI
rue des Sols 8 Stuiversstraat
B-1000 Brussels, BELGIUM
+32 2 515 08 35
www.cepani.be/

Bulgaria

Open Education Centre
Dobromir Hriz str.31
Sofia, 1124 BULGARIA
(359 2) 943 37 15; fax (359 2)943 3715
osfoem@bgcict.bitnet

Canada

Alberta Arbitration and Mediation Society (AAMS)
#405, 10707 100th Ave.
Edmonton, AB T5J 3M1 CANADA
(780) 433–4881; fax (780) 433–9024
(800) 232–7214
aams@aams.ab.ca
www.aams.ab.ca

British Columbia Mediator Roster Society
Ministry of the Attorney General
c/o Dispute Resolution Office
P.O. Box 9280 Stn. Prov. Govt.
Victoria, BC V8W 9J7 CANADA
(250) 356–8147; fax (250) 387–1189
(888) 713–0433
mediators@mediator-roster.bc.ca
www.mediator-roster.bc.ca

ADR Institute of Canada
Suite 500, 234 Eglinton Ave. East
Toronto, ON M4P 1K5 CANADA
(416) 487–4733; fax (416) 487–4429
admin@adrcanada.ca
www.adrcanada.ca/

Canadian Bar Association, National Alternative
Dispute Resolution Section
902–50 O'Connor St.
Ottawa, ON K1P 6L2 CANADA
(613) 237–2925; fax (613) 237–0185
(800) 267–8860
info@cba.org
www.cba.org/sections/adre/

Conflict Resolution Network Canada
Conrad Grebel College
University of Waterloo
Waterloo, ON N2L 3G6 CANADA
(519) 885–0880; fax (519) 885–0806
crnetwork@crnetwork.ca
www.crnetwork.ca/

Family Mediation Manitoba (FMM)
P.O. Box 2369
Winnipeg, MB R3C 4A6 CANADA
info@fmm.winnipeg.mb.ca
www.fmm.winnipeg.mb.ca/index.html

Family Mediation Canada
528 Victoria St. North
Kitchener, ON N2H 5G1 CANADA
(519) 585–3118; fax (519) 585–3121
fmc@fmc.ca
www.fmc.ca

Ontario Association for Family Mediation
P.O. Box 752, Station B
Sudbury, ON P5E 4S1 CANADA
(800) 989–3025; fax (705) 670–0905
oafm@oafm.on.ca
www.oafm.on.ca

China

Hong Kong Mediation Council
Hong Kong International Arbitration Centre
38th Floor, Two Exchange Square
8 Connaught Place
Hong Kong S.A.R. CHINA
(852) 2525–2381; fax (852) 2524–2171
adr@hkiac.org
www.hkiac.com

Denmark

Conflict Transformation Service
Albertslundvej 13
DK-2620 Albertslund/Copenhagen DENMARK
+45 2972 5435; fax +45 4366 1362
www.conflicttransform.org

Germany

Berghof Research Center for Constructive Conflict Management
Altensteinstrasse 48a
D-14195 Berlin GERMANY
+49 (30) 844 1540; fax +49 (30) 844 15499
info@berghof-center.org
www.berghof-center.org

Bundesverband für Familienmediation
c/o Dr. Hans Georg Maehler
Südliche Auffahrtsallee 57
D-80639 München GERMANY

German Platform for Peaceful Conflict Management
Hauptstr. 35
555491 Wahlenau GERMANY
+49 (6543) 980 096; fax +49 (6543) 500 636
www.konflictbearbeitung.net

Great Britain

Mediation UK
Alexander House
Telephone Avenue
Bristol BS1 4BS ENGLAND
(0117) 904 6661; fax (0117) 904 3331
enquiry@mediationuk.org.uk
www.mediationuk.org.uk/contact.htm

Indonesia

Indonesia Center for Environmental Law
Jl. Kerinci IX / 24, Kebayoran Baru
Jakarta, 12120 INDONESIA
+62 (21) 739–4432; fax +62 (21) 726–9331
icel@indosat.net.id
www.nrm.or.id/Content/NGO/ICEL.htm

Ireland

Mediators Institute Ireland
72 Beechpark Rd., Foxrock
Dublin 18 IRELAND
01 6618488
info@mediatorsinstituteireland.ie
www.mediatorsinstituteireland.ie

Italy

Centro Italiano per la Promozione della Mediazione
Via Gonin 8
20047 Milan ITALY
02/4830293739
www.mediazionesociale.com

Japan

Japan Center for Conflict Prevention
2–17–12–803 Akasaka Minato-Ku
Tokyo 107–0052 JAPAN
81-(0)3–3584–7457; fax 81-(0)3–3584–7528
tokyo@jccp.gr.jp
www.jccp.gr.jp

Kenya

Africa Peace Forum (APFO)
P.O. Box 63078
Nairobi KENYA
+254 (2) 574 092/6; fax +254 (2) 561 357
kilenem@users.aftricaonline.co.ke

Nairobi Peace Initiative
P.O. Box 14894
Nairobi KENYA
254(2) 441–444; fax 254(2) 442–533/445 177/440098
npi@africaonline.co.ke
www.unoy.org/ANWK_org_Kenya_Nairobi%20Peace%
20Initiative.htm

Kyrgyzstan

Foundation for Tolerance International (FTI)
Appt. 8 16 Orozbekova St.
Bishkek 720040 KYRGYZSTAN
+996 (312) 222 233/223 390/661 615; fax 996 (312) 222 233
Fti@infotel.kg

Lebanon

Center for Conflict Management (CCM)
Box 55215
Beirut LEBANON
+961 (1) 490 561; fax +961 (1) 601 787
psalem@icps.org.lb

Netherlands

Nederlands Mediation Instituut (NMI)
Beaurs—World Trade Center Beursplein 37 (12e verdieping)
Postbus 30137
Rotterdam, 3001 DC NETHERLANDS
+31 (0)10–405 69 89; fax +31 (0)10–405 53 45
info@nmi-mediation.nl
www.nmi-mediation.nl

New Zealand

Arbitrators' and Mediators' Institute of New Zealand (AMINZ)
Level 3, Hallenstein House
276–278 Lambton Quay
P.O. Box 1477
Wellington NEW ZEALAND
64 4 4999 384
0800 4 AMINZ (0800 426 469)
institute@aminz.org.nz
www.aminz.org.nz

LEADR New Zealand
New Zealand Chapter Office
6th Floor, Wool House
Cnr Featherstone & Brandon Sts.
Wellington, NEW ZEALAND
(P.O. Box 10991, Wellington, NEW ZEALAND)
64–4 470 0110; fax 64–4 470 0111
leadrnz@xtra.co.nz

Northern Ireland

Institute on Conflict Resolution and Ethnicity (INCORE)
Aberfoyle House, Northland Road
Derry/Londonderry BT48 7JA NORTHERN IRELAND
+44 (28) 7137 5500; fax +44 (28) 7137 5510
incore@incore.ulst.ac.uk
www.incore.ulst.ac.uk

Mediation Network for Northern Ireland
10 Upper Crescent
Belfast BT7 1NT NORTHERN IRELAND
(+44) 028 90 438614; fax (+44) 028 90 314430
www.mediation-network.org.uk/

Peru

Peruvian Institute for Resolution of Conflicts, Negotiation,
and Mediation (INPRECONM)
Apartado Postal 14–0035
Lima 14 PERU
+51 (1) 244 3728; fax +51 (1) 244 3725
iromachea@arnauta.rcp.net.po

Philippines

Gaston Z. Ortigas Peace Institute (GZOPI)
Quezon City 1108 PHILIPPINES
+63 (2) 426 6122/6001; fax +63 (2) 426 6064
peace@codewan.com.ph.gzopi@i-next.net

Senegal

Council for the Development of Social Science Research in Africa
(CODESRIA)
BP 3304
Dakar SENEGAL
(221) 825 98 14; fax (221) 824 12 89
CODESRIA@telecomplus.sn

Singapore

Community Mediation Centre
Block 161 #02–265
Ang Mo Kio Ave. 4
SINGAPORE 560161
65 553 1586; fax 65 553 0697
www.hdbhousing.com/cmc.htm

South Africa

African Center for the Constructive Resolution of Disputes
(ACCORD)
Private Bag X018
Umhlanga Rocks 4320 SOUTH AFRICA
+27 (31) 5023908; fax +27 (31) 5024160
info@accord.org.za
www.accord.org.za/web.nsf

Centre for Conflict Resolution
Private Bag
Rondebosch 7701 SOUTH AFRICA
+27 (21) 422 2512; fax +27 (21) 422 2622
mailbox@ccr.uct.ac.za
www.ccrweb.ccr.uct.ac.za

South African Association for Conflict Intervention (SAACI)
c/o Welma de Beer
41 Rhyn Ave.
Bayswater 9301 SOUTH AFRICA
27 51 311 423; 27 51 313 696

Spain

Gernika-Gogoratuz
Foru Plaza z/g
Gernika-Lumo Bizkaia 48300 SPAIN
34 4 625 3558; 34 4 625 6765

Turkey

Umut Foundation
Yildiz Posta Caddesi 52 Esentepe 80700
Istanbul TURKEY
(212) 275 76 00 (5708); fax (212) 275 76 05
www.umut.org.tr

Uganda

Center for Conflict Resolution (CECORE)
2nd Floor NIC Building
P.O. Box 5211
Kampala UGANDA
+256 (41) 255033; fax +256 (41) 234252
cecore@swiftuganda.com
www.cecore.org/contacts.html

United States and Territories

Alabama

Alabama Center for Dispute Resolution
415 Dexter Ave.
P.O. Box 671
Montgomery, AL 36101
(334) 269–1515 ext. 111; fax (334) 261–6310
alabar.org/adr/index.cfm

Alaska

Alaska Court System
820 West 4th Ave., Room 223
Anchorage, AK 99501
(907) 264–8236; fax 907–264–8291
www.state.ak.us/courts/mediat.htm

Alaska Dispute Settlement Association
P.O. Box 242922
Anchorage, AK 99524–2922
(907) 258–0624
www.adsa.ws

Alaska State Commission for Human Rights
800 A St., Suite 204
Anchorage, AK 99501–3669
(907) 276–3177; fax (907) 278–8588
www.gov.state.ak.us/aschr/aschr.htm

Arizona

Arizona Dispute Resolution Association
P.O. Box 7638
Phoenix, AZ 85011–7638
(480) 777–7562; fax (480) 649–3334
(888) 868–0979
info@azdra.org
www.azdra.org/

Arkansas

Arkansas Access and Visitation Mediation Program
625 Marshall St. Justice Building
Little Rock, AR 72201
(501) 682–9400; fax (501) 682–9410

Arkansas ADR Commission
Administrative Office of the Courts
Justice Building, 625 Marshall St.
Little Rock, AR 72201–1020
(510) 682–9400 ext. 1310; fax (510) 682–9401

California

California Academy of Mediation Professionals (CAMP)
16501 Ventura Blvd., Suite 606
Encino, CA 91436
(818) 377–7250; fax (818) 784–1836
www.conflict-resolution.net/cdrc

California Dispute Resolution Council
760 Market St., Suite 516
San Francisco, CA 94102–2406
(866) 285–6500; fax (866) 285–6600
cdrc@pachbell.net

Central California Dispute Resolution Association (CCDRA)
1717 South Chestnut Ave.
Fresno, CA 93702
(209) 455–5842; fax (209) 252–4800
ccdra@fresno.edu
www.fresno.edu/dept/pacs/ccdra/

Northern California Mediation Association
P.O. Box 544
Corte Madera, CA 94976
(650) 745–3842; fax (650) 745–3842
adr@admc.org
www.mediators-ncma.org

Southern California Mediation Association
195 South "C" St., Suite #250
Tustin, CA 92680
(877) 963–3428; fax (714) 669–9341
scma@scmediation.org
www.scmediation.org

Western Justice Center Foundation
85 South Grand Ave.
Pasadena, CA 91105
(626) 584–7494; fax (626) 568–8223
info@westernjustice.org
www.wjcf.org

Colorado

Colorado Council of Mediators (CCMO)
PMB 115
3100 South Sheridan Blvd., Suite 1C
Denver, CO 80227
(303) 322–9275; (800) 864–4317
ccmo@coloradomediation.org
www.coloradomediation.org

Office of Dispute Resolution
Colorado Judicial Department
1301 Pennsylvania St., Suite 110
Denver, CO 80203–2416
(303) 837–3667; fax (303) 837–2340
www.court.no/.org/odr/

Connecticut

Connecticut Council for Divorce Mediation
731 Hebcon Ave.
Glastonbury, CT 06033
(860) 633–5122; fax (860) 657–8241
(888) 236–2236
info@ctmediators.org
www.ctmediators.org

Delaware

Delaware Federation for Dispute Resolution
P.O. Box 2703
Newark, DE 19805
(302) 737–5395

Florida

Florida Academy of Professional Mediators
P.O. Box 488
Archer, FL 23618–0488
(800) 808–8494; fax (352) 373–6515
info@tfapm.org
www.tfapm.org/indx.shtml/

Florida Association of Professional Family Mediators (FAPFM)
P.O. Box 140249
Coral Gables, FL 33114–0249
(305) 442–6946; fax (305) 442–6946
fleischerj@igc.org

Florida Conflict Resolution Consortium (FCRC)
Shaw Building, Suite 132
2031 East Paul Dirac Dr.
Tallahassee, FL 32310
(850) 644–6320; fax (850) 644–4968
http://consensus.fsu.edu/

Florida Dispute Resolution Center
Supreme Court Building
500 South Duval St.
Tallahassee, FL 32399–1905
(850) 921–2910; fax (850) 922–9290
www.flcourts.org/osca/divisions/adr/brochure.html

Georgia

Georgia Office of Dispute Resolution
Supreme Court of Georgia
244 Washington St. S.W., Suite 423
Atlanta, GA 30334–5900
(404) 463–3788; fax (404) 463–3790
gaodr@mindspring.com
www.state.ga.us/courts/adr/adrhome.htm

Governor's Office of Georgia Human Relations
2 Martin Luther King Jr. Dr.
Suite 1306, West Tower
Atlanta, GA 30334
(404) 463–2500; fax (404) 463–2508

Hawaii

Ali'iolani Hale
417 South King St., Room 207
Honolulu, HI 96813-4769
(808) 539–4237; fax (808) 539–4416
www.courts.state.hi.us/page

State Judiciary of Hawaii
Center for Alternative Dispute Resolution
417 South King Street, Room 207
Honolulu, HI 96837-4769
(808) 539–4241; fax (808) 539–4985

Idaho

Idaho Mediation Association
P.O. Box 2504
Boise, ID 83701
(208) 238–0942; fax (208) 344–0758
adminstrator@idahomediation.org
www.idahomediation.org

Idaho Supreme Court
Supreme Court Building
451 W. State St.
Boise, ID 83702–6057
(208) 334–2246; fax (208) 334–2146
www2.state.id.us/cao/service.asp?service_id=3

Illinois

Center for Analysis of Alternative Dispute Resolution Systems
11 East Adams, Suite 500
Chicago, IL 60603
(312) 922–6475; fax (312) 922–6763
caadrs@caadrs.org
www.caadrs.org

Mediation Council of Illinois
60 B Terra Cotta Ave.
PMB 146
Crystal Lake, IL 60014
(312) 641–3000
www.mediationillinois.org

Indiana

Indiana Association of Mediators (IAM)
6526 Ralston Ave.
Indianapolis, IN 46220
(317) 571–0260
(800) 571–0260
www.mediation-indiana.org

Iowa

Iowa Association for Dispute Resolution
P.O. Box 3193
Iowa City, IA 52240–3193
(319) 358–6690

Iowa Peace Institute
P.O. Box 480
Grinnell, IA 50112
(641) 236–4880; fax (641) 236–6905
iapeace@netins.net
www.iapeace.org

Office of the Attorney General
Hoover State Office Building
Des Moines, IA 50319
(515) 281–5166; fax (515) 281–6771

Kansas

Office of State Long-Term Care Ombudsman
610 S.W. 10th St., 2nd Floor
Topeka, KS 66612–1616
(785) 296–3017; fax (785) 296–3916

Kentucky

Kentucky Personnel Cabinet Division of Communication and
Recognition
Kentucky Employee Mediation Program
200 Fair Oaks Lane, Suite 511
Frankfort, KY 40601
(502) 564–3433; fax (502) 564–4311
personnel.ky.gov/kemp.htm

Mediation Association of Kentucky
P.O. Box 1641
Frankfort, KY 40602–1641
(502) 581–1961

Natural Resources Environmental Protection Cabinet
Office of Administrative Hearings
35–36 Fountain Place
Frankfort, KY 40601
(502) 564–7312; fax (502) 564–4973
www.nr.state.ky.us/nrepc/hearings/guide.htm#16

Maine

Court ADR Service
147 New Meadows Rd.
West Bath, ME 04530
(207) 442–0227; fax (207) 422–0228

Maine State Bar Association ADR Section
P.O. Box 788
Augusta, ME 04332–0788
(207) 622–7523; fax (207) 623–0085
info@mainebar.org

Office of the Attorney General
Consumer Complaints ADR
Station 6, State House
Augusta, ME 04333
(207) 626–8800; fax (207) 626–8865

Maryland

Maryland Alternative Dispute Resolution Commission
113 Towsontown Blvd., Suite C
Towson, MD 21286
(410) 321–3298; fax (410) 321–2399
www.courts.state.md.us

Maryland Society of Professional Family Mediators
211 Massbury St.
Gaithersburg, MD 20878
(301) 947–0500; fax (301) 947–0501
info@familymediator.com
www.familymediator.com

Mediation and Conflict Resolution Office for the State of Maryland
113 Towsontown Blvd., Suite C
Towson, MD 21286
(410) 321–2398; fax (410) 321–2399
www.courts.state.md.us/adr.html

Massachusetts

Massachusetts Association of Mediation Practitioners and Programs
(MAMPP)
133 Federal St., 11th Floor
Boston, MA 02110
(617) 451–2093; fax (617) 451–0763
info@mampporg
www.mampp.org

Massachusetts Council on Family Mediation (MCFM)
23 Parker Rd.
Needham Heights, MA 02194–2001
(781) 449–4430
mcfm23@aol.com
www.mcfm.org

Massachusetts Office of Dispute Resolution (MODR)
One Asburton Place, Room 501
Boston, MA 02108
(617) 727–2224; fax (617) 727–6495
www.state.ma.us/modr/

Office of the Attorney General
Mediation Services Department
One Ashburton Place
Boston, MA 02108
(617) 727–2200 ext. 2916; fax (617) 727–5762

Michigan

Michigan Council for Family and Divorce Mediation
489 Berrypatch La.
White Lake, MI 48386
(248) 698–7921; (800) 827–4390
www.familymediation.com

Michigan Supreme Court
Office of Dispute Resolution
P.O. Box 30048
Lansing, MI 48909–7548
(517) 373–4839; fax (517) 373–8922
www.courts.michigan.gov/scao/dispute/odr.htm

State Court Administrative Office
Office of Dispute Resolution
Box 30048
Lansing, MI 48909
(517) 373–8922; fax (517) 373–8922
courts.michigan.gov/scao/dispute/odr.htm

Minnesota

Division of Alternative Dispute Resolution
340 Centennial Office Building
St. Paul, MN 55155
(651) 296–2633; fax (651) 282–6396
www.mnadr.state.mn.us

Minnesota Office of Dispute Resolution
340 Centennial Office Building
658 Cedar St.
St. Paul, MN 55155
(651) 296–2633; fax (651) 297–7200
mnodr@igc.apc.org
www.bms.state.mn.us/office_of_dispute_resolution

Missouri

Association of Missouri Mediators
P.O. Box 67
Liberty, MO 64069
(816) 792–7681
www.mediate.com/amm/

Mississippi

Office of the Attorney General
Department of Justice
P.O. Box 220
Jackson, MS 39205–0220
(601) 359–4209; fax (601) 359–3441

Nebraska

Office of Dispute Resolution
State Capitol Building, Room 1220
P.O. Box 98910
Lincoln, NE 68509–8910
(402) 471–3148; fax (402) 471–2197

Nevada

Mediators of Southern Nevada
333 N. Rancho Dr., #144
Las Vegas, NV 89106
(702) 631–2790; fax (702) 646–3412
mediatorsonv.com

Nevada Supreme Court
Civil Settlement Conference Program
201 South Carson St., Suite 201
Carson City, NV 89701–4702
(775) 684–1600; fax (775) 684–1601

New Hampshire

New Hampshire Court ADR Program
Superior Court ADR Committee
22 Main St.
Newport, NH 03773
(603) 863–3450; fax (603) 863–3204

New Hampshire Mediators Association
P.O. Box 7228
Concord, NH 03301–7228
NHmediator@aol.com

New Jersey

New Jersey Association of Professional Mediators (NJAPM)
203 Towne Center Dr.
Hillsborough, NJ 08844–4693
(908) 359–1184; fax (908) 359–7619
(800) 981–4800
info@njapm.org
www.njapm.org

Office of Dispute Settlement
25 Market St.
P.O. Box 850
Trenton, NJ 08625
(609) 292–7686; fax (609) 292–6292

New Mexico

New Mexico Mediation Association
P.O. Box 82384
Albuquerque, NM 87198
(505) 881–1141
www.lobo.net/~ergo/mediate/nmma000.htm

New York

New York Family and Divorce Mediation
Council of Greater New York
114 West 47th St., Suite 2200
New York, NY 10036
(212) 978–8590; fax (212) 242–0944
www.fdmcgny.org

New York State Council on Divorce Mediation
685 Stewart Ave.
Garden City, NY 11530
(800) 894–2646; fax (516) 745–5745
questions@nysmediate.org
www.nysmediate.org

New York State Dispute Resolution Association
182-A Washington Ave.
Albany, NY 12210
(518) 465–2500; fax (518) 465–0840
nysdra@nysdra.org
www.nysdra.org

New York State Unified Court System
Division of Court Operations—Office of ADR Programs
25 Beaver St., Room 859B
New York, NY 10004
(212) 428–2863; fax (212) 428–2696

North Carolina

Mediation Network of North Carolina
4208 Six Forks Rd., Suite 305
Raleigh, NC 27609
(919) 783–8483; fax (919) 783–8478
mnnc@mnnnc.org
www.mnnc.org

North Carolina Dispute Resolution Commission
1100 Navaho Dr., Suite 126
P.O. Box 2448
Raleigh, NC 27602
(919) 981–5077; fax (919) 981–5048

North Dakota

Conflict Resolution Center—UND
314 Cambridge St.
P.O. Box 8009
Grand Forks, ND 58202–8009
(701) 777–3664; fax (701) 777–6184
conflictresolution@und.nodak.edu
www.und.nodak.edu/dept/crc

Ohio

Ohio Commission on Dispute Resolution
and Conflict Management
77 South High St., 24th Floor
Columbus, OH 43215–6108
(614) 752–9595; fax (614) 752–9682
www.state.oh.us/cdr

Ohio Mediation Association
25 West Jefferson St.
Jefferson, OH 44047
(440) 576–3628; fax (440) 576–4639
www.mediateohio.org

Oklahoma

Oklahoma Academy of Mediators and Arbitrators (OAMA)
10435 South Sandusky
Tulsa, OK 74137–6242
(877) 508–6262
www.oama.org

Administrative Office of the Courts
1915 North Stiles, Suite 305
Oklahoma City, OK 73105
(405) 521–2450; fax (405) 521–6815

Oklahoma Victim Restitution/Juvenile Offender
Responsibility Program
P.O. Box 268812
3814 North Santa Fe
Oklahoma City, OK 73126–8812
(405) 530–2867; fax (405) 530–2800

Oregon

National Policy Consensus Center
Portland State University
P.O. Box 751
Portland, OR 97207–0751
(503) 725–9077
www.policyconsensus.org

Oregon Dispute Resolution Commission
1201 Court St., N.E., Suite 305
Salem, OR 97310
(503) 378–2877; fax (503) 373–0794
odrc.mail@state.or.us

Oregon Dispute Resolution Steering Committee
National Policy Consensus Center
P.O. Box 751
Portland, OR 97207–0751
(503) 725–9077

Oregon Judicial Department
Court Community Justice Services Division
Office of the State Court Administrator
1163 State St.
Salem, OR 97310
(503) 986–5935; fax (503) 986–6419

Oregon Mediation Association (OMA)
P.O. Box 2952
Portland, OR 97208–2952
(503) 872–9775; fax (503) 236–2973
omediate@teleport.com
www.omediate.org

Pennsylvania

Pennsylvania Council of Mediators
414 Barclay Rd.
Rosemont, PA 19010
(800) 861–9292
www.pamediation.org

Pennsylvania Public Utility Commission
Office of Administrative Law Judge
P.O. Box 3265
Harrisburg, PA 17105–3265
(717) 783–5428; fax (717) 787–0481

Pennsylvania Department of Corrections
Office of the Victim Advocate Mediation Program
for Victims of Violent Crime
P.O. Box 598
Camp Hill, PA 17001–0598
(717) 731–7060

Pennsylvania Department of Environmental Protection
Training and ADR Services Division, Bureau of Personnel
400 Market St., 2nd Floor RCSOB
P.O. Box 2357
Harrisburg, PA 17105–2357
(717) 783–5787; fax (717) 787–2938

Puerto Rico

Interventores Neutrales de Puerto Rico
(787) 873–6010
edjd@hotmail.com

Rhode Island

Department of Environmental Management
Administrative Adjudication Department
235 Promenade St., 3rd Floor
Providence, RI 02908
(401) 222–1357 ext. 4800; fax (401) 222–1398
www.state.ri.us/dem/programs/director/adminadj/
mediate/index.htm

Rhode Island Council of Family Mediators
500 Prospect St.
Pawtucket, RI 02903
(401) 463–9800; fax (401) 463–5907

South Carolina

Low Country Mediation Network
P.O. Box 1404
Charleston, SC 29402
(843) 727–6202; fax (843) 723–0420
brmelton@world.net.att.net

Office of Human Resources
South Carolina Statewide Mediators Pool
1201 Main St., Suite 1000
Columbia, SC 29201
(803) 737–0900

South Carolina Council for Conflict Resolution (SCCCR)
4630 North Main St.
Columbia, SC 29203
(803) 735–7150; fax (803) 735–3112
(888) 722–4030
info@scmediate.org
www.scmediate.org

Texas

Office of Administrative Hearings
300 West 15th St., Suite 502
Austin, TX 78701
(512) 858–7793

Texas Association of Mediators
P.O. Box 191208
Dallas, TX 75219–1208
www.txmediator.org

Texas Commission on Environmental Quality
Alternative Dispute Resolution Office
P.O. Box 13087
Austin, TX 78711
(512) 239–4010; fax (512) 239–4015

Utah

Administrative Office of the Courts
P.O. Box 140241
Salt Lake City, UT 84114–0241
(801) 578–3982; fax (801) 578–3843
courtlink.utcourts.gov/mediation/index.htm

Utah ADR Program
Administrative Office of the Courts
P.O. Box 140241
Salt Lake City, UT 84114–0241
(801) 578–3984; fax (801) 578–3843
www.courtlink.utcourts.gov/mediation/adr.htm

Vermont

Human Rights Commission
135 State St., Drawer 33
Montpelier, VT 05633–6301
(802) 828–2480; fax (802) 828–2481
www.hrc.state.vt.us/mediation.htm

Vermont Family Court Mediation Program
7 Mahady Ct.
Middlebury, VT 05357
(802) 388–5764
(800) 622–6359 (VT number)
vfcmp@mail.state.vt.us
www.state.vt.us/courts/vt_mediation

Virgin Islands

Virgin Islands Mediation Service
2118 Company St.
Christiansted, St. Croix VI 00820 VIRGIN ISLANDS
(340) 773–3031 Fax: (340) 773–3950

Virginia

Central Virginia Mediation Network
2246 Oak Bay La.
Richmond, VA 23233–3541
(804) 646–3451

Department of Employment Dispute Resolution
One Capitol Square
830 E. Main St., Suite 400
Richmond, VA 23219
(804) 786–7994; fax (804) 786–0100
cfarr@EDR.state.va.us
www.edr.state.va.us

Supreme Court of Virginia
Department of Dispute Resolution
100 North Ninth St.
Richmond, VA 23219
(804) 786–6455; fax (804) 786–4760

Virginia Mediation Network
8001 Franklin Farms Dr., Suite 120
Richmond, VA 23229
(804) 285–3373; fax (804) 285–3377
(888) 506–4VMN
Office@vamediation.org
www.vamediation.org

Washington

Christian Mediation Service
2612 North Bristol St.
Tacoma, WA 98407
(253) 475–2388
www.projectredemption.orf/cms.htm

Department of Health
Office of Professional Standards
P.O. Box 47879
Olympia, WA 98504–7879
(206) 389–2600; fax (360) 236–4677

Environmental Hearings Office
P.O. Box 40903
Olympia, WA 98504–0903
(360) 493–9223
www.eho.wa.gov/default2.asp?Page=mediatio.htm

Office of Community Development
Growth Management Division
P.O. Box 48300
Olympia, WA 98504–8300
(360) 725–3056

Office of the Attorney General
P.O. Box 40100
Olympia, WA 98504–0100
(360) 664–2475; fax (360) 586–7671

Washington Mediation Association
1122 East Pike St., PMB #1095
Seattle, WA 98122–3934
(206) 262–0600
www.washingtonmediation.org

Wisconsin

Wisconsin Association of Mediators
P.O. Box 44578
Madison, WI 53744–4578
(608) 848–1970; fax (608) 848–9266
wam@mailbag.com
www.wamediators.org

Wisconsin Department of Natural Resources
101 South Webster St.
Madison, WI 53707
(608) 267–7151

PROFESSIONAL JOURNALS

Arbitration and Mediation Institute Journal
ADR Institute of Canada
Suite 500, 234 Eglinton Ave. East
Toronto, ON M4P 1K5 CANADA
(416) 487–4733; fax (416) 487–4429
admin@adrcanada.ca
www.adrcnada.ca/

Canadian Arbitration and Mediation Journal
Arbitration and Mediation Institute of Canada
P.O. Box 462, Station U
Toronto, ON M8Z 5Y8 CANADA
(416) 849–8993

Conflict Resolution Quarterly
Wiley Subscription Services
Jossey-Bass Publishers
989 Market St.
San Francisco, CA 94103–1741
(888) 378–2537

Journal of Dispute Resolution
University of Missouri, Columbia
School of Law, 104 Hulston Hall
Columbia, MO 65211
(573) 882–9682
umclawjournal@missouri.edu
www.mail.law.missouri.edu/journal/

Negotiation Journal: On the Process of Dispute Settlement
Kluwer Academic/Plenum Publishers
233 Spring St.
New York, NY 10013–1578
(212) 620–8085; fax (212) 463–0742

Ohio State Journal on Dispute Resolution
Ohio State University
Moritz College of Law
55 West 12th Ave.
Columbus, OH 43210–1578
(614) 292–7170; fax (614) 292–3442
moritzlaw.osu.edu/jdr/

NEWSLETTERS

ACR Update
Association for Conflict Resolution
1527 New Hampshire Ave., N.W.
Washington, DC 20036
(202) 667–9700; fax (202) 265–1968
www.acresolution.org

Conciliation Quarterly Newsletter
Mennonite Central Committee
21 S. 12th St.
P.O. Box 500
Akron, PA 17501–0500
(717) 859–3889 ext. 112
www.mcc.org/us/peaceandjustice/mcs

Dispute Resolution
American Bar Association
Section of Dispute Resolution
740 15th St., N.W.
Washington, DC 20036
(202) 662–1680

Florida Growth Management
Florida Conflict Resolution Consortium
Shaw Building, STE 132
2031 East Paul Dirac Dr.
Tallahassee, FL 32310
(850) 644–6320; fax (850) 644–4968
flacrc@mailer.fsu.edu
http://consensus.fsu.edu/LeADRship_Letters/
leadrship_sep02.html

Interaction
Conflict Resolution Network Canada
Conrad Grebel College
University of Waterloo
Waterloo, ON N2L 3G6 CANADA
(519) 885–0880; fax (519) 885–0806
crnetwork@crnetwork.ca
www.nicr.ca/about/index.asp

The Mediator
Mediation Development Association of British Columbia
P.O. Box 2309
Vancouver, BC V6B-3Y4 CANADA
(604) 241–1460

TRAINING RESOURCES

CDR Associates
100 Arapahoe Ave., Suite 12
Boulder, CO 80302
(303) 442–7367; fax (303) 442–7442
(800) MEDIATE

References

"AAA Designs ADR Insurance Procedures." *Dispute Resolution*, 1984, *13*, 12.

Acland, A. *A Sudden Outbreak of Common Sense: Managing Conflict Through Mediation*. London: Hutchinson, 1990.

Adler, R., Rosen, B., and Silverstein, E., "Emotions in Negotiation: How to Manage Fear and Anger." *Negotiation Journal*, 1998, *14*(2), 161–179.

"Administrative Dispute Resolution Act." *Federal Register*, Jan. 23, 1990.

Afzal, M. "Community-Based Conflict Resolution (Pakistan Experience)." In C. Pe, G. Sosmeña, and A. Tadiar (eds.), *Transcultural Mediation in the Asia-Pacific*. Manila, Philippines: Asia-Pacific Organization for Mediators, 1988.

Aiken, M., and Mott, P. "Locating Centers of Power." In M. Aiken and P. Mott (eds.), *The Structure of Community Power*. New York: Random House, 1970.

All African Conference on African Principles of Conflict Resolution and Reconciliation, United Nations Conference Center, Addis Ababa, Ethiopia, November 8–12, 1999.

American Arbitration Association. *An Overview of Mediation*. New York: American Arbitration Association, n.d.

Aminuddin, M. *Malaysian Industrial Relations*. New York: McGraw-Hill, 1990.

Anacona, D., Friedman, R., and Kolb, D. "The Group and What Happens on the Way to 'Yes.'" *Negotiation Journal*, 1991, 7(2), 155–173.

Antoun, R. *Arab Village*. Bloomington: Indiana University Press, 1972.

Araki, C. "Dispute Management in the Schools." *Mediation Quarterly*, 1990, *8*(1), 51–62.

Argyris, C. *Intervention Theory and Method: A Behavioral Science View*. Reading, Mass.: Addison-Wesley, 1970.

Aryal, L. "Mediation in Nepal." In C. Pe, G. Sosmeña, and A. Tadiar (eds.), *Transcultural Mediation in the Asia-Pacific*. Manila, Philippines: Asia-Pacific Organization for Mediators, 1988.

Assefa, H. "The Politics of Reconciliation." *Track Two,* 1994, *3*(4), 1–7.

Aubert, V. "Competition and Dissensus: Two Types of Conflict and Conflict Resolution." *Journal of Conflict Resolution,* 1963, *7*(1), 26–42.

Auerbach, J. *Justice Without Law: Resolving Disputes Without Lawyers.* New York: Oxford University Press, 1983.

Augsburger, D. *Conflict Mediation Across Cultures.* Louisville, Ky.: Westminster/John Knox Press, 1992.

Ayendo, B., and others. *When You Are the Peacebuilder.* Harrisonburg, Va.: Conflict Transformation Program, Eastern Mennonite University, 2001.

Bach, G., and Goldberg, H. *Creative Aggression: The Art of Assertive Living.* New York: Doubleday, 1974.

Bacow, L., and Wheeler, M. *Environmental Dispute Resolution.* New York: Plenum Press, 1984.

Bagozzi, R., and Dholakia, R. "Mediational Mechanisms in Interorganizational Conflict." In D. Druckman (ed.), *Negotiations: Social Psychological Perspectives.* Thousand Oaks, Calif.: Sage, 1977.

Baldwin, P. (ed.). *Environmental Mediation: An Effective Alternative?* Palo Alto, Calif.: RESOLVE, Center for Environmental Conflict Resolution, 1978.

Barnes, B. E. "Conflict Resolution Across Cultures: A Hawaii Perspective and a Pacific Mediation Model." *Mediation Quarterly,* 1994, *12*(2), 117–133.

Barnes, B. "Building Conflict Resolution in Infrastructure in the Central and South Pacific: Indigenous Populations and Conflicts with Governments." *Conflict Resolution Quarterly,* 2002, *19,* 345–361.

Barsky, A. "Issues in the Termination of Mediation Due to Abuse." *Mediation Quarterly,* 1995, *13*(1), 19–35.

Batton, J. "Institutionalizing Conflict Resolution: The Ohio Model." *Conflict Resolution Quarterly,* 2002, *19*(4), 479–494.

Bazerman, M., and Lewicki, R. (eds.). *Negotiating in Organizations.* Thousand Oaks, Calif.: Sage, 1983.

Behn, R., and Vaupel, J. *Quick Analysis for Busy Decision Makers.* New York: Basic Books, 1982.

Bellman, H. "Mediation as an Approach to Resolving Environmental Disputes." In *Proceedings of the Environmental Conflict Management Practitioners Workshop.* Florissant, Colo., October 1982.

Bellows, G., and Moulton, B. "Assessment: Framing the Choices." In G. Bellows and B. Moulton (eds.), *The Lawyering Process.* Mineola, N.Y.: Foundation Press, 1981.

Benjamin, M., and Irving, H. "Research in Family Mediation: Review and Implications." *Mediation Quarterly,* 1995, *13*(1), 53–82.

Berger, P., and Luckmann, T. *The Social Construction of Reality: A Treatise on the Sociology of Knowledge.* New York: Doubleday, 1967.

Berkowitz, L. "Stimulus/Response: The Case for Bottling Up Rage." *Psychology Today*, 1973, *7*(2), 24–31.

Bernard, S., Folger, J., Weingarten, H., and Zumeta, Z. "The Neutral Mediator: Value Dilemmas in Divorce Mediation." *Mediation Quarterly*, 1984, no. 4, 61–74.

Bethel, C. "The Use of Separate Sessions in Family Mediation." *Negotiation Journal*, 1986, *2*(3), 257–271.

Bianchi, H. "Returning Conflict to the Community: The Alternative of Privatization." Unpublished manuscript, Amsterdam, Netherlands, 1978.

Biddle, A., and others. *Corporate Dispute Management 1982*. New York: Bender, 1982.

Bingham, G. "Does Negotiation Hold a Promise for Regulatory Reform?" *Resolve*, 1981, *10*, 1–8.

Bingham, G. *Resolving Environmental Disputes: A Decade of Experience*. Washington, D.C.: Conservation Foundation, 1984.

Blake, R., and Mouton, J. S. "Union Management Relations: From Conflict to Collaboration." *Personnel*, 1961, *38*, 38–51.

Blake, R., and Mouton, J. S. *Solving Costly Organizational Conflicts: Achieving Intergroup Trust, Cooperation, and Teamwork*. San Francisco: Jossey-Bass, 1984.

Blake, R., Mouton, J., and Sloma, R. "The Union-Management Intergroup Laboratory: Strategy for Resolving Intergroup Conflict." In W. Bennis and others (eds.), *The Planning of Change*. Austin, Tex.: Holt, Rinehart & Winston, 1961.

Blake, R., Shepard, H., and Mouton, J. *Managing Intergroup Conflict in Industry*. Houston: Gulf, 1964.

Bluehouse, P., and Zion, J. "Hozhooji Naat'aanii: The Navajo Justice and Harmony Ceremony." *Mediation Quarterly*, 1993, *10*(4), 321–325.

Bonner, M. *Group Dynamics*. New York: Ronald Press, 1959.

Boulding, K. *Conflict and Defense*. New York: HarperCollins, 1962.

Bowling, D., and Hoffman, D. "Bringing Peace into the Room: The Personal Qualities of the Mediator and Their Impact on Mediation." *Negotiation Journal*, 2000, *16*(1), 5–28.

Bradley, S., and Smith, M. (eds.). *Community Mediation: Past and Future*. *Mediation Quarterly*, 2000, *17*(4).

Brett, J. "Negotiating Group Decisions." *Negotiation Journal*, 1991, 7(3), 291–310.

Brett, J., and Goldberg, S. "Mediator Advisors: A New Third Party Role." In M. Bazerman and R. Lewicki (eds.), *Negotiating in Organizations*. Thousand Oaks, Calif.: Sage, 1983.

Bronstein, R. "Mediation and the Colorado Lawyer." *Colorado Lawyer*, 1982, *11*(9), 315–323.

Brookmire, D., and Sistrunk, F. "The Effects of Perceived Ability and

Impartiality of Mediators and Time Pressure on Negotiation." *Journal of Conflict Resolution,* 1980, *24*(2), 311–327.

Brown, B. "Face Saving and Face Restoration in Negotiation." In D. Druckman (ed.), *Negotiations: Social Psychological Perspectives.* Thousand Oaks, Calif.: Sage, 1977.

Brown, D. "Divorce and Family Mediation: History, Review, Future Directions." *Conciliation Courts Review,* 1982, *20*(2), 1–37.

Brown, L. D. *Managing Conflict of Organizational Interfaces.* Reading, Mass.: Addison-Wesley, 1983.

Brown, L. M. *How to Negotiate a Successful Contract.* Upper Saddle River, N.J.: Prentice Hall, 1955.

Brown, M. (ed.). *Ethnic Conflict and International Security.* Princeton: Princeton University Press, 1993.

Burgess, H. *The Foothills Water Treatment Project: A Case Study in Environmental Mediation.* Cambridge: Environmental Negotiation Project, Laboratory of Architecture and Planning, Massachusetts Institute of Technology, 1980.

Burrell, N. A., and Vogl, S. M. "Turf-Side Conflict Mediation for Students." *Mediation Quarterly,* 1990, *7*(3), 237–250.

Burton, J. *Conflict and Communication: The Use of Controlled Communication in International Relations.* London: Macmillan, 1969.

Bush, R., and Folger, J. *The Promise of Mediation: Responding to Conflict Through Empowerment and Recognition.* San Francisco: Jossey-Bass, 1994.

Calhoun, P., and Smith, W. "Integrative Bargaining: Does Gender Make a Difference?" *International Journal of Conflict Management,* 1999, *10,* 203–224.

Campbell, A. "Mediation of Children Issues When One parent Is Gay: A Cultural Perspective." *Mediation Quarterly,* 1996, *19,* 79–88.

Carpenter, S., and Kennedy, J. "Information Sharing and Conciliation: Tools for Environmental Conflict Management." *Environmental Comment,* 1977, 22–23.

Carpenter, S., and Kennedy, J. "Conflict Anticipation: A Site Specific Approach for Managing Environmental Conflict." Paper presented at fall meeting of the Society for Mining Engineers of AIME, Tucson, Ariz., Oct. 1979.

Carter, J. *Keeping the Faith: Memoirs of a President.* New York: Bantam Books, 1982.

CDR Associates. *Designing Dispute Resolution Systems.* Boulder, Colo.: CDR Associates, 1992.

CDR Associates. "Dispute Resolution and School Restructuring Project." (Report to National Institute for Dispute Resolution.) Boulder, Colo.: CDR Associates, 1993a.

CDR Associates. *Wolf summit materials.* Boulder, Colo.: CDR Associates, 1993b.

CDR Associates. *Furbearer dialogue materials.* Boulder, Colo.: CDR Associates, 1995.

Chandler, J. P. (ed.). *Teachings of Mahatma Gandhi.* Lahore, India: Indian Printing Works, 1945.

Cialdini, R. Influence: *Science and Practice.* (4th ed.) Boston: Allyn & Bacon, 2001.

Civil Rights Act, Title X. *U.S. Code,* vol. 42, sec. 2000, 1964.

Clark, P., and Cummings, F. "Selecting an Environmental Conflict Management Strategy." In P. Marcus and W. Emrich (eds.), *Working Papers in Conflict Management.* New York: American Arbitration Association, 1981.

Clark-McGlennon Associates. *Patuxent-River Cleanup Agreement.* Boston: Clark-McGlennon Associates, 1982.

Cloke, K. *Mediation: Revenge and the Magic of Forgiveness.* Santa Monica, Calif.: Center for Dispute Resolution, 1994.

Cloke, K., and Goldsmith, J. *Resolving Personal and Organizational Conflict.* San Francisco: Jossey-Bass, 2000.

Cloke, K., and Goldsmith, J. *Resolving Conflicts at Work.* San Francisco: Jossey-Bass, 2001.

Coates, R., and Gehm, J. "Victim Meets Offender: An Evaluation of Victim-Offender Reconciliation Programs." In M. Wright and B. Galaway (eds.), *Mediation and Criminal Justice.* London: Sage, 1989.

Cohen, A., and Smith, R. "The Critical-Incident Approach to Leadership Intervention in Training Groups." In W. Dyer (ed.), *Modern Theory and Method in Group Training.* New York: Van Nostrand Reinhold, 1972.

Cohen, H. *You Can Negotiate Anything.* Secaucus, N.J.: Lyle Stuart, 1980.

Colosi, T., and Berkeley, A. "The Negotiating Table: Bridging Troubled Waters." Unpublished manuscript, American Arbitration Association, Washington, D.C., 1980.

Comaroff, J., and Roberts, S. *Rules and Processes: The Cultural Logic of Dispute in an African Context.* Chicago: University of Chicago Press, 1981.

Comeau, E. "Procedural Controls in Public Sector Domestic Relations Mediation." In H. Davidson and others (eds.), *Alternative Means of Family Dispute Resolution.* Washington, D.C.: American Bar Association, 1982.

Compton, R. "Discovering the Promise of Curriculum Integration: The National Curriculum Integration Project." *Conflict Resolution Quarter,* 2002, *19*(4), 447–464.

Connors, J. "Resolving Disputes Locally in Rural Alaska." *Mediation Quarterly,* 1993, *10*(4), 367–385.

Constantino, C., and Merchant, C. S. *Designing Conflict Management Systems: A Guide to Creating Productive and Healthy Organizations.* San Francisco: Jossey-Bass, 1995.

Coogler, O. J. *Structured Mediation in Divorce Settlement.* Lexington, Mass.: Lexington Books, 1978.

Cook, J., Rochl, J., and Shepard, D. *Executive Summary Final Report.* Washington, D.C.: Neighborhood Justice Field Institute, U.S. Department of Justice, 1980.

Coover, V., Deacon, E., Esser, C., and Moore, C. W. *Resource Manual for a Living Revolution.* Philadelphia: New Society, 1977.

Corcoran, K., and Melamed, J. "From Coercion to Empowerment: Spousal Abuse and Mediation." *Mediation Quarterly,* 1990, *7*(4), 303–316.

Cormick, G. "Mediating Environmental Controversies: Perspectives and First Experience." *Earth Law Journal,* 1976, *2.*

Cormick, G. "Intervention and Self-Determination in Environmental Disputes: A Mediator's Perspective." *Resolve,* 1982, *11,* 1–7.

Cormick, G. "Strategic Issues in Structuring Multi-Party Public Policy Negotiations." *Negotiation Journal,* 1989, *5*(2), 125–132.

"Corps of Engineers Early Resolution Program." Circular 690–1–690. Washington, D.C.: Corps of Engineers, 1993.

Coser, L. *The Functions of Social Conflict.* New York: Free Press, 1956.

Coser, L. *Continuities in the Study of Social Conflict.* New York: Free Press, 1967.

Craver, C., and Barnes, D. "Gender, Risk Taking, and Negotiation Performance." *Michigan Journal on Gender and Law,* 1999, *5,* 299–352.

Creighton, J. *Communications.* Tulsa, Okla.: Synergy, 1972.

Creighton, J. "The Use of Values: Public Participation in the Planning Process." In *Public Involvement Techniques: A Reader of Ten Years Experience at the Institute of Water Resources.* (Research Report 82-R1.) Ft. Belvoir, Va.: Institute of Water Resources, May 1983.

Crohn, M. "Dispute Resolution in Higher Education." *Negotiation Journal,* 1985, *1*(4), 301–305.

Cross, J. *The Economics of Bargaining.* New York: Basic Books, 1969.

Cross, J. "Negotiation as a Learning Process." *Journal of Conflict Resolution,* 1977, *21*(4), 581–606.

Crowfoot, J. "Negotiations: An Effective Tool for Citizen Organizations?" *NRAG Papers,* 1980, *3*(4).

Curle, A. *Making Peace.* London: Tavistock, 1971.

Currie, C. "Mediators and Medical Practice Disputes." *Mediation Quarterly,* 1998, *15*(3), 215–216.

Dahl, R. *Who Governs? Democracy and Power in an American City.* New Haven, Conn.: Yale University Press, 1961.

Daily, J. "The Effects of Anger on Negotiations over Mergers and Acquisitions." *Negotiation Journal,* 1991, *7*(1), 31–39.

D'Antonio, W., Loomis, C., Form, W., and Erickson, E. "Institutional and Occupational Representations in Eleven Community Influence Systems." *American Sociological Review,* 1961, *26*(3), 440–446.

Dauer, E. "National Practitioner Data Bank: Implications for Reaching Settlement in Medical Malpractice Cases." In *Proceedings, 22nd Annual SPIDR Conference,* Dallas, 1994.

Davis, A., and Gadlin, H. "Mediators Gain Trust the Old-Fashioned Way— We Earn It!" *Negotiation Journal,* 1988, *4*(1), 55–62.

Davis, R., Tichane, M., and Grayson, D. "The Effects of Alternative Forms of Dispute Resolution on Recidivism in Felony Offenses Between Acquaintances." Unpublished manuscript, Brooklyn Dispute Resolution Center, 1980.

Delbecq, A., Vandeven, A., and Gustafson, D. *Group Techniques for Program Planning.* Glenview, Ill.: Scott, Foresman, 1975.

deLeon, L. "Using Mediation to Resolve Personnel Disputes in a State Bureaucracy." *Negotiation Journal,* 1994, *10*(1), 64–86.

Dembart, L., and Kwartler, R. "The Snoqualmie River Conflict: Bringing Mediation into Environmental Disputes." In R. Goldmann (ed.), *Roundtable Justice: Case Studies in Conflict Resolution.* Boulder, Colo.: Westview Press, 1980.

Deutsch, M. "Conflicts: Productive and Destructive." *Journal of Social Issues,* 1969, *25*(1), 7–41.

Deutsch, M. *Resolution of Conflict.* New Haven, Conn.: Yale University Press, 1974.

Dewdney, M., Sordo, B., and Chinkin, C. "Contemporary Developments in Mediation Within the Legal System and Evaluation of the 1992–93 Settlement Week Program." Sydney, Australia: Law Society of New South Wales, 1994.

Dispute Resolution Forum. Washington, D.C.: National Institute for Dispute Resolution, 1989.

Doelker, R. E., Jr. "Mediation in Academia: Practicing What We Preach." *Mediation Quarterly,* 1989, *7*(2), 157–161.

Donahue, W. *Communication, Marital Dispute, and Divorce Mediation.* Mahwah, N.J.: Erlbaum, 1991.

Douglas, A. *Industrial Peacemaking.* New York: Columbia University Press, 1962.

Downing, T. "Strategy and Tactics at the Bargaining Table." *Personnel,* 1960, *37*(1), 58–63.

Doyle, M., and Straus, D. *How to Make Meetings Work.* Chicago: Playboy Press, 1976.

Drake, W. "Statewide Offices of Mediation." *Negotiation Journal,* 1989, *5*(4), 359–364.

Dubois, R., and Mew, S. L. *The Art of Group Conversation.* New York: Association Press, 1963.

Dukes, E. F. *Reaching Higher Ground in Conflict Resolution.* San Francisco: Jossey-Bass, 2000.

Eckhoff, T. "The Mediator, the Judge, and the Administrator in Conflict Resolution." *Acta Sociologica: Scandinavian Review of Sociology,* 1966–67, *10,* 148–172.

Ehrman, J., and Lesnick, M. "The Policy Dialogue: Applying Mediation to the Policy Making Process." *Mediation Quarterly,* 1988, no. 20, 93–99.

Ellis, D., and Stuckless, N. "Pre-Separation Abuse, Marital Conflict Mediation and Post-Separation Abuse." *Mediation Quarterly,* 1992, *9*(3), 205–226.

Epstein, A. "Dispute Settlement Among the Tolai." *Oceana,* 1971, *41*(4), 157–170.

Erickson, S., and McKnight, M. "Mediating Spousal Abuse Divorces." *Mediation Quarterly,* 1990, *7*(4), 377–388.

Evans, G. *Cooperating for Peace.* St. Leonards, Australia: Allen & Unwin, 1993.

Faulkes, W. "Mediation in Australia: State of the Art 1987." In C. Pe, G. Sosmeña, and A. Tadiar (eds.), *Transcultural Mediation in the Asia-Pacific.* Manila, Philippines: Asia-Pacific Organization for Mediators, 1988.

Faulkes, W. "The Modern Development of Alternative Dispute Resolution in Australia." *Australian Dispute Resolution Journal,* 1990, *1*(2), 61–68.

Felsteiner, W., and Williams, L. "Mediation as an Alternative to Criminal Prosecution." *Law and Human Behavior,* 1978, *2*(3), 223–244.

Festinger, L. *A Theory of Cognitive Dissonance.* Stanford, Calif.: Stanford University Press, 1962.

Feuille, P. "Why Does Grievance Mediation Resolve Grievances?" *Negotiation Journal,* 1992, *8*(2), 131–145.

Feuille, P., and Kolb, D. "Waiting in the Wings: Mediation's Role in Grievance Mediation." *Negotiation Journal,* 1994, *10*(3), 249–261.

Filley, A. *Interpersonal Conflict Resolution.* Glenview, Ill.: Scott, Foresman, 1975.

Fisch, R., Weakland, J., and Segal, L. *The Tactics of Change: Doing Therapy Briefly.* San Francisco: Jossey-Bass, 1982.

Fisher, L. "Family (Divorce) Mediation in the United States of America." *Australian Journal of Dispute Resolution,* 1991, *2*(3), 186–197.

Fisher, R. "Fractionating Conflict." In R. Fisher (ed.), *International Conflict and Behavioral Sciences: The Craigville Papers.* New York: Basic Books, 1964.

Fisher, R. *International Conflict for Beginners*. New York: HarperCollins, 1969.

Fisher, R. *International Mediation: A Working Guide*. New York: International Peace Academy, 1978.

Fisher, R., and Brown, S. "How Can We Accept Those Whose Conduct Is Unacceptable?" *Negotiation Journal*, 1988, *4*(2), 125–136.

Fisher, R., and Ury, W. *Getting to Yes: Negotiating Agreement Without Giving In*. Boston: Houghton Mifflin, 1981.

Fisher, R. J. "Third Party Consultation: A Method for the Study and Resolution of Conflict." *Journal of Conflict Resolution*, 1982, *16*(1), 67–94.

Fisher, R. J. *Interactive Conflict Resolution*. Syracuse, N.Y.: Syracuse University Press, 1997.

Fisher, T. "Advice by Any Other Name . . ." *Conflict Resolution Quarterly*, 2001, *19*(2), 197–214.

Folberg, J., and Milne, A. *Divorce Mediation: Theory and Practice*. New York: Guilford Press, 1988.

Folberg, J., and Taylor, A. *Mediation: A Comprehensive Guide to Resolving Conflicts Without Litigation*. San Francisco: Jossey-Bass, 1984.

Ford, E. "Oregon's SCRIP Model: Building School Conflict Resolution Education Capacity Through Community Partnerships." *Conflict Resolution Quarterly*, 2002, *19*(4), 465–477.

Freedman, L., Haile, C., and Bookstaff, H. *Confidentiality in Mediation: A Practitioner's Guide*. Washington, D.C.: American Bar Association, 1985.

Freire, P. *Pedagogy of the Oppressed*. New York: Herder and Herder, 1970.

Freud, S. *A General Introduction to Psycho-Analysis*. Garden City, N.Y.: Garden City Publishing, 1943. (Originally published 1920)

Frost, J., and Wilmot, W. *Interpersonal Conflict*. Dubuque, Iowa: Brown, 1978.

Fucini, J., and Fucini, S. *Working for the Japanese*. New York: Free Press, 1990.

Fukuyama, F. *Trust: The Social Virtues and the Creation of Prosperity*. New York: Free Press, 1995.

Galper, M. *Joint Custody and Co-Parenting: Sharing Your Child Equally. A Source Book for the Separated or Divorced Family*. Philadelphia: Running Press, 1980.

Galtung, J. "On the Meaning of Nonviolence." In J. Galtung (ed.), *Peace: Research-Education-Action*. Copenhagen, Denmark: Ejlers, 1975.

Gardner, L. "Mediation Triage: Screening for Spouse Abuse in Divorce Mediation." *Mediation Quarterly*, 1990, *7*(4), 365-376.

Gentry, D. B. "The Certification Movement: Past, Present, and Future." *Mediation Quarterly*, 1994, *11*(3), 285–291.

Gentry, D. B. "Resolving Middle-Age Sibling Conflict Regarding Parent Care." *Conflict Resolution Quarterly,* 2001, *19*(1), 31–47.

Gewurz, I. "(Re)Designing Mediation to Address the Nuances of Power Imbalance." *Conflict Resolution Quarterly,* 2001, *19*(2), 135–162.

Gibson, K. "Mediator Attitudes Toward Outcomes: A Philosophical View." *Mediation Quarterly,* 1999, *17*(2), 197–211.

Gibson, K., Thompson, L., and Bozerman, M. "Shortcomings of Neutrality in Mediation: Solutions Based on Rationality." *Mediation Quarterly,* 1996, *12*(1), 69–80.

Ginsberg, R. B. "American Bar Association Delegation Visits the People's Republic of China." *American Bar Association Journal,* 1978, *64,* 1516–1525.

Girdner, L. "Mediation Triage: Screening for Spouse Abuse in Divorce Mediation." *Mediation Quarterly,* 1990, *4*(17), 365–376.

Givin, D. *Nonverbal Dictionary.* [http://members.aol.com/nonverbal2].

Goffman, E. *The Presentation of Self in Everyday Life.* New York: Doubleday, 1959.

Goffman, E. *Strategic Interaction.* Philadelphia: University of Pennsylvania Press, 1969.

Goldberg, S. "Grievance Mediation: A Successful Alternative to Labor Arbitration." *Negotiation Journal,* 1989, *5*(5), 9–15.

Golten, M. M., and Mayer, B. S. *Child Protection Mediation Project Manual.* Boulder, Colo.: CDR Associates, 1987.

Gordon, T. *Leadership Effectiveness Training.* New York: Wyden, 1978.

Gottman, J. *What Predicts Divorce? The Relationship Between Marital Processes and Marital Outcomes.* Hillsdale, N.J.: Erlbaum, 1994.

Graham, J., and Sano, Y. *Smart Bargaining: Doing Business with the Japanese.* New York: Ballinger, 1984.

Grebe, S. C. "Ethical Issues in Conflict Resolution: Divorce Mediation." *Negotiation Journal,* 1989, *5*(2), 179–190.

Grey, B. *Collaborating: Finding Common Ground for Multi-Party Problems.* San Francisco: Jossey-Bass, 1989.

Gulliver, P. H. *Neighbors and Networks.* Berkeley: University of California Press, 1971.

Gulliver, P. H. *Disputes and Negotiations.* San Diego, Calif.: Academic Press, 1979.

Gunning, I. "Mediation as an Alternative to Court for Lesbian and Gay Families: Some Thoughts on Douglas McIntyre's Article." *Mediation Quarterly,* 1995, *13*(1), 47–52.

Hall, E. T. *The Hidden Dimension.* New York: Doubleday, 1966.

Hall, E. *The Dance of Life.* New York: Anchor Press/Doubleday, 1983.

Hall, E., and Hall, M. *Hidden Differences: Doing Business with the Japanese.* New York: Doubleday, 1987.

Hamilton, P. "Counseling and the Legal Profession." *American Bar Association Journal*, 1972, *58*, 39–42.

Hamzeh, A. "The Role of Hizbullah in Conflict Management Within Lebanon's Shi'a Community." Unpublished manuscript, American University of Beirut, 1994.

Harter, P. "Regulatory Negotiation: The Experience So Far." *Resolve*, 1984, *16*, 1–10.

Hatfield, E., Cacioppo, J., and Rapson, R. *Emotional Contagion*. Paris: Cambridge University Press, 1992.

Haygood, L. "Negotiated Rule Making: Challenges for Mediators and Participants." *Mediation Quarterly*, 1988, *20*, 77–91.

Haynes, J. *Divorce Mediation: A Practical Guide for Therapists and Counselors*. New York: Springer, 1981.

Haynes, J. *Fundamentals of Family Mediation*. Albany: State University of New York Press, 1994.

Hecht, M. *Nonverbal Communication Research*. [http://euphrates.wpunj.edu/faculty/wagnerk/webagogy/hecht.htm].

Henderson, M. *The Forgiveness Factor: Stories of Hope in a World of Conflict*. Salem, Ore.: Grosvenor Books, 1996.

Henderson, M. *Forgiveness: Breaking the Chain of Hate*. Wilsonville, Ore.: Book Partners, 1999.

Henley, N. *Body Politics—Power, Sex, and Nonverbal Communication*. Upper Saddle River, N.J.: Prentice Hall, 1977.

Henry, J., and Lieberman, J. *The Manager's Guide to Resolving Legal Disputes*. New York: HarperCollins, 1985.

Herat, P. B. "Community-Based Dispute Resolution in Sri Lanka." *Forum* (National Institute of Dispute Resolution), winter 1993.

Herman, M., and others. "Supporting Accountability in the Field of Mediation." *Mediation Journal*, 2002, *18*(1), 29–50.

Hinde, R. (ed.). *Nonverbal Communication*. Cambridge, England: Cambridge University Press, 1972.

Hokanson, J. "Psychophysiological Evaluations of the Catharsis Hypothesis." In J. Hokanson and E. Megargee (eds.), *The Dynamics of Aggression*. New York: HarperCollins, 1970.

Holbrooke, R. *To End a War*. New York: Random House, 1998.

Horowitz, D. *Ethnic Groups in Conflict*. Berkeley: University of California Press, 1985.

Hourani, A. *A History of the Arab Peoples*. New York: Warner Books, 1991.

Hughes, M. "Beating Diversity Adversity in the Battle Against AIDS." *Consensus*, 1999, no. 28, 5–8.

Hughes, M., Forester, J., and Weiser, I. "Facilitating Statewide HIV/AIDS Policies and Priorities in Colorado." In L. Susskind, S. McKearnan, and J. Thomas-Larmer (eds.), *The Consensus Building Handbook: A*

Comprehensive Guide to Reaching Agreement. Thousand Oaks, Calif.: Sage, 1999.

Hunter, F. *Community Power Structure: A Study of Decision Makers.* Chapel Hill: University of North Carolina Press, 1953.

Hunter, L., and McKersie, R. "Can 'Mutual Gains' Training Change Labor-Management Relationships?" *Negotiation Journal,* 1992, *8*(4), 319–330.

Hunter, R. G. *Shakespeare and the Comedy of Forgiveness.* New York: Columbia University Press, 1965.

Huntington, S. *The Third Wave: Democratization in the Late Twentieth Century.* Norman: University of Oklahoma Press, 1991.

Ihromi, T. "Informal Methods of Dispute Settlement in Indonesia." In C. Pe, G. Sosmeña, and A. Tadiar (eds.), *Transcultural Mediation in the Asia-Pacific.* Manila, Philippines: Asia-Pacific Organization for Mediators, 1988.

Interim Rules 1992. Part 21 of the Industrial Court (Interim) Rules, Appendix A to the *Industrial Court Rules (Transitional) Regulation,* Australia, 1992.

International City Managers' Association. *Municipal Human Relations Commissions: Organizations and Programs.* (Report no. 270.) Chicago: International City Managers' Association, 1966.

Irving, H. *Divorce Mediation: A Rational Alternative to the Adversary System.* New York: Universe Books, 1980.

Islam, A. "Status of Mediation in Bangladesh in the Sub-Continental Settings." In C. Pe, G. Sosmeña, and A. Tadiar (eds.), *Transcultural Mediation in the Asia-Pacific.* Manila, Philippines: Asia-Pacific Organization for Mediators, 1988.

Jackins, H. *The Human Side of Human Beings.* Seattle: Rational Island Press, 1978.

Jennings, M. K. *Community Influentials: The Elites of Atlanta.* New York: Free Press, 1964.

Jones, T. "'Breaking Up Is Hard to Do': An Exploratory Study of Communication Behaviors in Child-Custody Divorce Mediation." Unpublished doctoral dissertation, Ohio State University, 1985.

Jones, T. "Phase Structures in Agreement and No-Agreement Mediation." *Communication Research,* 1988, *15,* 470–495.

Jones, T. "Mediating with Heart in Mind: Addressing Emotion in Mediation Practices." *Negotiation Journal,* 2001, *17* (3), 217–244.

Joseph, D. "Health Care Conflict Management Education." Unpublished manuscript, 1994.

Katsh, E., and Rifkin, J. *Online Dispute Resolution.* San Francisco: Jossey Bass, 2001.

Kelly, H. "A Classroom Study of the Dilemmas in Interpersonal Negotiations." In K. Archibald (ed.), *Strategic Interaction and Conflict: Original Papers and Discussion*. Berkeley, Calif.: Institute of International Studies, 1966.

Kelly, J. "Power Imbalance in Divorce and Interpersonal Mediation: Assessment and Intervention." *Mediation Quarterly*, 1995, *13*(2), 85–98.

Kelman, H. "Interactive Problem Solving: The Uses and Limits of a Therapeutic Model for the Resolution of International Conflicts." In V. Volkan, J. Montville, and D. Julius (eds.), *The Psychodynamics of International Relationships, Vol. 2*. Lexington, Mass.: Lexington, 1991.

Kelman, H. "Interactive Problem Solving as a Tool for Second Track Diplomacy." In J. Davies and E. Kaufman (eds.), *Second Track/Citizens' Diplomacy*. Lanham, Md.: Rowman & Littlefield, 2001.

Keltner, J. "Communications and the Labor-Management Mediation Process: Some Aspects and Hypotheses." *Journal of Communication*, 1965, *15*(2), 64–80.

Kerr, C. "Industrial Conflict and Its Mediation." *American Journal of Sociology*, 1954, *60*, 230–245.

Kessler, S. *Creative Conflict Resolution: Mediation*. Unpublished workbook, 1978.

Khor, K. "Cost Savings Propel Proliferation of States' Conflict Resolution Programs." *Consensus*, 1995, no. 27, 1–12.

Klamath Basin Issues: Situation Assessment and Prospect for Mediation. Boulder, Colo.: CDR Associates, 2001.

Klugman, J. "Negotiating Agreements and Resolving Disputes Across Cultures." *Mediation Quarterly*, 1992, *9*(4), 387–390.

Kochan, T., and Jick, T. "The Public Sector Mediation Process: A Theory and Empirical Examination." *Journal of Conflict Resolution*, 1978, *22*(2), 209–237.

Kochman, T. *Black and White Styles in Conflict*. Chicago: University of Chicago Press, 1981.

Kolb, D. *The Mediators*. Cambridge, Mass.: MIT Press, 1983.

Kolb, D. "More Than Just a Footnote: Constructing a Theoretical Framework for Teaching About Gender in Mediation." *Negotiation Journal*, 2000, *16*(4), 347–356.

Kolb, D., and Coolidge, G. "Her Place at the Table: A Consideration of Gender Issues in Negotiation." In J. Broslin and J. Rubin (eds.), *Negotiation Theory and Practice*. Cambridge, Mass.: PON Books, 1992.

Kolb, D., and Sheppard, B. "Do Managers Mediate, or Even Arbitrate?" *Negotiation Journal*, 1985, *1*(4), 379–388.

Kolb, D., and Williams, J. *The Shadow Negotiation: How Women Can Master the Hidden Agendas That Determine Bargaining Success*. New York: Simon & Schuster, 2000.

Kosambi Jataka, no. 428, book IX, 486–490, n.d.

Krapp, T. Presentation at the First European Conference on Peacemaking and Conflict Resolution, Antalya, Turkey, May 1992.

Kraybill, R. "Institutionalizing Mediation as an Alternative Dispute Settlement Mechanism: An Ethical Critique." In R. Kraybill and L. Buzzard (eds.), *Christian Conciliation Sourcebook*. Oak Park, Ill.: Christian Legal Society, 1979.

Kriesberg, L. *The Sociology of Social Conflicts*. Upper Saddle River, N.J.: Prentice Hall, 1973.

Kriesberg, L. *Constructive Conflict: From Escalation to Resolution*. Lanham, Md.: Rowman & Littlefield, 1998.

Kriesberg, L., Northrup, T., and Thorson, S. (eds.). *Intractable Conflicts and Their Transformation*. Syracuse, N.Y.: Syracuse University Press, 1989.

Kushner, H. *How Good Do We Have to Be? A New Understanding of Guilt and Forgiveness*. New York: Little, Brown, 1996.

Kwartler, R. "This Land Is Our Land: The Mohawk Indians v. the State of New York." In R. Goldmann (ed.), *Roundtable Justice: Case Studies in Conflict Resolution*. Boulder, Colo.: Westview Press, 1980.

Labor-Management Relations Act (Taft-Hartley Act). *U.S. Code*, sec. 203(b), 1947.

Lake, L. *Environmental Mediation: The Search for Consensus*. Boulder, Colo.: Westview Press, 1980.

Lake, R. *Resolving Locational Conflict*. New Brunswick, N.J.: Center for Urban Policy Research, 1987.

Landry, E. "Scrolling Around the New Organization: The Potential for Conflict in the On-Line Environment." *Negotiation Journal*, 2000, *16*(2), 133–142.

Landsberger, H. "Final Report on a Research Project in Mediation." *Labor Law Journal*, 1956, *7*(8).

Lansford, H. *The Metropolitan Water Roundtable: A Case Study in Environmental Conflict Management*. Boulder, Colo.: ACCORD Associates, 1983.

Laue, J. "Using Mediation to Shape Public Policy." *Mediation Quarterly*, 1988, no. 20.

Laue, J., and Cormick, G. "The Ethics of Intervention in Community Disputes." In G. Bermont and others (eds.), *The Ethics of Social Intervention*. New York: Wiley, 1978.

Lax, D., and Sebenius, J. "The Power of Alternatives or the Limits to Negotiation." *Negotiation Journal*, 1985, *1*(2), 163–179.

Lazrus, R. *Emotion and Adaptation*. New York: Oxford University Press, 1991.

Lazrus, R. "Meaning and Emotional Development." In P. Ekman and R. J. Davidson (eds.), *The Nature of Emotion: Fundamental Questions.* New York: Oxford University Press, 1994.

Lederach, J. P. *"La regulacion del conflicto: interpersonal y de grupos reduidos"* ["The Regulation of Conflict: Interpersonal and Small Groups"]. Unpublished manuscript, University of Colorado, 1984.

Lederach, J. P. "Mediation in North America: An Examination of the Profession's Cultural Assumptions." Paper presented at the National Conference on Peacemaking and Conflict Resolution, Denver, 1985.

Lederach, J. P. "Of Nails, Nets, and Problemas." Ph.D. dissertation, University of Colorado, 1988.

Lederach, J. P. "Comprehensive Approach in Somalia." Presentation at the North American Conference on Peacemaking and Conflict Resolution, Portland, Oregon, May 1993.

Lederach, J. P. *Preparing for Peace: Conflict Transformation Across Cultures.* Syracuse, N.Y.: Syracuse University Press, 1995.

Lederach, J. P. *Building Peace: Sustainable Reconciliation in Divided Societies.* Washington, D.C.: United States Institute of Peace, 1997.

Lederach, J. P. *The Journey Toward Reconciliation.* Scottsdale, Pa.: Harold Press, 1999.

Lemmon, J. (ed.). "Community Mediation." (Special issue.) *Mediation Quarterly,* 1984, no. 5.

Lemmon, J. *Family Mediation Practice.* New York: Macmillan, 1985.

Leone, A. "Is ADR the Rx for Malpractice?" *Dispute Resolution Journal,* 1994, *4*(3), 7–13.

LeResche, D. "Editor's Notes." *Mediation Quarterly,* 1993, *10*(14), 327–337.

Levinson, D. "The Intergroup Relations Workshop: Its Psychological Aims and Effects." *Journal of Psychology,* 1954, *38,* 103–126.

Levinson, D., and Schermerhorn, R. "Emotional Attitudinal Effects of an Intergroup Relations Workshop on Its Members." *Journal of Psychology,* 1951, *31,* 243–256.

Levy, J. "Conflict Resolution in Elementary and Secondary Education." *Mediation Quarterly,* 1989, *7*(1), 73–87.

Li, M. Q. "Mediation in China." In C. Pe, G. Sosmeña, and A. Tadiar (eds.), *Transcultural Mediation in the Asia-Pacific.* Manila, Philippines: Asia-Pacific Organization for Mediators, 1988.

Li, V. *Law Without Lawyers: A Comparative View of Law in China and the United States.* Boulder, Colo.: Westview Press, 1978.

Lincoln, W. F. Mediation: *A Transferable Process for the Prevention and Resolution of Racial Conflict in Public Secondary Schools.* New York: American Arbitration Association, 1976.

Lincoln, W. F. "Presenting Initial Positions." Unpublished manuscript, National Center for Collaborative Planning and Community Services, Watertown, Mass., 1981.

Lincoln, W. F. "Types of Negotiations." Unpublished manuscript, National Center for Collaborative Planning and Community Services, Watertown, Mass., n.d.

Lindsay, P. "Conflict Resolution and Peer Mediation in Public Schools: What Works?" *Mediation Quarterly*, 1998, *16*(1), 85–99.

Lovell, H. "The Pressure Lever in Mediation." *Industrial and Labor Relations Review*, 1952, *6*(1), 20–29.

Lynch, J. "Beyond ADR: A Systems Approach to Conflict Management." *Negotiation Journal*, 2001, *17*(3), 207–216.

Macduff, I. "Mediation in New Zealand: Legislating for Community?" In C. Pe, G. Sosmeña, and A. Tadiar (eds.), *Transcultural Mediation in the Asia-Pacific*. Manila, Philippines: Asia-Pacific Organization for Mediators, 1988.

Macduff, I. "Resources, Rights and Recognition." *Cultural Survival*, 1995, *19*(3), 30–32.

Madonik, B. *I Hear What You Say, But What Are You Telling Me? The Strategic Use of Communication in Mediation*. San Francisco: Jossey-Bass, 2001.

Maggiolo, W. *Techniques of Mediation in Labor Disputes*. Dobbs Ferry, N.Y.: Oceana, 1972.

Maier, N., and Hoffman, L. "Quality of First and Second Solutions in Group Problem Solving." *Journal of Applied Psychology*, 1960, *44*, 278–283.

Mann, J. *Beijing Jeep*. New York: Simon & Schuster, 1989.

Mansbridge, J. *Beyond Adversary Democracy*. Chicago: University of Chicago Press, 1983.

Mansfield, E. "Balance and Harmony: Peacemaking in Coast Salish Tribes of the Pacific Northwest." *Mediation Quarterly*, 1993, *10*(4), 339–353.

Marcus, L., and others. *Renegotiating Health Care: Resolving Conflict to Build Collaboration*. San Francisco: Jossey-Bass, 1995.

Mares-Dixon, J. "Building Consensus for Change Within a Major Corporation: The Case of Levi Strauss and Co." In L. Susskind, S. McKearnan, and J. Thomas-Larmer (eds.), *The Consensus Building Handbook: A Comprehensive Guide to Reaching Agreement*. Thousand Oaks, Calif.: Sage, 1999.

Maslow, A. *Toward a Psychology of Being*. New York: Van Nostrand Reinhold, 1968.

Massip, J. *Nonverbal Behavior/Nonverbal Communication*. [www.3.usal.es/~nonverbal/introduction.htm].

Matz, D. "ADR and Life in Israel." *Negotiation Journal*, 1991, *7*(1), 11–16.

Maxwell, D. "Gender Differences in Mediation Style and Their Impact on Mediator Effectiveness." *Mediation Quarterly*, 1992, *9*(4), 353–364.

Maxwell, J., and Maxwell, D. "Male and Female Mediation Styles and Their Effectiveness." Paper presented at the National Conference on Peacemaking and Conflict Resolution Conference, Montreal, Feb. 28–Mar. 5, 1989.

Mayer, B., and others. *Reaching for Peace: Lessons Learned from Mott Foundation's Conflict Resolution Grantmaking*. Flint, Mich.: Charles Stewart Mott Foundation, 1999.

Mayer, B., Wildau, S., and Valchev, R. "Promoting Multi-Cultural Consensus Building in Bulgaria." *Cultural Survival*, 1995, *19*(3), 64–68.

Mayer, B. S. "Conflict Resolution in Child Protection and Adoption." *Mediation Quarterly*, 1985, no. 7, 69–81.

Mayer, B. S. "The Dynamics of Power in Mediation." *Mediation Quarterly*, 1987, no. 16, 75–85.

Mayer, B. S. *The Dynamics of Conflict Resolution: A Practitioner's Guide*. San Francisco: Jossey-Bass, 2000.

Mayer, B. S., Moore, C., and Todd, S. "The Alaska Wolf Summit." In P. Adler and K. Lowery (eds.), *Finding the Common Good*. Forthcoming.

Mayor's Office, City of Portland, Oregon. *Police-Citizen Mediation Program*. Portland, Oreg.: Mayor's Office, 1994.

McCarthy, J. (ed.). *Resolving Conflict in Higher Education*. New Directions for Higher Education, no. 32. San Francisco: Jossey-Bass, 1980.

McCarthy, J., and others. *Managing Faculty Disputes: A Guide to Issues, Procedures, and Practices*. San Francisco: Jossey-Bass, 1984.

McConnell, J. *Mindful Mediation: A Handbook for Buddhist Peacemakers*. Bangkok, Thailand: Buddhist Research Institute and Manachula Buddhist University, 1995.

McCreary, S. "Independent Fact Finding as a Catalyst for Cross-Cultural Dialogue." *Cultural Survival*, 1995, *19*(3), 30–32.

McIntyre, D. "Gay Parents and Child Custody: A Struggle Under the Legal System." *Mediation Quarterly*, 1994, *12*(2), 135–149.

McIsaac, H. "Mandatory Conciliation Custody/Visitation Matters: California's Bold Stroke." *Conciliation Courts Review*, 1983, *19*(2), 51–73.

McKnight, M., and Erikson, S. *Mediating Divorce: A Client's Workbook*. Jossey-Bass, 1998.

McKnight, M., and Erikson, S. *Mediating Divorce: A Step-by-Step Manual*. Jossey-Bass, 2002.

McSurely, A. *How to Negotiate*. Louisville, Ky.: Southern Conference Educational Fund, 1967.

Meeks, G. "Negotiating a State Environmental Quality Act: The Arizona Groundwater Case." *Mediation Quarterly*, 1988, no. 20, 57–73.

Menkel-Meadow, C. "Teaching About Gender and Negotiation: Sex, Truth, and Videotapes." *Negotiation Journal,* 2000, *16*(4), 357–376.

Menocal, M. R. *The Ornament of the World: How Muslims, Jews and Christians Created a Culture of Tolerance in Medieval Spain.* New York: Little, Brown, 2002.

Mernitz, S. *Mediation of Environmental Disputes: A Sourcebook.* New York: Praeger, 1980.

Millhauser, M., and Pou, C. (eds.). *Sourcebook: Federal Agency Use of Alternative Means of Dispute Resolution.* Washington, D.C.: Office of the Chairman, Administrative Conference of the United States, 1987.

Milne, A. "Family Self-Determination: An Alternative to the Adversarial System in Custody Disputes." Paper presented at the winter meeting of the Association of Family and Conciliation Courts, Fort Lauderdale, Fla., Dec. 1981.

Minow, M. *Between Vengeance and Forgiveness: Facing History After Genocide and Mass Violence.* Boston: Beacon Press, 1998.

Moore, C. W. *Mediator Checklist.* Denver, Colo.: Center for Dispute Resolution, 1981.

Moore, C. W. *Code of Professional Conduct.* Denver: Colorado Council of Mediation Organizations and the Center for Dispute Resolution, 1982a.

Moore, C. W. *Natural Resources Conflict Management.* Boulder, Colo.: ACCORD Associates, 1982b.

Moore, C. W. "The Caucus: Private Meetings That Promote Settlement." *Mediation Quarterly,* 1987, no. 16, 87–101.

Moore, C. W. "Obstacles to Effective Divorce Mediation." In J. Folberg and A. Milne (eds.), *Divorce Mediation.* New York: Guilford Press, 1988.

Moore, C. W. "Utilizing Negotiations to Resolve Complex Environmental Disputes." In W. Viessman and E. Smerdon (eds.), *Managing Water-Related Conflicts.* New York: American Society of Civil Engineers, 1989.

Moore, C. W. *Corps of Engineers Uses Mediation to Settle Hydropower Dispute.* (Case study 91-ADR-CS6.) Ft. Belvoir, Va.: Institute for Water Resources, 1991.

Moore, C. W. "Implementing Peace Accords on the Ground." *Track Two,* 1993, *2*(2), 10–13.

Moore, C. W. "Mediating Environmental Enforcement and Compliance Issues." In G. Martin and W. Hamacher (eds.), *Lessons Learned in Environmental Mediation: Practical Experiences in North and South.* Geneva, Switzerland: International Academy of the Environment, 1997.

Moore, C. W., and Santosa, A. "Developing Appropriate Environmental Conflict Management Procedures in Indonesia." *Cultural Survival,* 1995, *19*(3), 23–29.

Moore, C. W., and Woodrow, P. "Collaborative Problem Solving Within Organizations." In L. Susskind, S. McKearnan, and J. Thomas-Larmer (eds.), *The Consensus Building Handbook: A Comprehensive Guide to Reaching Agreement.* Thousand Oaks, Calif.: Sage, 1999.

Morril, C. *The Executive Way.* Chicago: University of Chicago Press, 1995.

Morrow, D., and Wilson, D. "Three into Two Won't Go? From Mediation to New Relationships in Northern Ireland." *Forum* (National Institute of Dispute Resolution), 1993.

Mulcahy, N. "Conciliation and Race Complaints." *Australian Dispute Resolution Journal,* 1992, *3*(1), 21–30.

Müller-Fahrenholz, G. *The Art of Forgiveness: Theological Reflections on Healing and Reconciliation.* Geneva: World Council of Churches, 1997.

Muntarbhorn, V. "Prospects and Trends of Mediation as an Alternative to Dispute Resolution in Thailand." In C. Pe, G. Sosmeña, and A. Tadiar (eds.), *Transcultural Mediation in the Asia-Pacific.* Manila, Philippines: Asia-Pacific Organization for Mediators, 1988.

Murphy, J. "Forgiveness and Resentment." In J. Murphy and J. Hampton, *Forgiveness and Mercy.* New York: Cambridge University Press, 1988.

Murray, J. "The Cairo Stories: Some Reflections on Conflict Resolution in Egypt." *Negotiation Journal,* 1997, *13*(1), 39–60.

Nadler, J. "Electronically-Mediated Dispute Resolution and E-Commerce." *Journal of Negotiation,* 2001, *17*(4), 333–347.

Nader, L. "Styles of Court Procedure: To Make the Balance." In L. Nader (ed.), *Law in Culture and Society.* Hawthorne, N.Y.: Aldine de Gruyter, 1969.

Nathan, L. "An Imperfect Bridge: Crossing to Democracy on the Peace Accord." *Track Two,* 1993, *2*(2), 1–5.

Nelson, M., and Sharp, W. R. "Mediating Conflicts of Persons at Risk of Homelessness: The Helping Hand Project." *Mediation Quarterly,* 1995, *12*(4), 317–325.

New York State Special Commission on Attica. *Attica: The Official Report of the New York State Special Commission on Attica.* New York: Praeger, 1972.

Ngoh-Tiong, T. "Community Mediation in Singapore: Principles for Community Conflict Resolution." *Conflict Resolution Quarterly,* 2002, *19*(3), 289–301.

Northrup, T. "The Dynamic of Identity in Personal and Social Conflict." In L. Kriesberg, T. Northrup, and S. Thorson (eds.), *Intractable Conflicts and Their Transformation.* Syracuse, N.Y.: Syracuse University Press, 1989.

O'Hare, M., Bacow, L., and Sanderson, D. *Facility Siting and Public Opposition.* New York: Van Nostrand Reinhold, 1983.

Oren, G. *Persuasion: The Art and Science of Effective Influence.* Cambridge, Mass.: John F. Kennedy School of Government, Harvard University, 2001.

Orenstein, S. G. "The Role of Mediation in Domestic Violence Cases." In H. Davidson and others (eds.), *Alternative Means of Family Dispute Resolution.* Washington, D.C.: American Bar Association, 1982.

Owen, D. *Balkan Odyssey.* Orlando: Harcourt Brace, 1995.

Patai, R. *The Arab Mind.* New York: Scribner, 1983.

Pe, C., and Tadiar, A. *Katarungang Pambarangay: Dynamics of Compulsory Conciliation.* Quezon City, Philippines: Publishers' Printing Press, 1988.

Pearce, W. B., and Littlejohn, S. *Moral Conflict: When Social Worlds Collide.* Thousand Oaks, Calif.: Sage, 1997.

Pearson, J. "Divorce Mediation: Strengths and Weaknesses over Time." In H. Davidson and others (eds.), *Alternative Means of Family Dispute Resolution.* Washington, D.C.: American Bar Association, 1982.

Pearson, J. "Denver Child Custody Project: Final Report to the Piton Foundation and Colorado Bar Association." Denver, Colo.: Center for Policy Research, 1984.

Perez, F. A. "Evaluation of Mediation Techniques." *Labor Law Journal,* 1959, *10*(10), 716–720.

Phillips, B. A. *The Mediation Field Guide: Transcending Litigation and Resolving Conflicts in Your Business or Organization.* San Francisco: Jossey-Bass, 2001.

Polsby, N. "How to Study Community Power." *Journal of Politics,* 1960, *22,* 474–484.

President. "Memorandum on Use of Alternative Dispute Resolution." *Federal Register,* Sept. 30, 1993.

Princen, T. *Intermediaries in International Conflict.* Princeton, N.J.: Princeton University Press, 1992.

Pruitt, D. *Negotiation Behavior.* San Diego, Calif.: Academic Press, 1981.

Pruitt, D., and Lewis, S. "The Psychology of Integrative Bargaining." In D. Druckman (ed.), *Negotiations: A Social Psychological Perspective.* Thousand Oaks, Calif.: Sage, 1977.

Pruitt, D., Parker, J., and Mikolic, J. "Escalation as a Reaction to Persistent Annoyance." *International Journal of Conflict Management,* 1997, *8*(3), 252–270.

Putnam, R. *Making Democracy Work: Civic Traditions in Modern Italy.* Princeton, N.J.: Princeton University Press, 1993.

Pye, L. *Chinese Commercial Negotiating Style.* Cambridge, Mass.: Oelgeschlager, Gunn & Hain, 1982.

Qualifying Neutrals: The Basic Principles. Washington, D.C.: Society of Professionals in Dispute Resolution, 1989.

Quayle, D. "Less Litigation, More Justice." *Wall Street Journal,* Aug. 14, 1991, p. A8.

Ray, L. "Community Mediation Centers: Delivering First-Class Services to Low-Income People for the Past Twenty Years." *Mediation Quarterly,* 1997, *15*(1), 71–77.

Ray, L., and Smolover, D. *Consumer Dispute Resolution: Exploring the Alternatives.* Washington, D.C.: American Bar Association and U.S. Department of Consumer Affairs, 1983.

Reeves, J. "ADR Relieves Pain of Health Care Disputes." *Dispute Resolution Journal,* 1994, *49*(3), 14–20.

Remland, M. Book review of B. Madonik, *I Hear What You Say, But What Are You Telling Me?* Conflict Resolution Quarterly, 2002, 20(1), 121–127.

Renouf, E. "Family Conciliation/Mediation in Australia: Which Way Forward?" *Australian Dispute Resolution Journal,* 1991, *2*(2), 108–116.

Reynolds, W., and Tonry, M. "Professional Mediation Services for Prisoners' Complaints." *American Bar Association Journal,* 1981, *67,* 294–297.

Ricci, I. *Mom's House, Dad's House.* New York: Collier Books, 1980.

Richardson, J., and Margulis, J. *The Magic of Rapport: The Business of Negotiation.* New York: Avon Books, 1984.

Richardson, S., Dohrenwend, B. S., and Klein, D. *Interviewing: Its Forms and Functions.* New York: Basic Books, 1965.

Rifkin, J. "Online Dispute Resolution: Theory and Practice of the Fourth Party." *Conflict Resolution Quarterly,* 2001, *19*(4).

Riley, H., and Sebenius, J. "Stakeholder Negotiations over Third World Natural Resource Projects." *Cultural Survival,* 1995, *19*(3), 39–43.

Riskin, L. "Mediation and Lawyers." *Ohio State Law Journal,* 1982, *43,* 29–60.

Roberts, K., and Lundy, C. "The ADA and NLRA: Resolving Accommodation Disputes in Unionized Workplaces." *Negotiation Journal,* 1995, *11*(1), 29–41.

Rogan, R., Donahue, W., and Lyles, J. "Gaining and Exercising Control in Hostage Negotiations Using Empathic Perspective Taking." *International Journal of Group Tensions,* 1990, *20*(1), 77–90.

Rogers, C. "The Non-Directive Method as a Technique of Social Research." *American Journal of Sociology,* 1945, *50*(4), 279–283.

Ross, H. "Aboriginal Australian's Cultural Norms for Negotiating Natural Resources." *Cultural Survival,* 1995, *19*(3), 33–38.

Rothman, J. *From Confrontation to Cooperation: Resolving Ethnic and Regional Conflict.* Thousand Oaks, Calif.: Sage, 1992.

Rothman, J. *Resolving Identity-Based Conflict in Nations, Organizations, and Communities.* San Francisco: Jossey-Bass, 1997.

Roubana, N., and Korper, S. "Dealing with Dilemmas Posed by Power Asymmetry in Intergroup Conflict." *Mediation Quarterly,* 1996, *12*(4), 353–366.

Rowe, M. "Harassment: A Systems Approach." Unpublished manuscript, Massachusetts Institute of Technology, 1994.

Rowe, M. "Dispute Resolution in the Non-Union Environment." Unpublished manuscript, Massachusetts Institute of Technology, 1995.

Rubin, J. (ed.). *Dynamics of Third Party Intervention: Kissinger in the Middle East.* New York: Praeger, 1981.

Rubin, J., and Brown, B. *The Social Psychology of Bargaining and Negotiation.* San Diego, Calif.: Academic Press, 1975.

Rule, C. *Online Dispute Resolution for Business.* San Francisco: Jossey-Bass, 2002.

Salacuse, J. "Your Draft or Mine?" *Negotiation Journal,* 1989, *5*(4), 337–341.

Salem, P. (ed.). *Conflict Resolution in the Arab World: Selected Essays.* Beirut, Lebanon: American University of Beirut, 1997.

Sandy, S. "Conflict Resolution Education in the Schools: Getting There." *Conflict Resolution Quarterly,* 2001, *19*(2), 237–250.

Saposnek, D. T. *Mediating Child Custody Disputes: A Systematic Guide for Family Therapists, Court Counselors, Attorneys, and Judges.* San Francisco: Jossey-Bass, 1983.

Saposnek, D. T. *Mediating Child Custody Disputes.* San Francisco: Jossey-Bass, 1998.

Saunders, H. *A Public Peace Process: Sustained Dialogue to Transform Racial and Ethnic Conflicts.* New York: St. Martin's Press, 1999.

Savage, C. A. "Future Lawyers: Adversaries or Problem Solvers? Two Law School Programs in Alternative Dispute Resolution." *Mediation Quarterly,* 1989, *7*(1), 89–101.

Sawyer, J., and Guetzkow, H. "Bargaining and Negotiating in International Relations." In H. Kelman (ed.), *International Behavior: A Social Psychological Analysis.* Austin, Tex.: Holt, Rinehart & Winston, 1965.

Schecter, J. *Russian Negotiating Behavior.* Washington, D.C.: U.S. Institute of Peace, 1998.

Schein, E. *Process Consultation: Its Role in Organization Development.* Reading, Mass.: Addison-Wesley, 1969.

Schelling, T. "An Essay on Bargaining." *American Economic Review,* 1956, *46*(3), 281–306.

Schelling, T. *The Strategy of Conflict.* Cambridge, Mass.: Harvard University Press, 1960.

Schmitz, S. "Mediation and the Elderly: What Mediators Need to Know." *Mediation Quarterly,* 1998, *16*(1), 71–84.

Schneider, C. "What It Means to Be Sorry: The Power of Apology in Mediation." *Mediation Quarterly,* 2000, *17*(3), 265–279.

Schön, D. *The Reflective Practitioner: How Professionals Think in Action.* New York: Basic Books, 1983.

Schreiber, F. B. *Domestic Disturbances: Officer Safety and Calming Techniques.* St. Cloud, Minn.: Center for Studies in Criminal Justice, St. Cloud University, 1971.

Schwarz, A. *Nation in Waiting: Indonesia in the 1990s.* St. Leonards, Australia: Allen & Unwin, 1994.

Seligman, S. *Dealing with the Chinese: A Practical Guide to Business Etiquette in the People's Republic Today.* New York: Warner Books, 1989.

Senger, J. "Tales of the Bazaar: Interest-Based Negotiation Across Cultures." *Negotiation Journal*, 2002, *18*(3).

Shanahan, J., and others. *Negotiated Investment Strategy.* Dayton, Ohio: Kettering Foundation, 1982.

Shapiro, F. "Profiles: Mediator." *New Yorker*, Aug. 1, 1970, pp. 36–58.

Shapiro, I. "New Approaches to Old Problems: Lessons from an Ethnic Conciliation Project in Four Central and Eastern European Countries." *Negotiation Journal*, 1999, *15*(2), 149–167.

Sharon, N., and Schwentzman, O. "Professional and Traditional Collaboration in Mediation of Family Conflicts: The Case of Ethiopian Immigrants in Israel." *Mediation Quarterly*, 1998, *16*(1), 3–13.

Sharp, G. *The Politics of Nonviolent Action.* Boston: Porter Sargent, 1973.

Shaughnessey, E. *Conflict Management in Norway: Practical Dispute Resolution.* Lanham, Md.: University Press of America, 1992.

Shaw, M. "Mediating Between Parents and Children." In H. Davidson and others (eds.), *Alternative Means of Family Dispute Resolution.* Washington, D.C.: American Bar Association, 1982.

Shell, G. *Bargaining for Advantage.* New York: Penguin, 1999.

Sherif, M., and others. *Intergroup Conflict and Cooperation: The Robbers Cave Experiment.* Norman: University of Oklahoma Book Exchange, 1961.

Shonholtz, R. "Neighborhood Justice Systems: Work, Structure, and Guiding Principles." *Mediation Quarterly*, 1984, no. 5, 3–30.

Shonholtz, R. (ed.). "Developing Mediating Processes in the New Democracies." Special issue of *Mediation Quarterly*, 1993, *10*(3).

Shook, V., and Kwan, K. "Straightening Relationships and Resolving Disputes in Hawai'i. Ho'Oponopono and Mediation." In C. Pe, G. Sosmeña, and A. Tadiar (eds.), *Transcultural Mediation in the Asia-Pacific.* Manila, Philippines: Asia-Pacific Organization for Mediators, 1988.

Shourie, H. "Mediation Sans Legislation: An Experiment in India." In C. Pe, G. Sosmeña, and A. Tadiar (eds.), *Transcultural Mediation in the Asia-Pacific.* Manila, Philippines: Asia-Pacific Organization for Mediators, 1988.

Shrestha, K. "Community Forestry in Nepal: An Overview of Conflicts." Unpublished paper presented at a conference on community forestry in Kathmandu, Nepal, January 1995.

Simkin, W. *Mediation and the Dynamics of Collective Bargaining.* Washington, D.C.: Bureau of National Affairs, 1971.

Simmel, G. *Conflict and the Web of Intergroup Affiliations.* New York: Free Press, 1955.

Simokaitis, M. *Preparing for Negotiations.* St. Louis, Mo.: Washington University Community Crisis Intervention Project, n.d.

Skratek, S. "Grievance Mediation: Does It Really Work?" *Negotiation Journal,* 1990, *6*(3), 269–280.

Slaiku, K. "Designing Dispute Resolution Systems in the Health Care Industry." *Negotiation Journal,* 1989, *5*(4), 395–400.

Slatts, H., and Porter, K. *Traditional Decision Making and Law.* Yogyakarta, Indonesia: Gadja Mada University Press, 1992.

Smart, L. "Mediator Strategies for Dealing with Dirty Tricks." *Mediation Quarterly,* 1987, *16,* 53–63.

Smith, M., and Sidwell, J. *Training and Implementation Guide for Student Mediation in Secondary Schools.* Albuquerque: New Mexico Center for Dispute Resolution, 1990.

Smith, R. F. *Negotiating with the Soviets.* Bloomington and Indianapolis: Indiana University Press, 1989.

Smith, W. "Effectiveness of the Biased Mediator." *Negotiation Journal,* 1985, *1*(4), 363–372.

Society of Professionals in Dispute Resolution. *Qualifying Neutrals: The Basic Principles.* (Report of the SPIDR Commission on Qualification.) Washington, D.C.: Society of Professionals in Dispute Resolution, 1989.

Society of Professionals in Dispute Resolution. *Ensuring Competence and Quality in Dispute Resolution Practice.* Washington, D.C.: Society of Professionals in Dispute Resolution, 1995.

Sommer, R. "Further Studies of Small Group Ecology." *Sociometry,* 1965, *28,* 337–348.

Sommer, R. *Personal Space: The Behavioral Basis of Design.* Upper Saddle River, N.J.: Prentice Hall, 1969.

Stamato, L. "Voice, Place, and Process: Research on Gender, Negotiation, and Conflict Resolution." *Mediation Quarterly,* 1992, *9*(4), 375–386.

Stamato, L., and Jaffe, S. "Mediation and Public Policy: Variations on a Consensus Theme." *Mediation Quarterly,* 1991, *9*(2), 165–178.

Steinmetz, S., and Straus, M. *Violence in the Family.* New York: HarperCollins, 1974.

Stevens, C. *Strategy in Collective Bargaining Negotiations.* New York: McGraw-Hill, 1963.

Stevenson, E. "The Use of Community Mediation in the Family Mediation Centre (NSW)." *Australian Dispute Resolution Journal,* 1990, *1*(1), 24–30.

Stewart, C., and Cash, W. *Interviewing: Principles and Practices.* Dubuque, Iowa: Brown, 1974.

Straus, D. "Managing Environmental Complexity: A New Look at Environmental Mediation." *Environment Science and Technology,* 1979, *13*(6), 661–665.

Straus, D., Clark, P., and Susskind, L. *Guidelines to Identify, Manage and Resolve Environmental Disputes.* New York: Research Institute, American Arbitration Association, n.d.

Straus, M. "A Sociological Perspective on the Prevention and Treatment of Wifebeatings." In M. Roy (ed.), *Battered Women.* New York: Van Nostrand Reinhold, 1977.

Stuhlmacher, A., and Walters, A. "Gender Differences in Negotiation Outcome: A Meta-Analysis." *Personnel Psychology,* 1999, *52,* 653–677.

Stulberg, J. *Citizen Dispute Settlement: A Mediator's Manual.* Tallahassee: Supreme Court of Florida, 1981a.

Stulberg, J. "The Theory and Practice of Mediation: A Reply to Professor Susskind." *Vermont Law Review,* 1981b, *6*(1), 85–117.

Sullivan, T. *Resolving Development Disputes Through Negotiations.* New York: Plenum, 1984.

Survey Research Center. *Interviewer's Manual.* Ann Arbor: Survey Research Center, Institute for Social Research, University of Michigan, 1969.

Susskind, L. "Environmental Mediation and the Accountability Problem." *Vermont Law Review,* 1981, *6*(1), 1–47.

Susskind, L. "NIDR's State Office of Mediation Experiment." *Negotiation Journal,* 1986, *2*(4), 323–327.

Susskind, L. *Environmental Diplomacy: Negotiating More Effective Global Agreements.* New York: Oxford University Press, 1994.

Susskind, L., Babbit, E., and Segal, P. "When ADR Becomes the Law: A Review of Federal Practice." *Negotiation Journal,* 1993, *9*(1), 59–75.

Susskind, L., and Cruikshank, J. *Breaking the Impasse: Consensual Approaches to Resolving Public Disputes.* New York: Basic Books, 1987.

Susskind, L., and Field, P. *Dealing with an Angry Public: The Mutual Gains Approach to Resolving Disputes.* New York: Free Press, 1996.

Talbot, A. *Settling Things: Six Case Studies in Environmental Mediation.* Washington, D.C.: Conservation Foundation, 1983.

Taylor, A. *The Handbook of Family Dispute Resolution: Mediation Theory and Practice.* San Francisco: Jossey-Bass, 2002.

Thibaut, J., and Kelly, H. *The Social Psychology of Groups.* New York: Wiley, 1959.

Thomas, K. "Conflict and Conflict Management." In M. Dunnette (ed.), *Handbook of Industrial and Organizational Psychology.* Skokie, Ill.: Rand McNally, 1976.

Thompson, L. *The Mind and Heart of the Negotiator.* Upper Saddle River, N.J.: Prentice Hall, 2001.

Tomain, J. "Land Use Mediation for Planners." *Mediation Quarterly,* 1989, 7(2), 163–173.

Tutu, D. *No Future Without Forgiveness.* New York: Doubleday, 1999.

Umbreit, M. *Victim Offender Mediation: Conflict Resolution and Restitution.* Washington, D.C.: National Institute of Corrections, U.S. Department of Justice, 1985.

Umbreit, M. *Victim Meets Offender: The Impact of Restorative Justice and Mediation.* Monsey, N.Y.: Criminal Justice Press, 1994.

Umbreit, M. *The Handbook of Victim-Offender Mediation.* San Francisco: Jossey-Bass, 2000.

Umbreit, M., and Greenwood, J. "National Survey of Victim-Offender Mediation Programs in the United States." *Mediation Quarterly,* 1999, 16(3), 235–251.

Ury, W., Brett, J., and Goldberg, S. *Getting Disputes Resolved: Designing Systems to Cut the Costs of Conflict.* San Francisco: Jossey-Bass, 1988.

Valtin, R. "The 'Real and Substantial' Benefits of Grievance Mediation." *Negotiation Journal,* 1993, 9(2), 179–184.

Van Hook, M. P., "Resolving Conflict Between Farmers and Creditors: An Analysis of the Farmer-Creditor Mediation Process." *Mediation Quarterly,* 1990, 8(1), 63–72.

Van Zandt, H. "How to Negotiate in Japan." *Harvard Business Review,* Nov.–Dec. 1970, 45–56.

Viessman, W., and Smerdon, E. *Managing Water-Related Conflicts.* New York: American Society of Civil Engineers, 1989.

Volpe, M. R., and Chandler, D. "Resolving and Managing Conflicts in Academic Communities: The Emerging Role of the 'Pracademic.'" *Negotiation Journal,* 2001, 17(3), 245–256.

Volpe, M. R., and Witherspoon, R. "Mediation and Cultural Diversity on College Campuses." *Mediation Quarterly,* 1992, 9(4), 341–351.

Von Benda-Beckmann, K. *The Broken Stairways to Consensus: Village Justice and State Courts in Mjnangkabau.* Cinnaminson, N.J.: Foris, 1984.

Vorenberg, E. W. *State of the Art Survey of Dispute Resolution Programs Involving Juveniles.* (Dispute Resolution Papers, Section 1.) Washington, D.C.: American Bar Association, Special Committee on Alternative Means of Dispute Resolution (Division of Public Service Activities), 1982.

Votchal, V. "The Movement Toward Conflict Resolution in the Former Soviet Union." *Forum* (National Institute for Dispute Resolution), winter 1993.

Wade, J. "Forever Bargaining in the Shadow of the Law: Who Sells Solid Shadows? (Who Advises What, How and When?)" *Australian Journal of Family Law,* 1998, 12(3), 256–296.

Wade, J. "Don't Waste My Time on Negotiation and Mediation: This Dispute Needs a Judge." *Mediation Quarterly*, 2001, *18*(3), 259–280.

Wahrhaftig, P. "Gang-Related Conflict Resolving Process." *Conflict Resolution Notes*, 1995, *13*(1), 4–5.

Wall, J. "Mediation: An Analysis Review and Proposed Research." *Journal of Conflict Resolution*, 1981, *25*(1), 157–180.

Walteres, A., Stahlmacher, A., and Mayer, L. "Gender and Negotiator Competitiveness: A Meta-Analysis." *Organizational Behavior and Human Development Process*, 1998, *76*, 1–29.

Walton, J. "Substance and Artifact: The Current Research on Community Power Structure." *American Journal of Sociology*, 1966, *71*(4), 430–438.

Walton, R. *Interpersonal Peacemaking: Confrontations and Third Party Consultation.* Reading, Mass.: Addison-Wesley, 1969.

Walton, R., and McKersie, R. *A Behavioral Theory of Labor Negotiations.* New York: McGraw-Hill, 1965.

Warren, C. "The Hopeful Future of Mediation: Resolving Environmental Disputes Outside the Courts." In P. Baldwin (ed.), *Environmental Mediation: An Effective Alternative?* Palo Alto, Calif.: RESOLVE, Center for Environmental Conflict Resolution, 1978.

Watkins, M., and Winters, K. "Intervenors with Interests and Power." *Negotiation Journal*, 1997, *13*(2), 119–142.

Watzlawick, P. *The Language of Change.* New York: Basic Books, 1978.

Wehr, P. *Conflict Regulation.* Boulder, Colo.: Westview Press, 1979.

Weidner, H., and Fietkau, H. J. *Environmental Mediation: The Mediation Procedure on the Waste Management Plan in the District of Neuss, North Rhine-Westphalia.* Berlin: Social Science Research Centre, 1995.

Weingarten, H., and Douvan, E. "Male and Female Visions of Mediation." *Mediation Journal*, 1985, *4*, 349–358.

Werner, L. *International Politics: Foundations of the System.* Minneapolis: University of Minnesota Press, 1974.

Westin, A., and Feliu, A. *Resolving Employment Disputes Without Litigation.* Washington, D.C.: Bureau of National Affairs, 1988.

Wheeler, M. Lecture in a CDR Associates divorce mediation seminar, Boulder, Colo., 1982.

Wicker, T. *A Time to Die.* New York: Quadrangle/New York Times, 1975.

Wildau, S. T. *Guidelines for Mediating Domestic Violence Cases.* Denver, Colo.: Center for Dispute Resolution, 1984.

Wildau, S. "Transitions: Moving Parties Between Stages." *Mediation Quarterly*, 1987, *16*, 3–13.

Wildau, S., and Mayer, B. "Introduction to Dispute Systems Design." In CDR Associates, *Designing Dispute Resolution Systems.* Boulder, Colo.: CDR Associates, 1992.

Wildau, S., Moore, C., and Mayer, B. "Developing Democratic Decision-Making and Dispute Resolution Procedures Abroad." *Mediation Quarterly,* 1993, *10*(3), 303–320.

Williams, G. *Legal Negotiations and Settlement.* St. Paul, Minn.: West, 1983.

Wilson, I. "The Waitangi Tribunal." *Australian Dispute Resolution Journal,* 1992, *3*(4), 240–254.

Wixted, S. "The Children's Hearings Project: A Mediation Program for Children and Families." In H. Davidson and others (eds.), *Alternative Means of Family Dispute Resolution.* Washington, D.C.: American Bar Association, 1982.

Yang, J. "Role of the Korea Legal Aid Center in Promoting Mediation as an Alternative to the Court." In C. Pe, G. Sosmeña, and A. Tadiar (eds.), *Transcultural Mediation in the Asia-Pacific.* Manila, Philippines: Asia-Pacific Organization for Mediators, 1988.

Young, O. "Intermediaries: Additional Thoughts on Third Parties." *Journal of Conflict Resolution,* 1972, *16*(1), 51–65.

Zartman, I. W., and Berman, M. *The Practical Negotiator.* New Haven, Conn.: Yale University Press, 1982.

Ziegenfuss, J. *Organizational Troubleshooters: Resolving Problems with Customers and Employees.* San Francisco: Jossey-Bass, 1988.

About the Author

CHRISTOPHER W. MOORE is a partner in CDR Associates, an international collaborative decision-making and conflict management firm based in Boulder, Colorado. He is an internationally known mediator and facilitator, dispute systems designer, trainer, and author in the field of conflict management.

He received his B.A. degree from Juniata College in history, an M.A.T. in social change from Antioch-Putney Graduate School, and a Ph.D. degree from Rutgers University in political sociology and development. He was trained as a mediator by the U.S. Federal Mediation and Conciliation Service and the American Arbitration Association.

Moore has consulted in the field of conflict management in more than twenty-five countries in Africa, Asia, Latin America, Western and Eastern Europe, North America, and the South Pacific Region. He has mediated and facilitated international agreements over river management issues in Africa, economic development in Russia, commercial trade dispute resolution procedures under the North American Free Trade Agreement, political/ethnic disputes, and conflicts within international organizations. Moore has also trained United Nations diplomats, Organization of American States officials, and foreign service officers from nations around the world in international mediation.

In the United States, his work has encompassed negotiated rule making at the federal and state levels; site-specific disputes in the public policy and environmental arenas; and conflicts over growth management planning, water conservation, wildlife protection, energy development, and air quality. His extensive experience in organizational mediation and dispute systems design includes labor-management disputes, cases of alleged discrimination and sexual harassment, and conflicts between headquarters and regional offices. Some of his clients have included AT&T, Sprint, U.S. West, DuPont, the U.S. Army Corps of Engineers, the U.S. Environmental Protection Agency, and the states of California, Colorado, and Minnesota. He has also mediated interpersonal and family disputes.

Moore has consulted on the design of dispute resolution systems for domestic companies such as Levi Strauss and Co., Pitney Bowes, the Army Corps of Engineers, and the U.S. Bureau of Reclamation and in the international arena for participants in the North American Free Trade Agreement, the Royal Canadian Mounted Police, the Barangay Justice System in the Philippines, the Ministry of the Environment and the Environmental Impact Management Agency of Indonesia, the Ministry of Justice in Sri Lanka, the Ministry of Justice in Haiti, and the Land and Property Directorate of East Timor.

His books include *An Executive Seminar on Alternative Dispute Resolution (ADR)*, *Negotiating Bargaining and Conflict Management*, *Decision Making and Conflict Management*, *Natural Resources Conflict Management*, and *Resource Manual for a Living Revolution* (1976, with coauthors). His articles on conflict management and dispute resolution have appeared in such journals as *Mediation Quarterly*, *Forum (National Institute for Dispute Resolution)*, *Pacifica Review*, and *Cultural Survival*.

Name Index

Subject Index